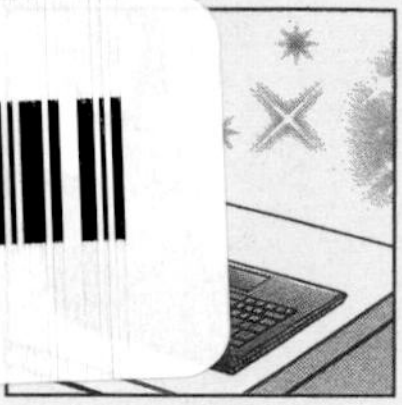

SHIN YOSHIDA

A new enemy bars Yuya's way. What is Eve's goal? The mystery is reaching its climax! But my personal enemy is *Yu-Gi-Oh! Duel LInks*. I'm way too absorbed in that game!

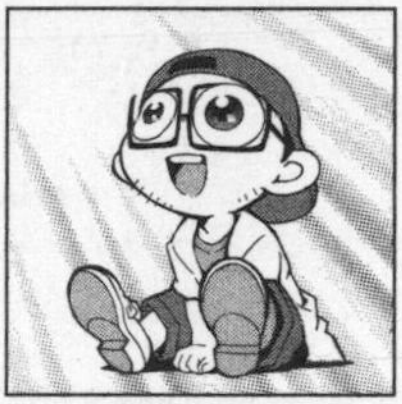

NAOHITO MIYOSHI

At Jump Victory Carnival in Osaka, lots of people cheered for me and gave me encouraging letters. I'm exhausted, but I'll keep doing my best! I'll eat myself out of house and home and get some power into my system! *Yu-Gi-Oh! ARC-V* is going full speed ahead!!

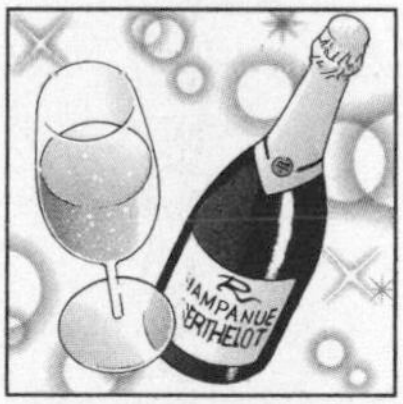
CHAMPANUE
BERTHELOT

MASAHIRO HIKOKUBO

When they make original cards from the manga into official game cards, it makes me so happy! Ren's White monsters are already showing up!! I do feel a little apologetic toward the preexisting Great White, though.

4

SHONEN JUMP MANGA EDITION

ORIGINAL CONCEPT BY
Kazuki Takahashi

PRODUCTION SUPPORT: **STUDIO DICE**

STORY BY
Shin Yoshida

ART BY
Naohito Miyoshi

DUEL COORDINATOR
Masahiro Hikokubo

TRANSLATION + ENGLISH ADAPTATION
Taylor Engel and John Werry, HC Language Solutions, Inc.
TOUCH-UP ART + LETTERING **John Hunt**
DESIGNER **Stacie Yamaki**
EDITOR **Mike Montesa**

YU-GI-OH! ARC-V © 2014 by Kazuki Takahashi, Shin Yoshida, Naohito Miyoshi, Masahiro Hikokubo/SHUEISHA Inc.
Based on Animation TV series YU-GI-OH! ARC-V
© 1996 Kazuki Takahashi
© 2014 NAS • TV TOKYO

Printed in the U.S.A.

Published by VIZ Media, LLC
P.O. Box 77010
San Francisco, CA 94107

10 9 8 7 6 5 4 3 2 1
First printing, November 2018

viz.com

shonenjump.com

PARENTAL ADVISORY
YU-GI-OH! ARC-V is rated T
for Teen and is recommended
for ages 13 and up.

Yu-Gi-Oh! ARC-V

4

Immortal Beings!!

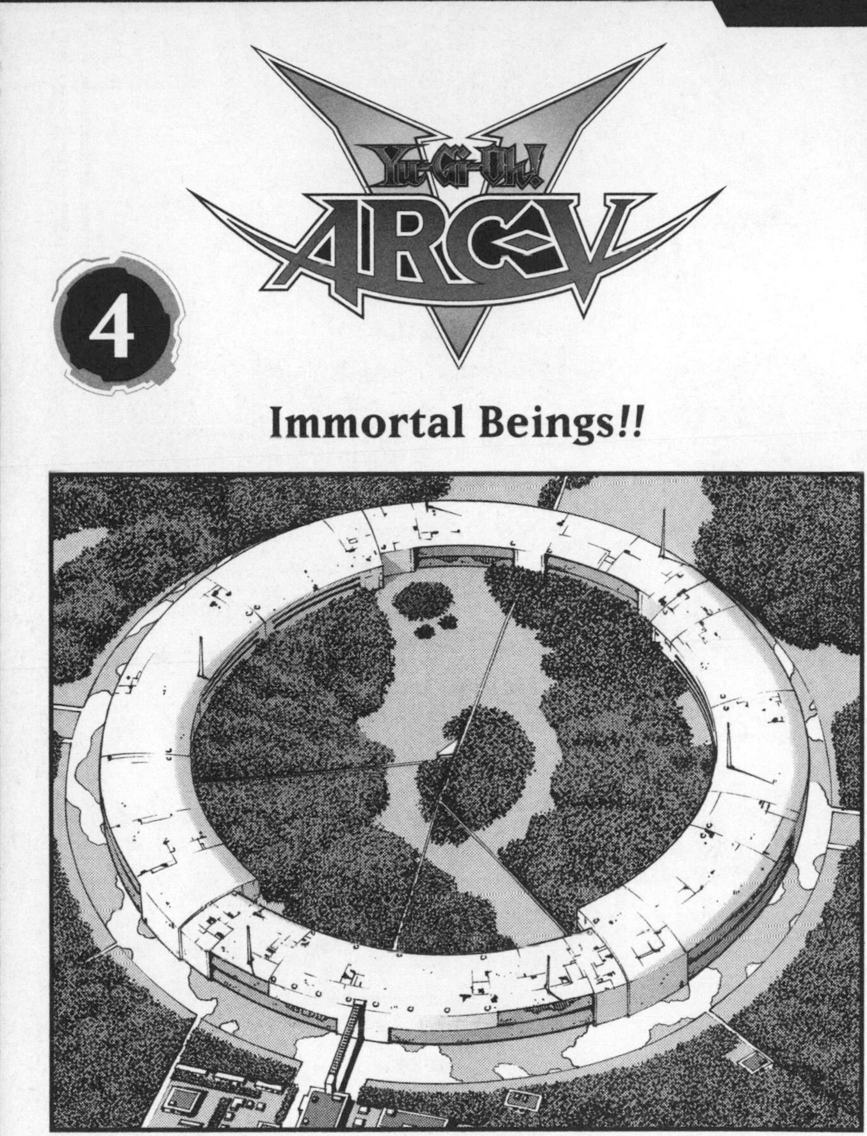

ORIGINAL CONCEPT BY **Kazuki Takahashi**

PRODUCTION SUPPORT: **STUDIO DICE**

STORY BY **Shin Yoshida**

ART BY **Naohito Miyoshi**

DUEL COORDINATOR **Masahiro Hikokubo**

CHARACTERS

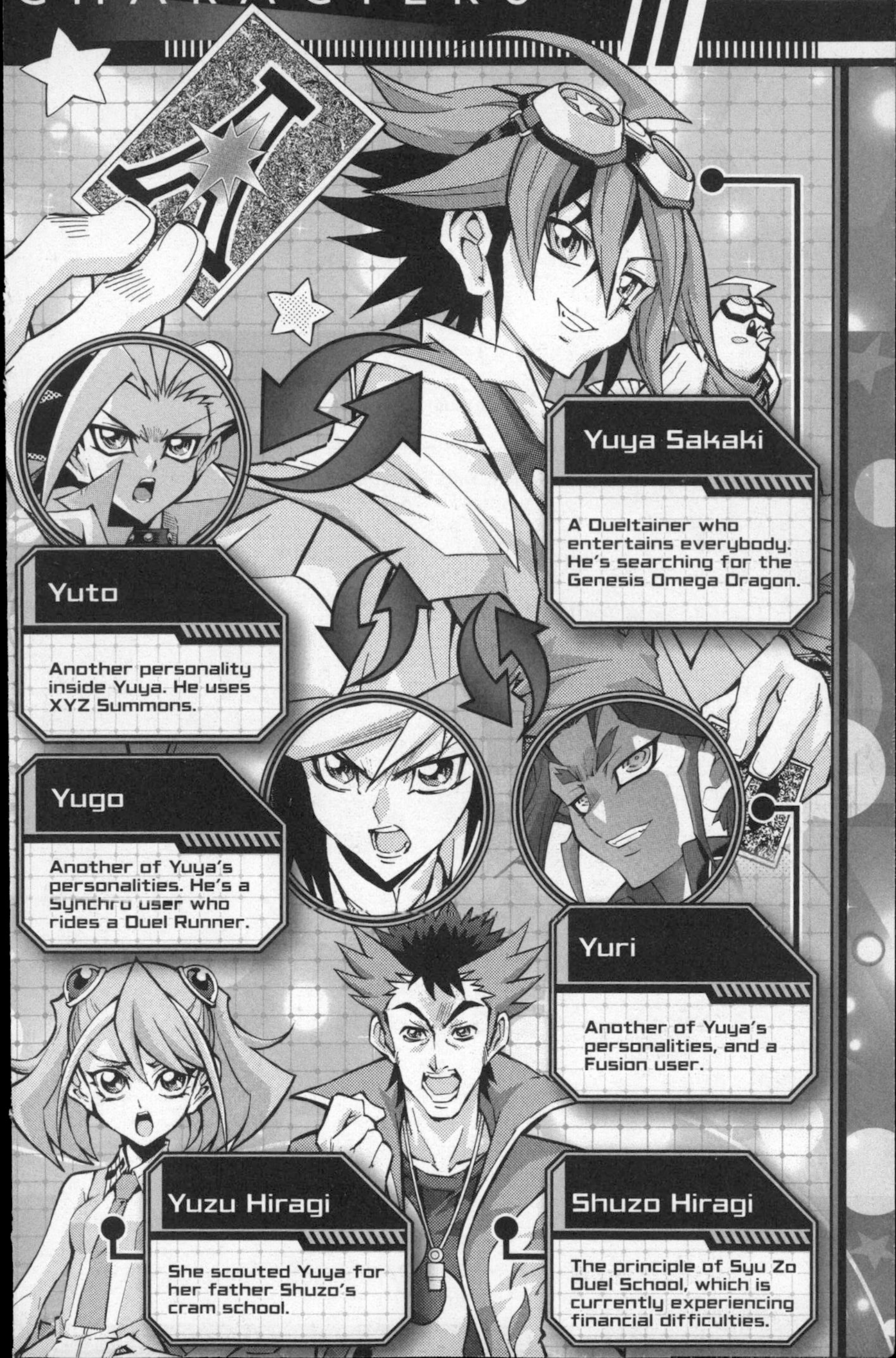
Yuya Sakaki
A Dueltainer who entertains everybody. He's searching for the Genesis Omega Dragon.
Yuto
Another personality inside Yuya. He uses XYZ Summons.
Yugo
Another of Yuya's personalities. He's a Synchro user who rides a Duel Runner.
Yuri
Another of Yuya's personalities, and a Fusion user.
Yuzu Hiragi
She scouted Yuya for her father Shuzo's cram school.
Shuzo Hiragi
The principle of Syu Zo Duel School, which is currently experiencing financial difficulties.

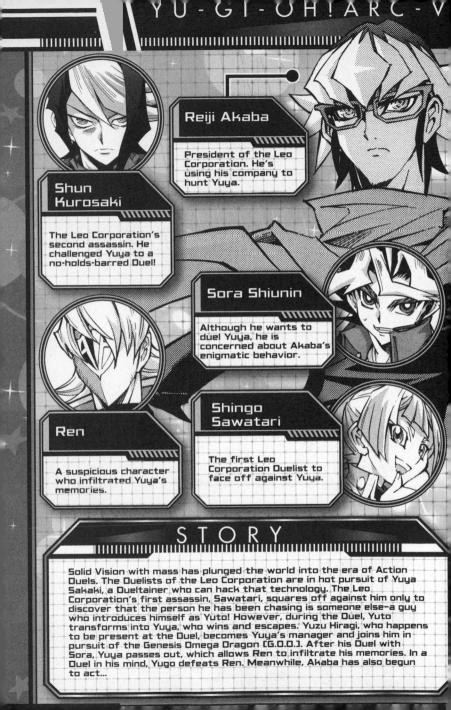

Reiji Akaba
President of the Leo Corporation. He's using his company to hunt Yuya.

Shun Kurosaki
The Leo Corporation's second assassin. He challenged Yuya to a no-holds-barred Duel!

Sora Shiunin
Although he wants to duel Yuya, he is concerned about Akaba's enigmatic behavior.

Shingo Sawatari
The first Leo Corporation Duelist to face off against Yuya.

Ren
A suspicious character who infiltrated Yuya's memories.

STORY

Solid Vision with mass has plunged the world into the era of Action Duels. The Duelists of the Leo Corporation are in hot pursuit of Yuya Sakaki, a Dueltainer who can hack that technology. The Leo Corporation's first assassin, Sawatari, squares off against him only to discover that the person he has been chasing is someone else—a guy who introduces himself as Yuto! However, during the Duel, Yuto transforms into Yuya, who wins and escapes. Yuzu Hiragi, who happens to be present at the Duel, becomes Yuya's manager and joins him in pursuit of the Genesis Omega Dragon (G.O.D.). After his Duel with Sora, Yuya passes out, which allows Ren to infiltrate his memories. In a Duel in his mind, Yugo defeats Ren. Meanwhile, Akaba has also begun to act...

Yu-Gi-Oh! ARC-V

4 Immortal Beings!!

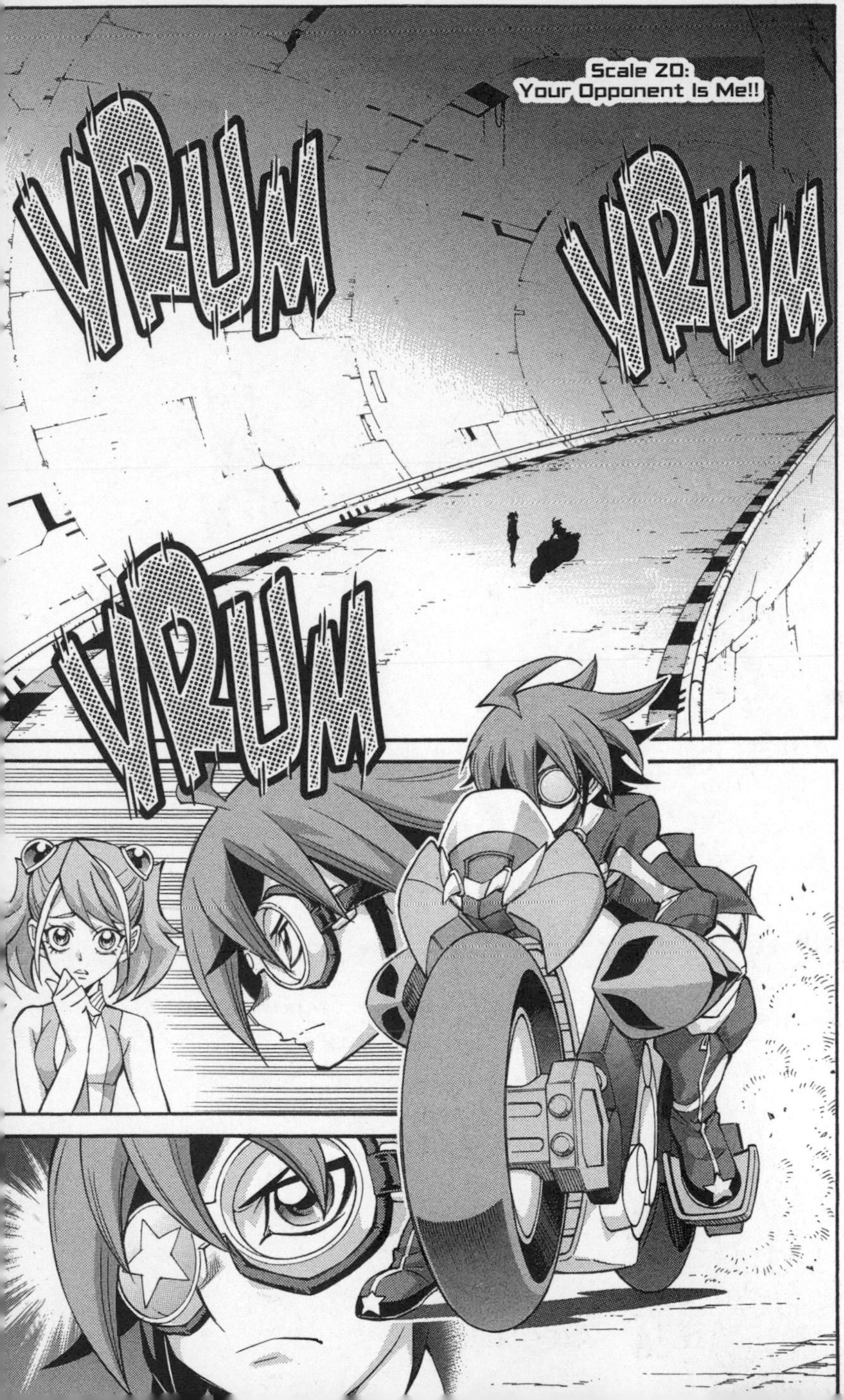
Scale 20:
Your Opponent Is Me!!
VRUM
VRUM
VRUM

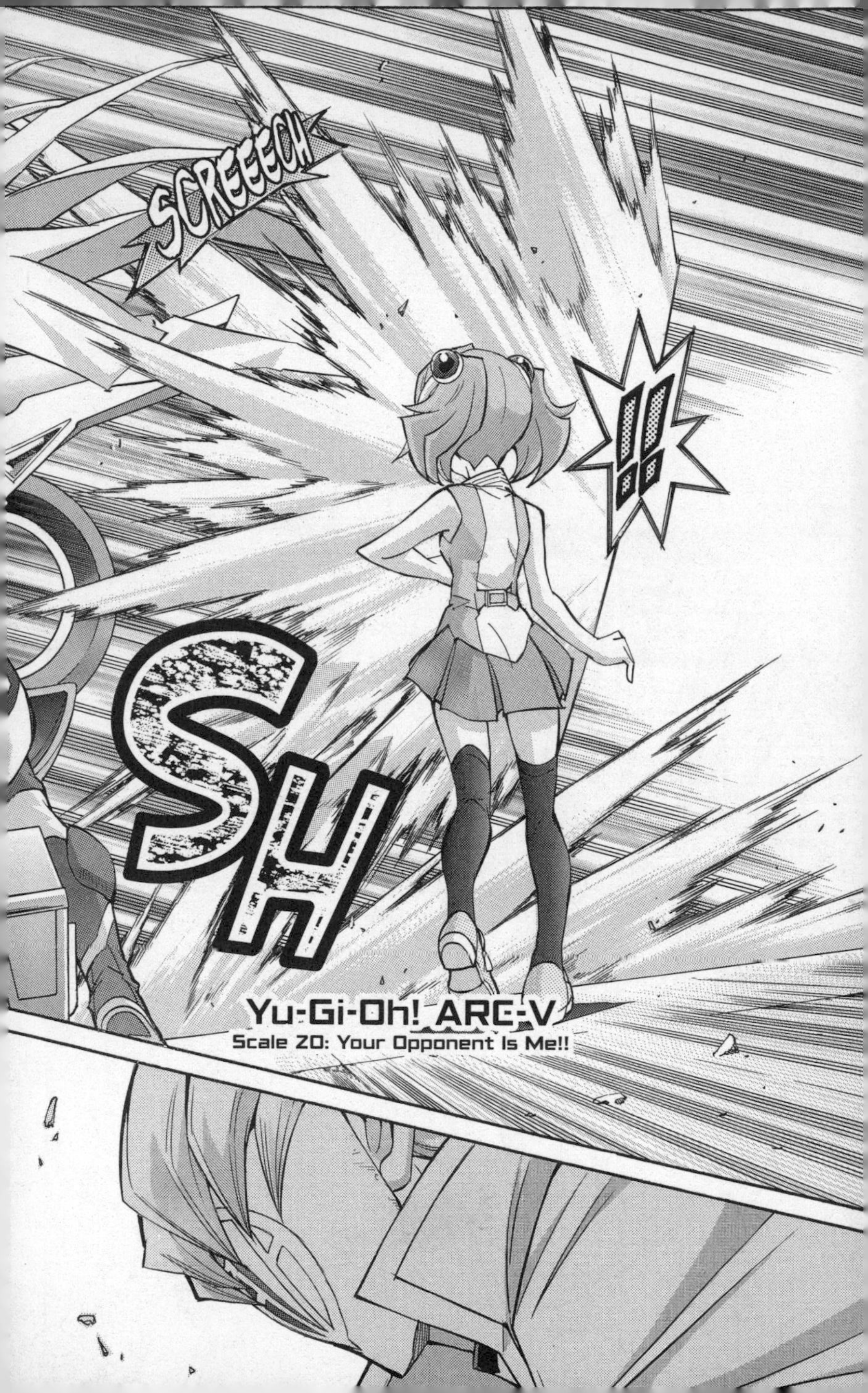
SCREEECH
!!
SH
Yu-Gi-Oh! ARC-V
Scale 20: Your Opponent Is Me!!

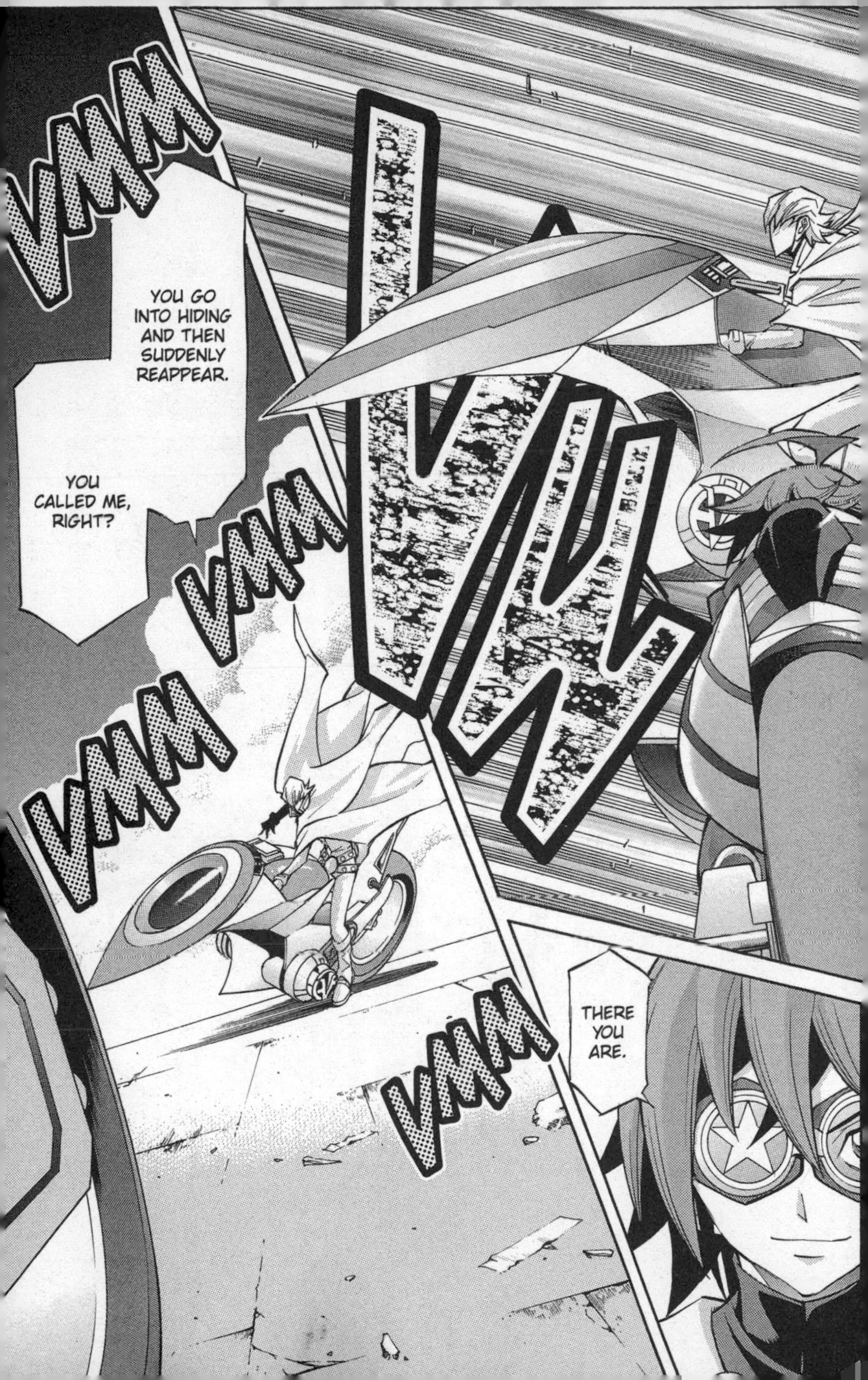
VMM
THERE YOU ARE.
VMM
VMMM
VMMM
VMMM
YOU GO INTO HIDING AND THEN SUDDENLY REAPPEAR.
YOU CALLED ME, RIGHT?

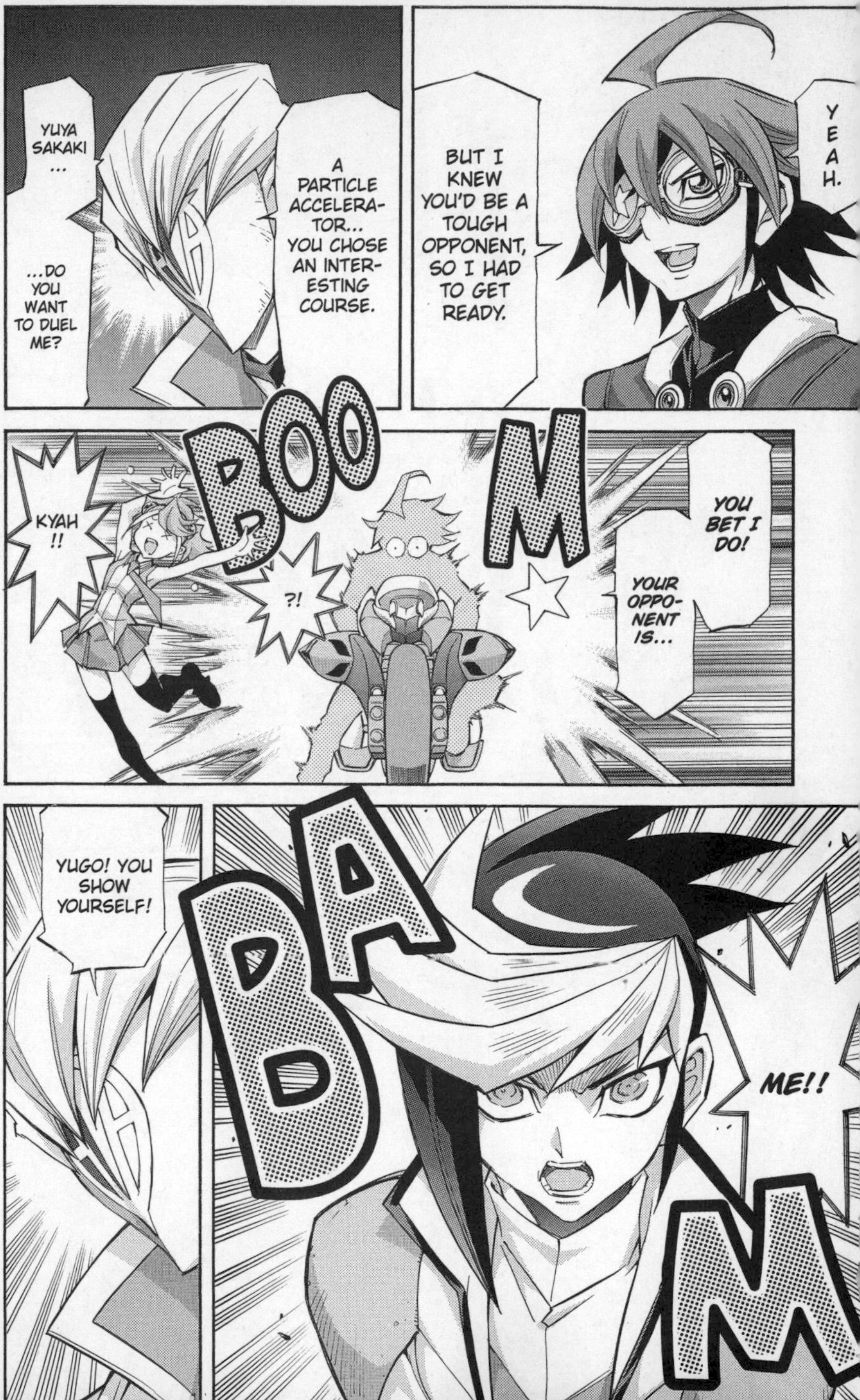
YEAH.
BUT I KNEW YOU'D BE A TOUGH OPPONENT, SO I HAD TO GET READY.
A PARTICLE ACCELERATOR... YOU CHOSE AN INTERESTING COURSE.
YUYA SAKAKI...
...DO YOU WANT TO DUEL ME?
YOU BET I DO!
YOUR OPPONENT IS...
BOOM
?!
KYAH!!
BAM
ME!!
YUGO! YOU SHOW YOURSELF!

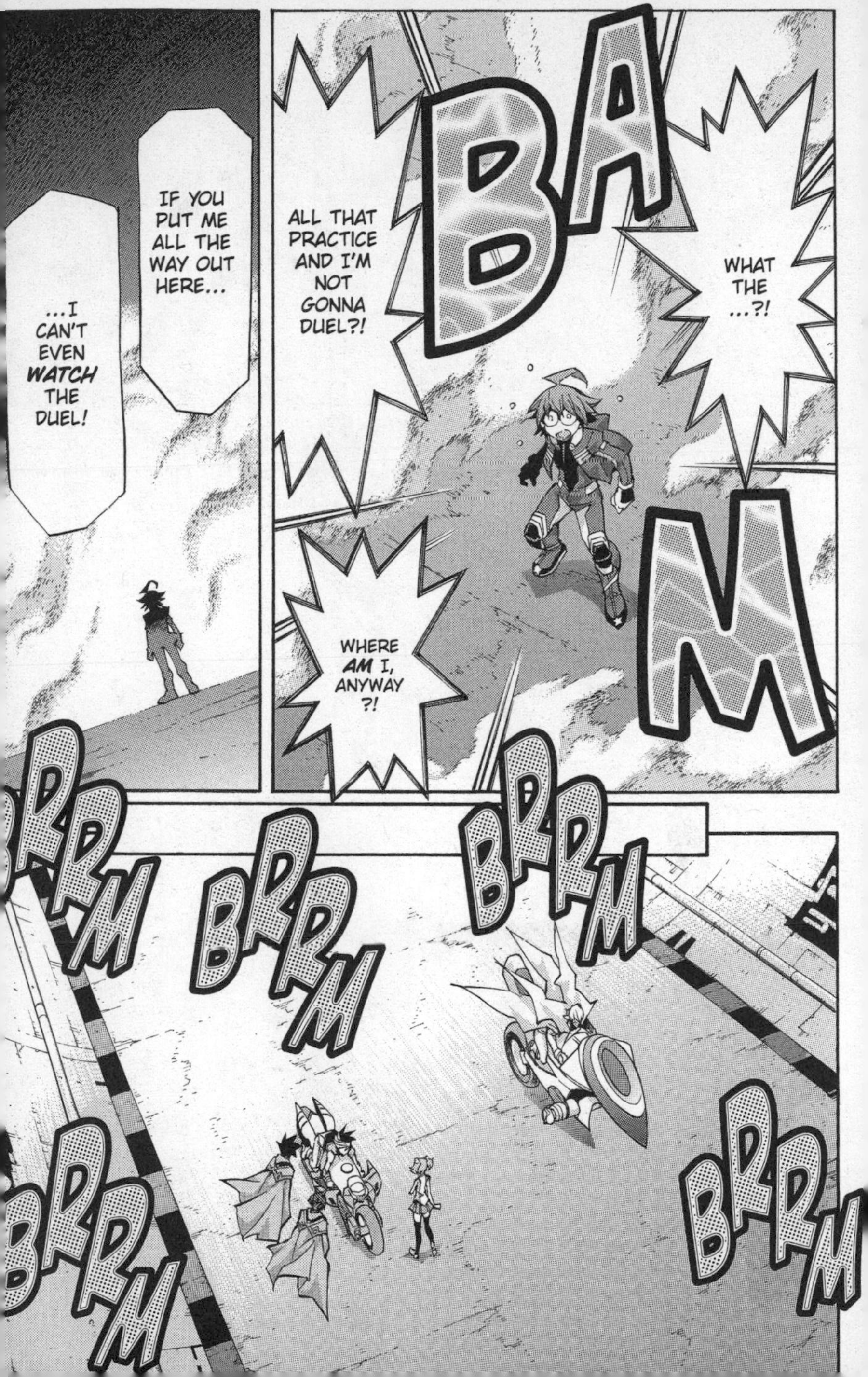
BAM
WHAT THE ...?!
ALL THAT PRACTICE AND I'M NOT GONNA DUEL?!
WHERE *AM* I, ANYWAY ?!
IF YOU PUT ME ALL THE WAY OUT HERE...
...I CAN'T EVEN *WATCH* THE DUEL!
BRRRM
BRRRM
BRRRM
BRRRM
BRRRM

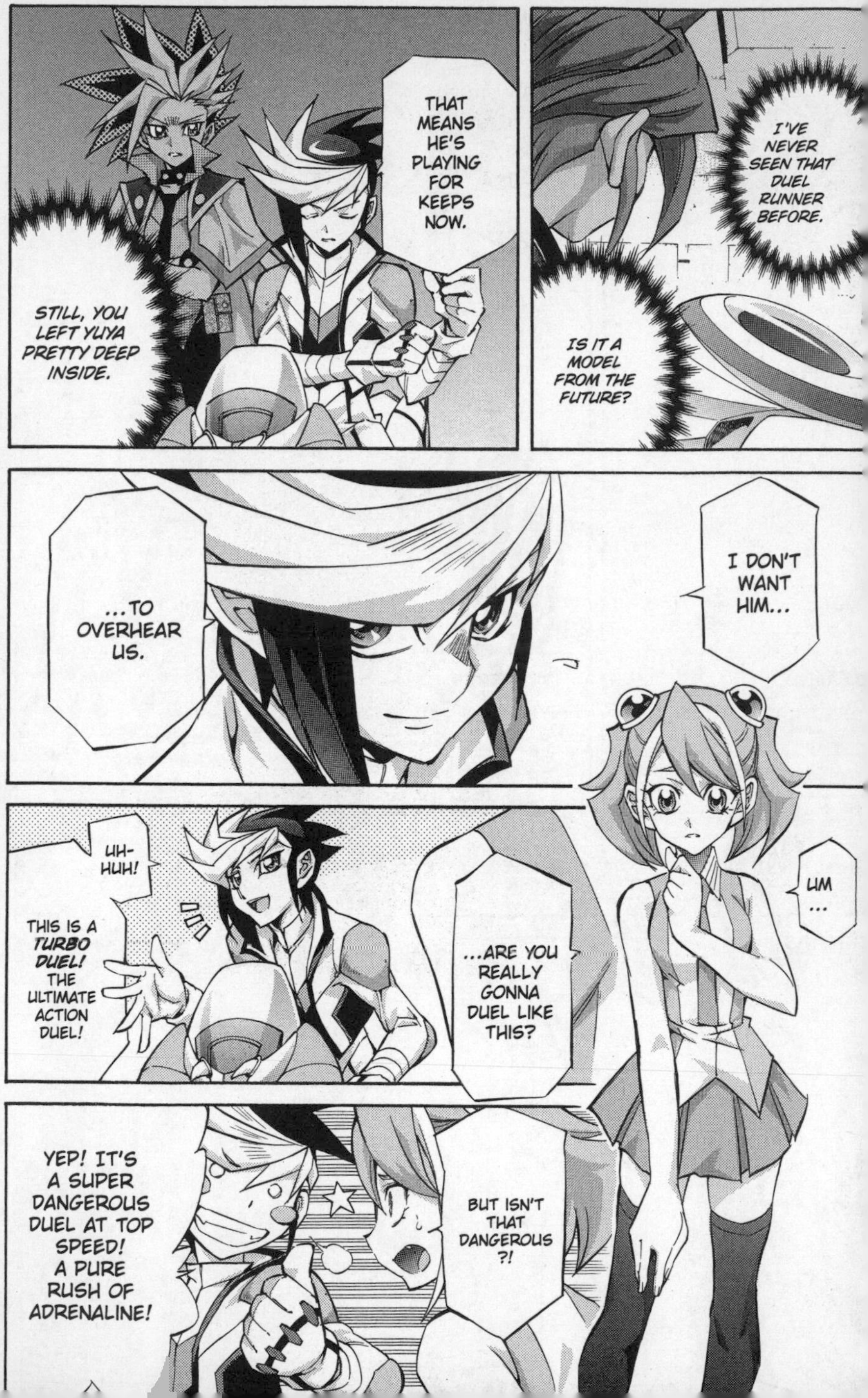

I'VE NEVER SEEN THAT DUEL RUNNER BEFORE.
IS IT A MODEL FROM THE FUTURE?
THAT MEANS HE'S PLAYING FOR KEEPS NOW.
STILL, YOU LEFT YUYA PRETTY DEEP INSIDE.
I DON'T WANT HIM...
...TO OVERHEAR US.
UM...
...ARE YOU REALLY GONNA DUEL LIKE THIS?
UH-HUH!
THIS IS A TURBO DUEL! THE ULTIMATE ACTION DUEL!
BUT ISN'T THAT DANGEROUS?!
YEP! IT'S A SUPER DANGEROUS DUEL AT TOP SPEED! A PURE RUSH OF ADRENALINE!

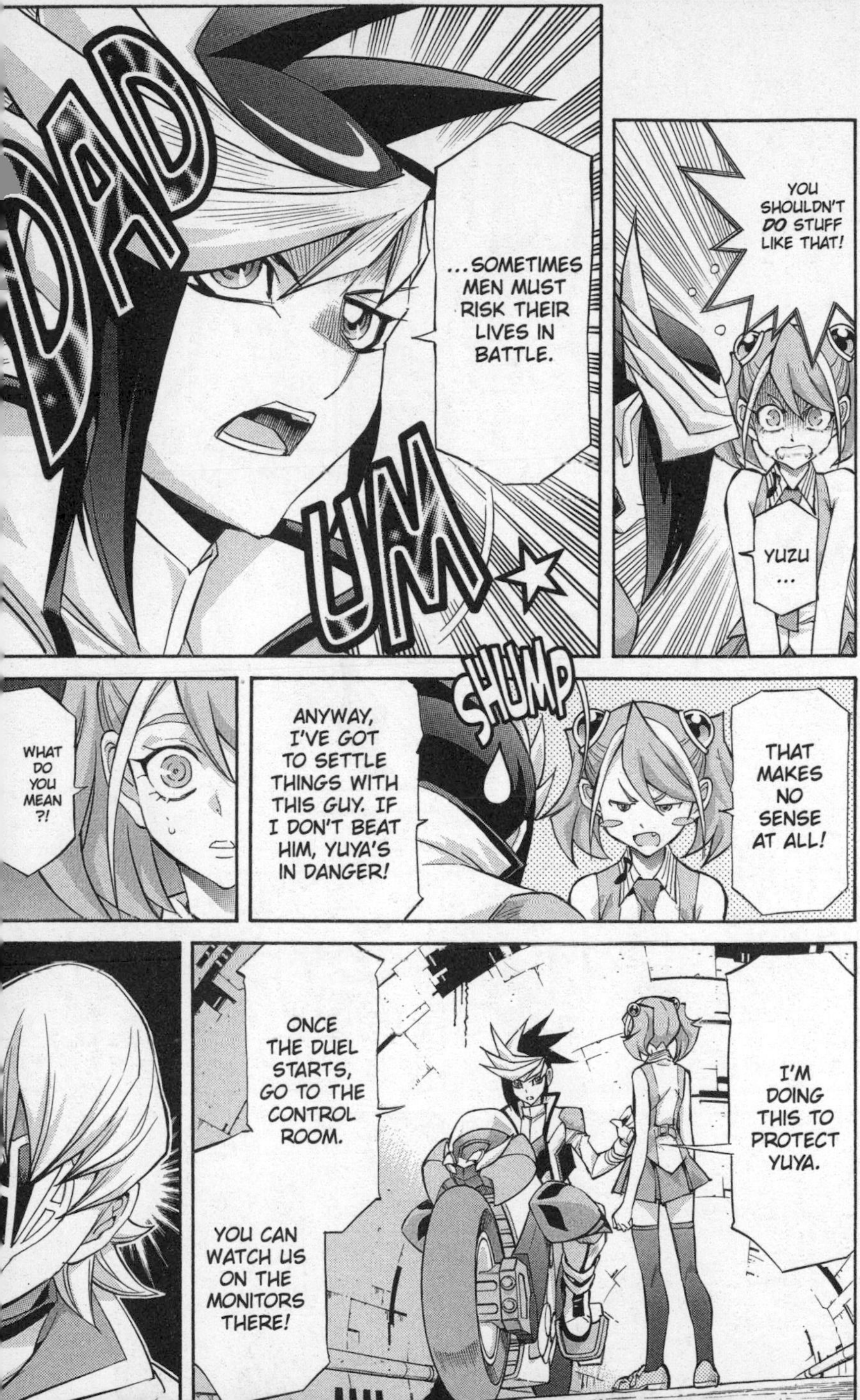
YOU SHOULDN'T DO STUFF LIKE THAT!
YUZU ...
...SOMETIMES MEN MUST RISK THEIR LIVES IN BATTLE.
DAD
UM★
THAT MAKES NO SENSE AT ALL!
SHUMP
ANYWAY, I'VE GOT TO SETTLE THINGS WITH THIS GUY. IF I DON'T BEAT HIM, YUYA'S IN DANGER!
WHAT DO YOU MEAN ?!
I'M DOING THIS TO PROTECT YUYA.
ONCE THE DUEL STARTS, GO TO THE CONTROL ROOM.
YOU CAN WATCH US ON THE MONITORS THERE!

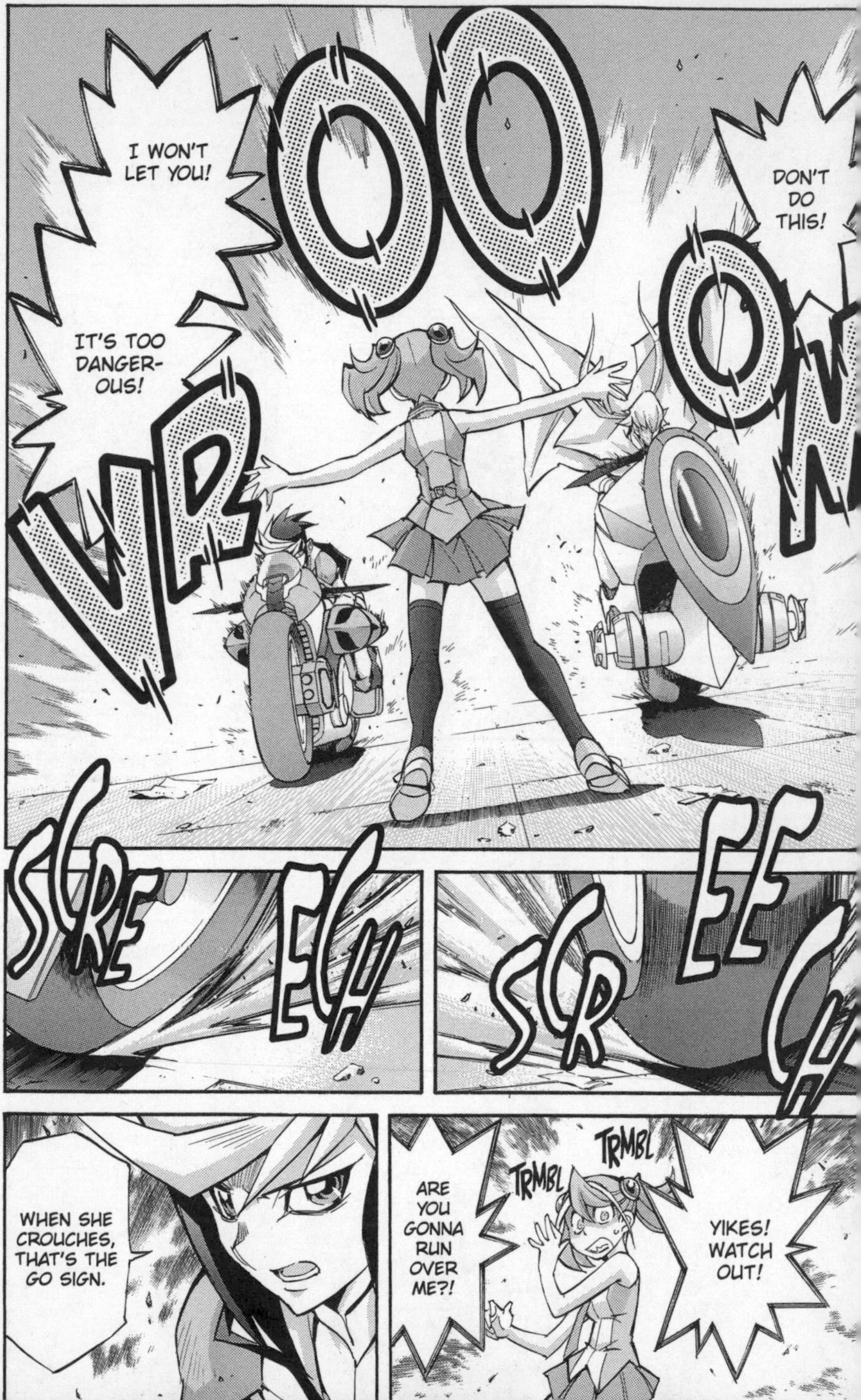
DON'T DO THIS!
VROOOM
I WON'T LET YOU!
IT'S TOO DANGER-OUS!
SCREECH
SCREECH
TRMBL
YIKES! WATCH OUT!
ARE YOU GONNA RUN OVER ME?!
TRMBL
WHEN SHE CROUCHES, THAT'S THE GO SIGN.

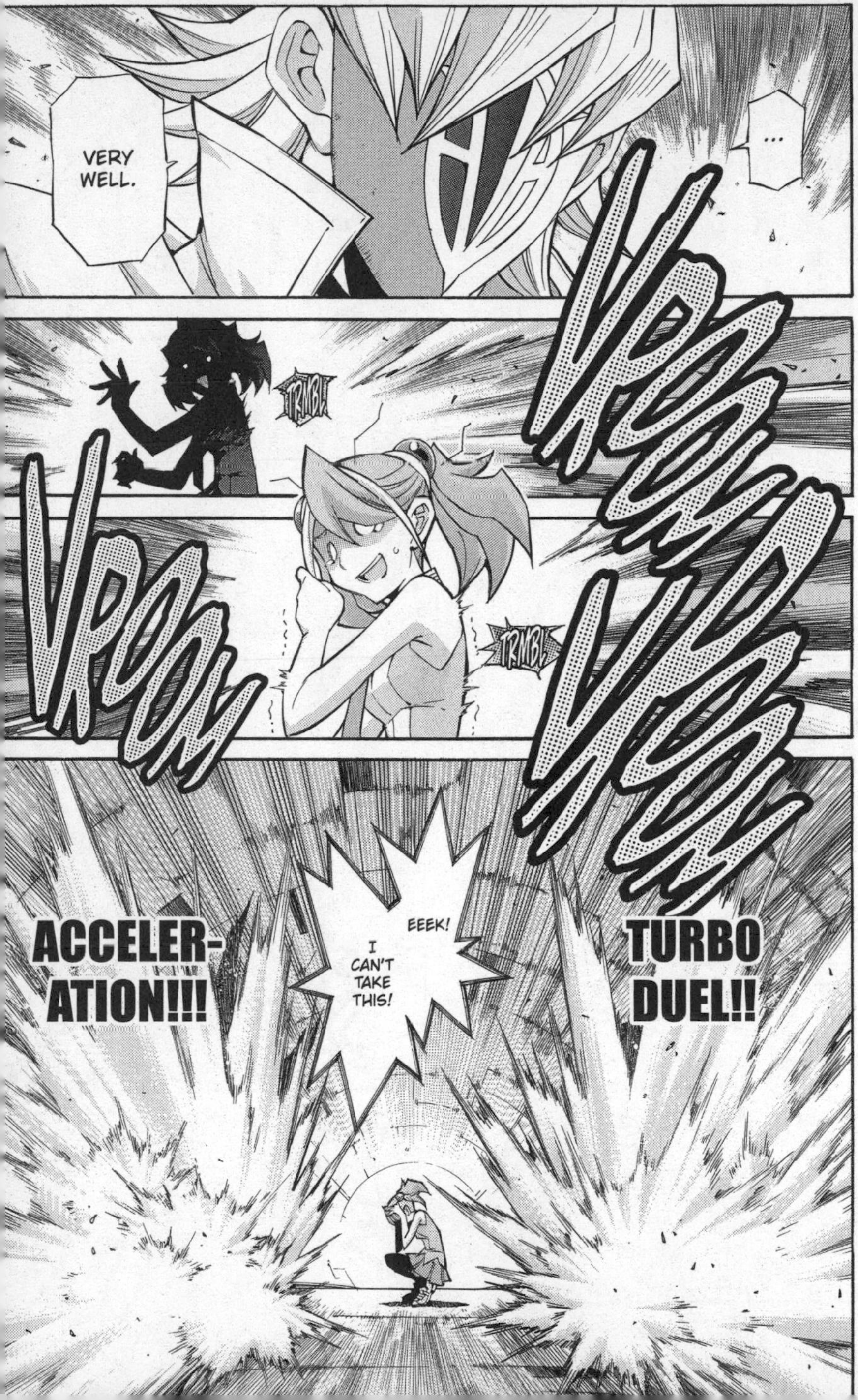
...
VERY WELL.
TRMBL
TRMBL
TURBO DUEL!!
EEEK!
I CAN'T TAKE THIS!
ACCELER-ATION!!!

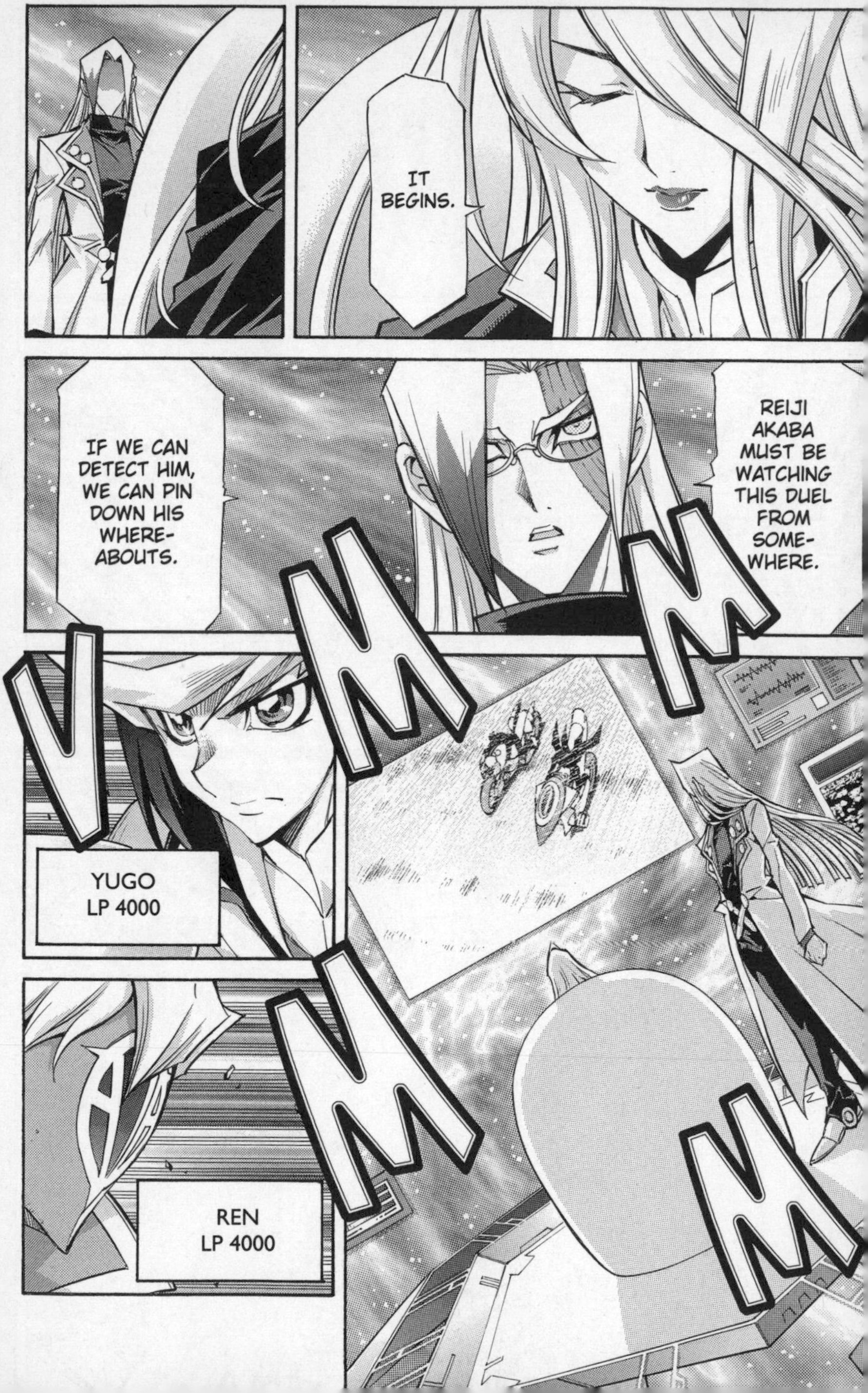
IT BEGINS.
REIJI AKABA MUST BE WATCHING THIS DUEL FROM SOME-WHERE.
IF WE CAN DETECT HIM, WE CAN PIN DOWN HIS WHERE-ABOUTS.
VMMMM
YUGO
LP 4000
REN
LP 4000

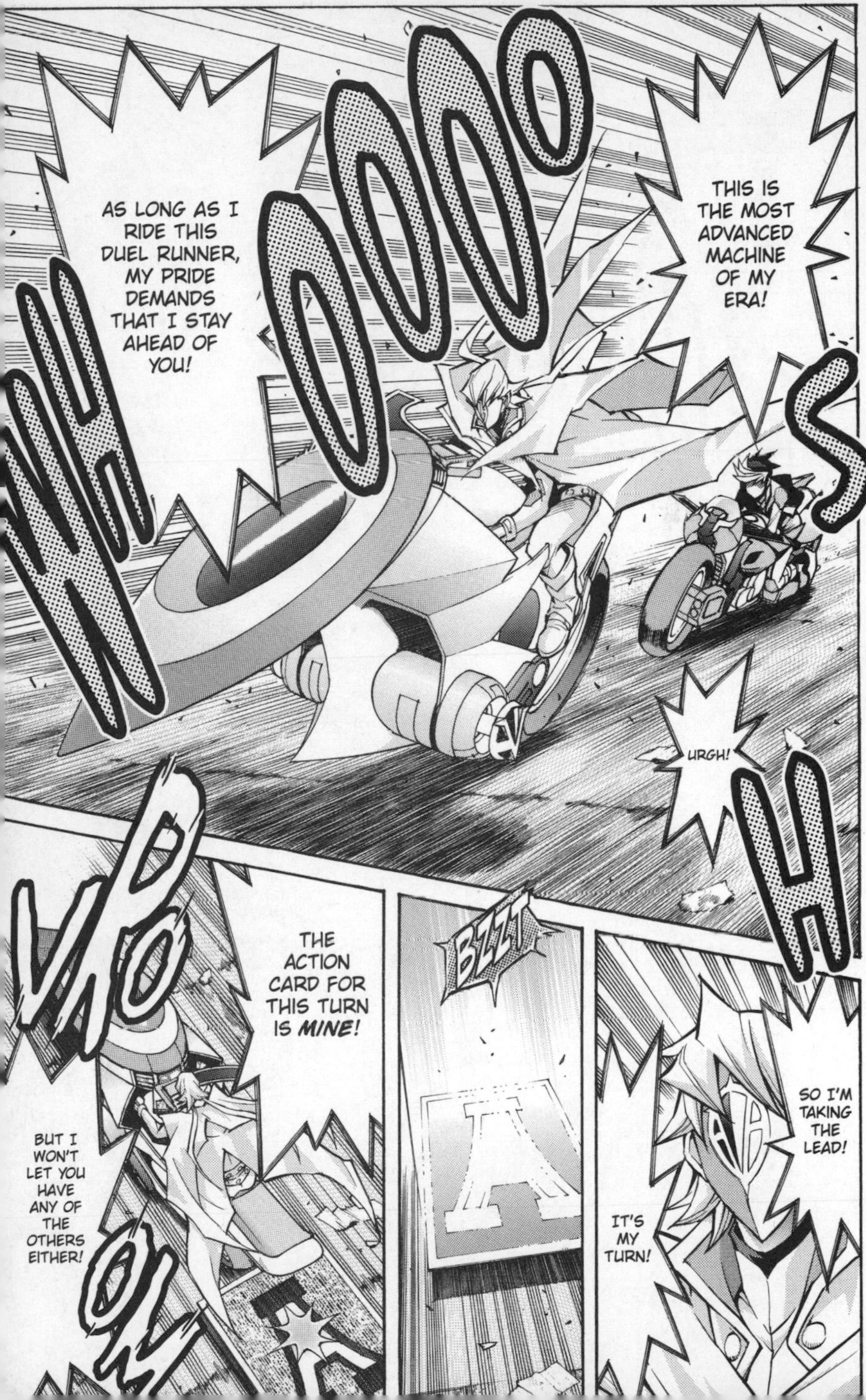
THIS IS THE MOST ADVANCED MACHINE OF MY ERA!
AS LONG AS I RIDE THIS DUEL RUNNER, MY PRIDE DEMANDS THAT I STAY AHEAD OF YOU!
WHOOOOOSH
URGH!
SO I'M TAKING THE LEAD!
IT'S MY TURN!
BZZT
THE ACTION CARD FOR THIS TURN IS *MINE*!
BUT I WON'T LET YOU HAVE ANY OF THE OTHERS EITHER!

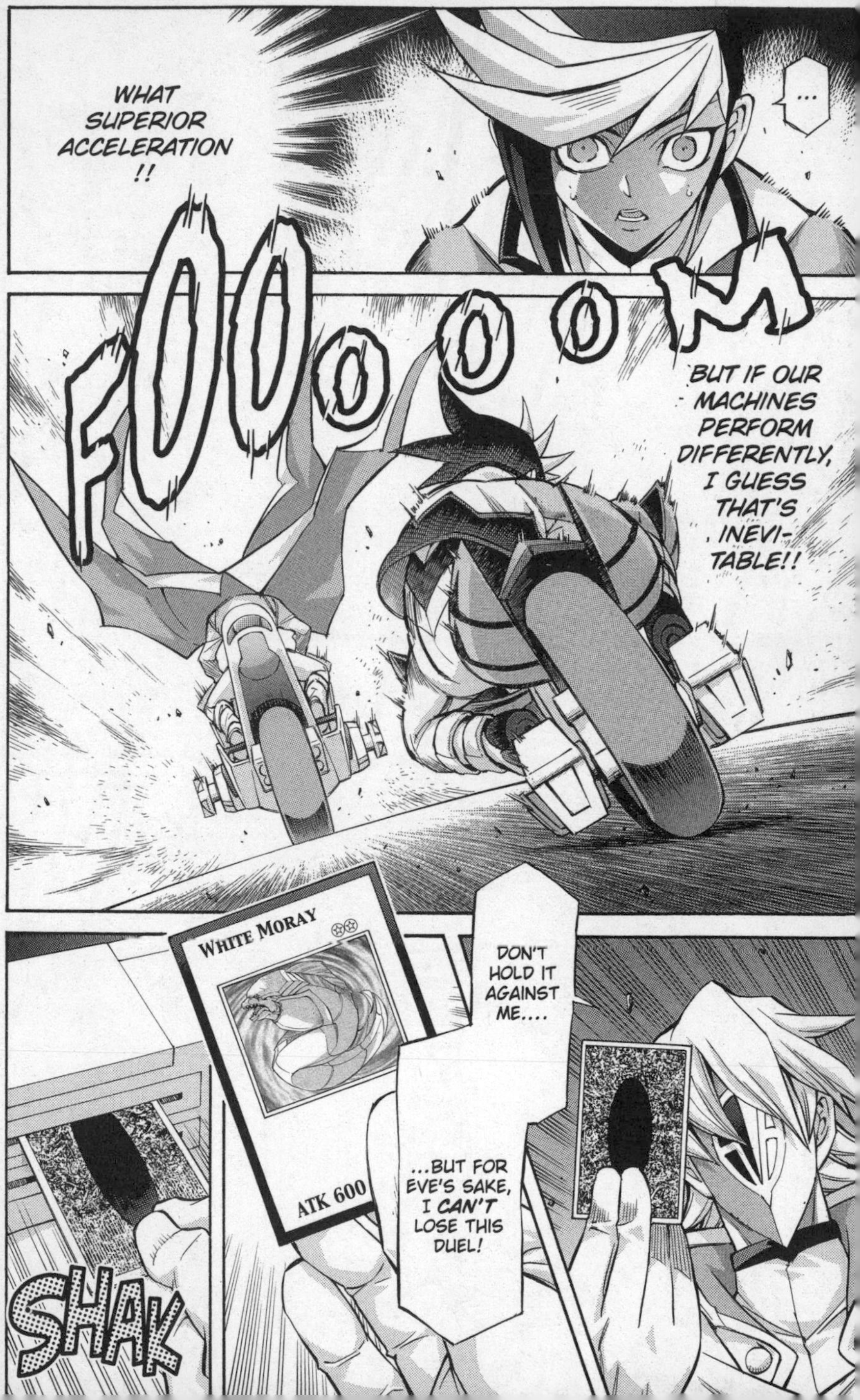
...
WHAT SUPERIOR ACCELERATION!!
FOOOOOOM
BUT IF OUR MACHINES PERFORM DIFFERENTLY, I GUESS THAT'S INEVITABLE!!
DON'T HOLD IT AGAINST ME....
...BUT FOR EVE'S SAKE, I *CAN'T* LOSE THIS DUEL!
WHITE MORAY
ATK 600
SHAK

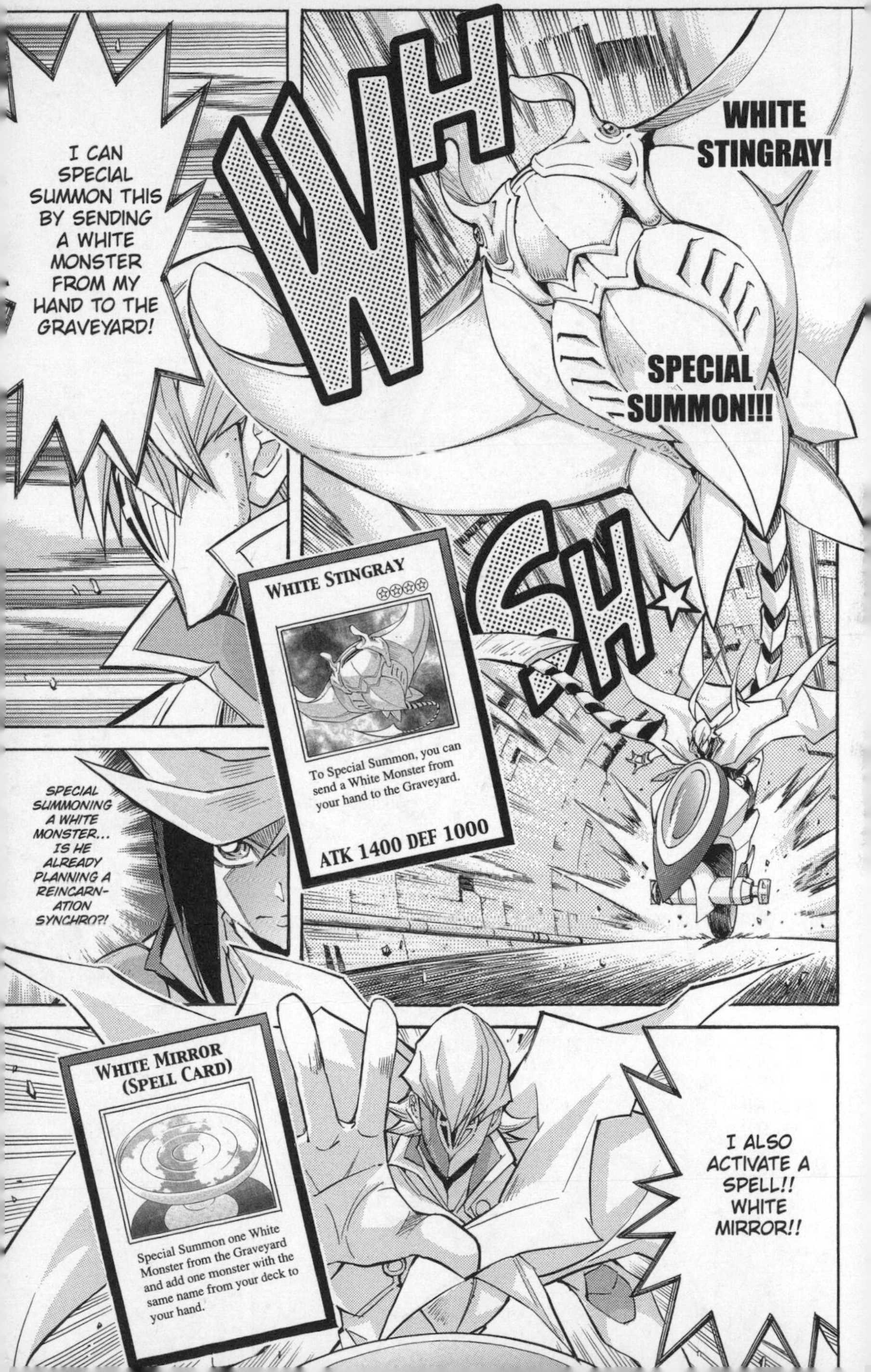
WHITE STINGRAY!
WH
SPECIAL SUMMON!!!
SH
WHITE STINGRAY
To Special Summon, you can send a White Monster from your hand to the Graveyard.
ATK 1400 DEF 1000
I CAN SPECIAL SUMMON THIS BY SENDING A WHITE MONSTER FROM MY HAND TO THE GRAVEYARD!
SPECIAL SUMMONING A WHITE MONSTER... IS HE ALREADY PLANNING A REINCARN-ATION SYNCHRO?!
I ALSO ACTIVATE A SPELL!! WHITE MIRROR!!
WHITE MIRROR (SPELL CARD)
Special Summon one White Monster from the Graveyard and add one monster with the same name from your deck to your hand.

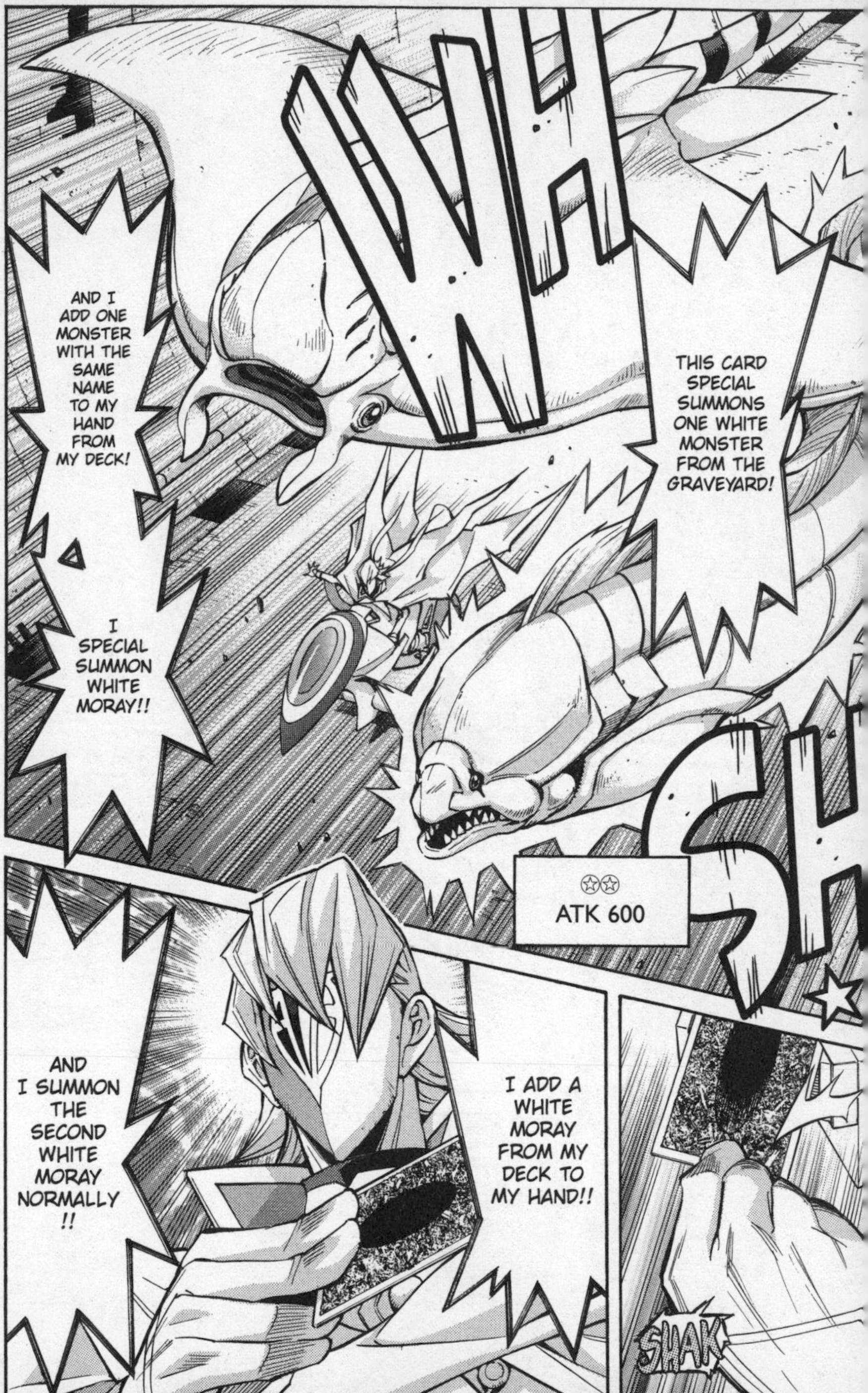
WHA
THIS CARD SPECIAL SUMMONS ONE WHITE MONSTER FROM THE GRAVEYARD!
AND I ADD ONE MONSTER WITH THE SAME NAME TO MY HAND FROM MY DECK!
I SPECIAL SUMMON WHITE MORAY!!
SH
☆☆ ATK 600
SHAK
I ADD A WHITE MORAY FROM MY DECK TO MY HAND!!
AND I SUMMON THE SECOND WHITE MORAY NORMALLY !!

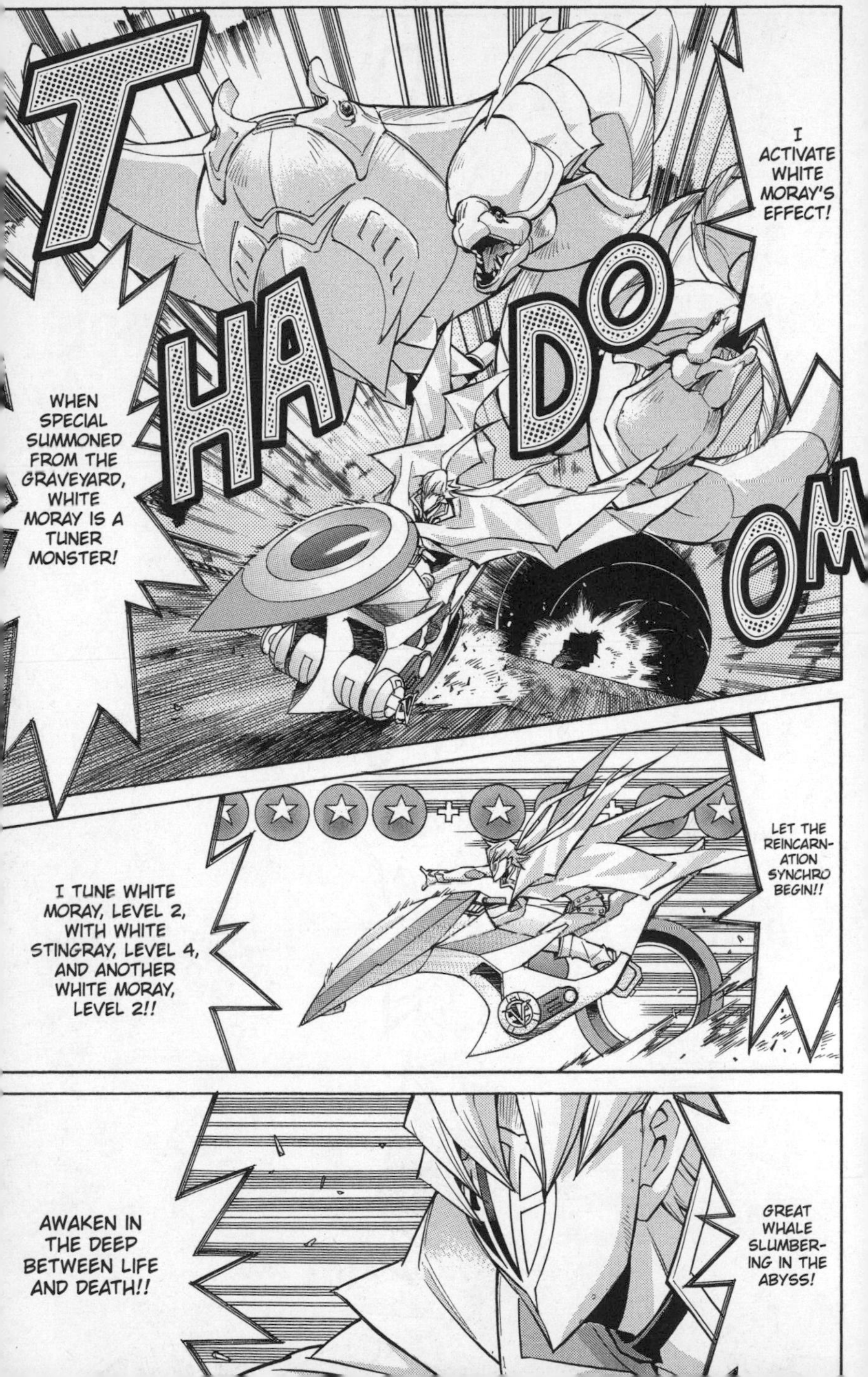
I ACTIVATE WHITE MORAY'S EFFECT!
THADOOM
WHEN SPECIAL SUMMONED FROM THE GRAVEYARD, WHITE MORAY IS A TUNER MONSTER!
LET THE REINCARNATION SYNCHRO BEGIN!!
I TUNE WHITE MORAY, LEVEL 2, WITH WHITE STINGRAY, LEVEL 4, AND ANOTHER WHITE MORAY, LEVEL 2!!
GREAT WHALE SLUMBERING IN THE ABYSS!
AWAKEN IN THE DEEP BETWEEN LIFE AND DEATH!!

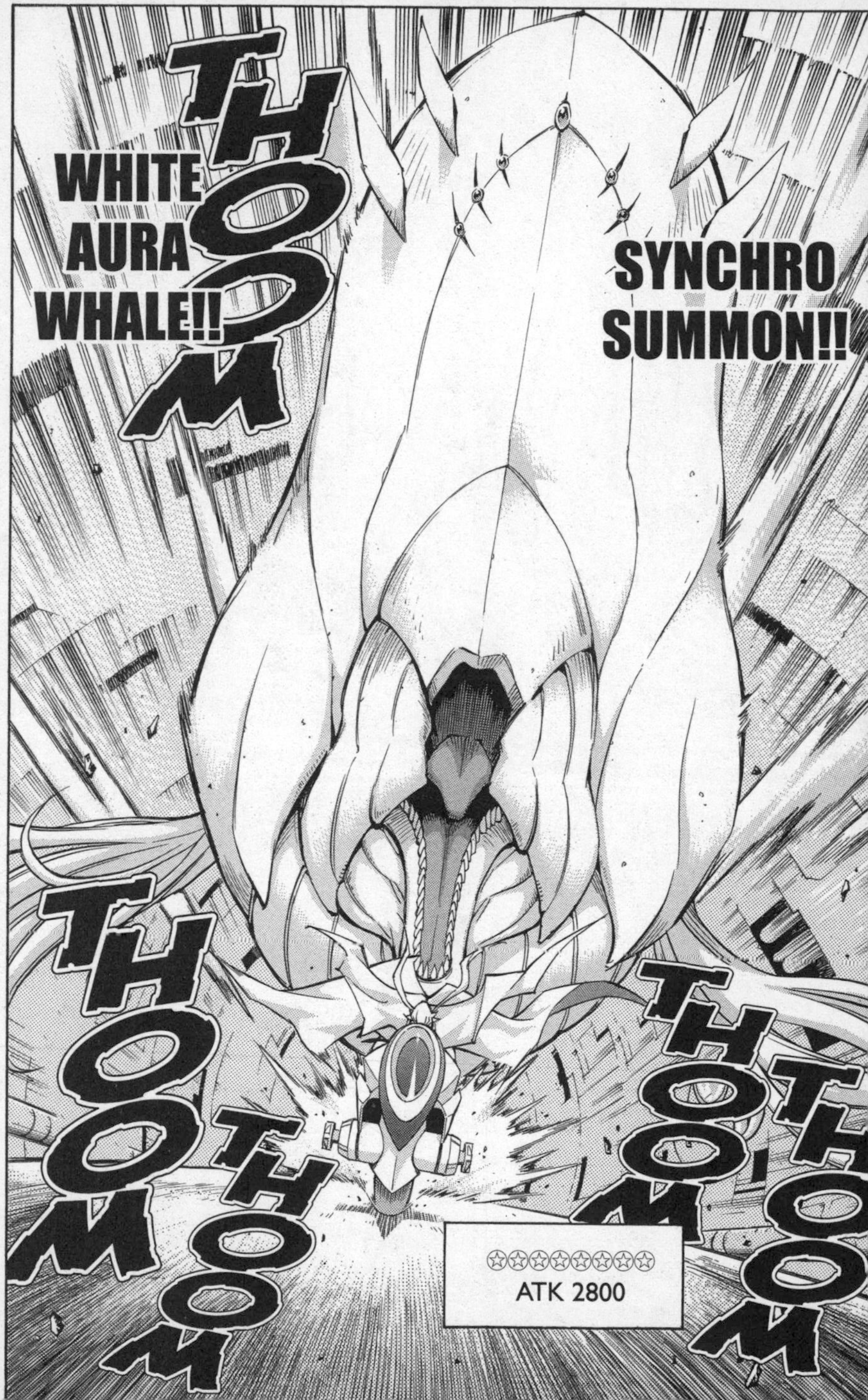
SYNCHRO SUMMON!!
WHITE AURA WHALE!!
THOOM
THOOOM
THOOOM
THOOOM
THOOOM
☆☆☆☆☆☆☆☆
ATK 2800

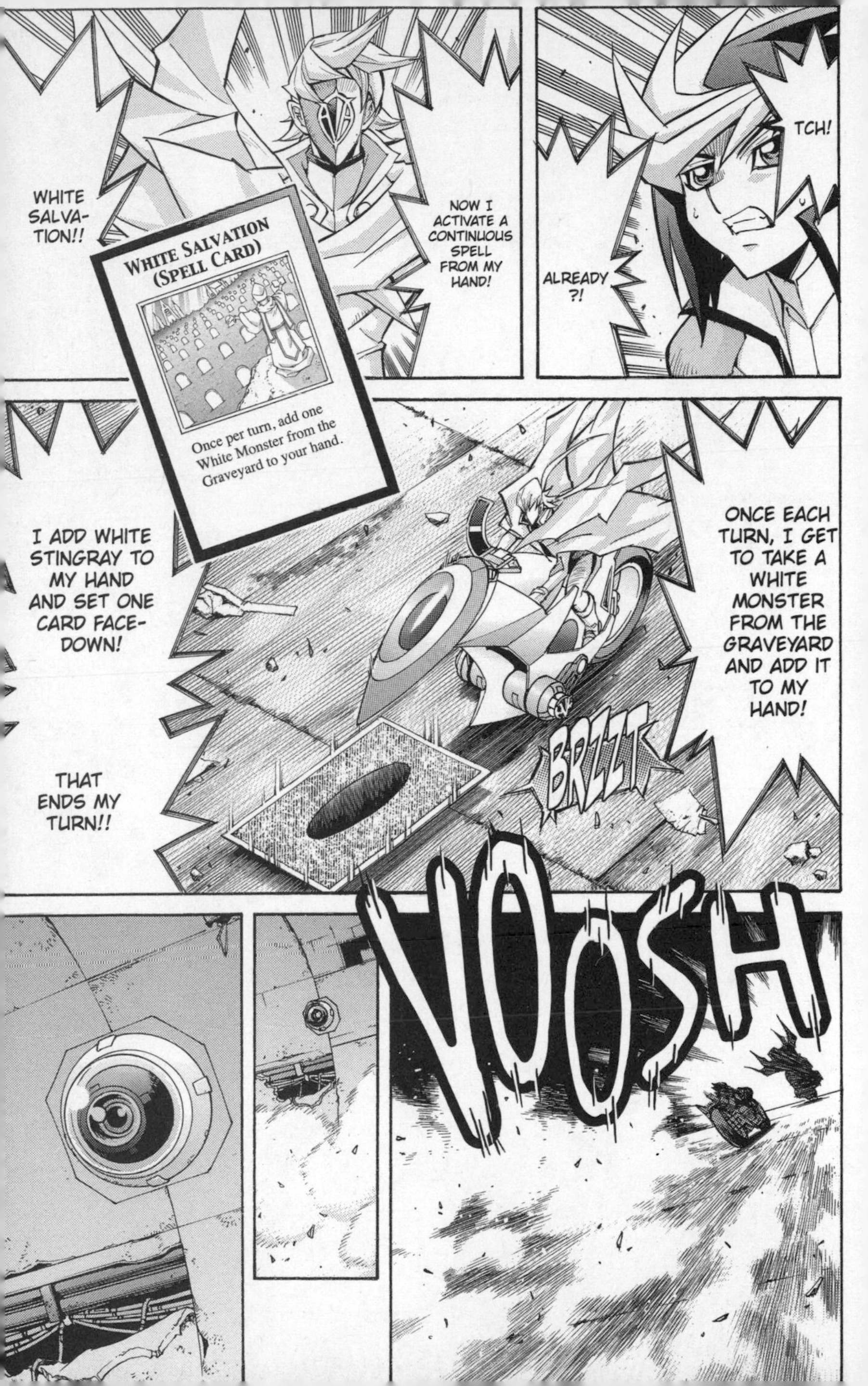
TCH!
ALREADY?!
NOW I ACTIVATE A CONTINUOUS SPELL FROM MY HAND!
WHITE SALVATION!!
WHITE SALVATION (SPELL CARD)
Once per turn, add one White Monster from the Graveyard to your hand.
ONCE EACH TURN, I GET TO TAKE A WHITE MONSTER FROM THE GRAVEYARD AND ADD IT TO MY HAND!
I ADD WHITE STINGRAY TO MY HAND AND SET ONE CARD FACE-DOWN!
BRZZT
THAT ENDS MY TURN!!
VOOSH

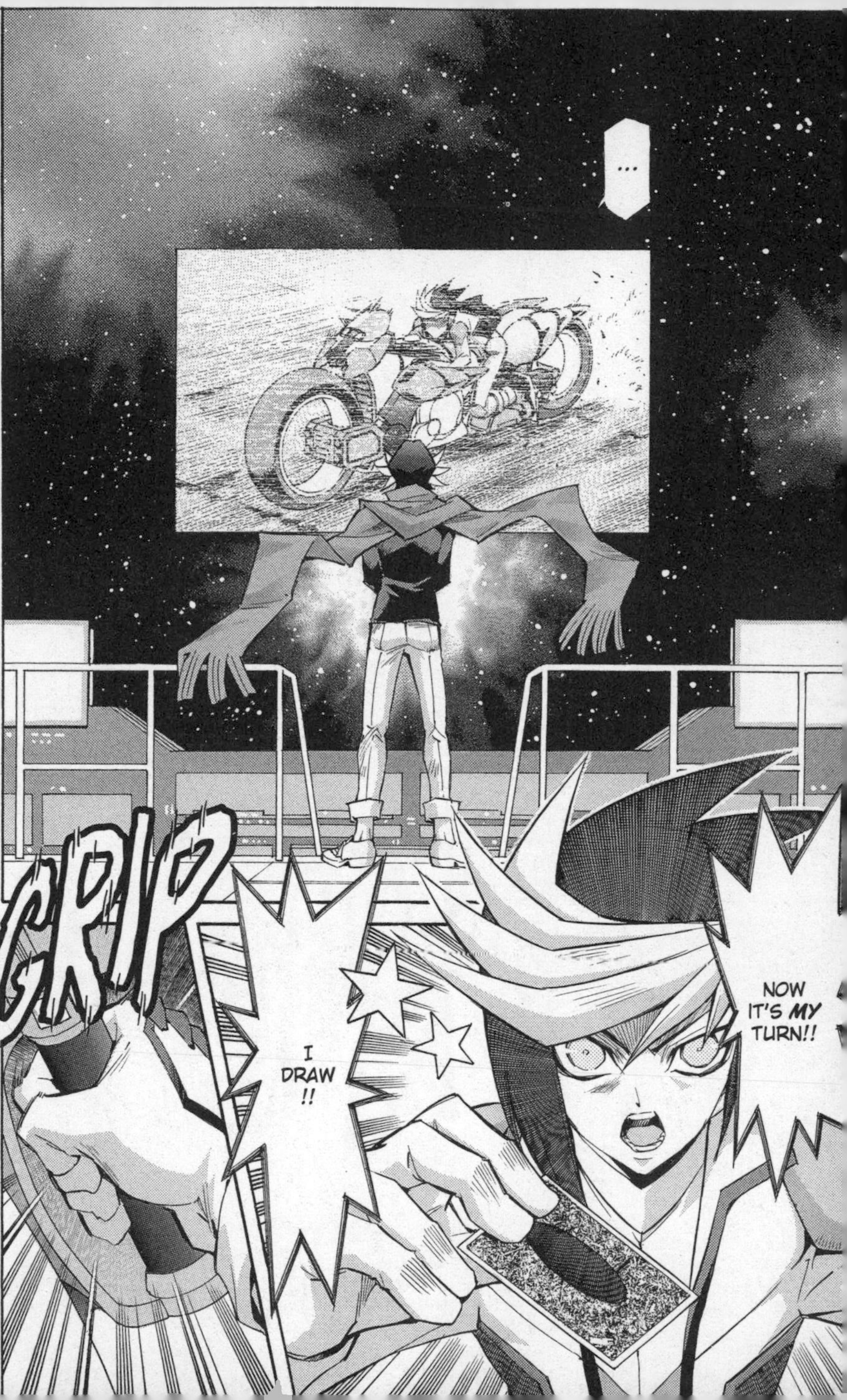
...
NOW IT'S *MY* TURN!!
I DRAW!!
GRIP

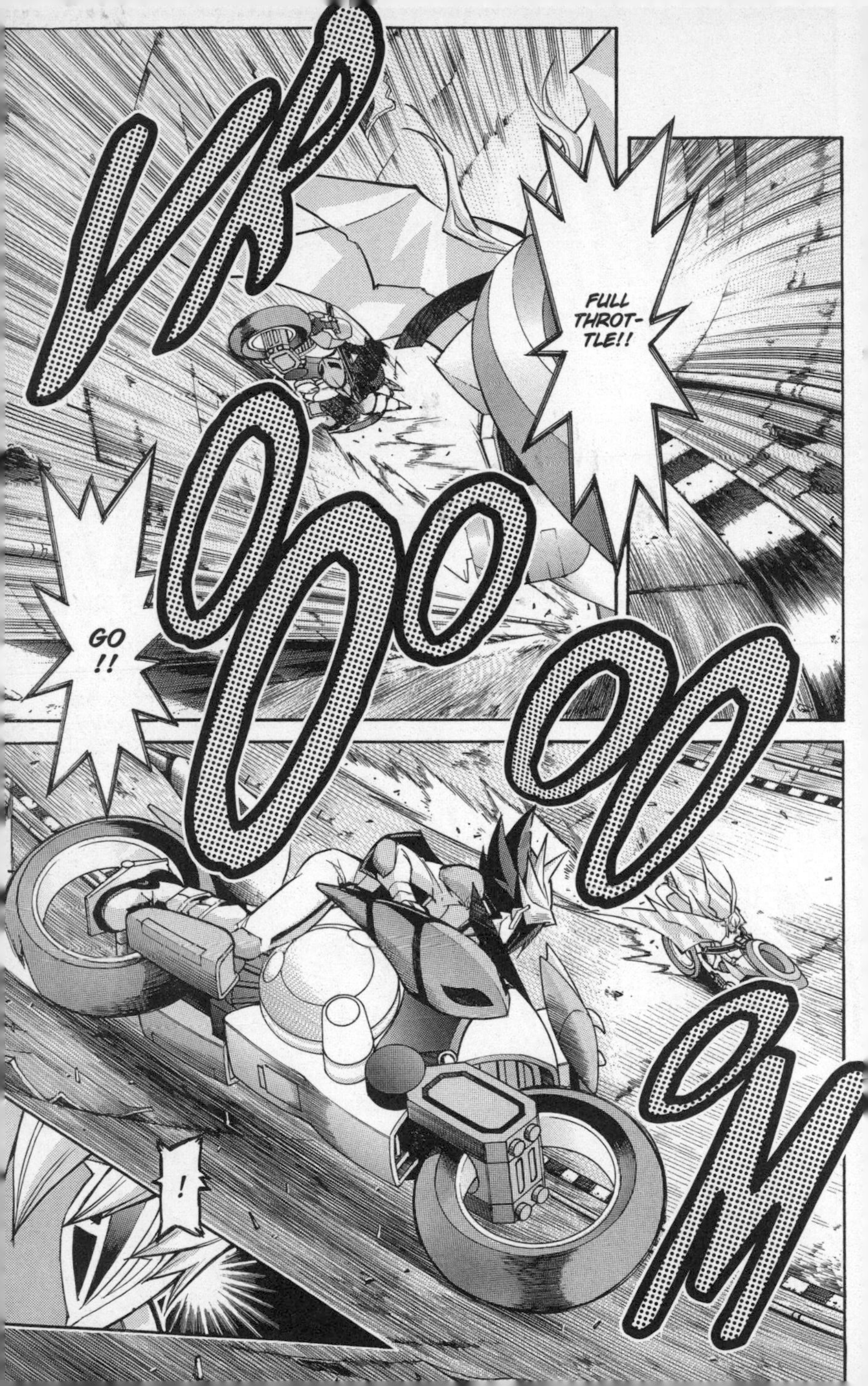
FULL THROT-TLE!!
GO!!
!

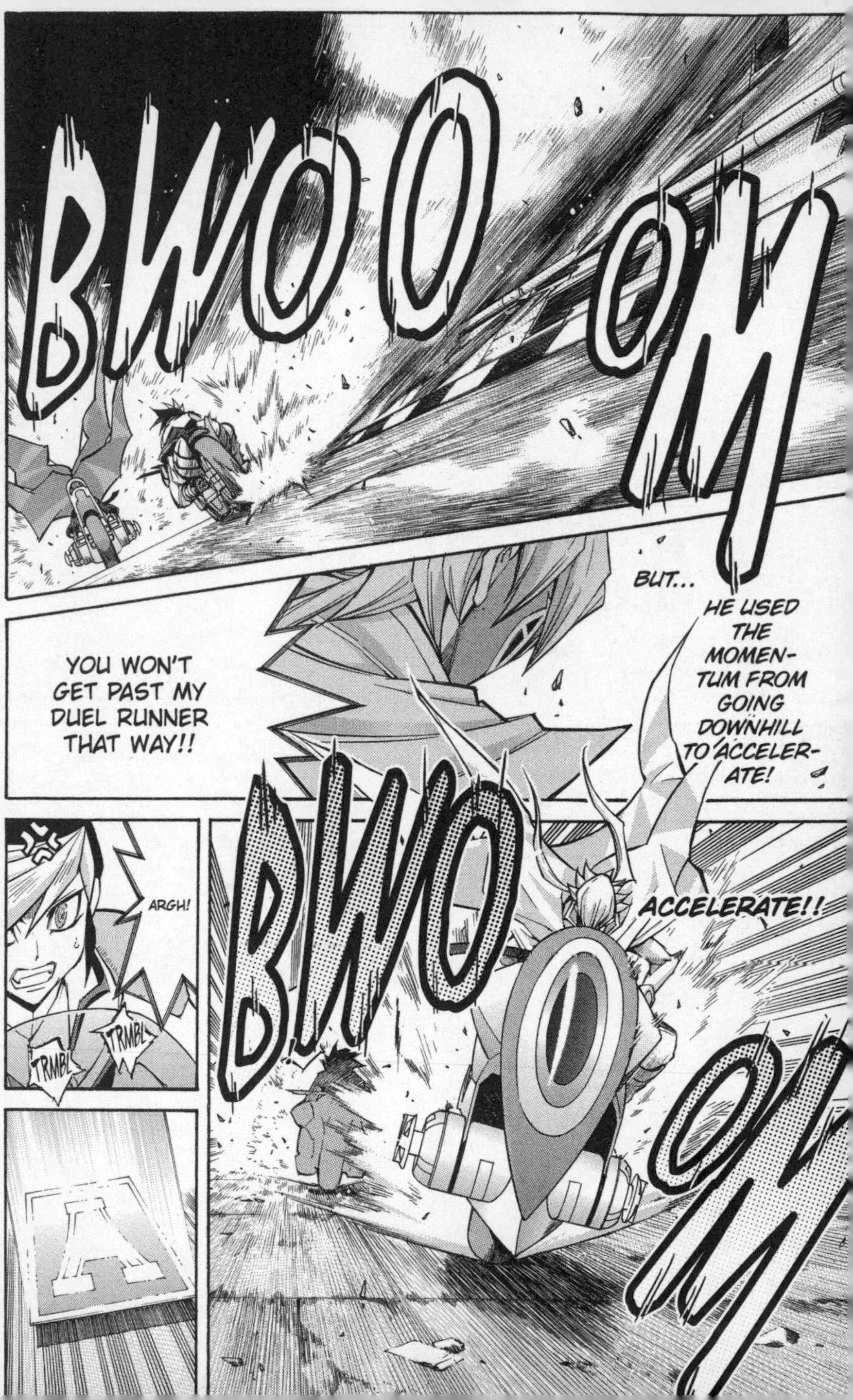
BWOOOOM
BUT...
HE USED THE MOMENTUM FROM GOING DOWNHILL TO ACCELERATE!
YOU WON'T GET PAST MY DUEL RUNNER THAT WAY!!
ACCELERATE!!
BWOOOOM
ARGH!
TRMBL
TRMBL

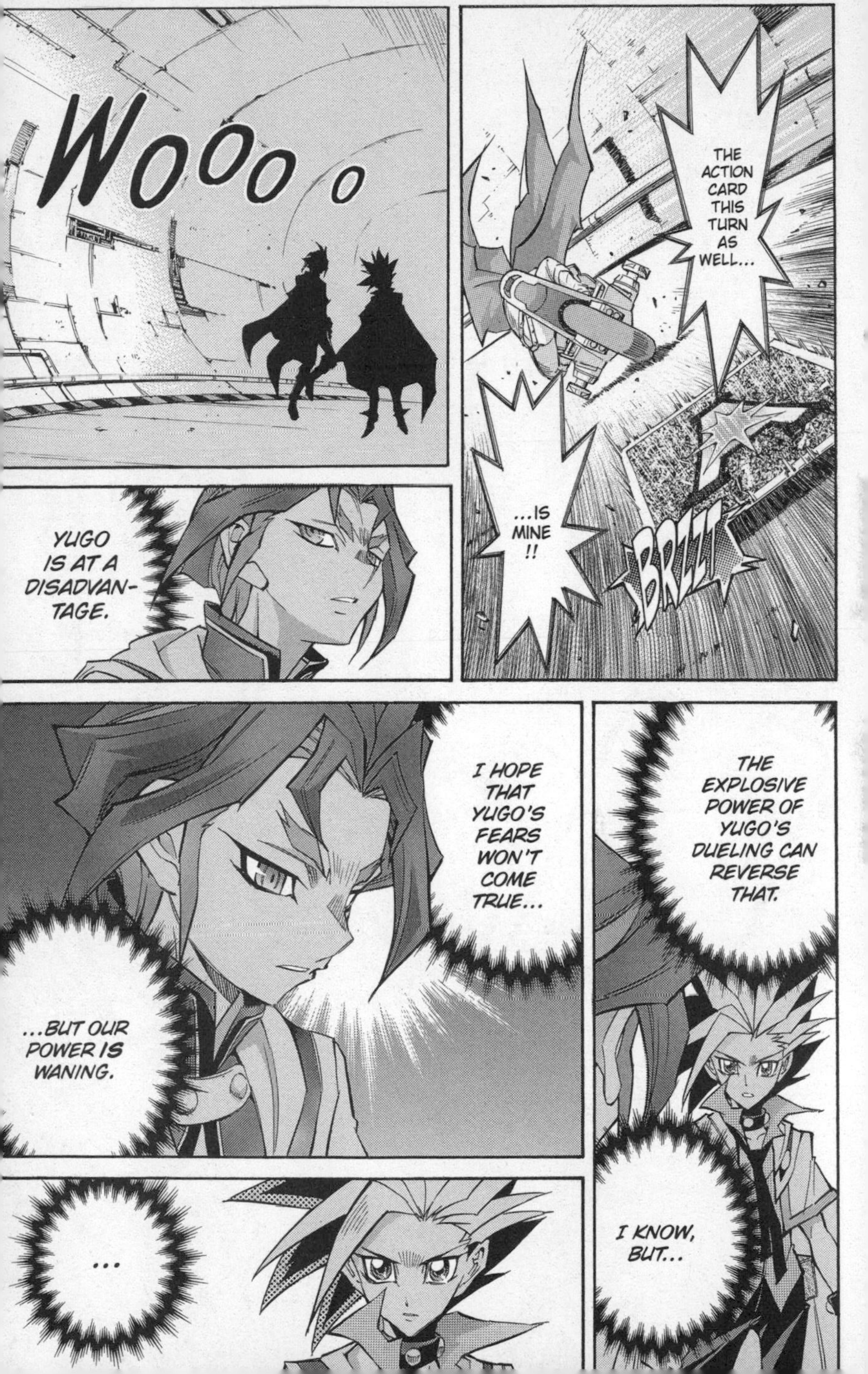
THE ACTION CARD THIS TURN AS WELL...
...IS MINE!!
BRZZT
WOOOO
YUGO IS AT A DISADVAN-TAGE.
THE EXPLOSIVE POWER OF YUGO'S DUELING CAN REVERSE THAT.
I KNOW, BUT...
I HOPE THAT YUGO'S FEARS WON'T COME TRUE...
...BUT OUR POWER IS WANING.
...

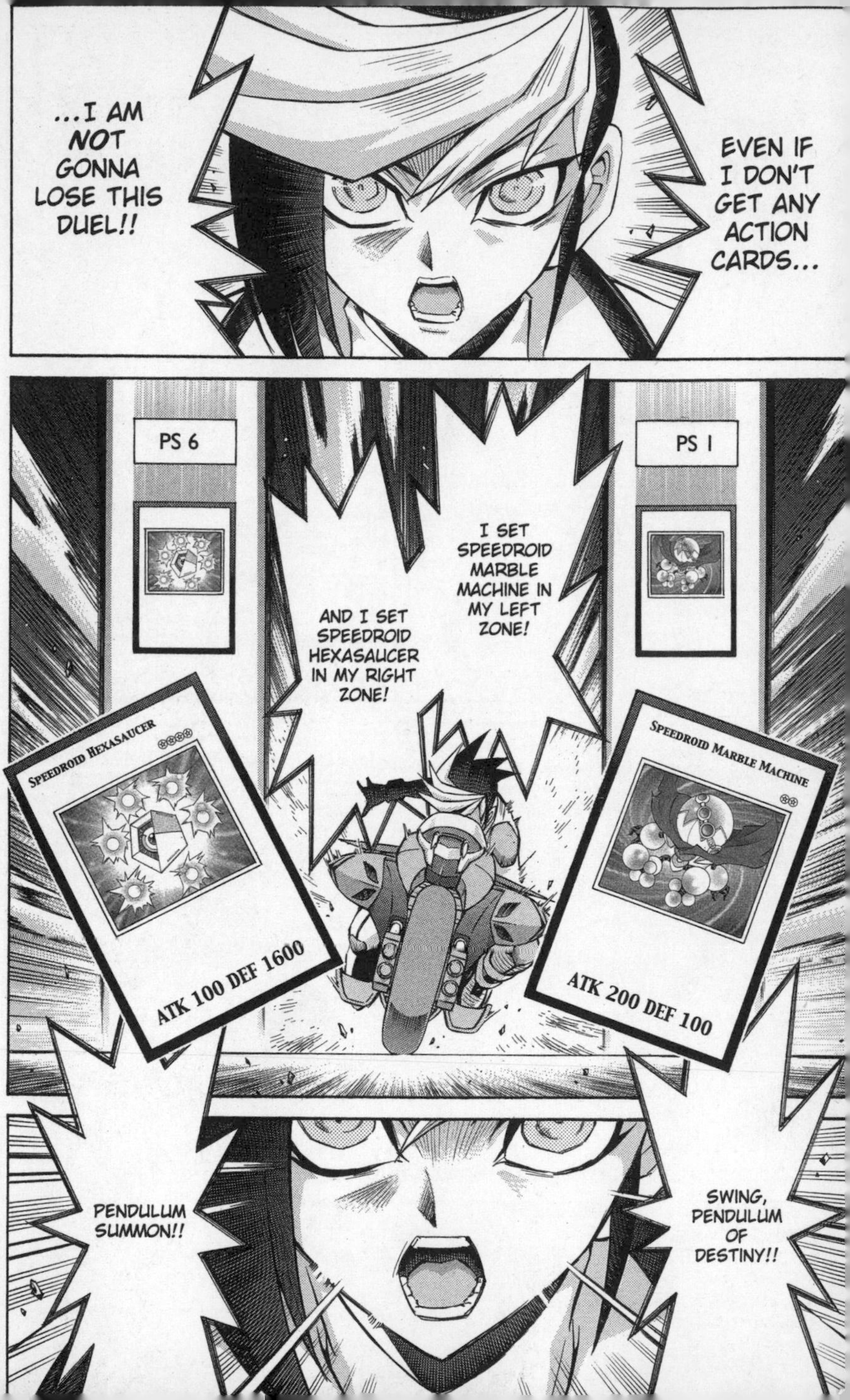
EVEN IF I DON'T GET ANY ACTION CARDS...
...I AM NOT GONNA LOSE THIS DUEL!!
PS 1
PS 6
I SET SPEEDROID MARBLE MACHINE IN MY LEFT ZONE!
AND I SET SPEEDROID HEXASAUCER IN MY RIGHT ZONE!
SPEEDROID MARBLE MACHINE
ATK 200 DEF 100
SPEEDROID HEXASAUCER
ATK 100 DEF 1600
SWING, PENDULUM OF DESTINY!!
PENDULUM SUMMON!!

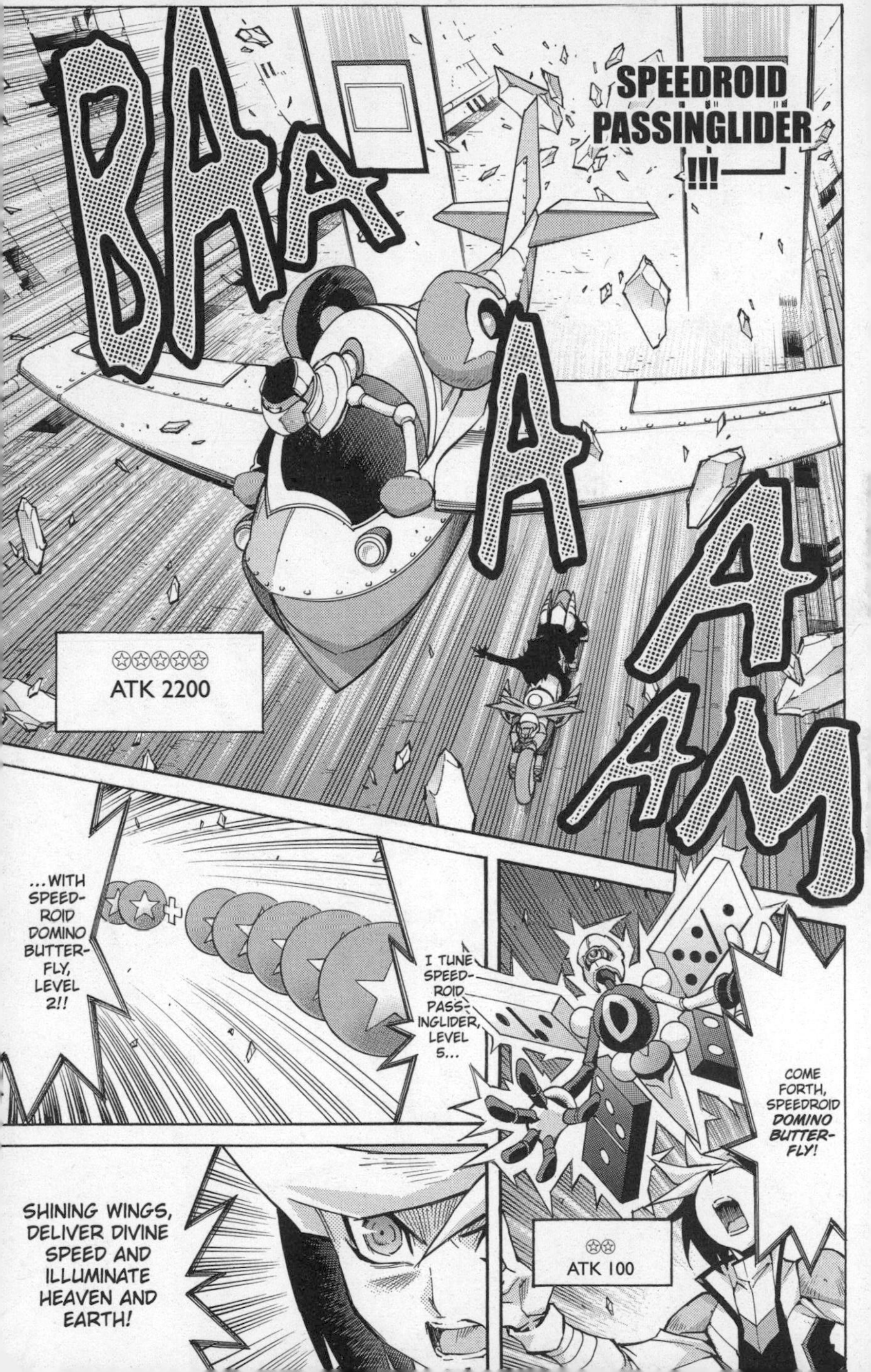
SPEEDROID PASSINGLIDER !!!
BRAAAAM
ATK 2200
I TUNE SPEEDROID PASSINGLIDER, LEVEL 5...
...WITH SPEEDROID DOMINO BUTTERFLY, LEVEL 2!!
SHINING WINGS, DELIVER DIVINE SPEED AND ILLUMINATE HEAVEN AND EARTH!
COME FORTH, SPEEDROID *DOMINO BUTTERFLY*!
ATK 100

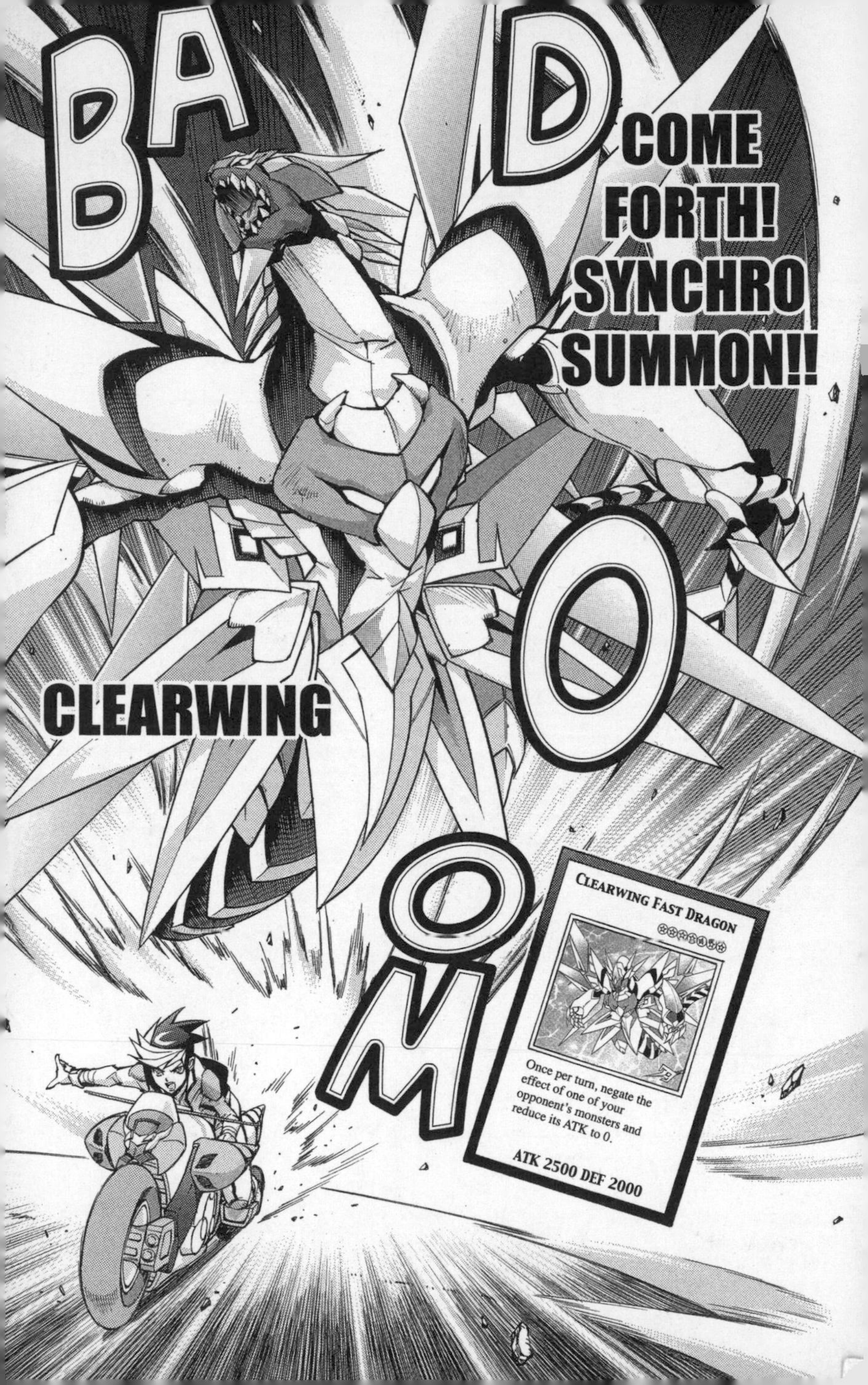
BADOOM
COME FORTH! SYNCHRO SUMMON!!
CLEARWING
CLEARWING FAST DRAGON
Once per turn, negate the effect of one of your opponent's monsters and reduce its ATK to 0.
ATK 2500 DEF 2000

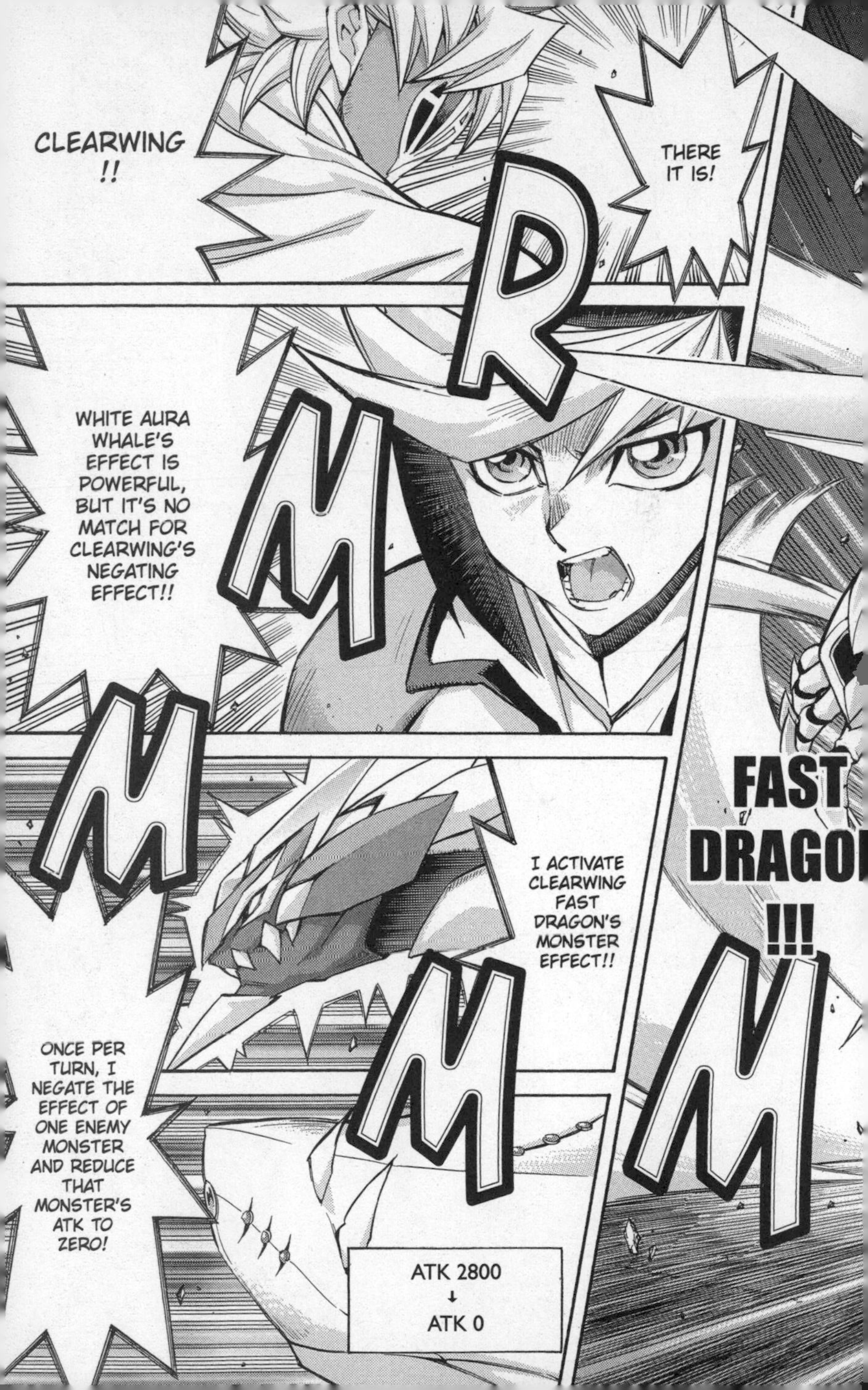

THERE IT IS!
CLEARWING !!
FAST DRAGON !!!
RMMMM
WHITE AURA WHALE'S EFFECT IS POWERFUL, BUT IT'S NO MATCH FOR CLEARWING'S NEGATING EFFECT!!
I ACTIVATE CLEARWING FAST DRAGON'S MONSTER EFFECT!!
ONCE PER TURN, I NEGATE THE EFFECT OF ONE ENEMY MONSTER AND REDUCE THAT MONSTER'S ATK TO ZERO!
ATK 2800 ↓ ATK 0

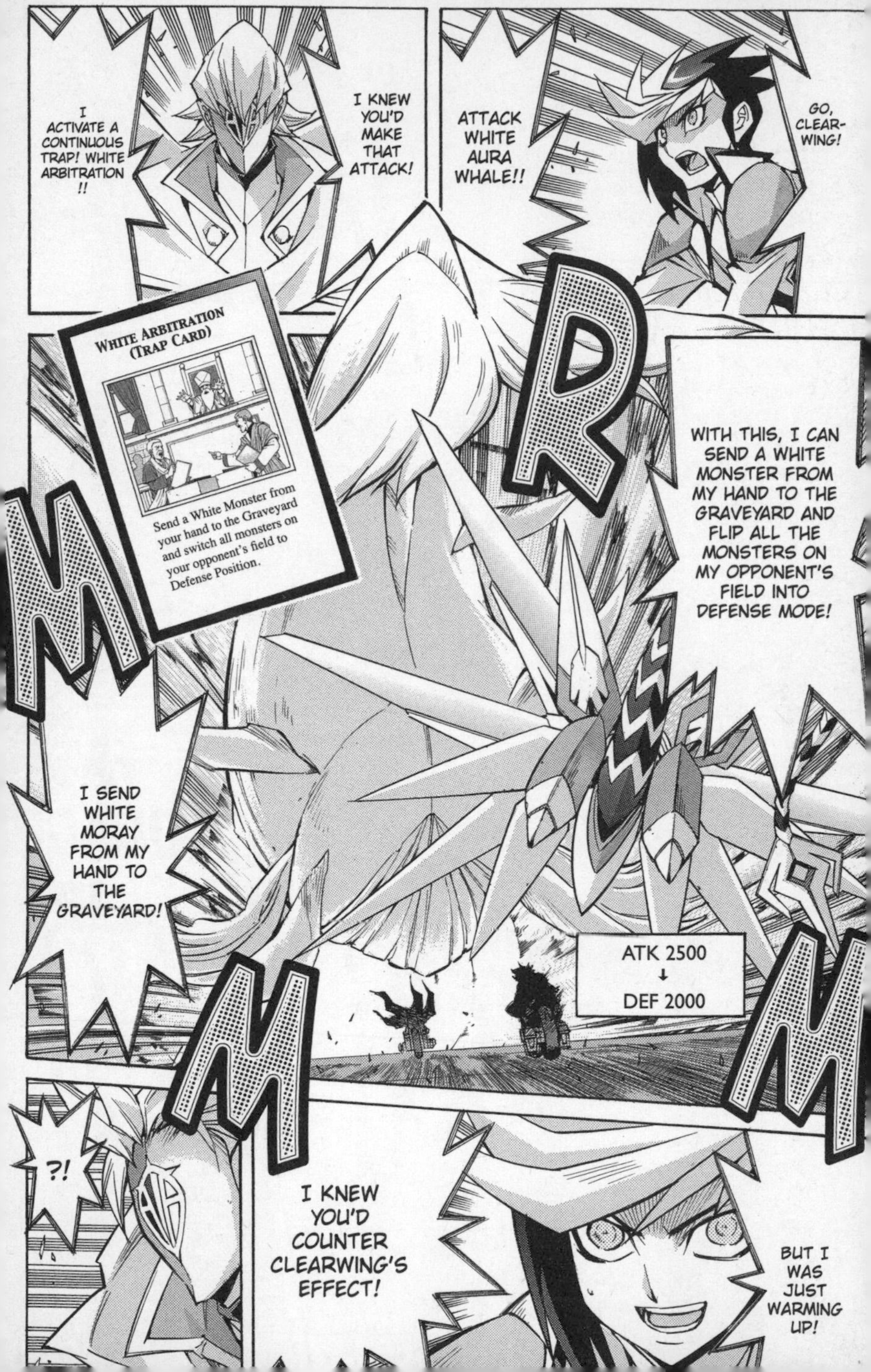
GO, CLEAR-WING!
ATTACK WHITE AURA WHALE!!
I KNEW YOU'D MAKE THAT ATTACK!
I ACTIVATE A CONTINUOUS TRAP! WHITE ARBITRATION !!
WHITE ARBITRATION (TRAP CARD)
Send a White Monster from your hand to the Graveyard and switch all monsters on your opponent's field to Defense Position.
WITH THIS, I CAN SEND A WHITE MONSTER FROM MY HAND TO THE GRAVEYARD AND FLIP ALL THE MONSTERS ON MY OPPONENT'S FIELD INTO DEFENSE MODE!
I SEND WHITE MORAY FROM MY HAND TO THE GRAVEYARD!
ATK 2500 ↓ DEF 2000
I KNEW YOU'D COUNTER CLEARWING'S EFFECT!
BUT I WAS JUST WARMING UP!
?!

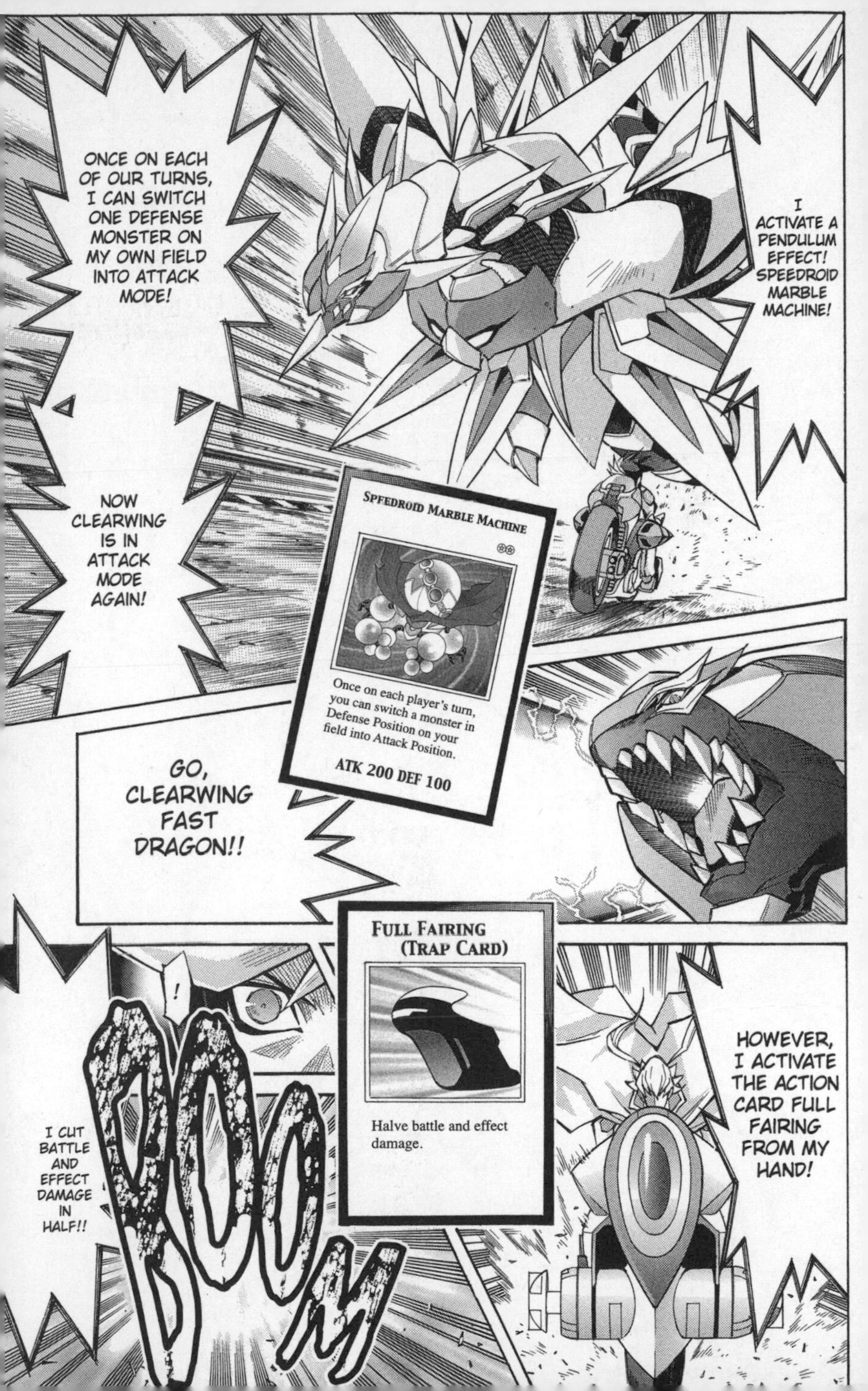
I ACTIVATE A PENDULUM EFFECT! SPEEDROID MARBLE MACHINE!
ONCE ON EACH OF OUR TURNS, I CAN SWITCH ONE DEFENSE MONSTER ON MY OWN FIELD INTO ATTACK MODE!
SPFEDROID MARBLE MACHINE
Once on each player's turn, you can switch a monster in Defense Position on your field into Attack Position.
ATK 200 DEF 100
NOW CLEARWING IS IN ATTACK MODE AGAIN!
GO, CLEARWING FAST DRAGON!!
HOWEVER, I ACTIVATE THE ACTION CARD FULL FAIRING FROM MY HAND!
FULL FAIRING (TRAP CARD)
Halve battle and effect damage.
!
I CUT BATTLE AND EFFECT DAMAGE IN HALF!!
BOOM

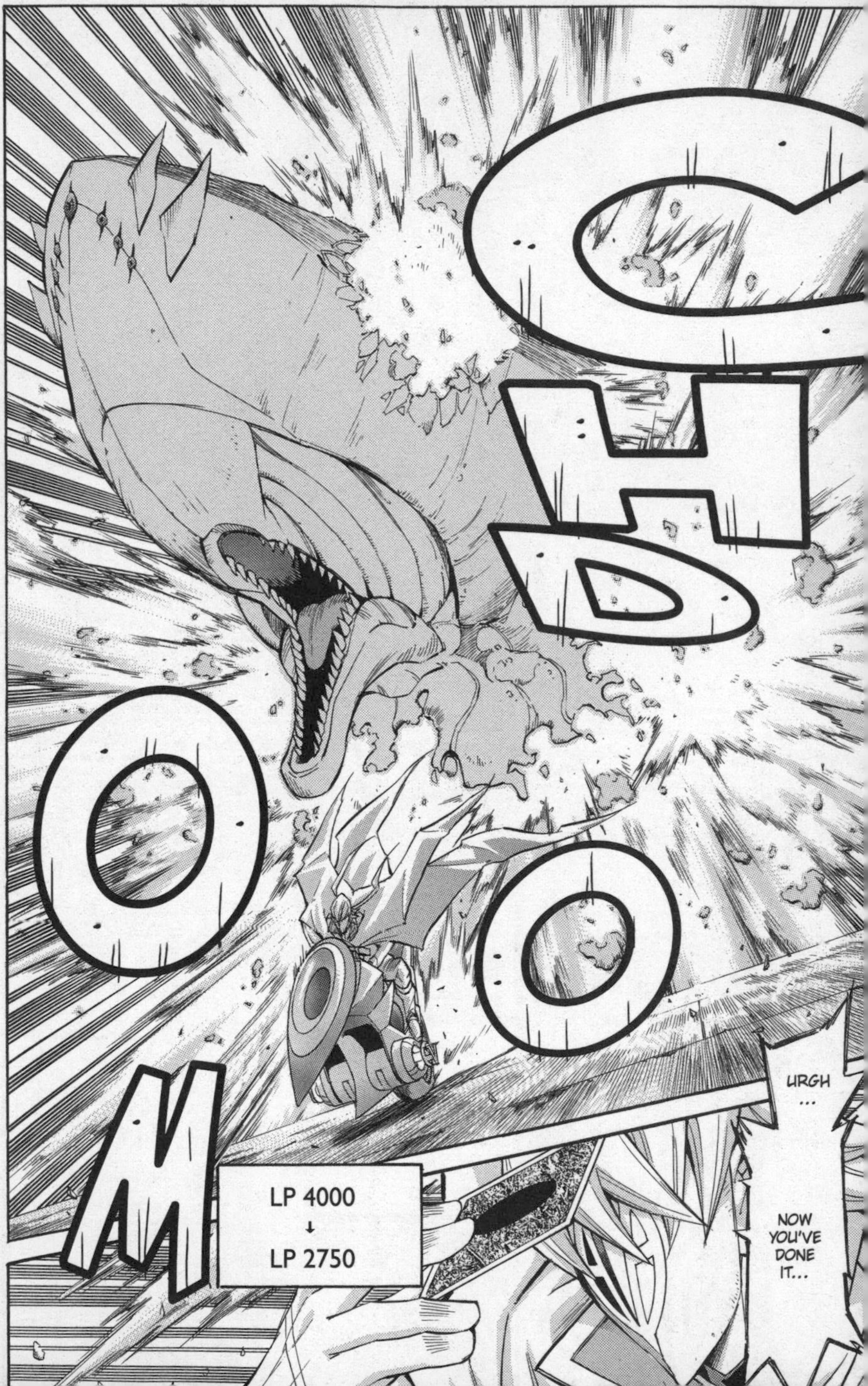
URGH ...
NOW YOU'VE DONE IT...
LP 4000 ↓ LP 2750

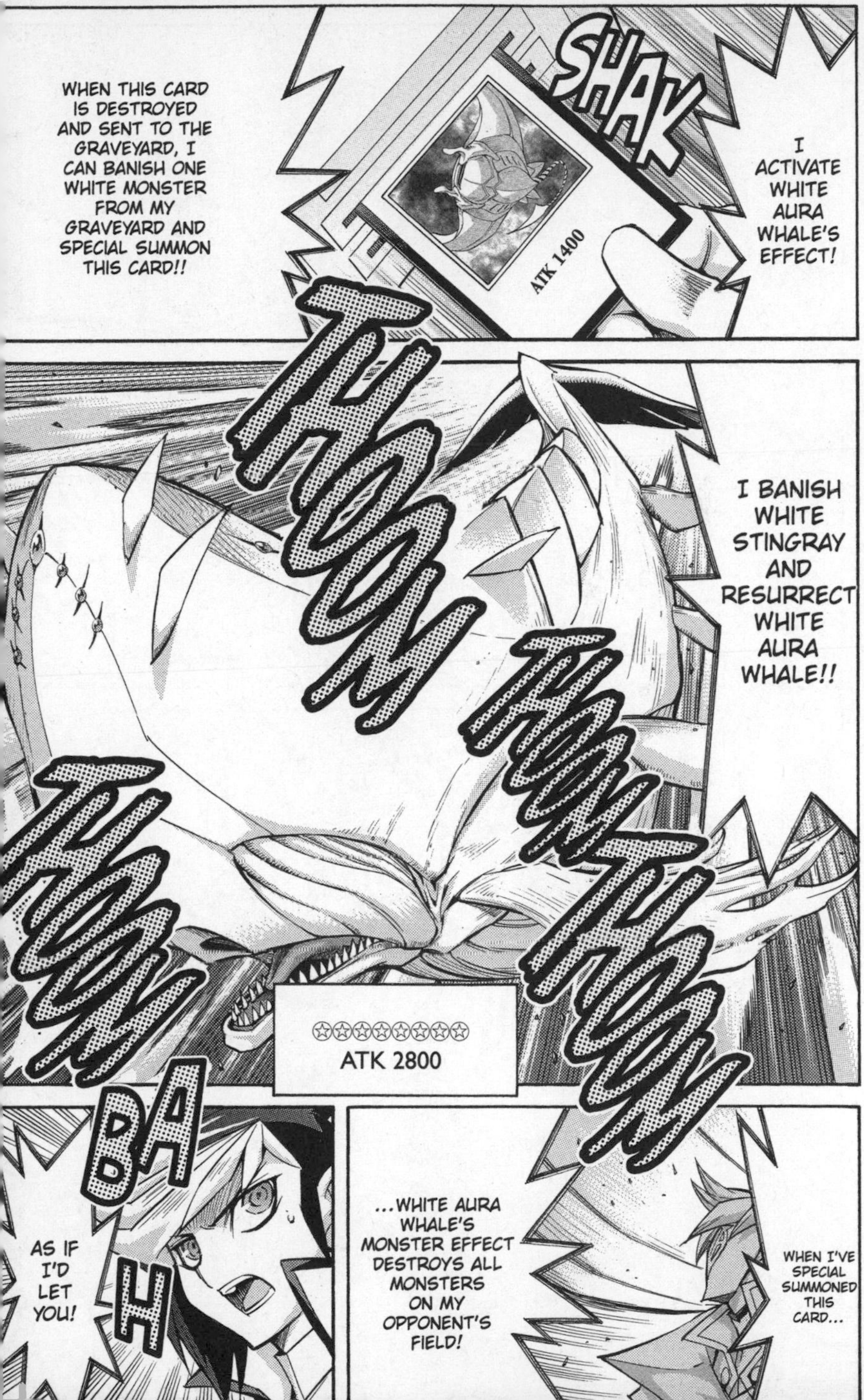
SHAK
I ACTIVATE WHITE AURA WHALE'S EFFECT!
ATK 1400
WHEN THIS CARD IS DESTROYED AND SENT TO THE GRAVEYARD, I CAN BANISH ONE WHITE MONSTER FROM MY GRAVEYARD AND SPECIAL SUMMON THIS CARD!!
I BANISH WHITE STINGRAY AND RESURRECT WHITE AURA WHALE!!
THOOM
THOOM THOOM
THOOM
ATK 2800
WHEN I'VE SPECIAL SUMMONED THIS CARD...
...WHITE AURA WHALE'S MONSTER EFFECT DESTROYS ALL MONSTERS ON MY OPPONENT'S FIELD!
BADH
AS IF I'D LET YOU!

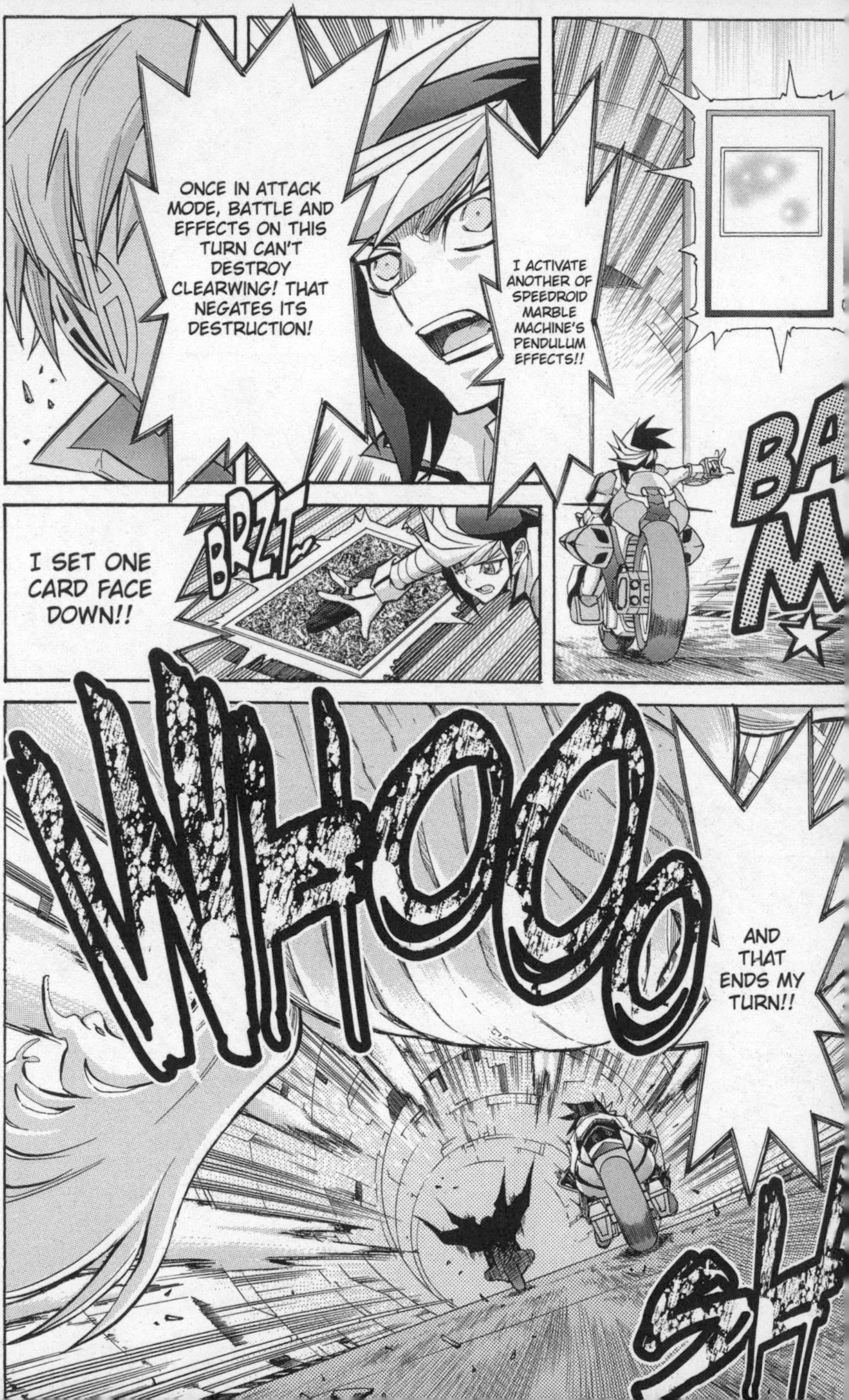
I ACTIVATE ANOTHER OF SPEEDROID MARBLE MACHINE'S PENDULUM EFFECTS!!
ONCE IN ATTACK MODE, BATTLE AND EFFECTS ON THIS TURN CAN'T DESTROY CLEARWING! THAT NEGATES ITS DESTRUCTION!
BAM
BRZZT
I SET ONE CARD FACE DOWN!!
AND THAT ENDS MY TURN!!
WHOOSH

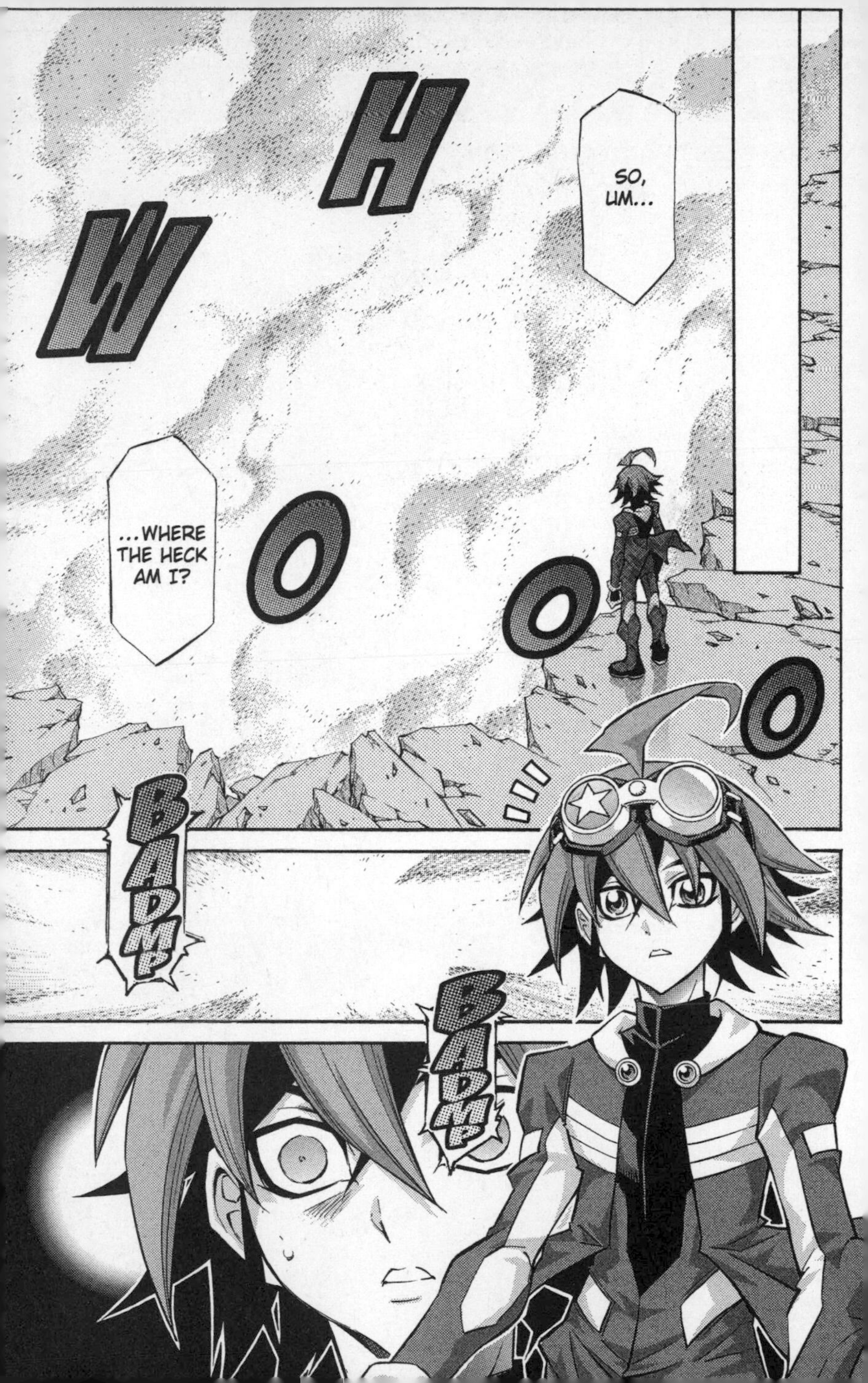
SO, UM...
WHOOOO
...WHERE THE HECK AM I?
BADMP
BADMP

ODD-EYES PHANTOM DRAGON

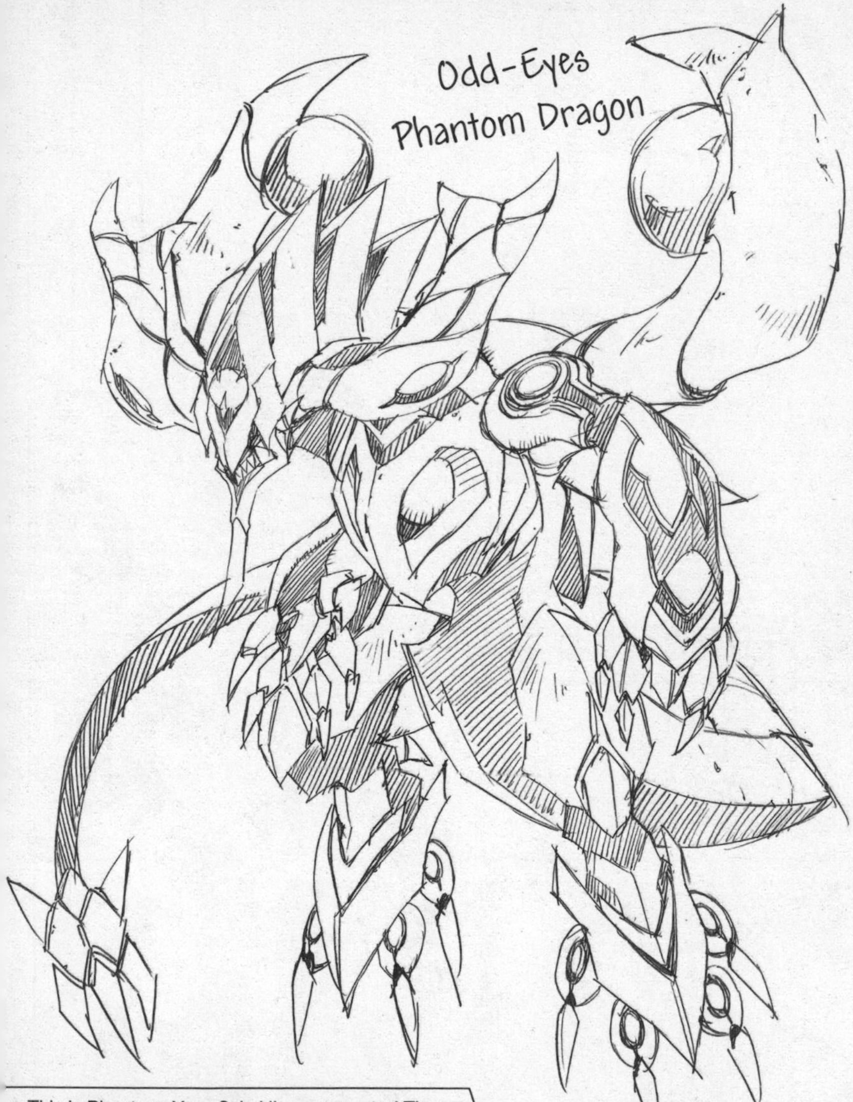
Odd-Eyes
Phantom Dragon

This is Phantom, Yuya Sakaki's ace monster! The overall design of its body is meant to remind you of bones, and a blue flame is in its eyes. The name "Phantom" is perfect for this dragon!

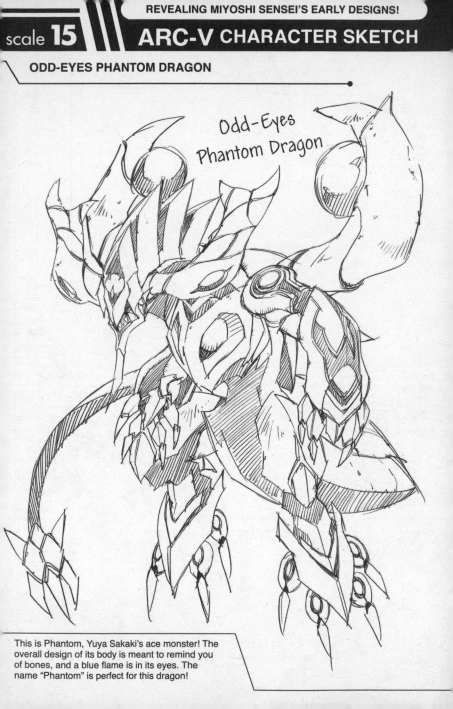

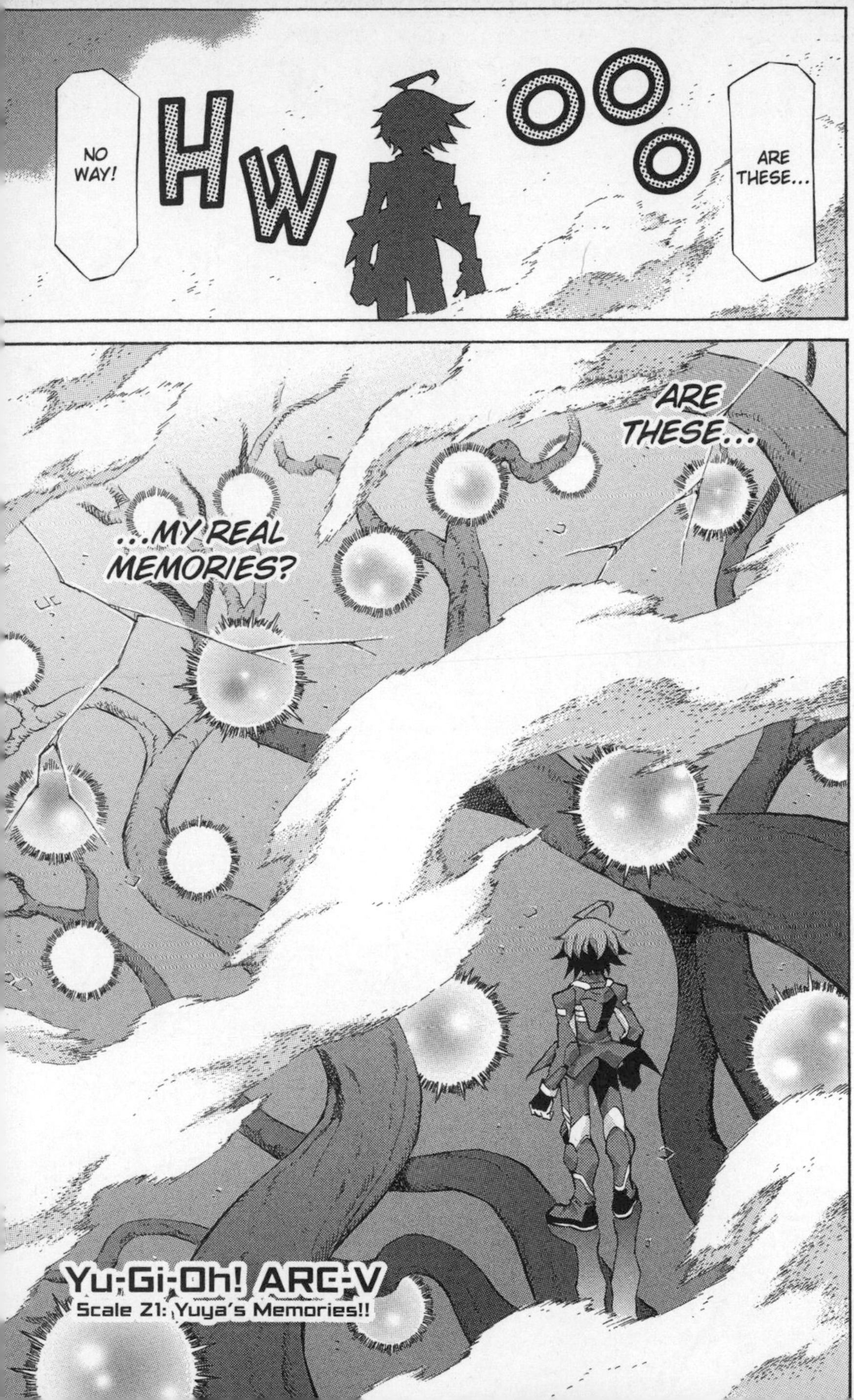
ARE THESE...
HWOOOO
NO WAY!
ARE THESE...
...MY REAL MEMORIES?
Yu-Gi-Oh! ARC-V
Scale 21: Yuya's Memories!!

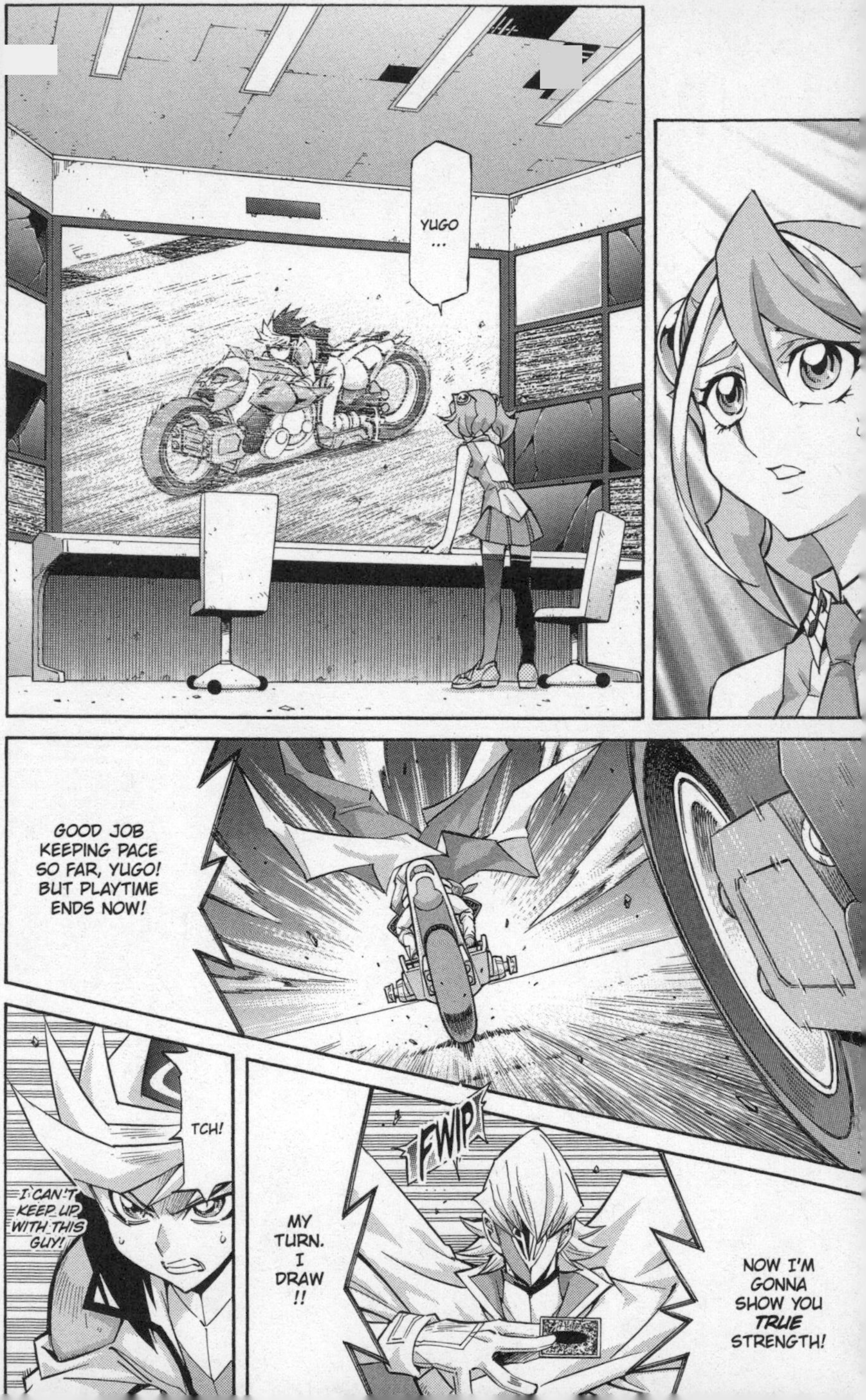
YUGO ...
GOOD JOB KEEPING PACE SO FAR, YUGO! BUT PLAYTIME ENDS NOW!
FWIP
MY TURN. I DRAW !!
NOW I'M GONNA SHOW YOU TRUE STRENGTH!
TCH!
I CAN'T KEEP UP WITH THIS GUY!

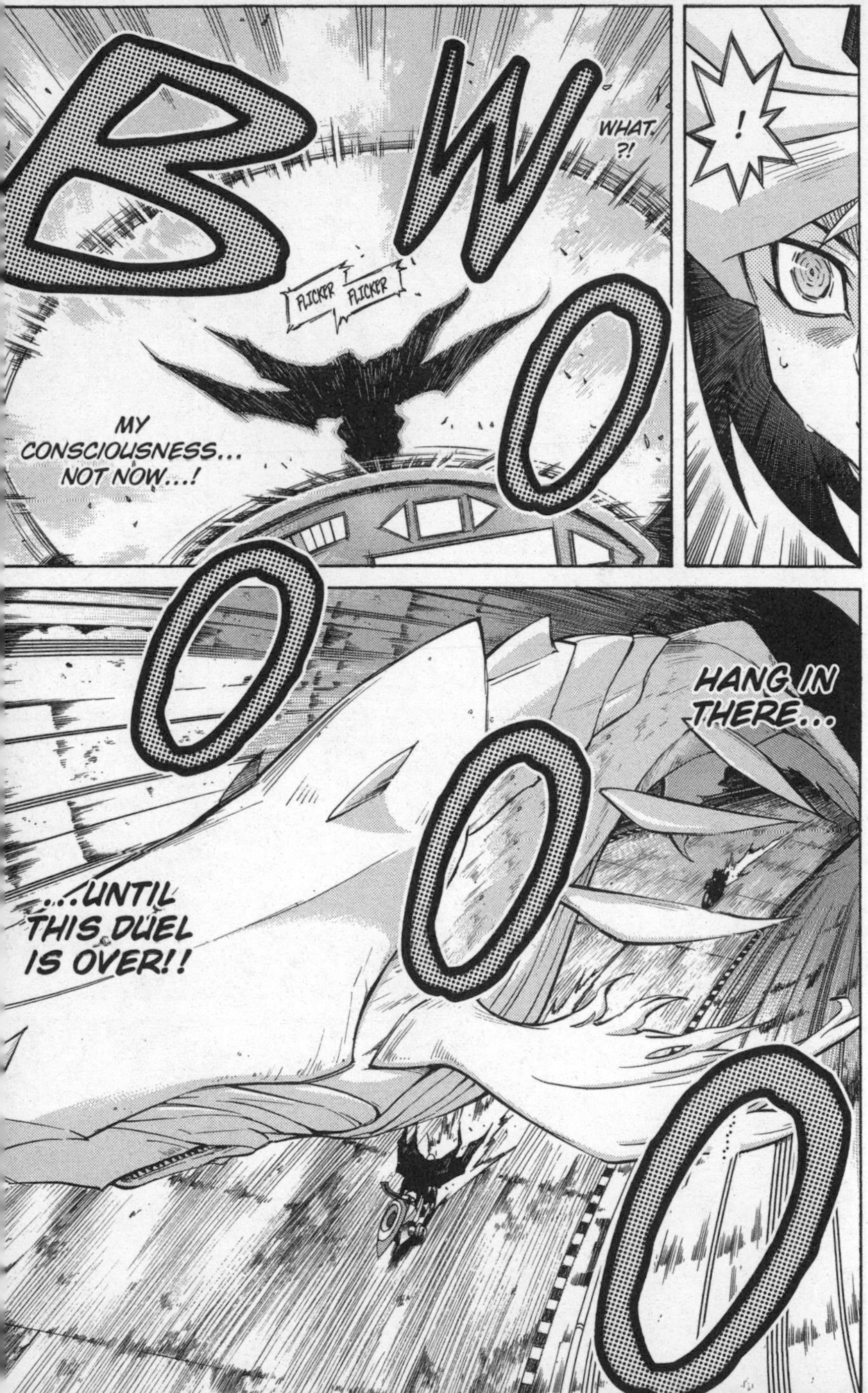
!
WHAT ?!
BWOOOOO
FLICKER FLICKER
MY CONSCIOUSNESS... NOT NOW...!
HANG IN THERE...
...UNTIL THIS DUEL IS OVER!!

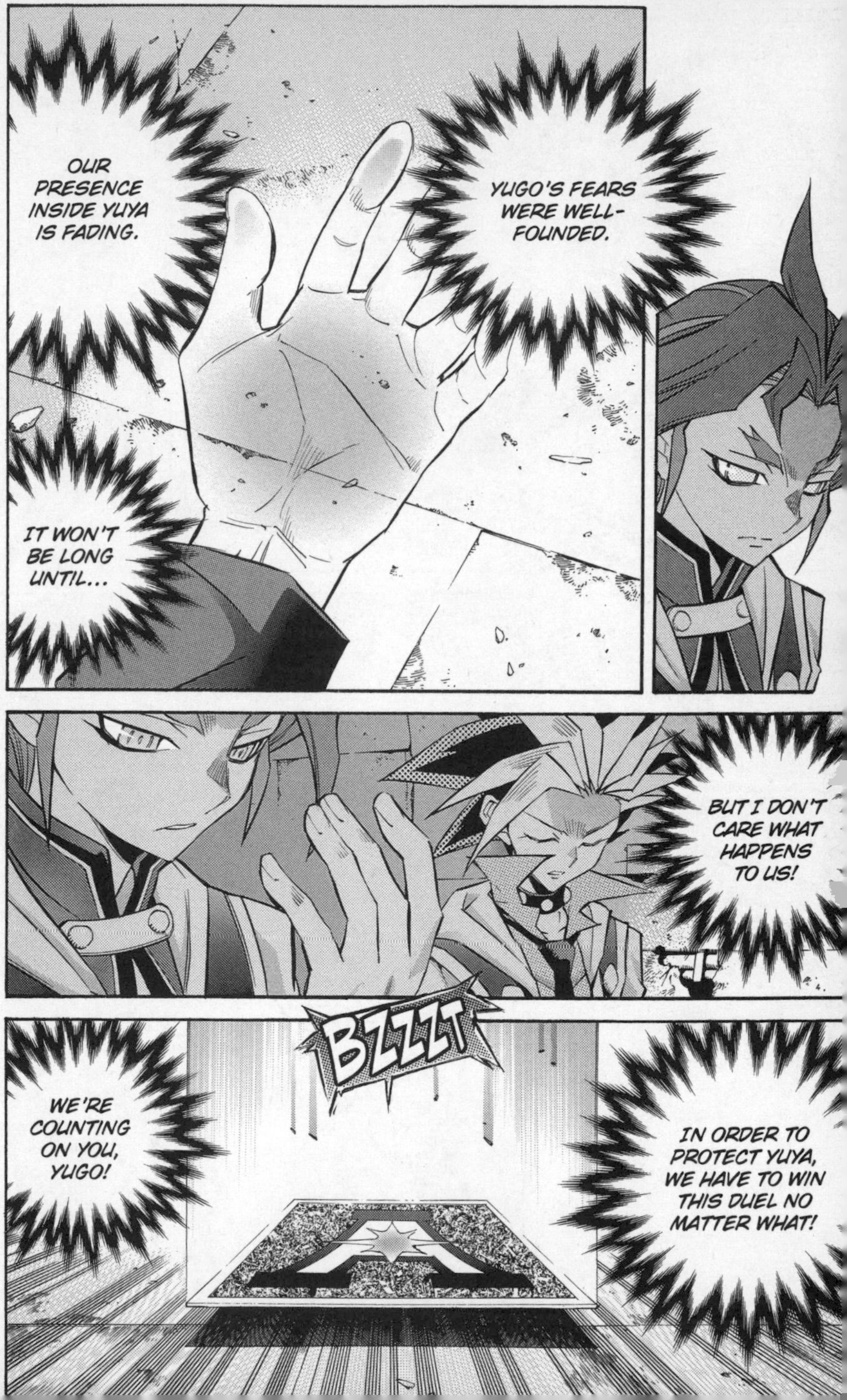
YUGO'S FEARS WERE WELL-FOUNDED.
OUR PRESENCE INSIDE YUYA IS FADING.
IT WON'T BE LONG UNTIL...
BUT I DON'T CARE WHAT HAPPENS TO US!
BZZZT
IN ORDER TO PROTECT YUYA, WE HAVE TO WIN THIS DUEL NO MATTER WHAT!
WE'RE COUNTING ON YOU, YUGO!

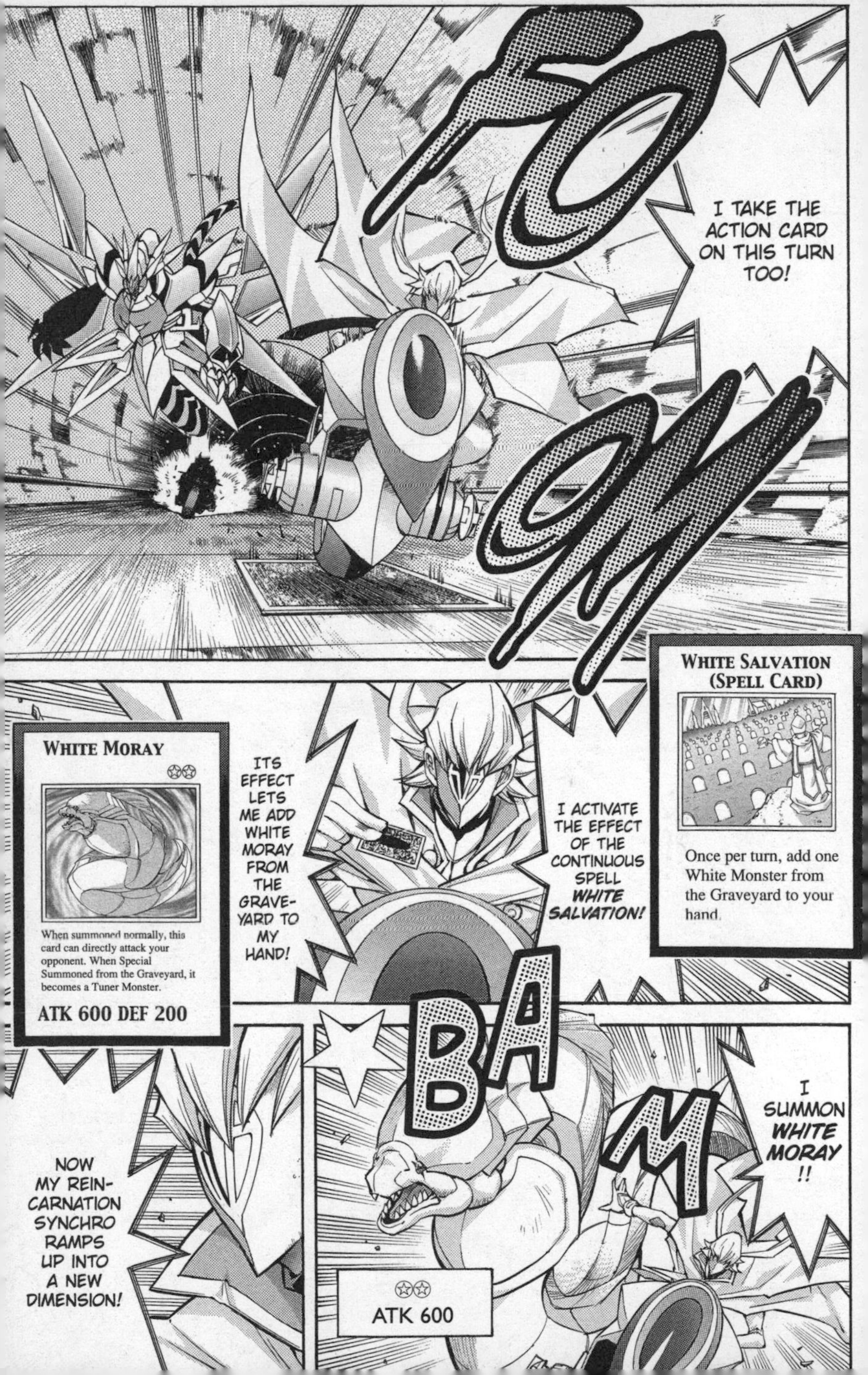
FOOM
I TAKE THE ACTION CARD ON THIS TURN TOO!
White Salvation (Spell Card)
Once per turn, add one White Monster from the Graveyard to your hand.
I ACTIVATE THE EFFECT OF THE CONTINUOUS SPELL WHITE SALVATION!
ITS EFFECT LETS ME ADD WHITE MORAY FROM THE GRAVEYARD TO MY HAND!
White Moray
When summoned normally, this card can directly attack your opponent. When Special Summoned from the Graveyard, it becomes a Tuner Monster.
ATK 600 DEF 200
BAM
I SUMMON WHITE MORAY!!
ATK 600
NOW MY REIN-CARNATION SYNCHRO RAMPS UP INTO A NEW DIMENSION!

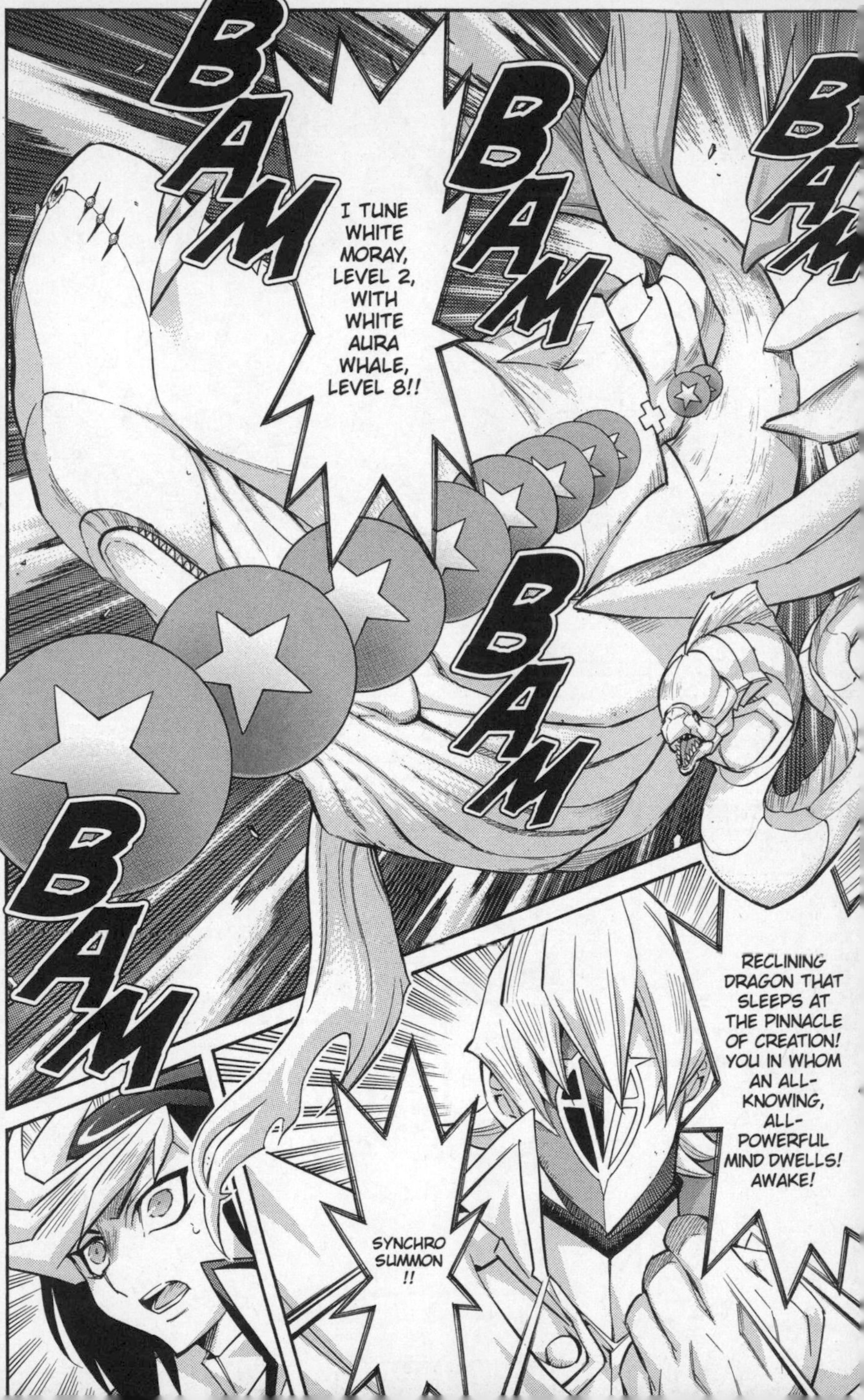

BAM
BAM
I TUNE WHITE MORAY, LEVEL 2, WITH WHITE AURA WHALE, LEVEL 8!!
BAM
BAM
BAM
RECLINING DRAGON THAT SLEEPS AT THE PINNACLE OF CREATION! YOU IN WHOM AN ALL-KNOWING, ALL-POWERFUL MIND DWELLS! AWAKE!
SYNCHRO SUMMON!!

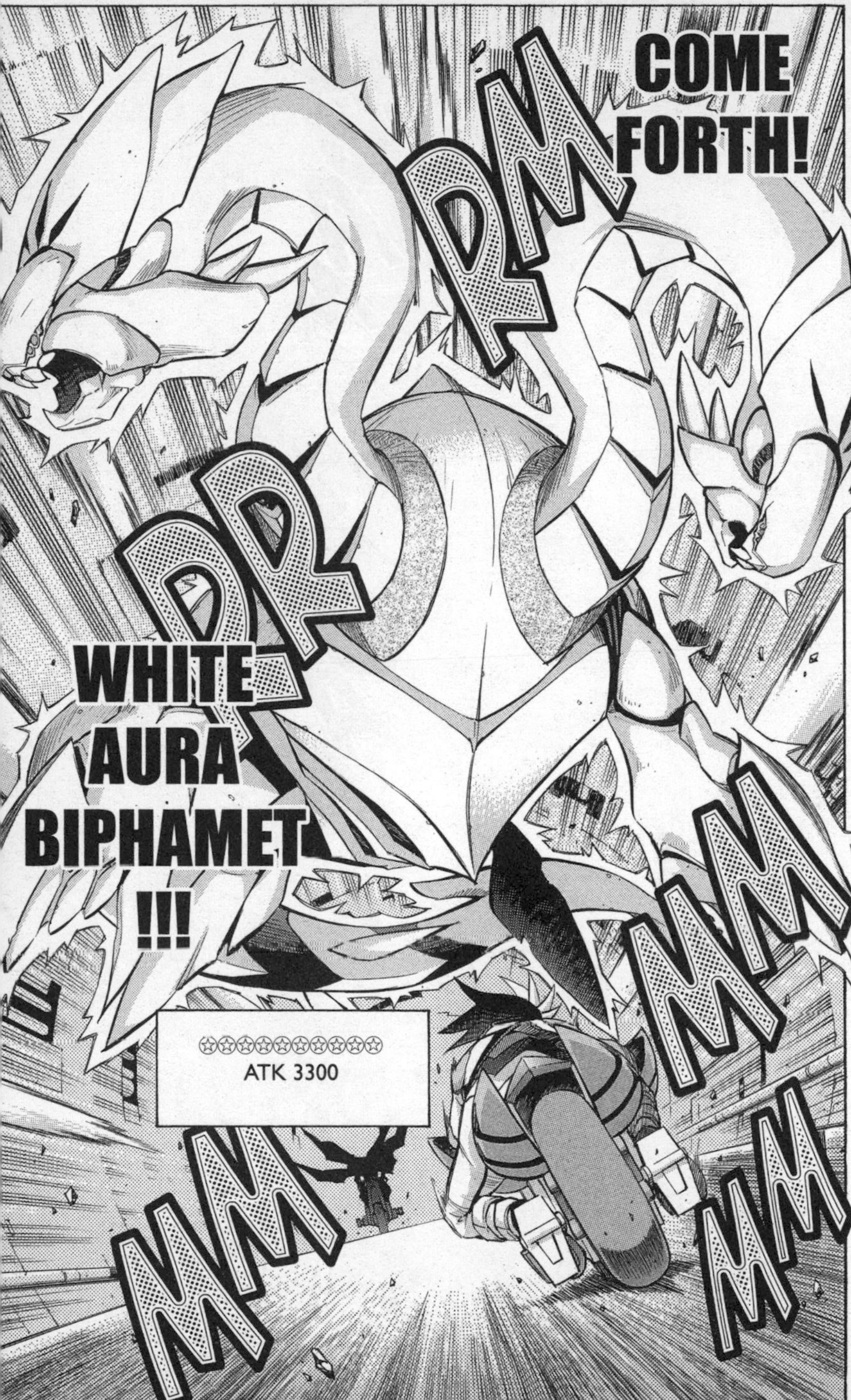
COME FORTH!
WHITE AURA BIPHAMET!!!
ATK 3300

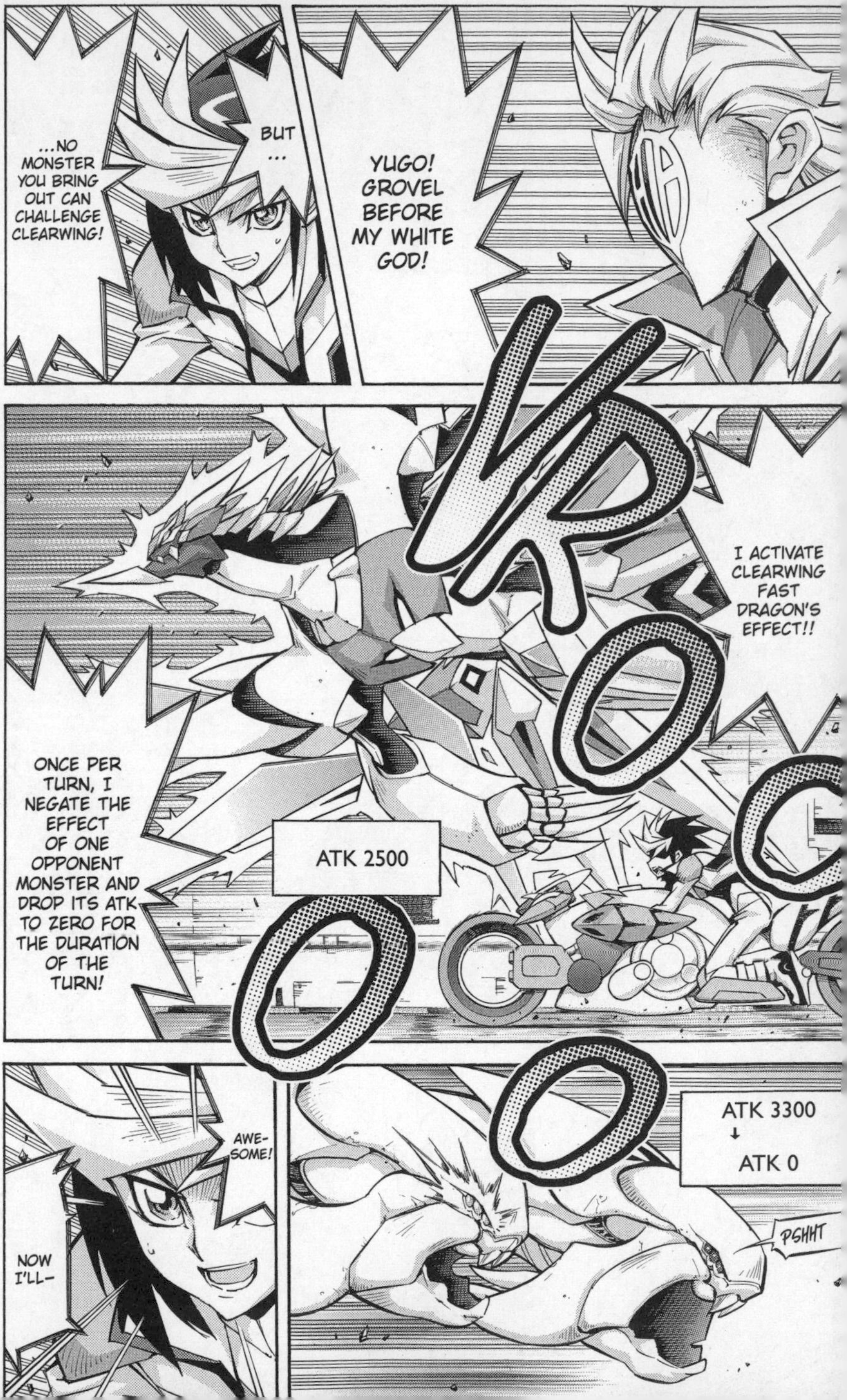
YUGO! GROVEL BEFORE MY WHITE GOD!
BUT ...
...NO MONSTER YOU BRING OUT CAN CHALLENGE CLEARWING!
VROOOO
I ACTIVATE CLEARWING FAST DRAGON'S EFFECT!!
ONCE PER TURN, I NEGATE THE EFFECT OF ONE OPPONENT MONSTER AND DROP ITS ATK TO ZERO FOR THE DURATION OF THE TURN!
ATK 2500
ATK 3300 ↓ ATK 0
PSHHT
AWESOME!
NOW I'LL—

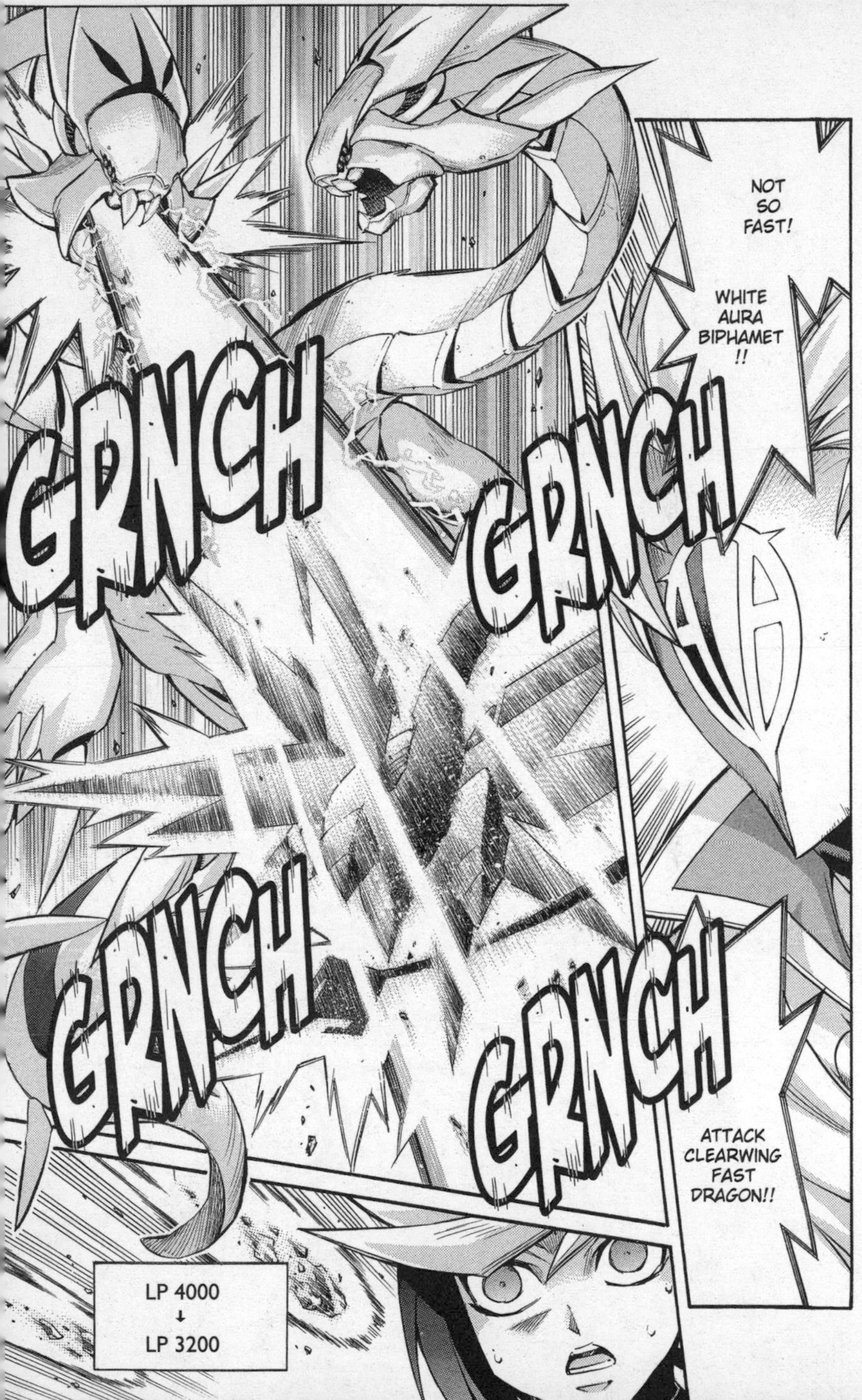
NOT SO FAST!
WHITE AURA BIPHAMET!!
GRNCH
GRNCH
GRNCH
GRNCH
ATTACK CLEARWING FAST DRAGON!!
LP 4000 ↓ LP 3200

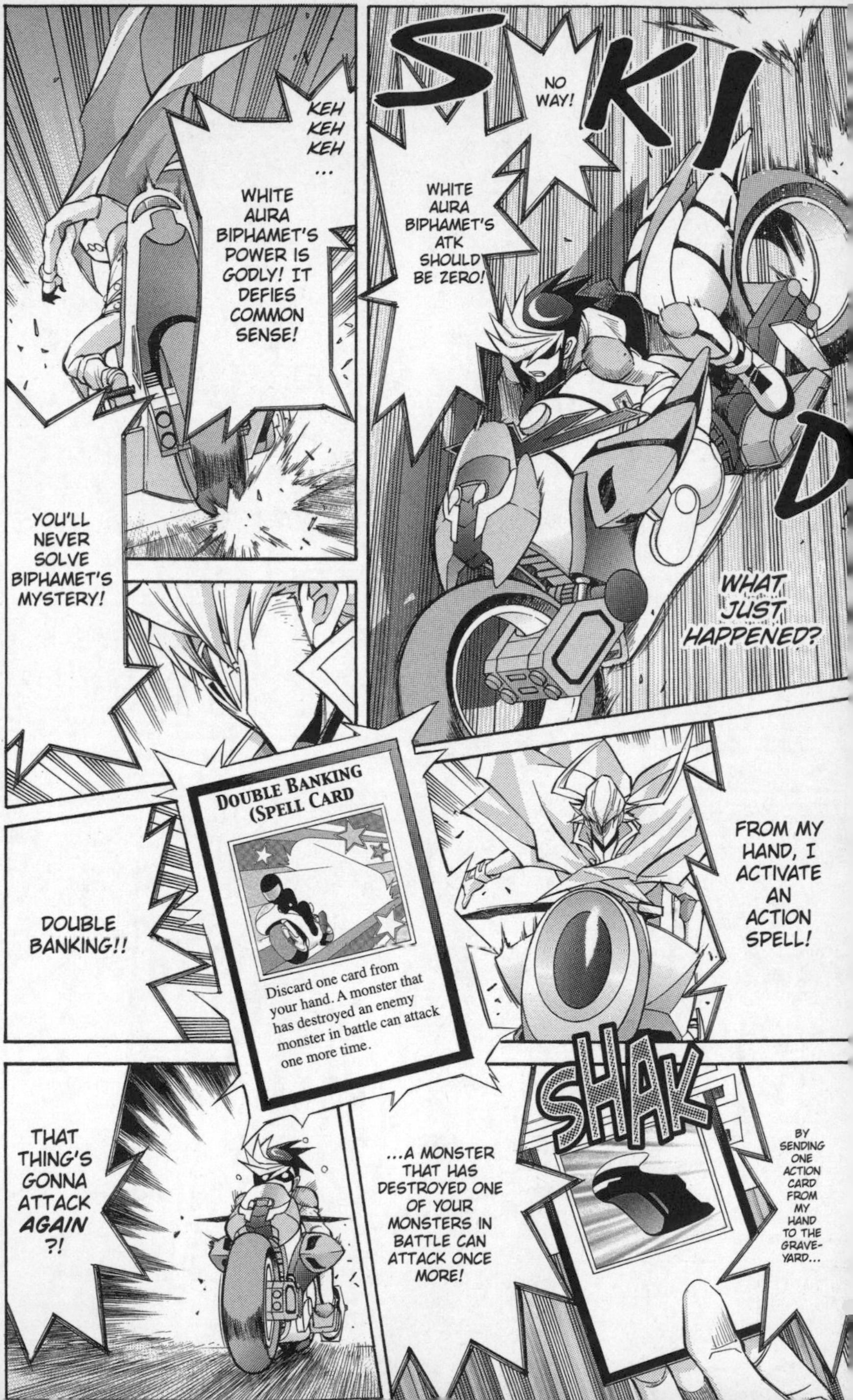
SKID
NO WAY!
WHITE AURA BIPHAMET'S ATK SHOULD BE ZERO!
WHAT JUST HAPPENED?
KEH KEH KEH...
WHITE AURA BIPHAMET'S POWER IS GODLY! IT DEFIES COMMON SENSE!
YOU'LL NEVER SOLVE BIPHAMET'S MYSTERY!
FROM MY HAND, I ACTIVATE AN ACTION SPELL!
DOUBLE BANKING!!
DOUBLE BANKING (SPELL CARD
Discard one card from your hand. A monster that has destroyed an enemy monster in battle can attack one more time.
SHAK
BY SENDING ONE ACTION CARD FROM MY HAND TO THE GRAVE-YARD...
...A MONSTER THAT HAS DESTROYED ONE OF YOUR MONSTERS IN BATTLE CAN ATTACK ONCE MORE!
THAT THING'S GONNA ATTACK *AGAIN* ?!

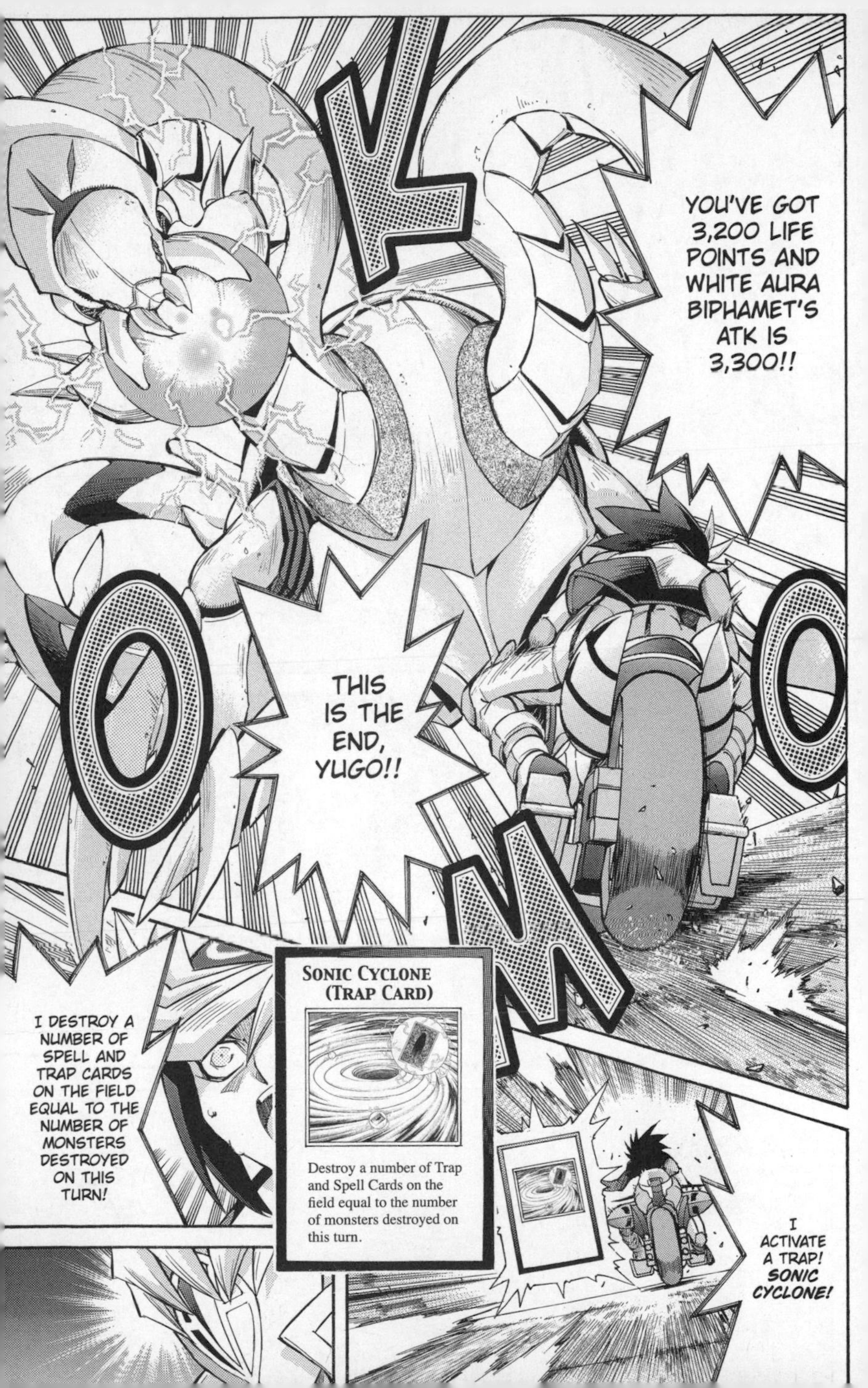
YOU'VE GOT 3,200 LIFE POINTS AND WHITE AURA BIPHAMET'S ATK IS 3,300!!
THIS IS THE END, YUGO!!
I ACTIVATE A TRAP! SONIC CYCLONE!
SONIC CYCLONE (TRAP CARD)
Destroy a number of Trap and Spell Cards on the field equal to the number of monsters destroyed on this turn.
I DESTROY A NUMBER OF SPELL AND TRAP CARDS ON THE FIELD EQUAL TO THE NUMBER OF MONSTERS DESTROYED ON THIS TURN!

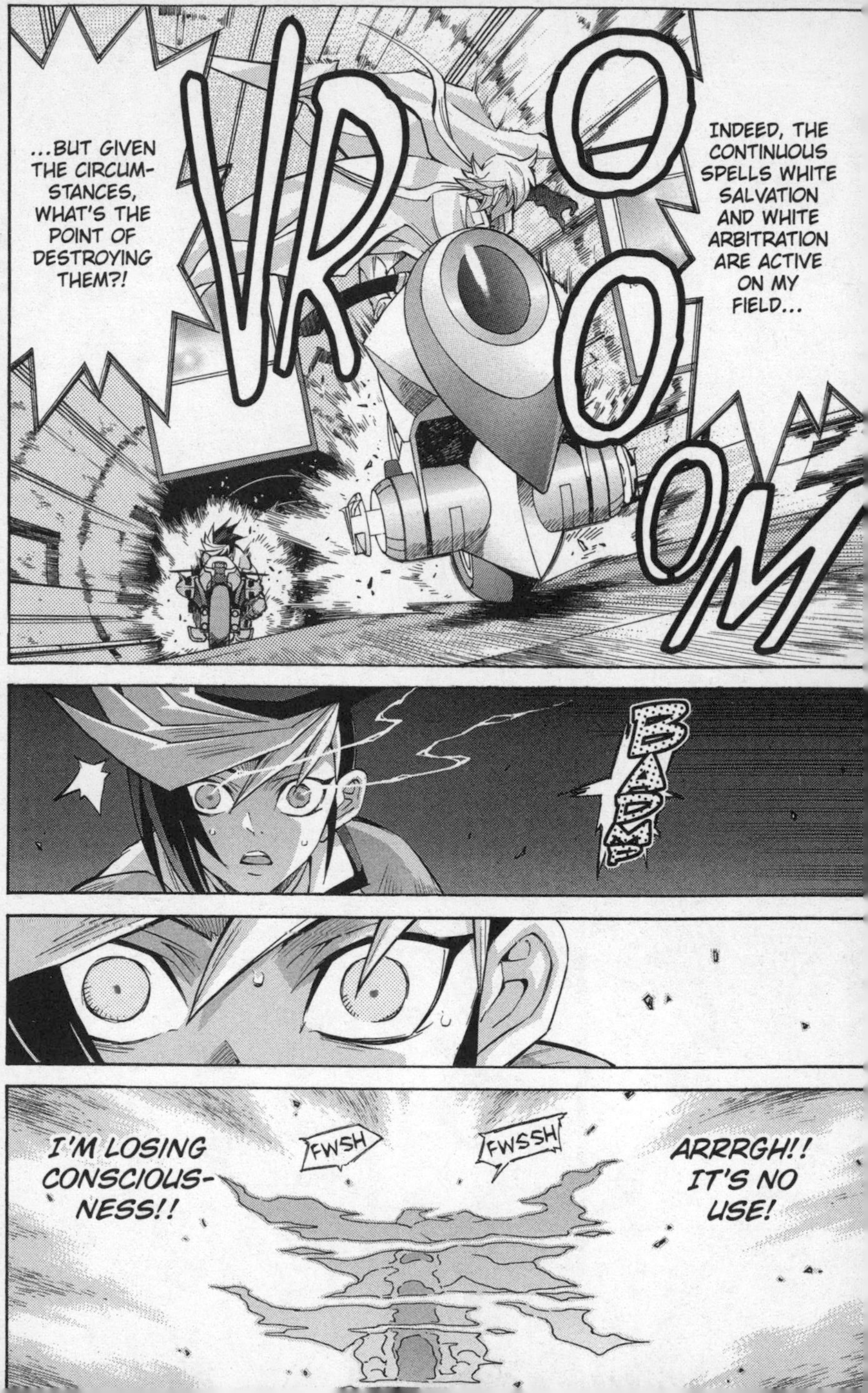
INDEED, THE CONTINUOUS SPELLS WHITE SALVATION AND WHITE ARBITRATION ARE ACTIVE ON MY FIELD...
...BUT GIVEN THE CIRCUM-STANCES, WHAT'S THE POINT OF DESTROYING THEM?!
VROOOOM
BADA
ARRRGH!! IT'S NO USE!
FWSSH
FWSH
I'M LOSING CONSCIOUS-NESS!!

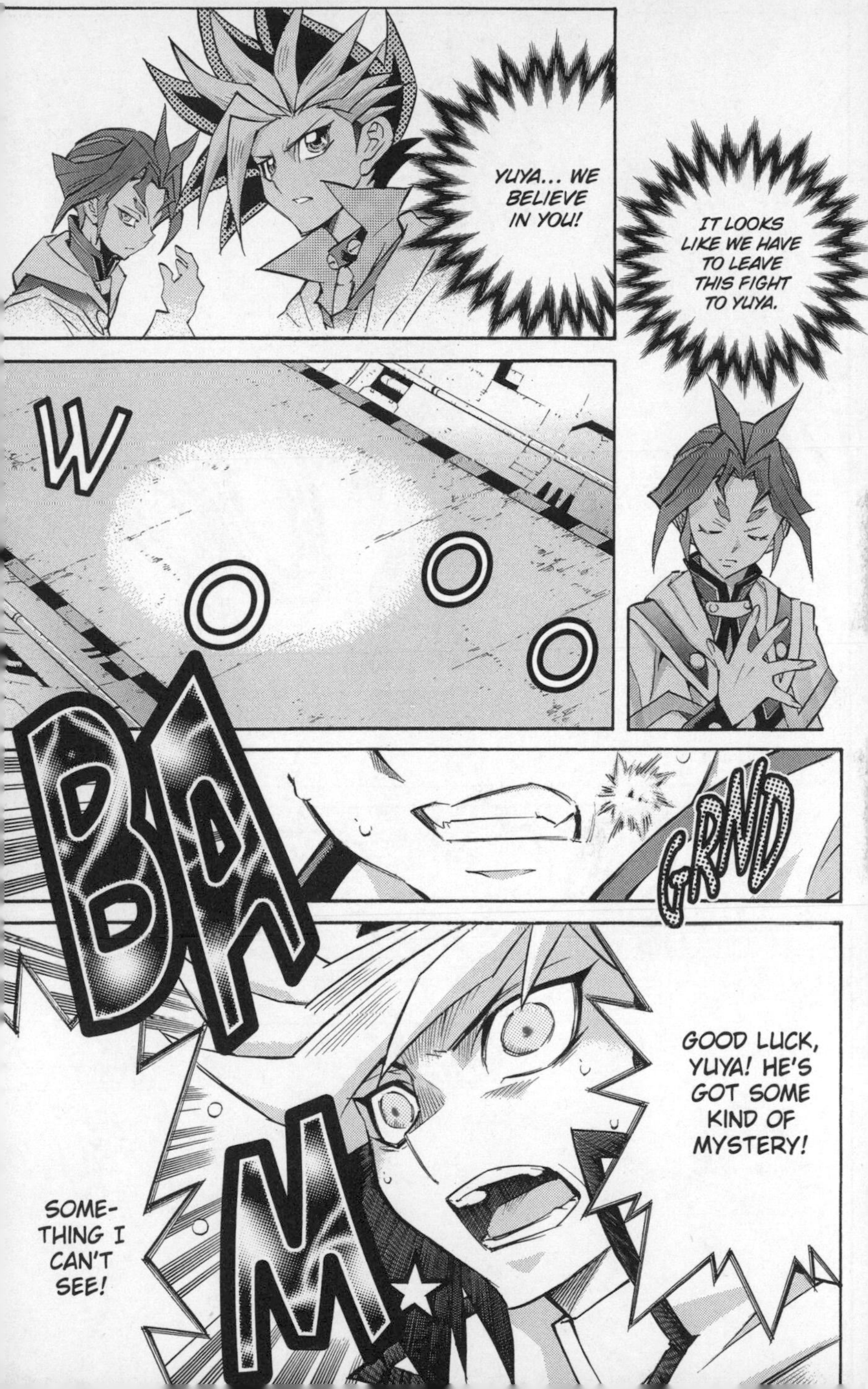
YUYA... WE BELIEVE IN YOU!
IT LOOKS LIKE WE HAVE TO LEAVE THIS FIGHT TO YUYA.
WOOOO
GRND
BOOM
GOOD LUCK, YUYA! HE'S GOT SOME KIND OF MYSTERY!
SOME-THING I CAN'T SEE!

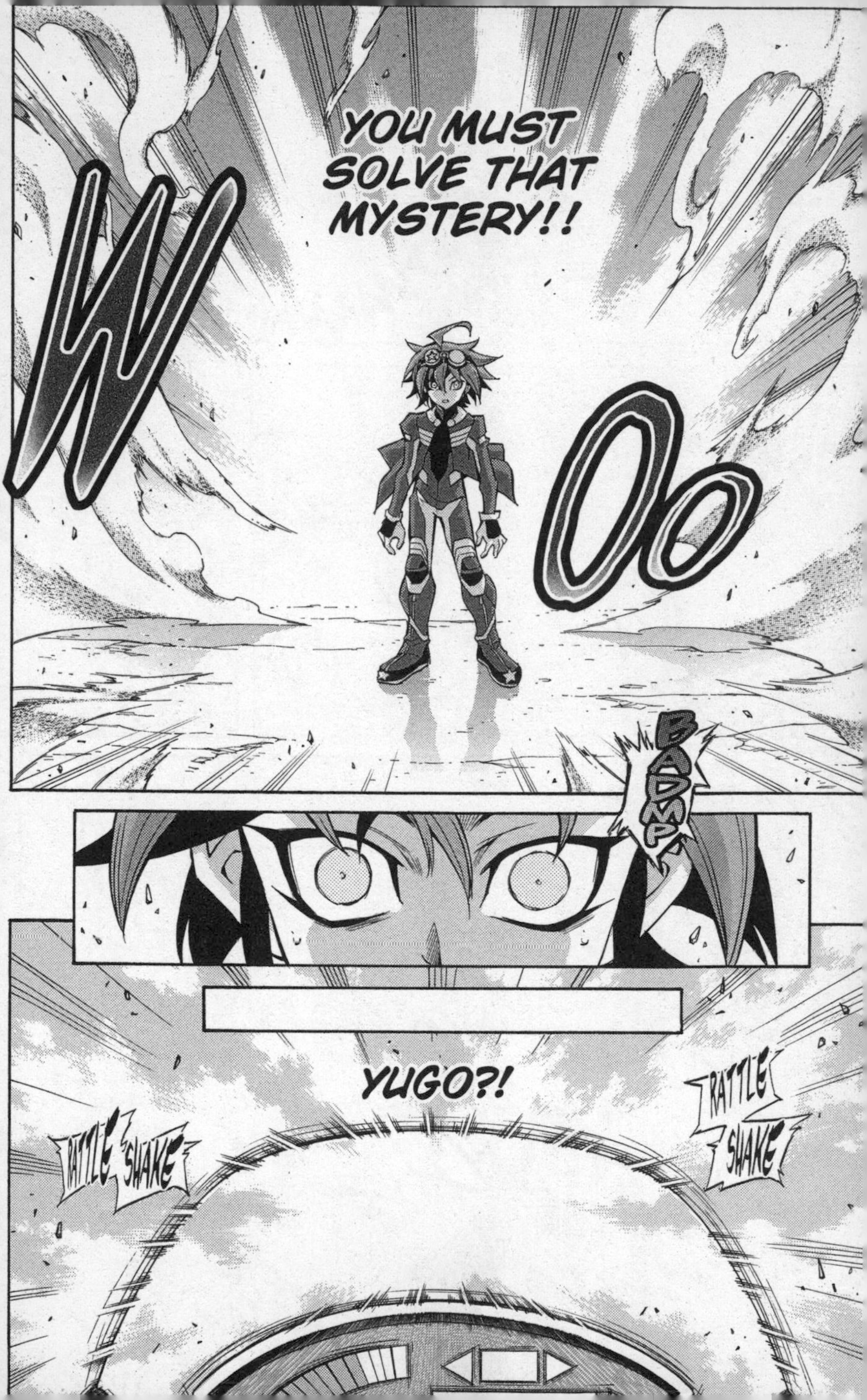
YOU MUST SOLVE THAT MYSTERY!!
WOO
BADMP
YUGO?!
RATTLE SHAKE
RATTLE SHAKE

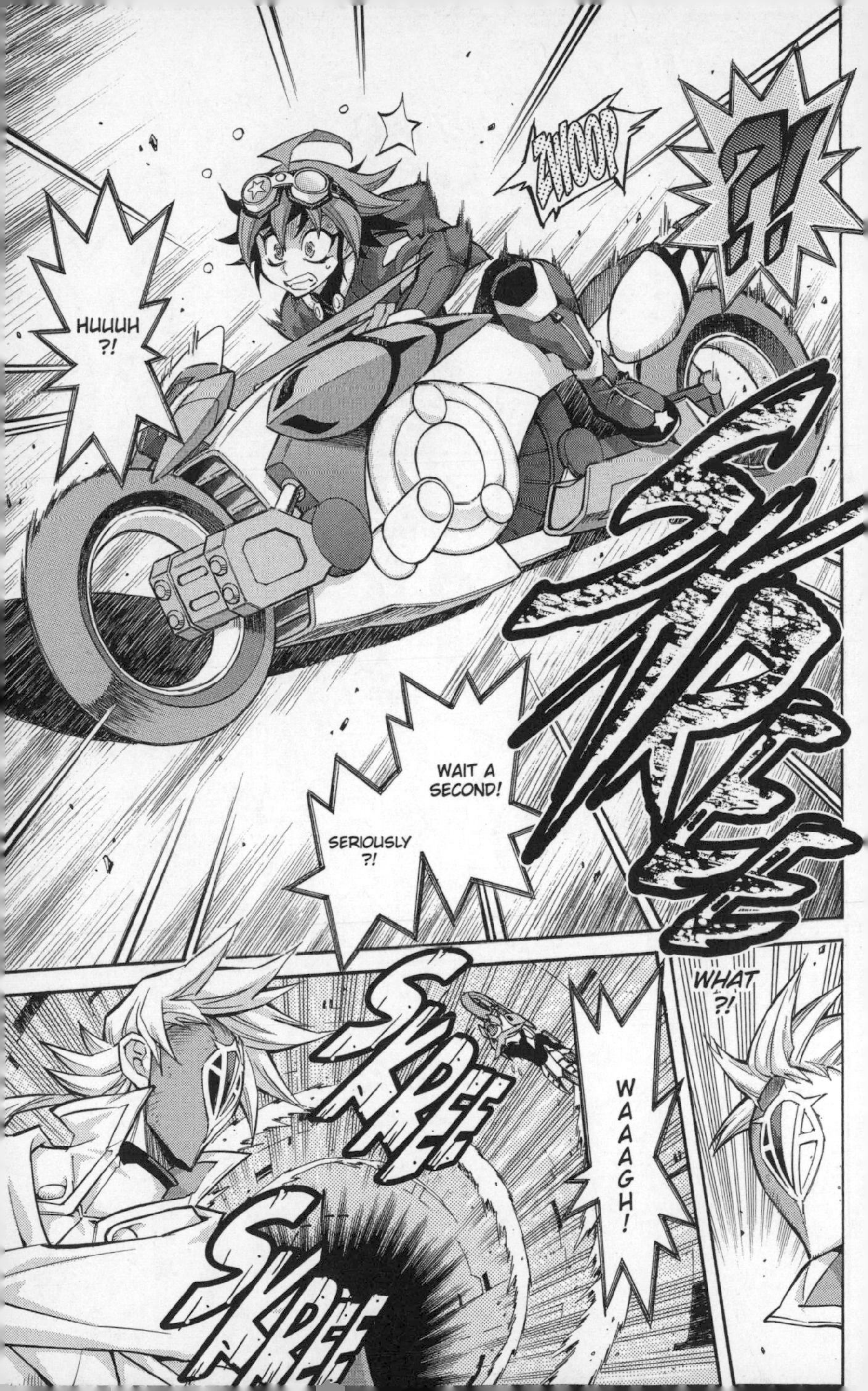
?!
ZWOOP
HUUUH ?!
WAIT A SECOND!
SERIOUSLY ?!
WHAT ?!
WAAAAGH!

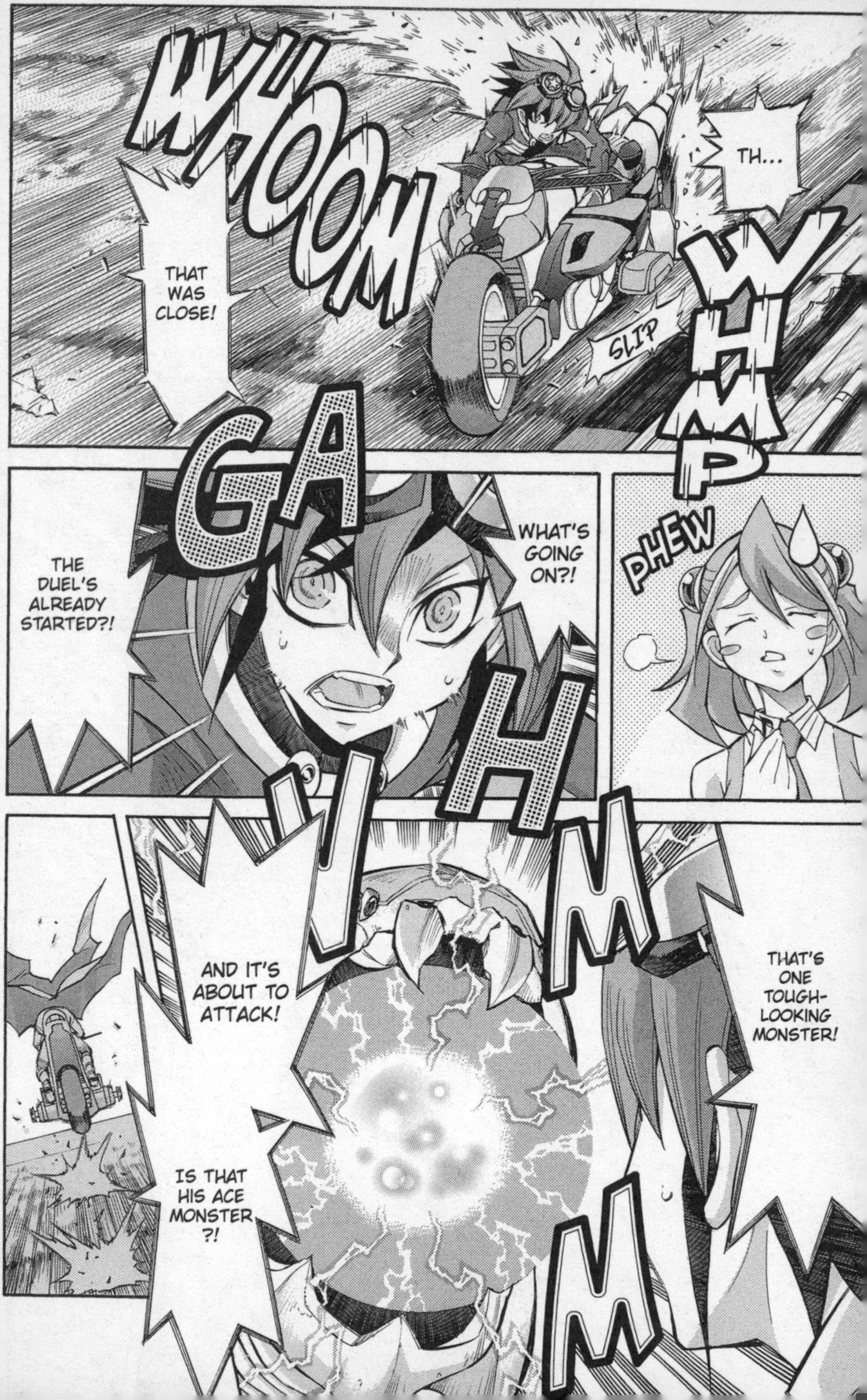
TH...
WHUMP
SLIP
WHOOM
THAT WAS CLOSE!
PHEW
GAH
WHAT'S GOING ON?!
THE DUEL'S ALREADY STARTED?!
THAT'S ONE TOUGH-LOOKING MONSTER!
AND IT'S ABOUT TO ATTACK!
IS THAT HIS ACE MONSTER?!

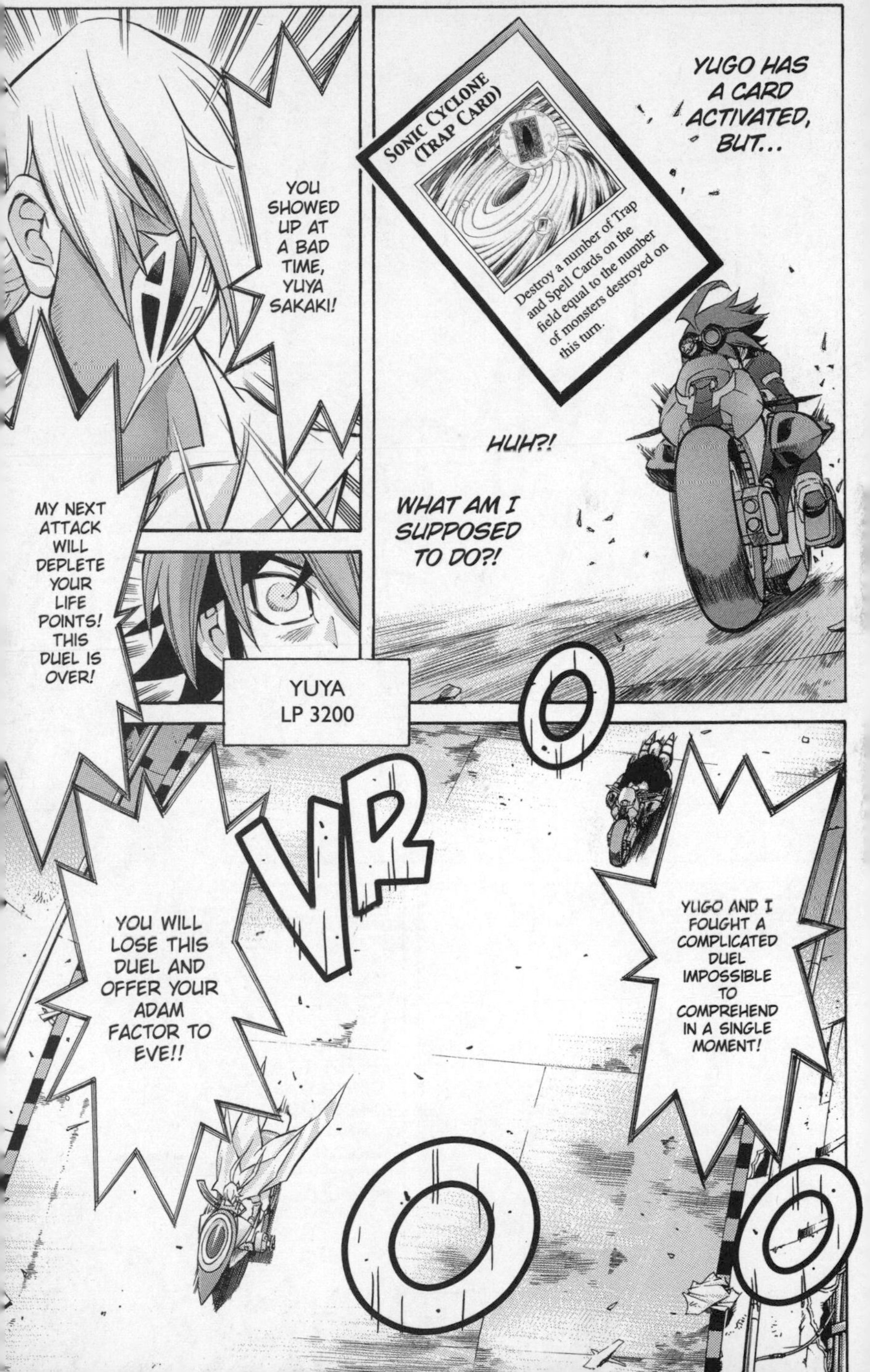
YUGO HAS A CARD ACTIVATED, BUT...
SONIC CYCLONE (TRAP CARD)
Destroy a number of Trap and Spell Cards on the field equal to the number of monsters destroyed on this turn.
HUH?!
WHAT AM I SUPPOSED TO DO?!
YOU SHOWED UP AT A BAD TIME, YUYA SAKAKI!
MY NEXT ATTACK WILL DEPLETE YOUR LIFE POINTS! THIS DUEL IS OVER!
YUYA LP 3200
YUGO AND I FOUGHT A COMPLICATED DUEL IMPOSSIBLE TO COMPREHEND IN A SINGLE MOMENT!
VROOO
YOU WILL LOSE THIS DUEL AND OFFER YOUR ADAM FACTOR TO EVE!!

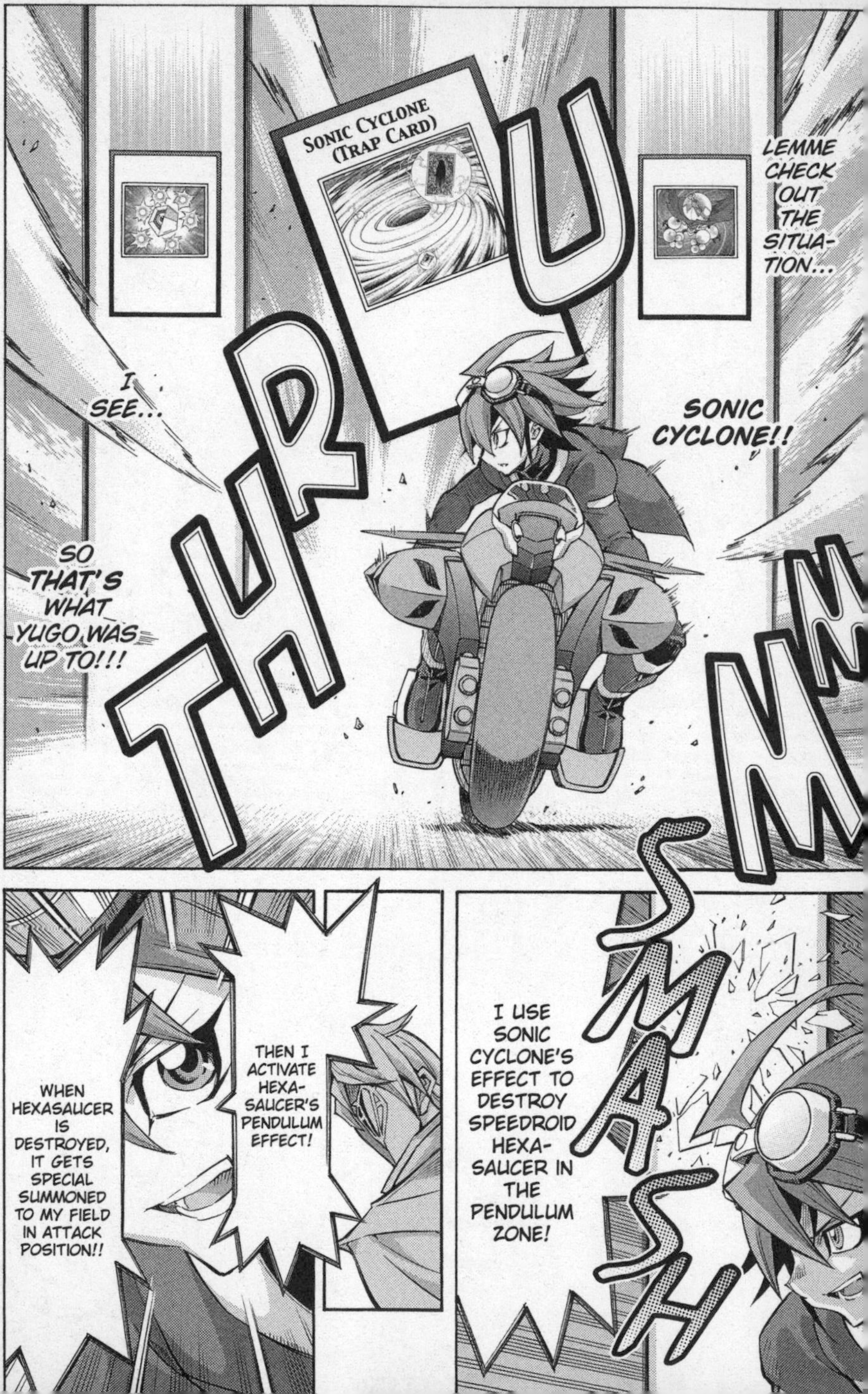
LEMME CHECK OUT THE SITUATION...
SONIC CYCLONE (TRAP CARD)
SONIC CYCLONE!!
THRUMM
I SEE...
SO THAT'S WHAT YUGO WAS UP TO!!!
SMASH
I USE SONIC CYCLONE'S EFFECT TO DESTROY SPEEDROID HEXA-SAUCER IN THE PENDULUM ZONE!
THEN I ACTIVATE HEXA-SAUCER'S PENDULUM EFFECT!
WHEN HEXASAUCER IS DESTROYED, IT GETS SPECIAL SUMMONED TO MY FIELD IN ATTACK POSITION!!

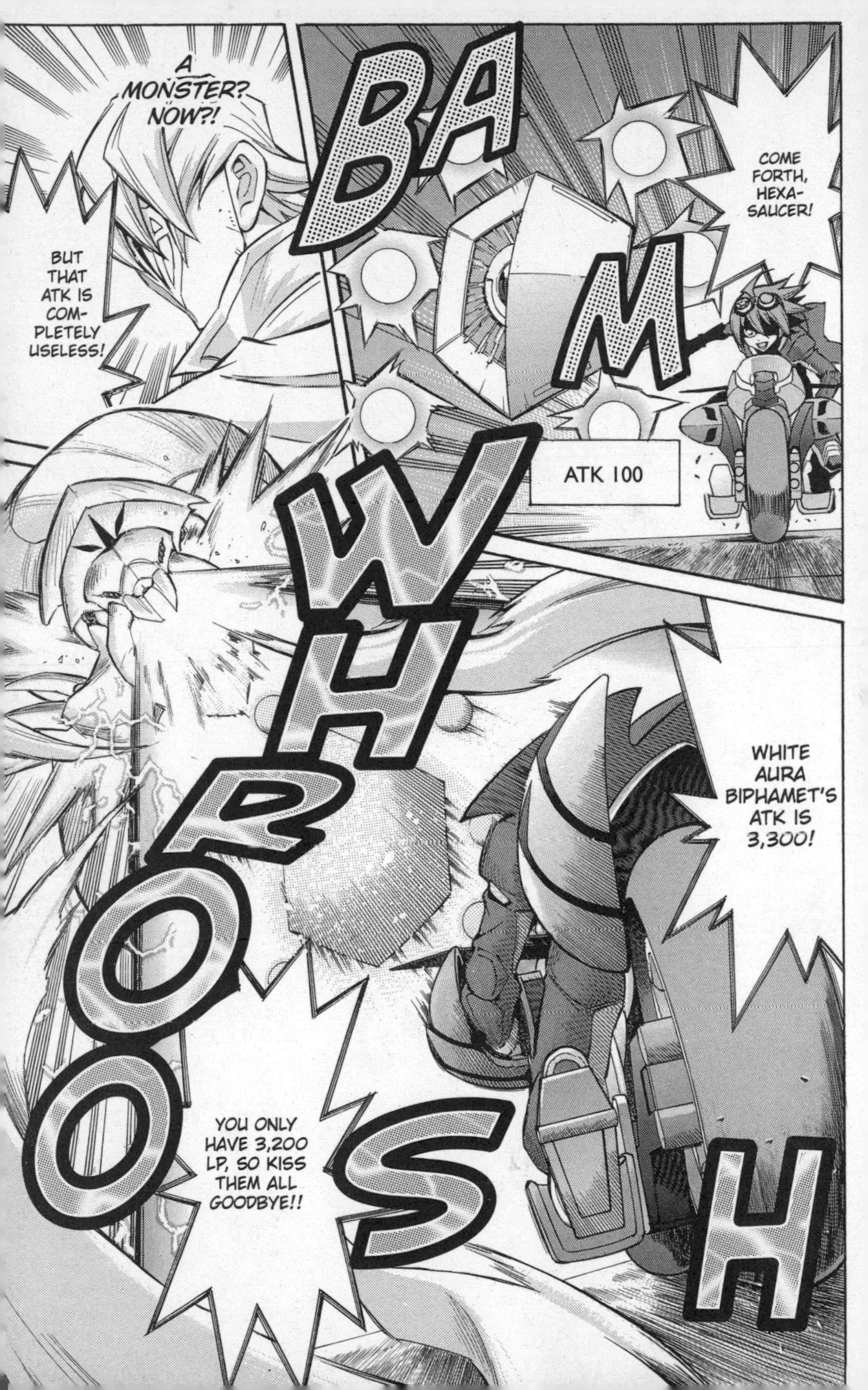
COME FORTH, HEXA-SAUCER!
BAM
ATK 100
A MONSTER? NOW?!
BUT THAT ATK IS COMPLETELY USELESS!
WHITE AURA BIPHAMET'S ATK IS 3,300!
WHROOSH
YOU ONLY HAVE 3,200 LP, SO KISS THEM ALL GOODBYE!!

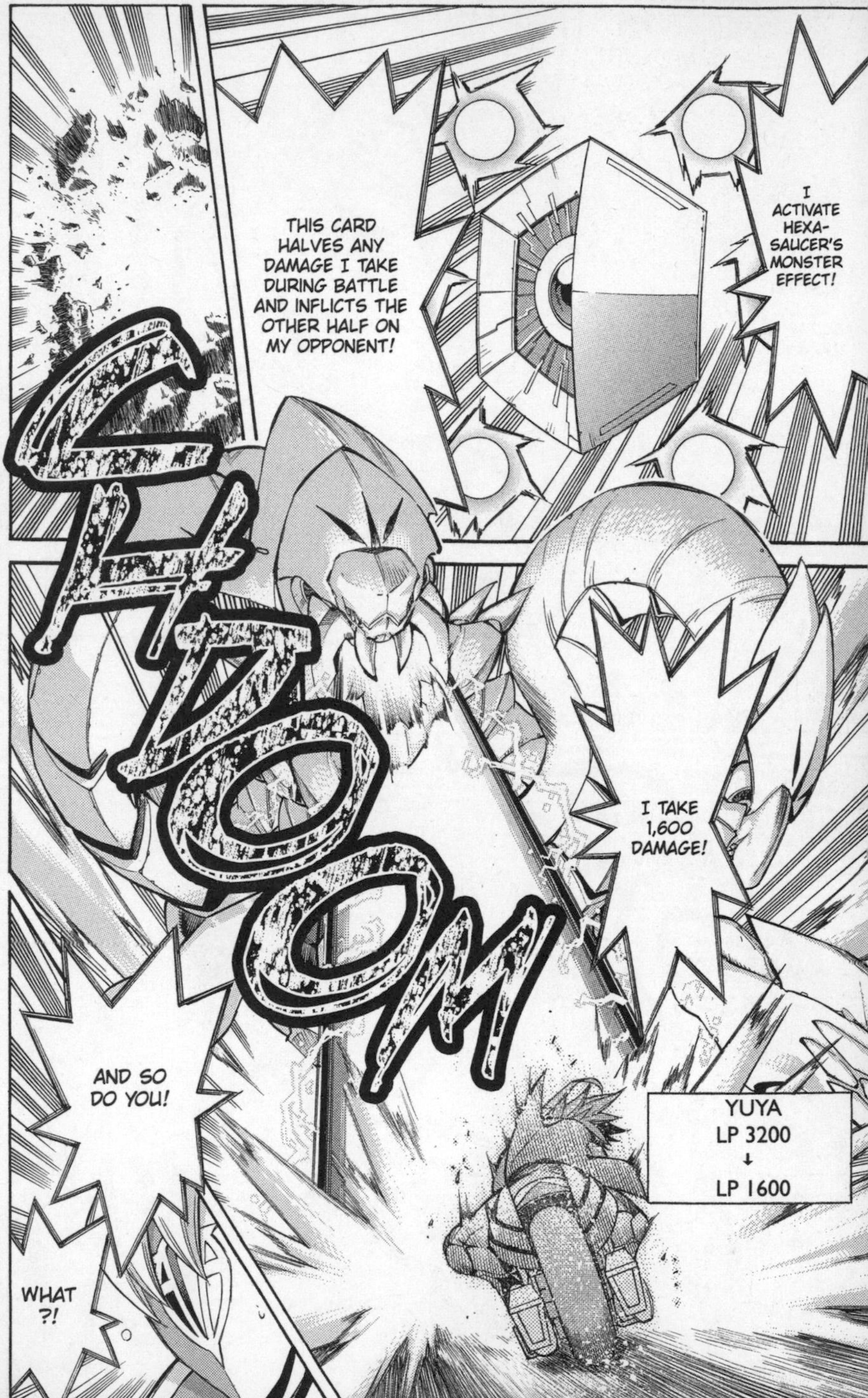
I ACTIVATE HEXA-SAUCER'S MONSTER EFFECT!
THIS CARD HALVES ANY DAMAGE I TAKE DURING BATTLE AND INFLICTS THE OTHER HALF ON MY OPPONENT!
I TAKE 1,600 DAMAGE!
CHVOOM
YUYA LP 3200 ↓ LP 1600
AND SO DO YOU!
WHAT?!

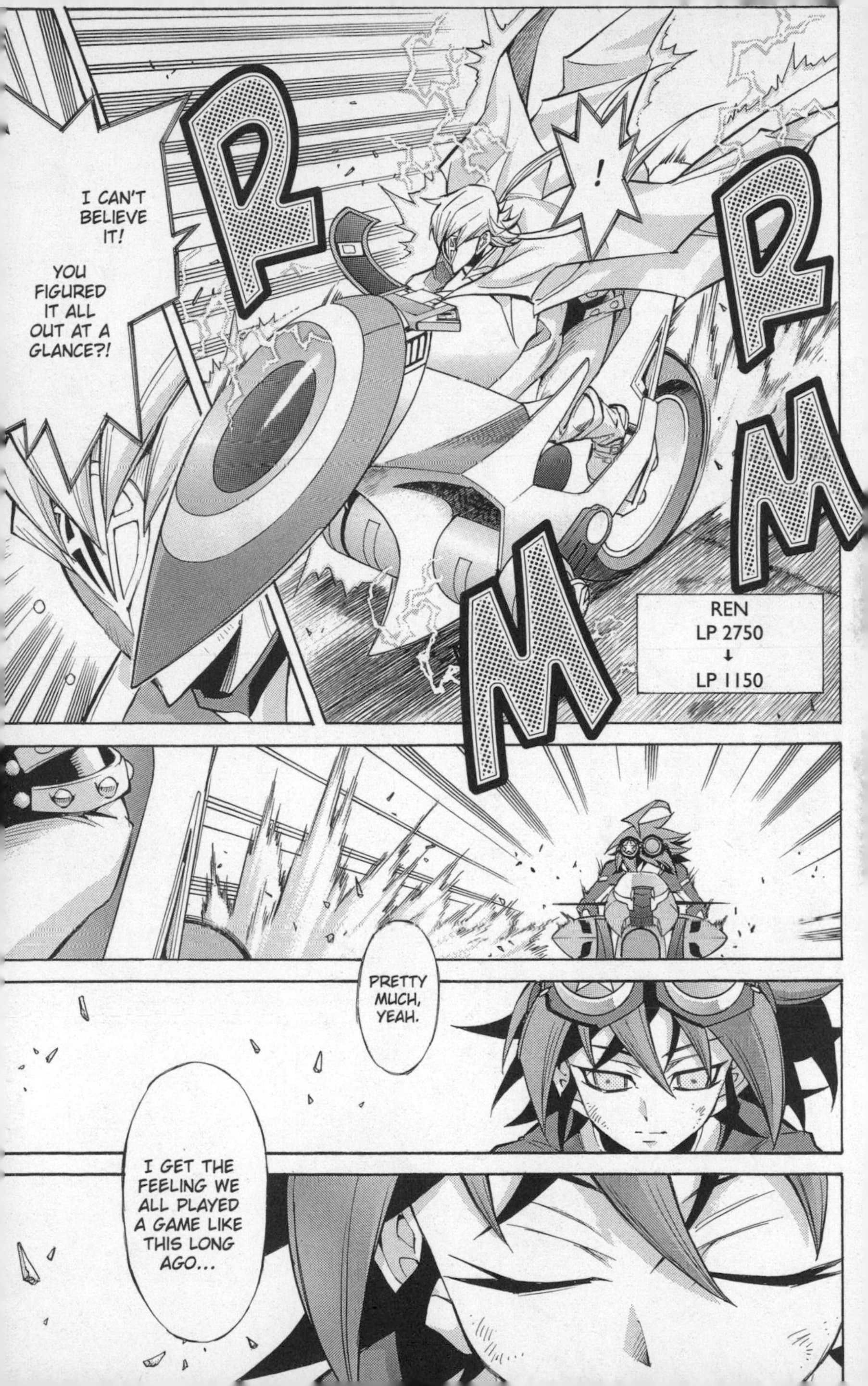
!
DRMM
I CAN'T BELIEVE IT!
YOU FIGURED IT ALL OUT AT A GLANCE?!
REN LP 2750 ↓ LP 1150
PRETTY MUCH, YEAH.
I GET THE FEELING WE ALL PLAYED A GAME LIKE THIS LONG AGO...

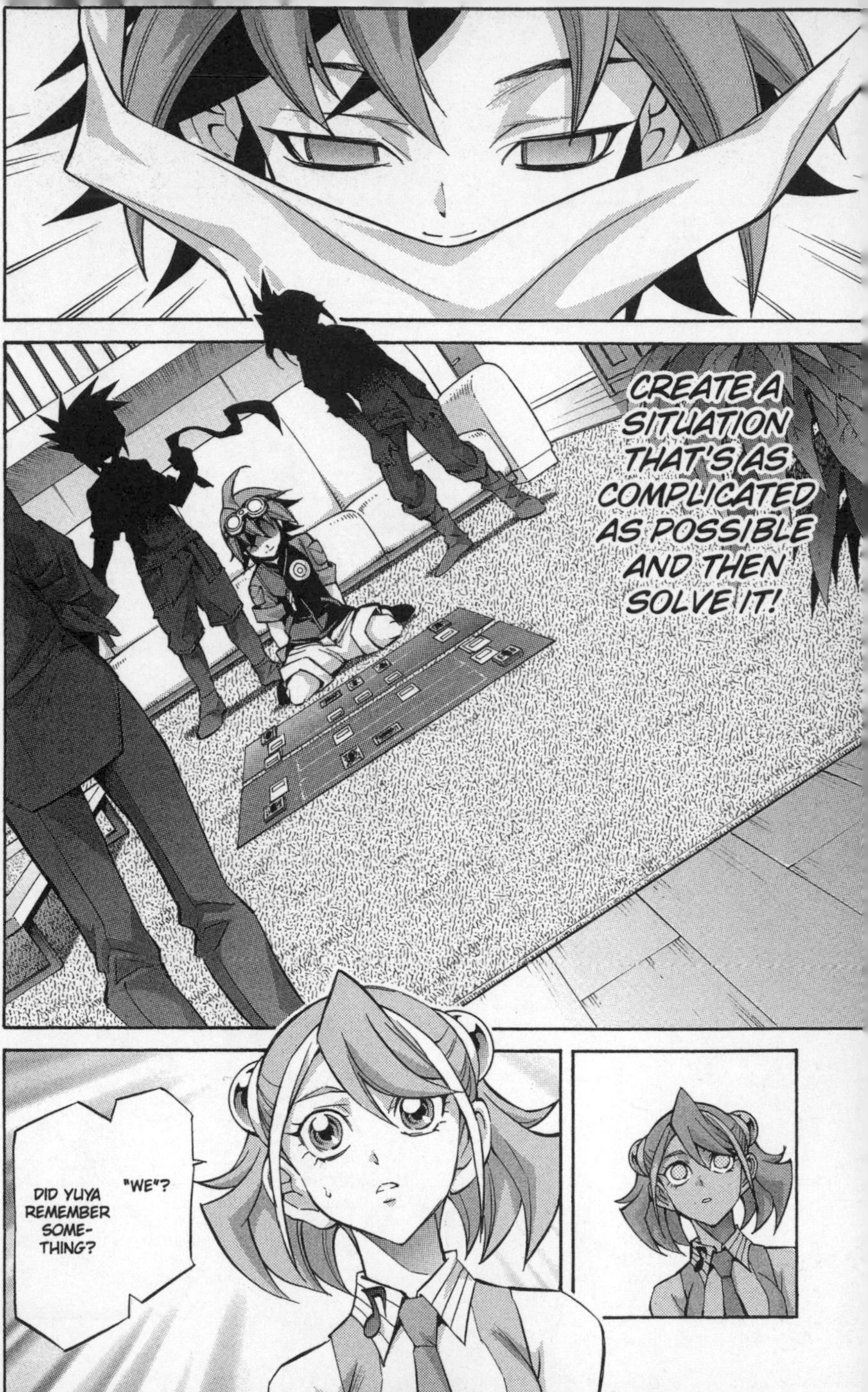
CREATE A SITUATION THAT'S AS COMPLICATED AS POSSIBLE AND THEN SOLVE IT!
"WE"?
DID YUYA REMEMBER SOME-THING?

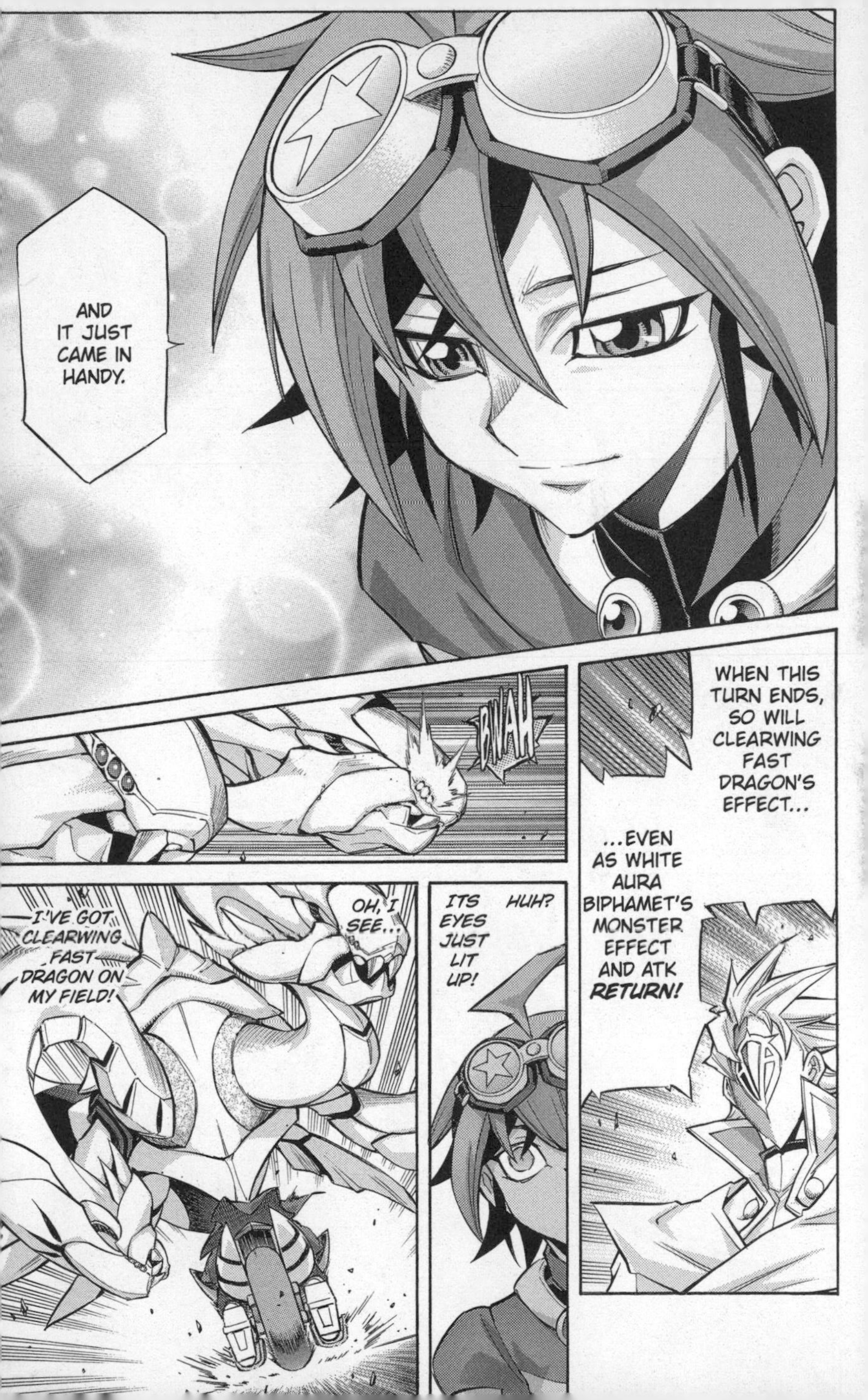
AND IT JUST CAME IN HANDY.
WHEN THIS TURN ENDS, SO WILL CLEARWING FAST DRAGON'S EFFECT...
...EVEN AS WHITE AURA BIPHAMET'S MONSTER EFFECT AND ATK RETURN!
BWAH
HUH?
ITS EYES JUST LIT UP!
OH, I SEE...
I'VE GOT CLEARWING FAST DRAGON ON MY FIELD!

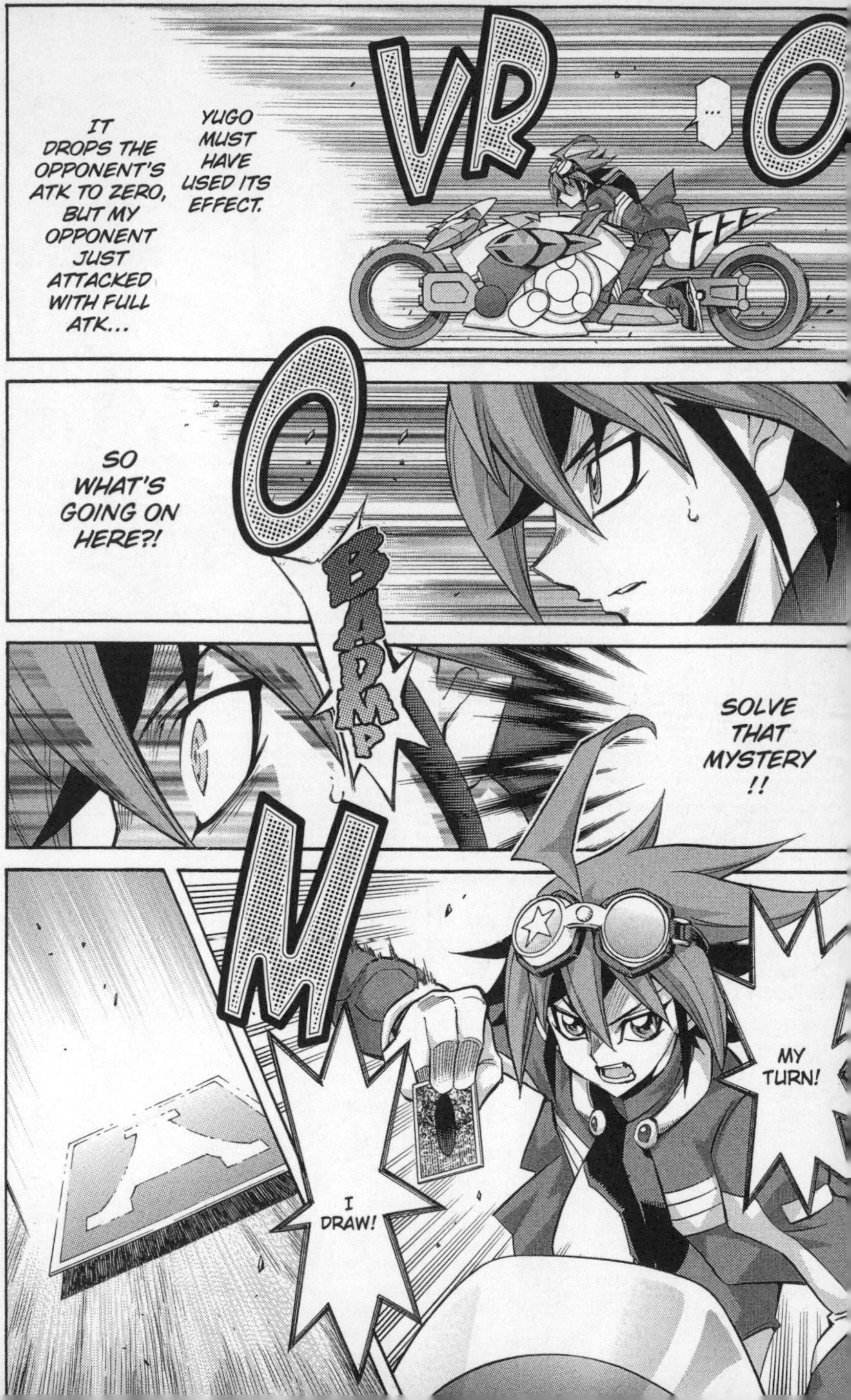
...
YUGO MUST HAVE USED ITS EFFECT.
IT DROPS THE OPPONENT'S ATK TO ZERO, BUT MY OPPONENT JUST ATTACKED WITH FULL ATK...
VROOM
SO WHAT'S GOING ON HERE?!
BADMP
SOLVE THAT MYSTERY !!
MY TURN!
I DRAW!

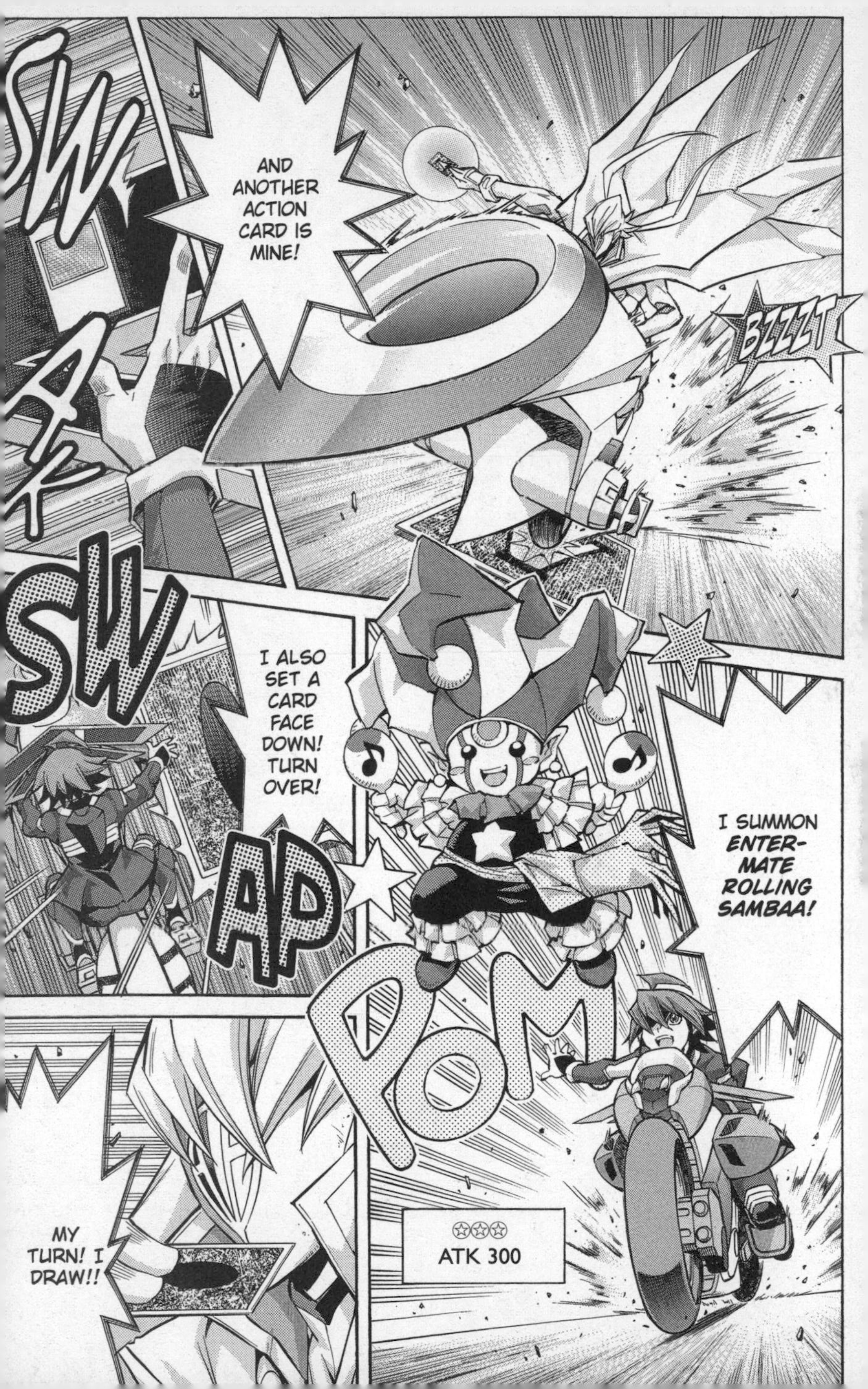
BZZZT
AND ANOTHER ACTION CARD IS MINE!
SWAK
I SUMMON ENTERMATE ROLLING SAMBAA!
POM
☆☆☆
ATK 300
I ALSO SET A CARD FACE DOWN! TURN OVER!
SWAP
MY TURN! I DRAW!!

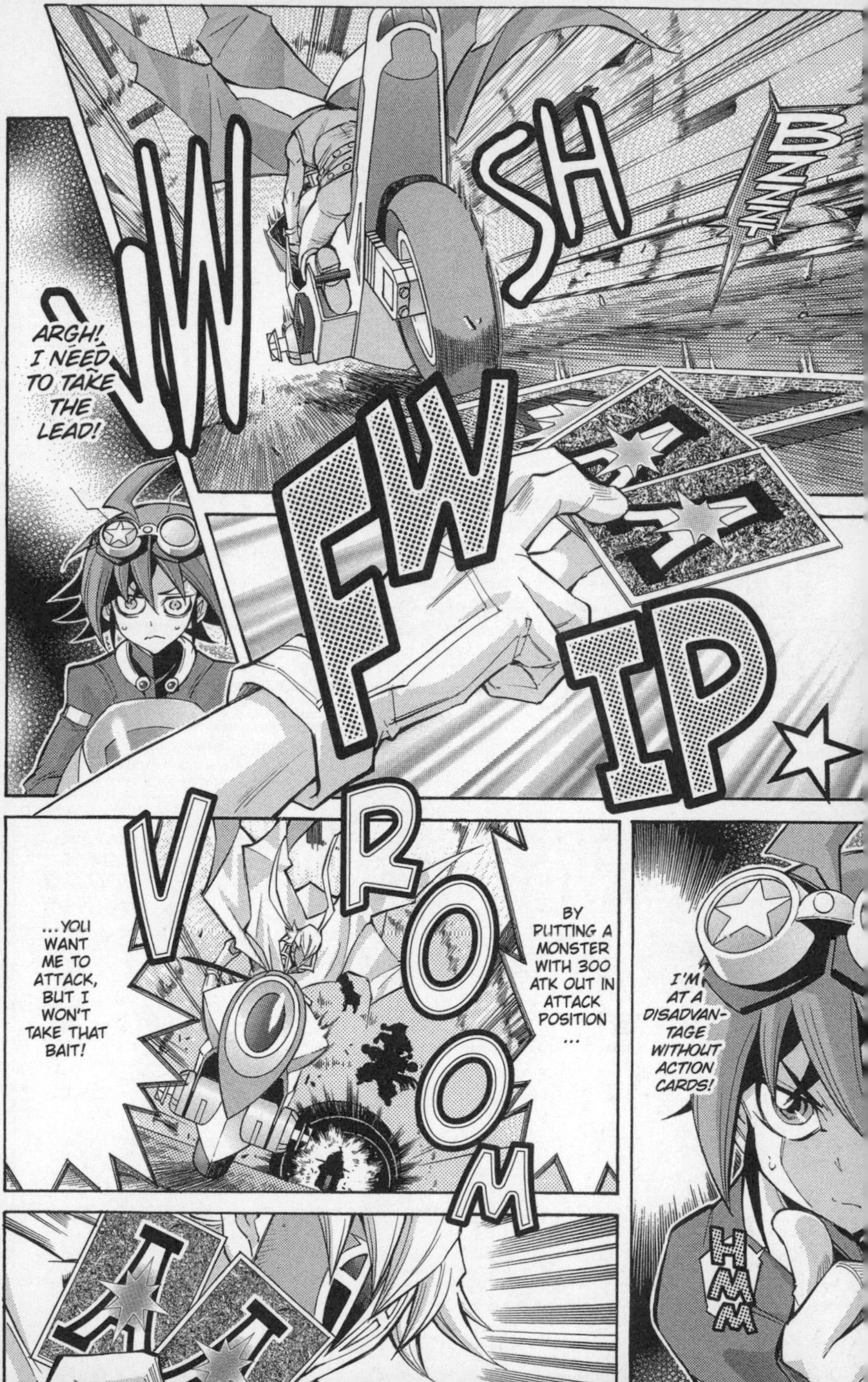
BZZZT
WSH
ARGH! I NEED TO TAKE THE LEAD!
FWIP
I'M AT A DISADVANTAGE WITHOUT ACTION CARDS!
HMM
BY PUTTING A MONSTER WITH 300 ATK OUT IN ATTACK POSITION...
...YOU WANT ME TO ATTACK, BUT I WON'T TAKE THAT BAIT!
VROOOM

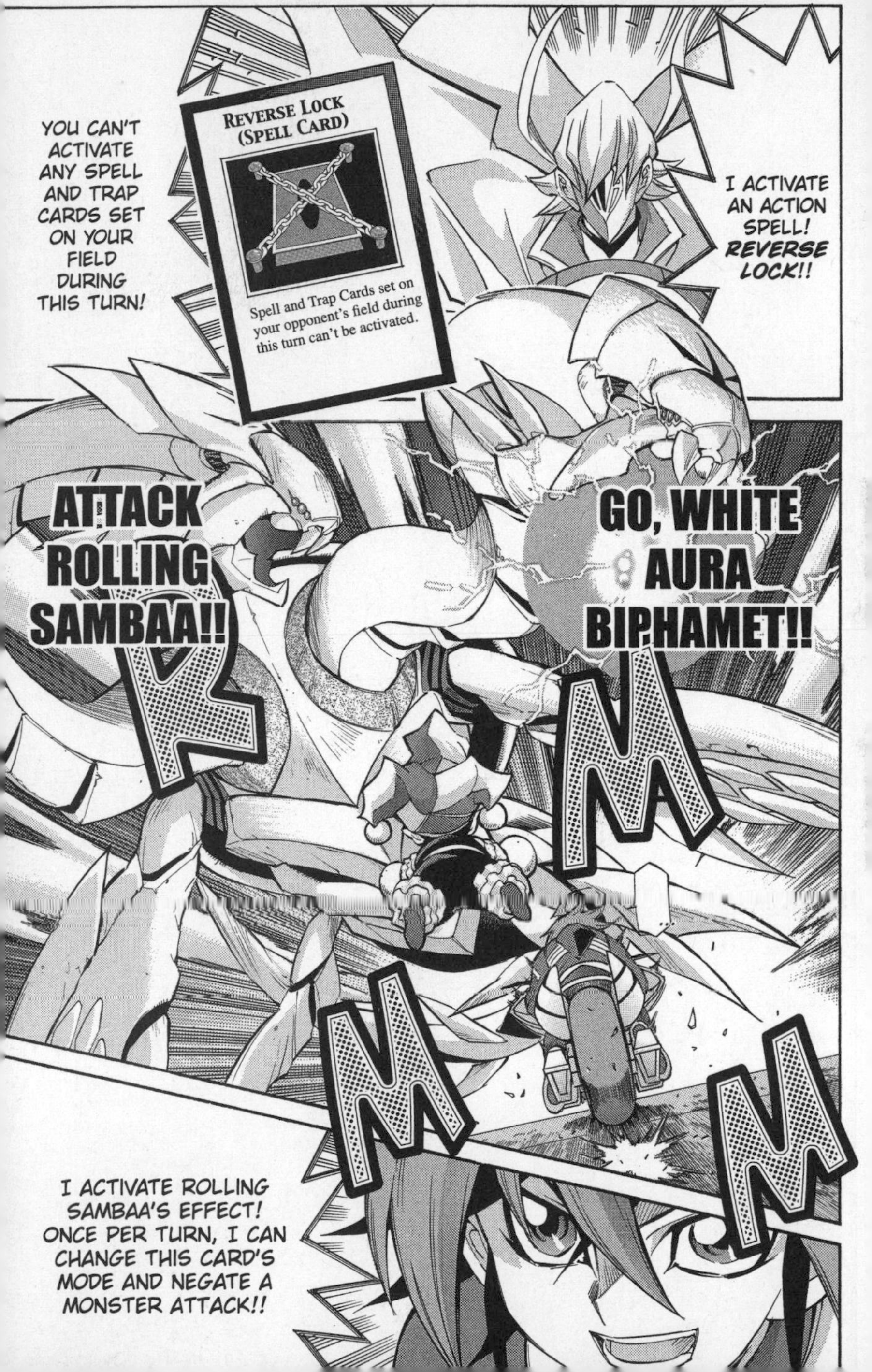

I ACTIVATE AN ACTION SPELL! REVERSE LOCK!!
REVERSE LOCK (SPELL CARD)
Spell and Trap Cards set on your opponent's field during this turn can't be activated.
YOU CAN'T ACTIVATE ANY SPELL AND TRAP CARDS SET ON YOUR FIELD DURING THIS TURN!
GO, WHITE AURA BIPHAMET!!
ATTACK ROLLING SAMBAA!!
I ACTIVATE ROLLING SAMBAA'S EFFECT! ONCE PER TURN, I CAN CHANGE THIS CARD'S MODE AND NEGATE A MONSTER ATTACK!!

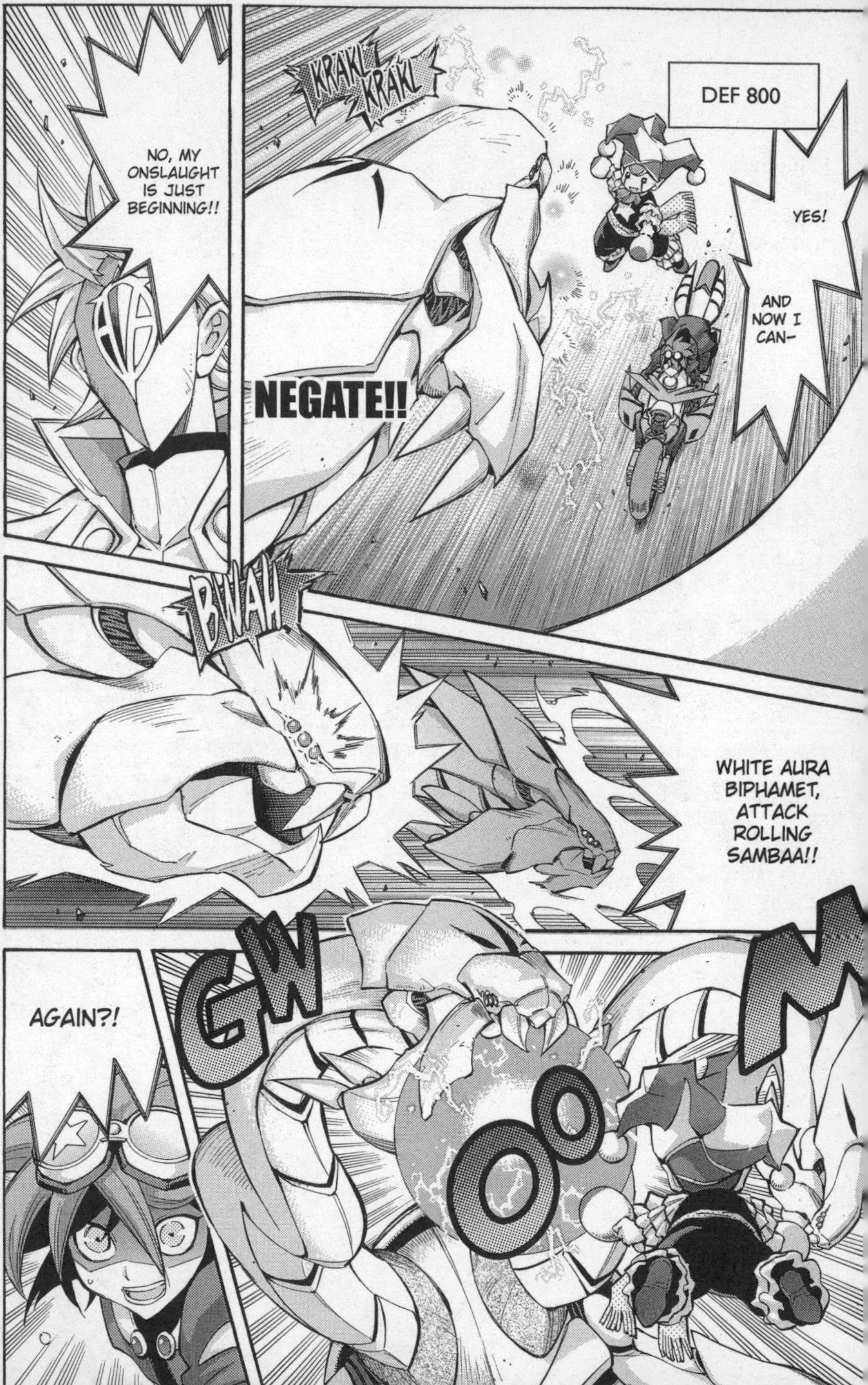
DEF 800
YES!
AND NOW I CAN-
KRAKL KRAKL
NEGATE!!
NO, MY ONSLAUGHT IS JUST BEGINNING!!
WHITE AURA BIPHAMET, ATTACK ROLLING SAMBAA!!
BWAH
GWOOOM
AGAIN?!

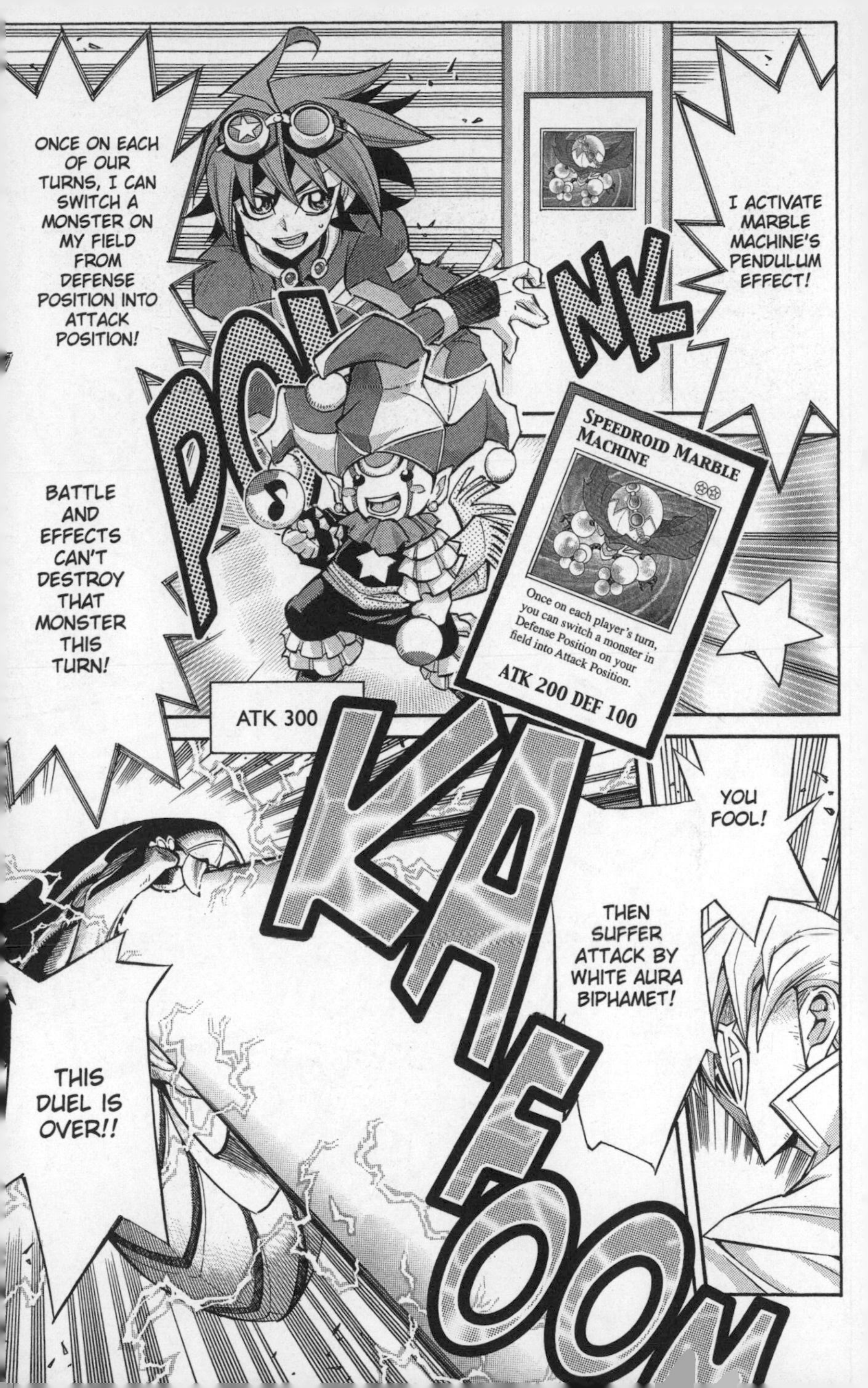
I ACTIVATE MARBLE MACHINE'S PENDULUM EFFECT!
ONCE ON EACH OF OUR TURNS, I CAN SWITCH A MONSTER ON MY FIELD FROM DEFENSE POSITION INTO ATTACK POSITION!
BATTLE AND EFFECTS CAN'T DESTROY THAT MONSTER THIS TURN!
SPEEDROID MARBLE MACHINE
Once on each player's turn, you can switch a monster in Defense Position on your field into Attack Position.
ATK 200 DEF 100
ATK 300
YOU FOOL!
THEN SUFFER ATTACK BY WHITE AURA BIPHAMET!
THIS DUEL IS OVER!!

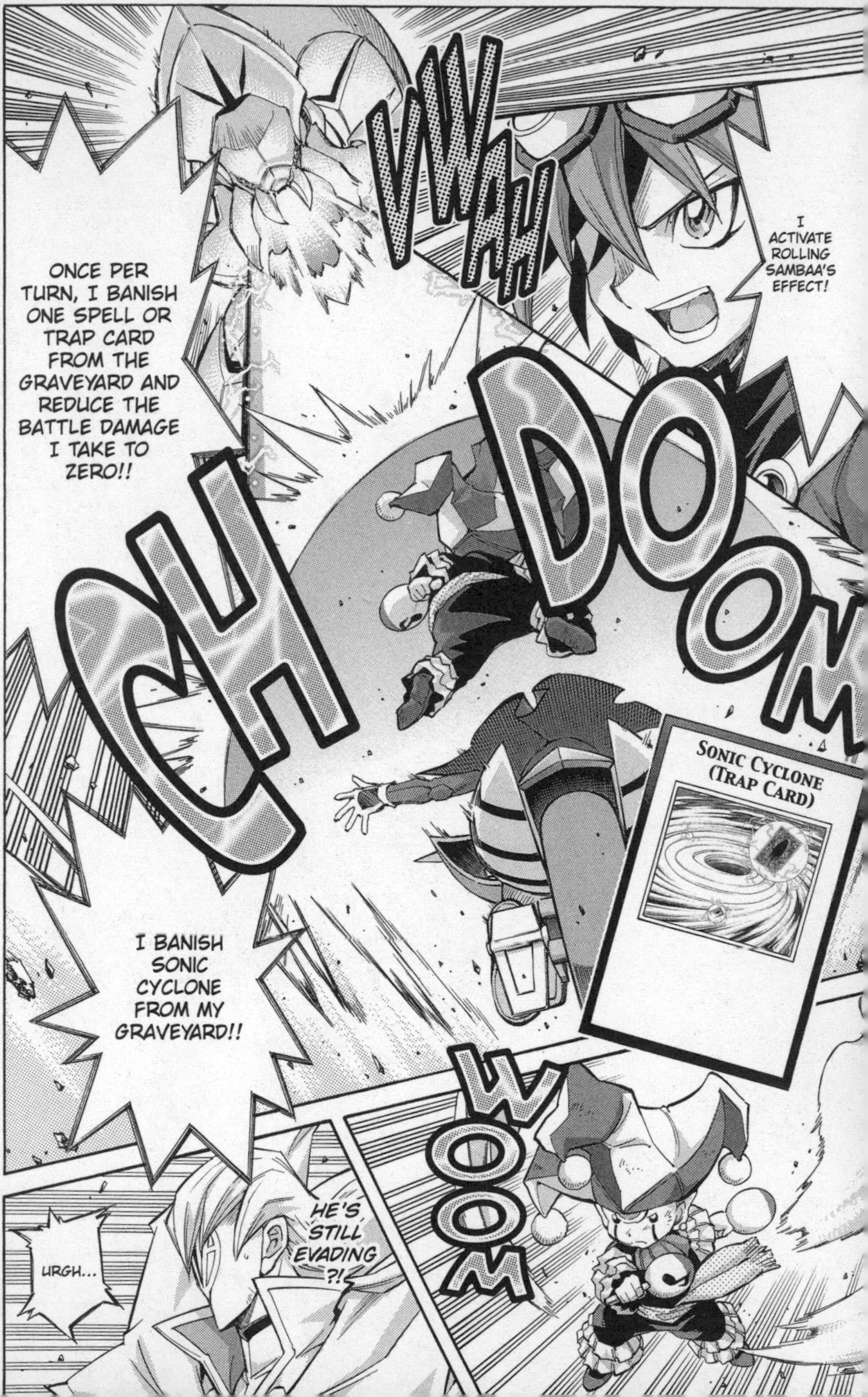
VWAH
I ACTIVATE ROLLING SAMBAA'S EFFECT!
ONCE PER TURN, I BANISH ONE SPELL OR TRAP CARD FROM THE GRAVEYARD AND REDUCE THE BATTLE DAMAGE I TAKE TO ZERO!!
CHDOOM
SONIC CYCLONE (TRAP CARD)
I BANISH SONIC CYCLONE FROM MY GRAVEYARD!!
WOOM
HE'S STILL EVADING?!
URGH...

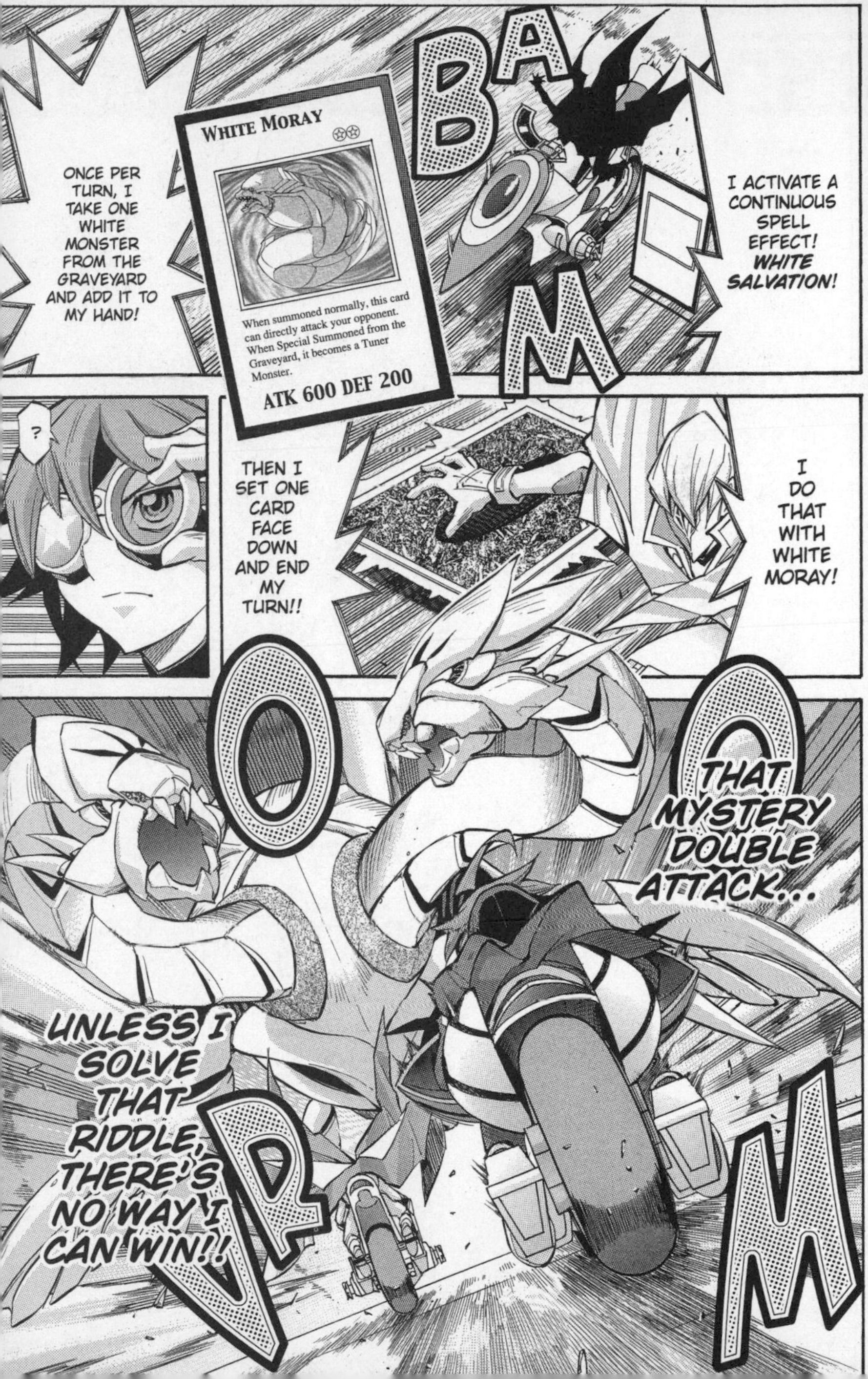
I ACTIVATE A CONTINUOUS SPELL EFFECT! WHITE SALVATION!
BAM
ONCE PER TURN, I TAKE ONE WHITE MONSTER FROM THE GRAVEYARD AND ADD IT TO MY HAND!
I DO THAT WITH WHITE MORAY!
WHITE MORAY
When summoned normally, this card can directly attack your opponent. When Special Summoned from the Graveyard, it becomes a Tuner Monster.
ATK 600 DEF 200
THEN I SET ONE CARD FACE DOWN AND END MY TURN!!
?
VROOM
THAT MYSTERY DOUBLE ATTACK...
UNLESS I SOLVE THAT RIDDLE, THERE'S NO WAY I CAN WIN!!

DARK ANTHELION DRAGON

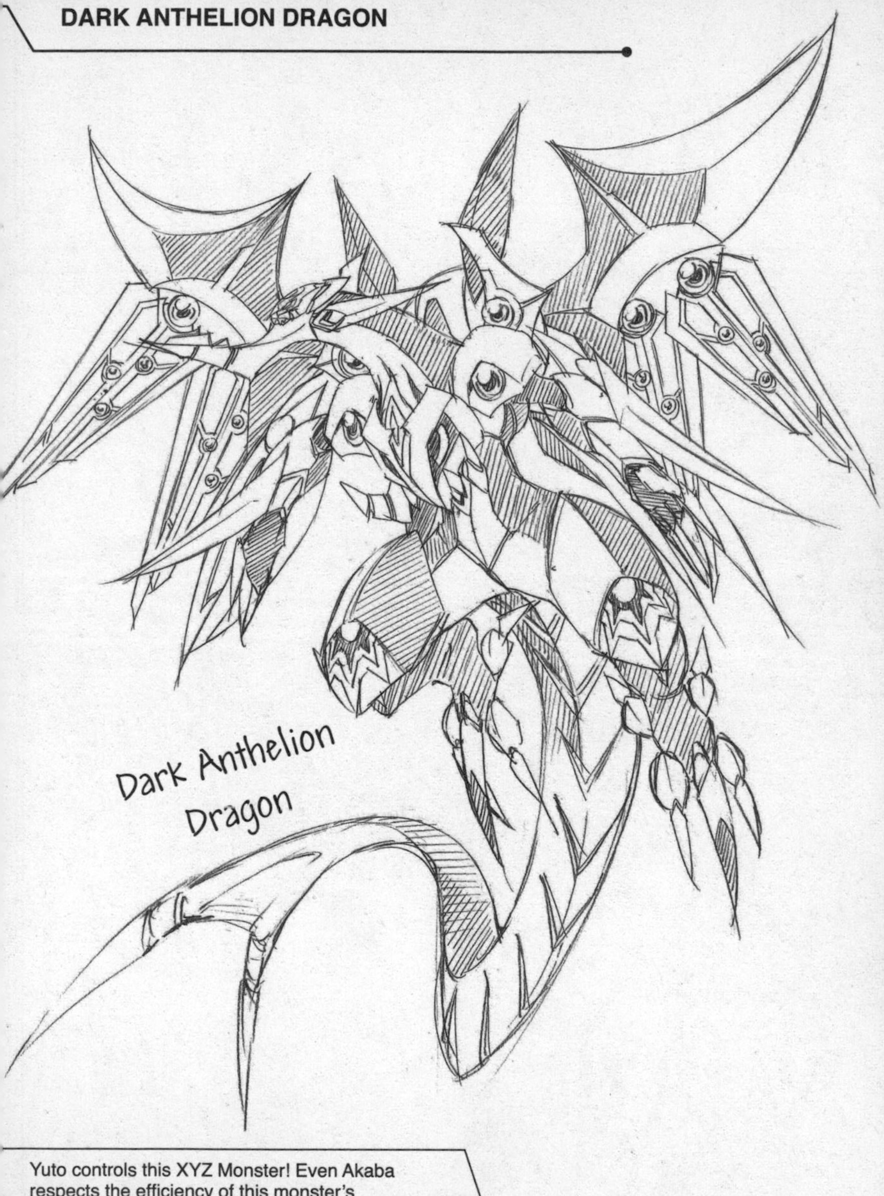
Dark Anthelion
Dragon

Yuto controls this XYZ Monster! Even Akaba respects the efficiency of this monster's effects. The blade-like design of its jaw and wings sets it apart.

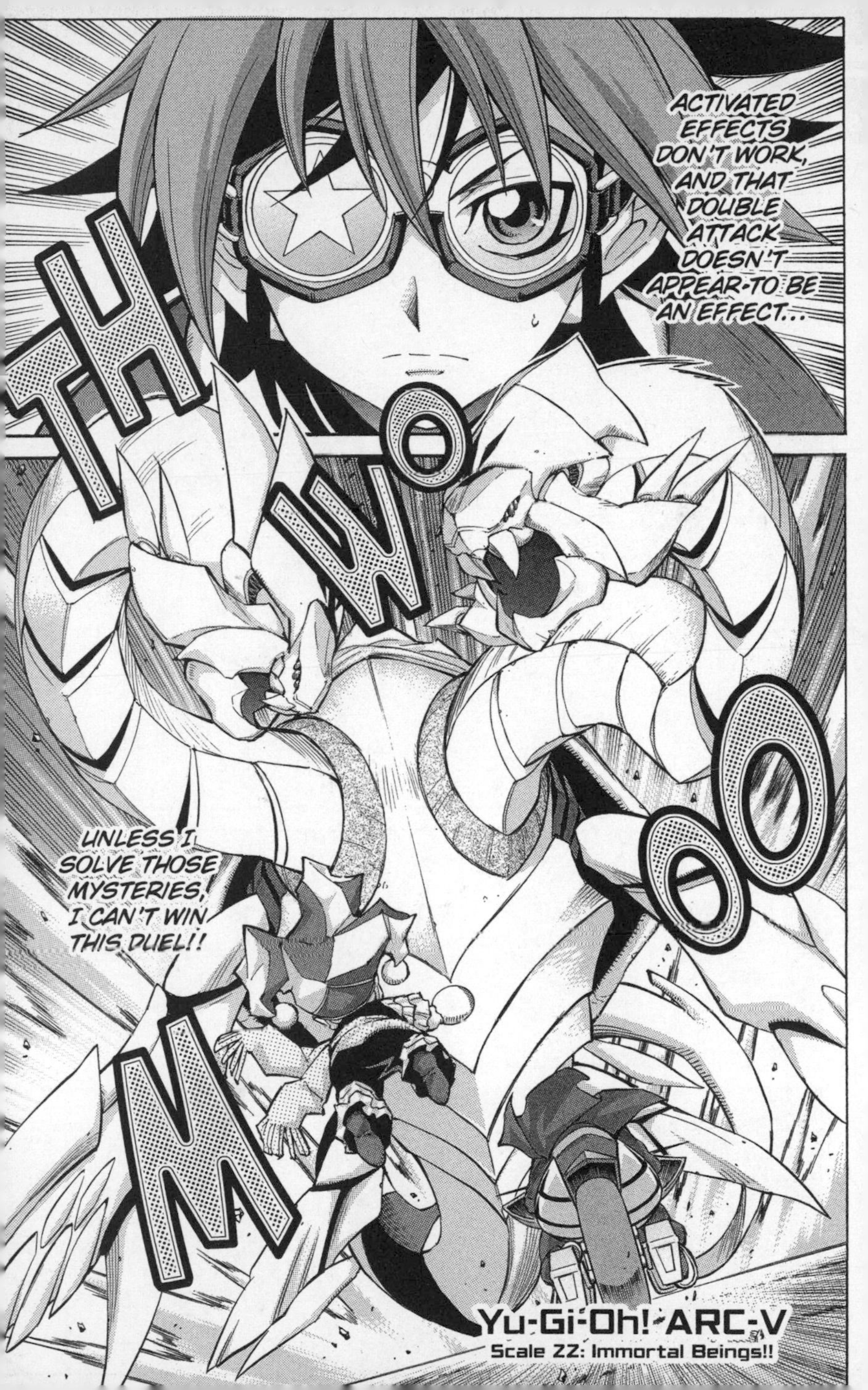
ACTIVATED EFFECTS DON'T WORK, AND THAT DOUBLE ATTACK DOESN'T APPEAR TO BE AN EFFECT...
THWOOOM
UNLESS I SOLVE THOSE MYSTERIES, I CAN'T WIN THIS DUEL!!
Yu-Gi-Oh! ARC-V
Scale 22: Immortal Beings!!

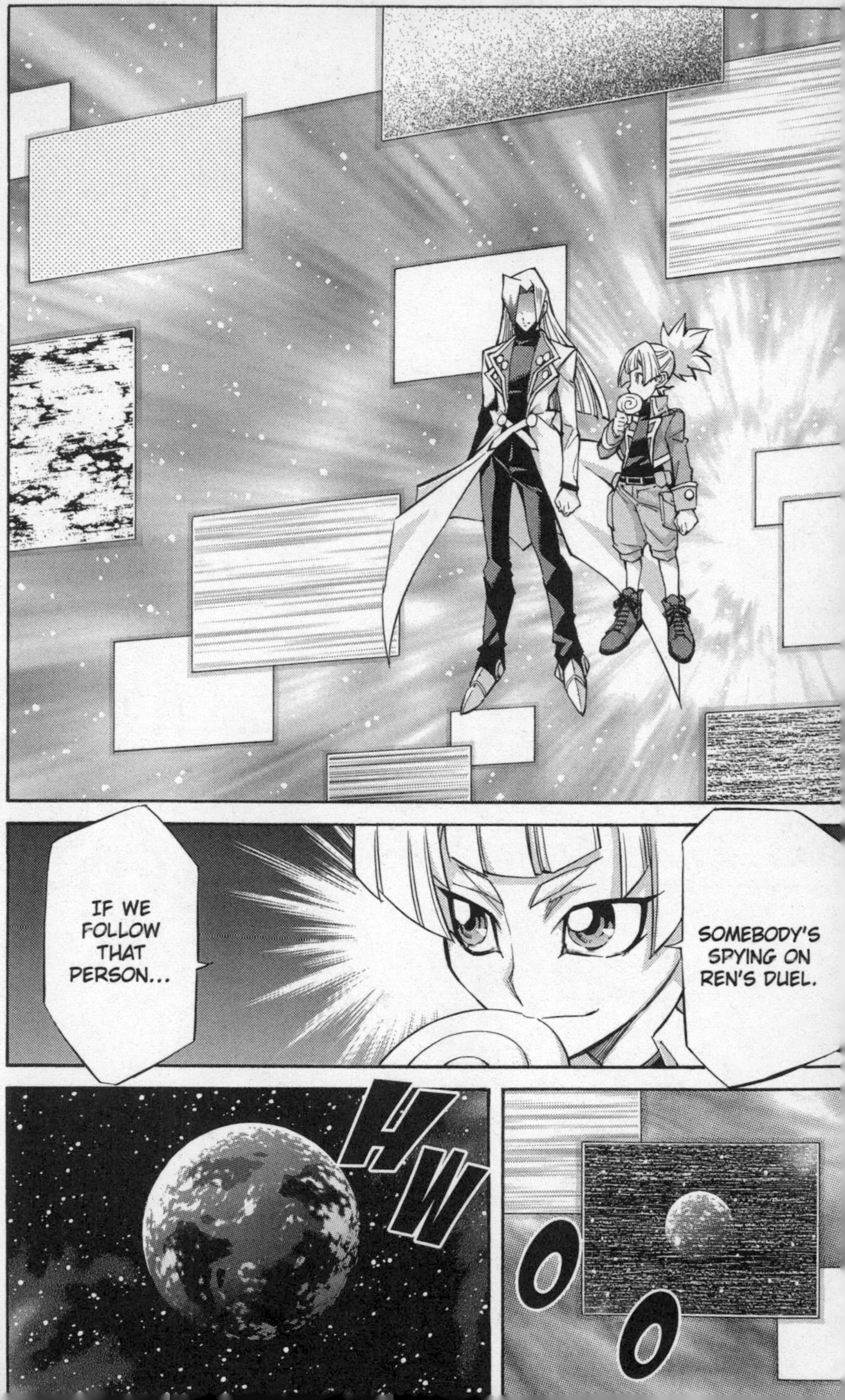
SOMEBODY'S SPYING ON REN'S DUEL.
IF WE FOLLOW THAT PERSON...
HWOOO

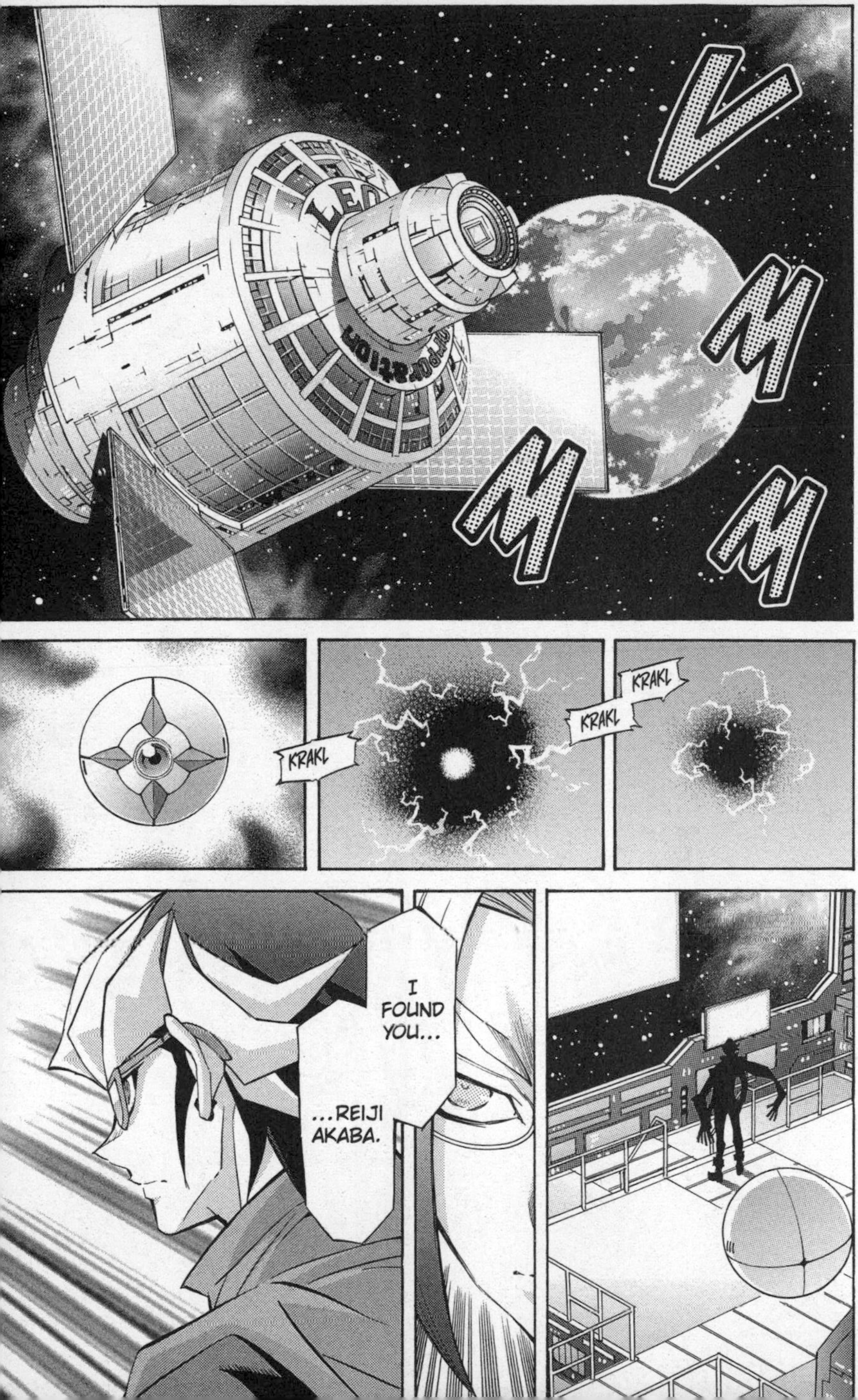
VMMM
KRAKL
KRAKL
KRAKL
I FOUND YOU...
...REIJI AKABA.

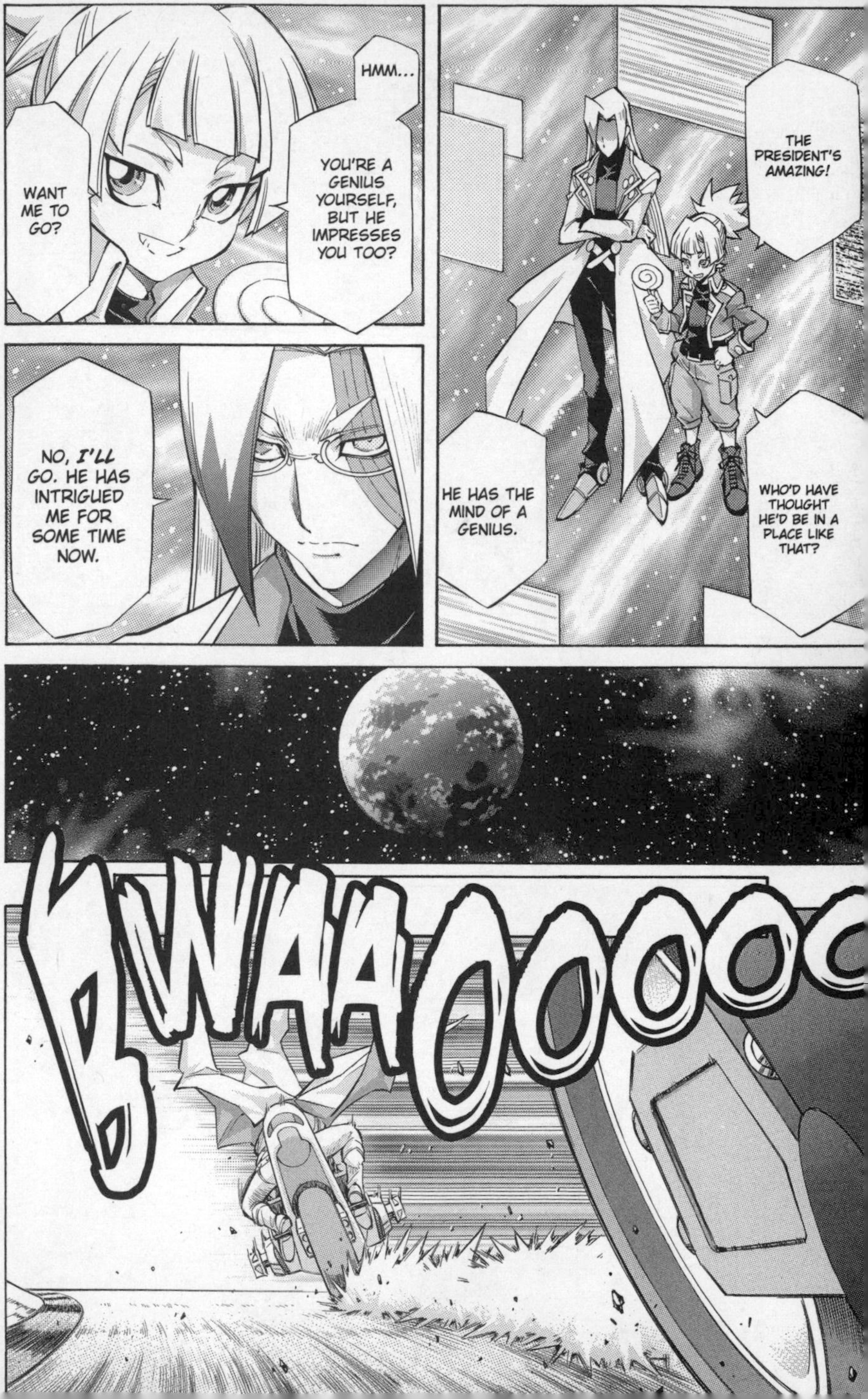
THE PRESIDENT'S AMAZING!
WHO'D HAVE THOUGHT HE'D BE IN A PLACE LIKE THAT?
HE HAS THE MIND OF A GENIUS.
HMM...
YOU'RE A GENIUS YOURSELF, BUT HE IMPRESSES YOU TOO?
WANT ME TO GO?
NO, *I'LL* GO. HE HAS INTRIGUED ME FOR SOME TIME NOW.
BWAAOOOOO

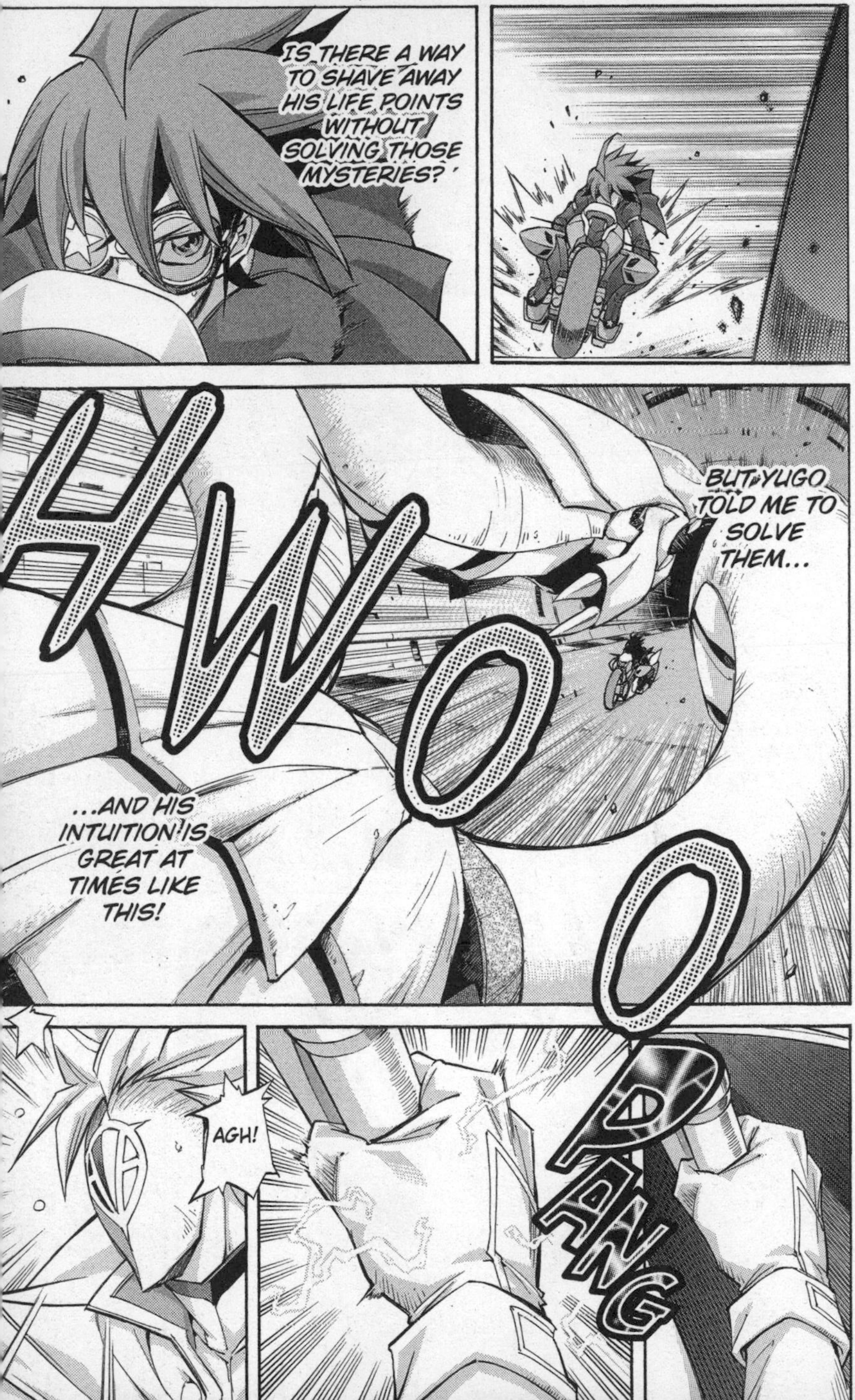
IS THERE A WAY TO SHAVE AWAY HIS LIFE POINTS WITHOUT SOLVING THOSE MYSTERIES?
BUT YUGO TOLD ME TO SOLVE THEM...
HWOOO
...AND HIS INTUITION IS GREAT AT TIMES LIKE THIS!
PANG
AGH!

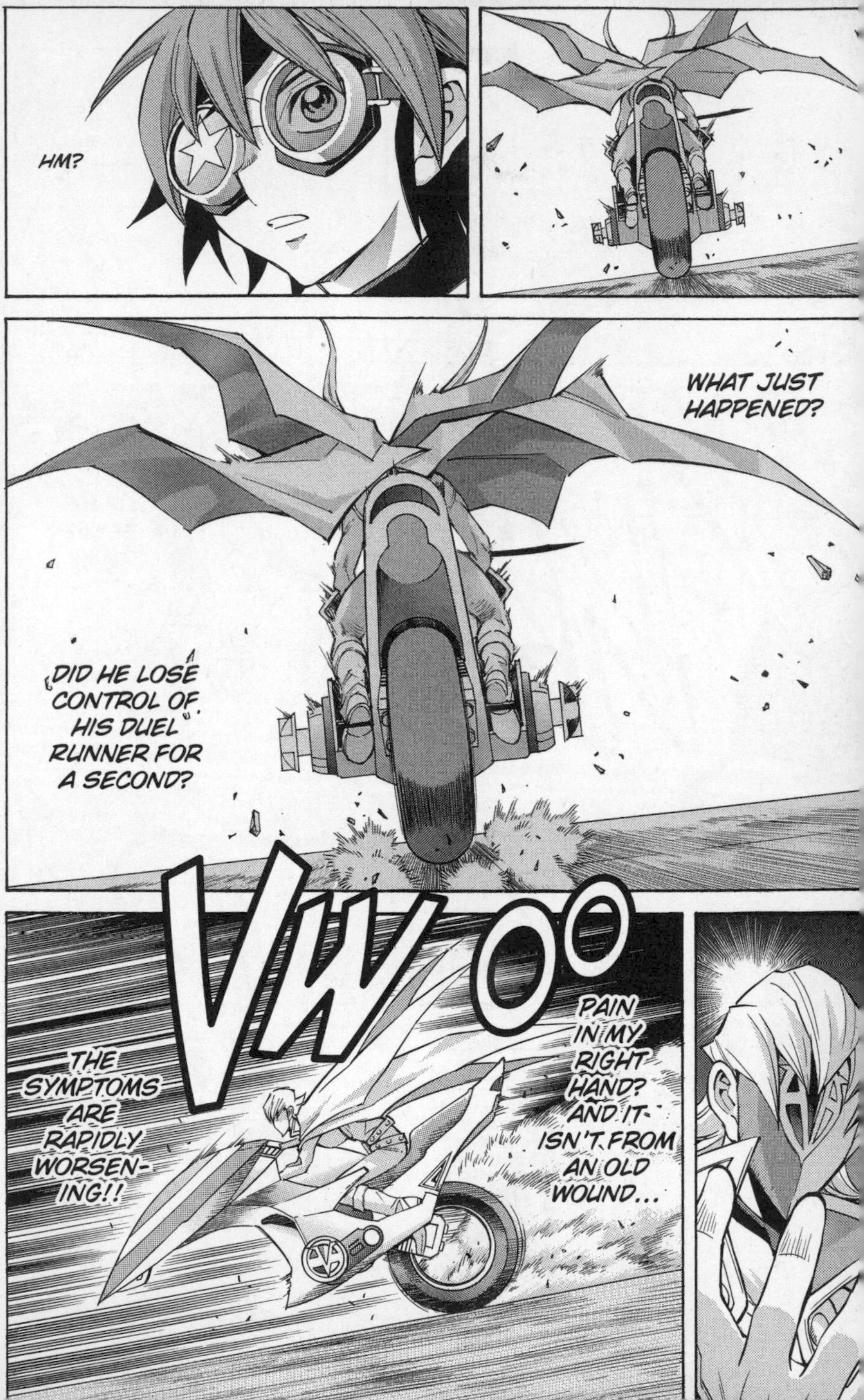
HM?
WHAT JUST HAPPENED?
DID HE LOSE CONTROL OF HIS DUEL RUNNER FOR A SECOND?
VWOO
PAIN IN MY RIGHT HAND? AND IT ISN'T FROM AN OLD WOUND...
THE SYMPTOMS ARE RAPIDLY WORSEN-ING!!

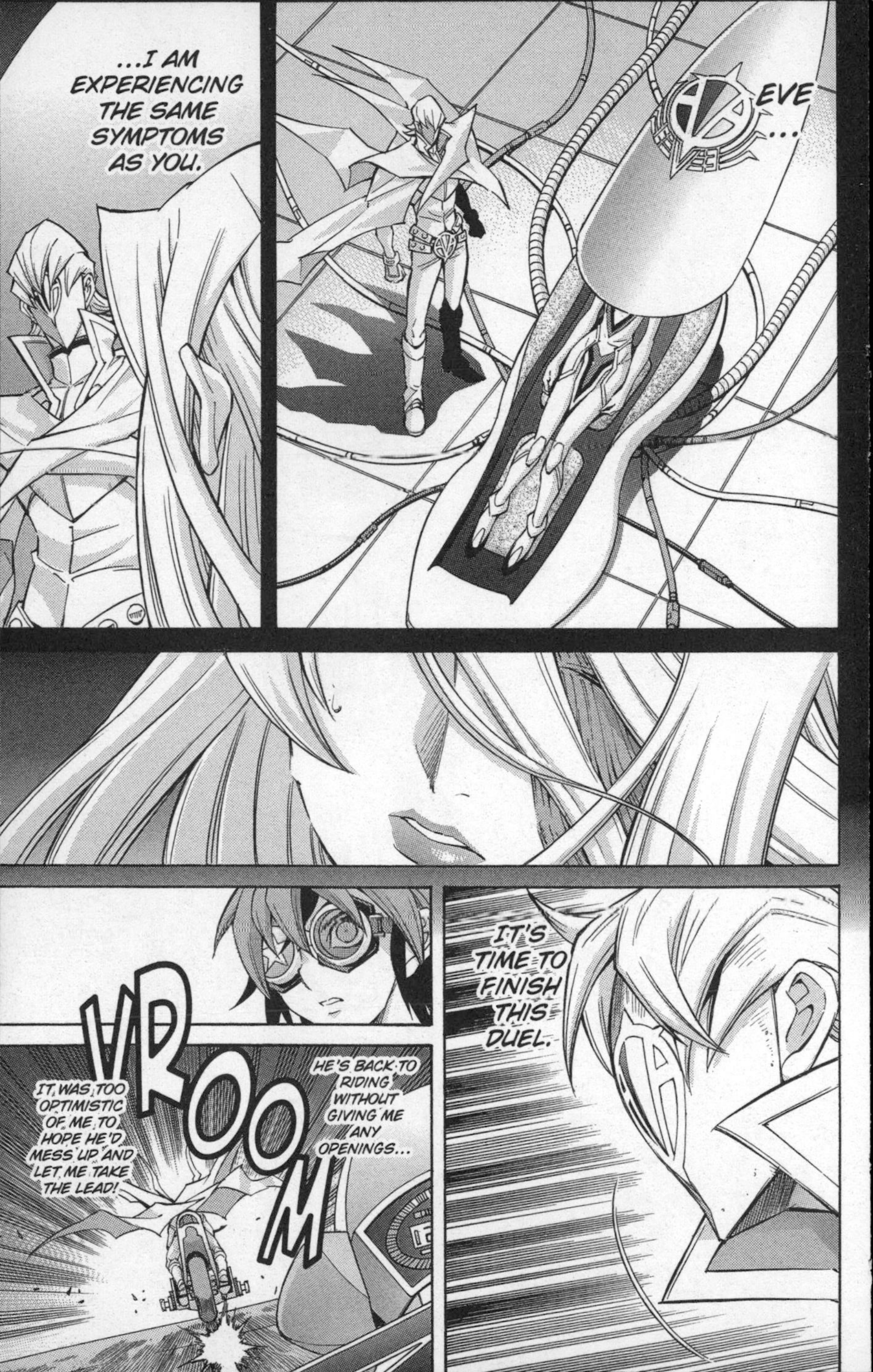
EVE...
...I AM EXPERIENCING THE SAME SYMPTOMS AS YOU.
IT'S TIME TO FINISH THIS DUEL.
VROOOM
HE'S BACK TO RIDING WITHOUT GIVING ME ANY OPENINGS...
IT WAS TOO OPTIMISTIC OF ME TO HOPE HE'D MESS UP AND LET ME TAKE THE LEAD!

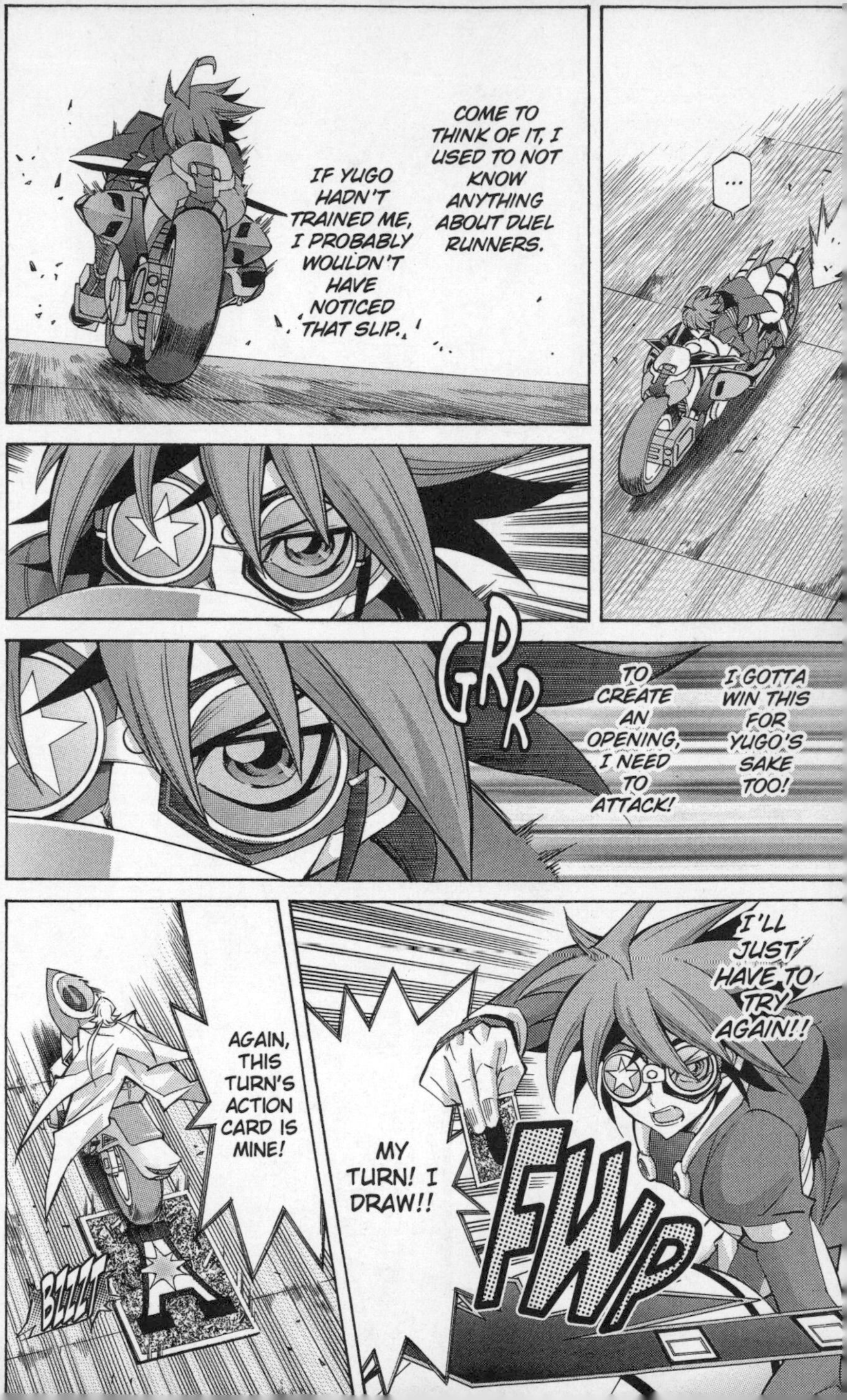
...
COME TO THINK OF IT, I USED TO NOT KNOW ANYTHING ABOUT DUEL RUNNERS.
IF YUGO HADN'T TRAINED ME, I PROBABLY WOULDN'T HAVE NOTICED THAT SLIP.
I GOTTA WIN THIS FOR YUGO'S SAKE TOO!
TO CREATE AN OPENING, I NEED TO ATTACK!
GRR
I'LL JUST HAVE TO TRY AGAIN!!
MY TURN! I DRAW!!
FWP
AGAIN, THIS TURN'S ACTION CARD IS MINE!
BZZZT

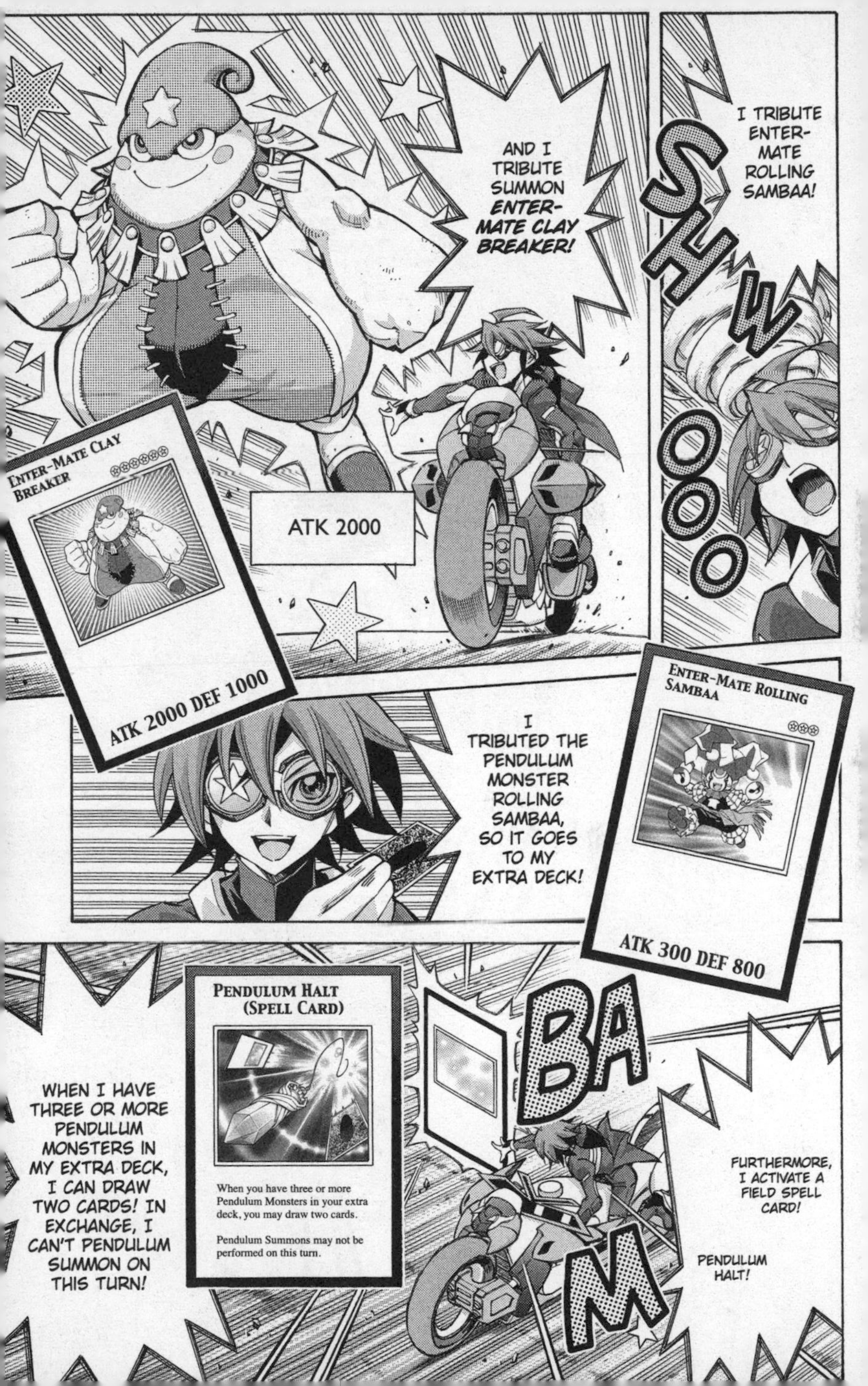
I TRIBUTE ENTER-MATE ROLLING SAMBAA!
SHWOOOOO
AND I TRIBUTE SUMMON ENTER-MATE CLAY BREAKER!
ENTER-MATE CLAY BREAKER
ATK 2000 DEF 1000
ATK 2000
I TRIBUTED THE PENDULUM MONSTER ROLLING SAMBAA, SO IT GOES TO MY EXTRA DECK!
ENTER-MATE ROLLING SAMBAA
ATK 300 DEF 800
FURTHERMORE, I ACTIVATE A FIELD SPELL CARD!
PENDULUM HALT!
BAM
PENDULUM HALT (SPELL CARD)
When you have three or more Pendulum Monsters in your extra deck, you may draw two cards.
Pendulum Summons may not be performed on this turn.
WHEN I HAVE THREE OR MORE PENDULUM MONSTERS IN MY EXTRA DECK, I CAN DRAW TWO CARDS! IN EXCHANGE, I CAN'T PENDULUM SUMMON ON THIS TURN!

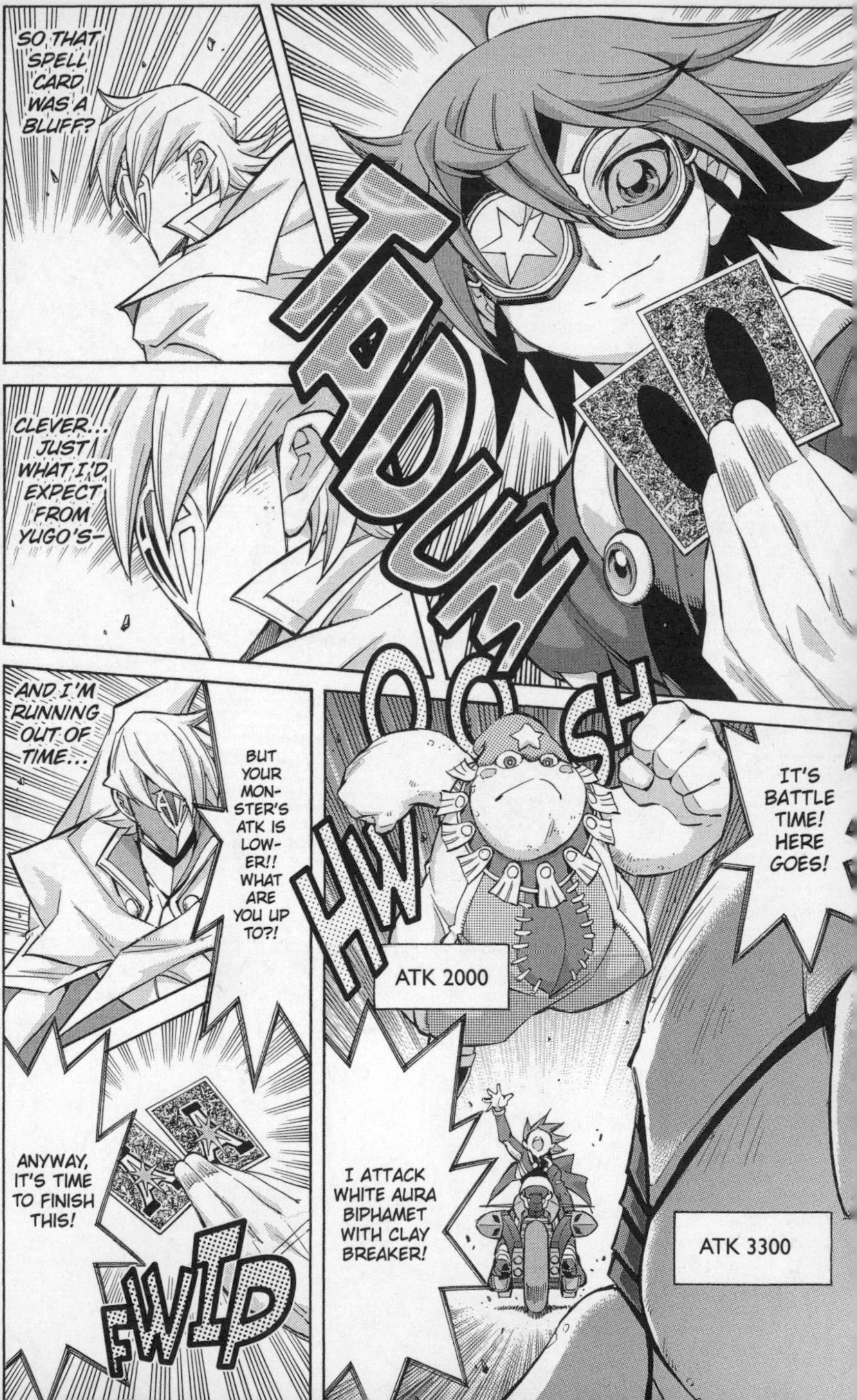
TADUM
SO THAT SPELL CARD WAS A BLUFF?
CLEVER... JUST WHAT I'D EXPECT FROM YUGO'S-
IT'S BATTLE TIME! HERE GOES!
HWOOSH
ATK 2000
ATK 3300
I ATTACK WHITE AURA BIPHAMET WITH CLAY BREAKER!
AND I'M RUNNING OUT OF TIME...
BUT YOUR MON-STER'S ATK IS LOW-ER!! WHAT ARE YOU UP TO?!
ANYWAY, IT'S TIME TO FINISH THIS!
FWIP

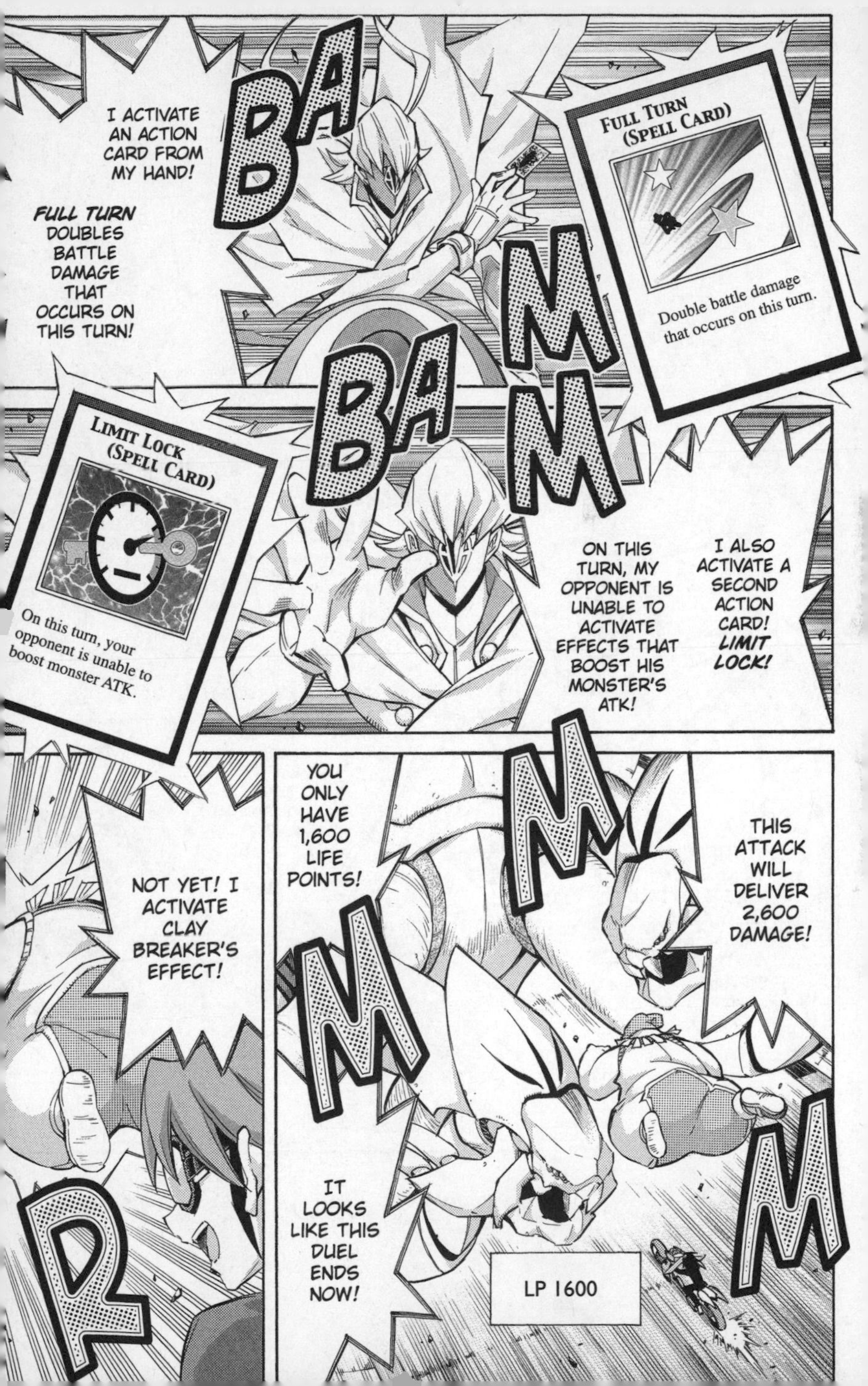

Full Turn (Spell Card)
Double battle damage that occurs on this turn.
BA
I ACTIVATE AN ACTION CARD FROM MY HAND!
FULL TURN DOUBLES BATTLE DAMAGE THAT OCCURS ON THIS TURN!
BAMM
MM
I ALSO ACTIVATE A SECOND ACTION CARD! *LIMIT LOCK!*
ON THIS TURN, MY OPPONENT IS UNABLE TO ACTIVATE EFFECTS THAT BOOST HIS MONSTER'S ATK!
Limit Lock (Spell Card)
On this turn, your opponent is unable to boost monster ATK.
THIS ATTACK WILL DELIVER 2,600 DAMAGE!
YOU ONLY HAVE 1,600 LIFE POINTS!
MMMM
IT LOOKS LIKE THIS DUEL ENDS NOW!
LP 1600
NOT YET! I ACTIVATE CLAY BREAKER'S EFFECT!
R

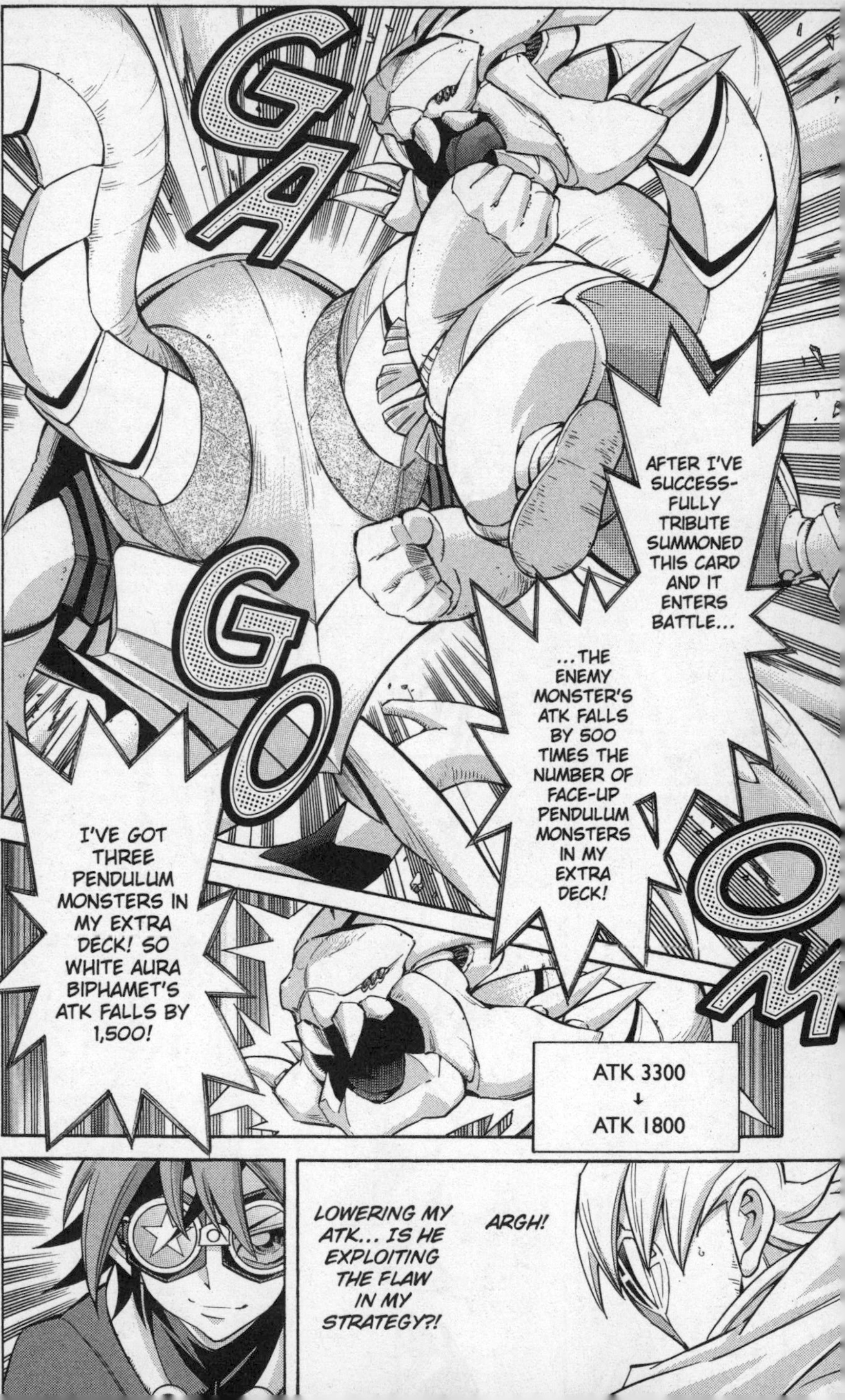
GAGOOM
AFTER I'VE SUCCESSFULLY TRIBUTE SUMMONED THIS CARD AND IT ENTERS BATTLE...
...THE ENEMY MONSTER'S ATK FALLS BY 500 TIMES THE NUMBER OF FACE-UP PENDULUM MONSTERS IN MY EXTRA DECK!
I'VE GOT THREE PENDULUM MONSTERS IN MY EXTRA DECK! SO WHITE AURA BIPHAMET'S ATK FALLS BY 1,500!
ATK 3300 ↓ ATK 1800
ARGH!
LOWERING MY ATK... IS HE EXPLOITING THE FLAW IN MY STRATEGY?!

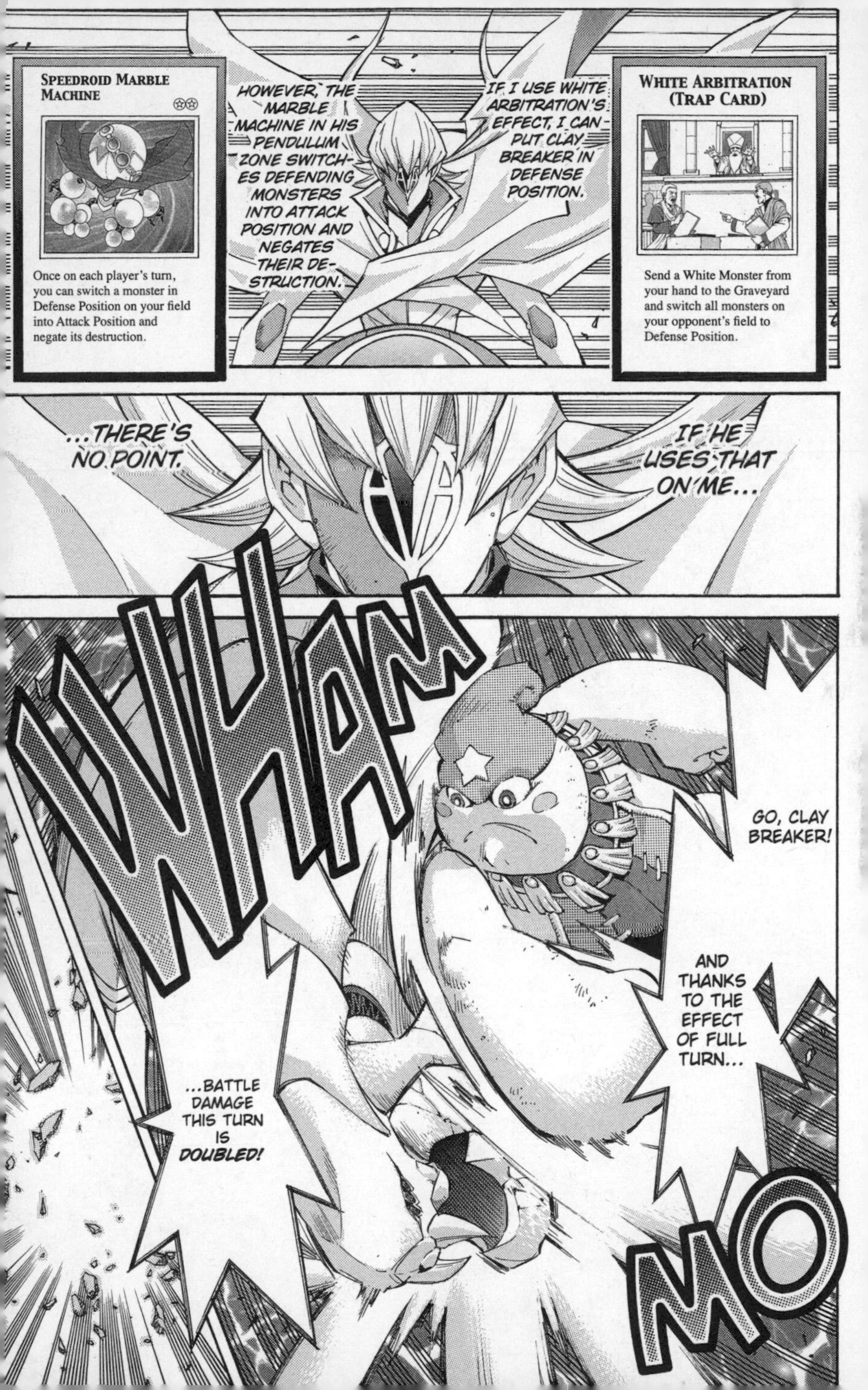

White Arbitration (Trap Card)
Send a White Monster from your hand to the Graveyard and switch all monsters on your opponent's field to Defense Position.
IF I USE WHITE ARBITRATION'S EFFECT, I CAN PUT CLAY BREAKER IN DEFENSE POSITION.
HOWEVER, THE MARBLE MACHINE IN HIS PENDULUM ZONE SWITCHES DEFENDING MONSTERS INTO ATTACK POSITION AND NEGATES THEIR DESTRUCTION.
Speedroid Marble Machine
Once on each player's turn, you can switch a monster in Defense Position on your field into Attack Position and negate its destruction.
IF HE USES THAT ON ME...
...THERE'S NO POINT.
GO, CLAY BREAKER!
WHAM
AND THANKS TO THE EFFECT OF FULL TURN...
...BATTLE DAMAGE THIS TURN IS DOUBLED!
MO

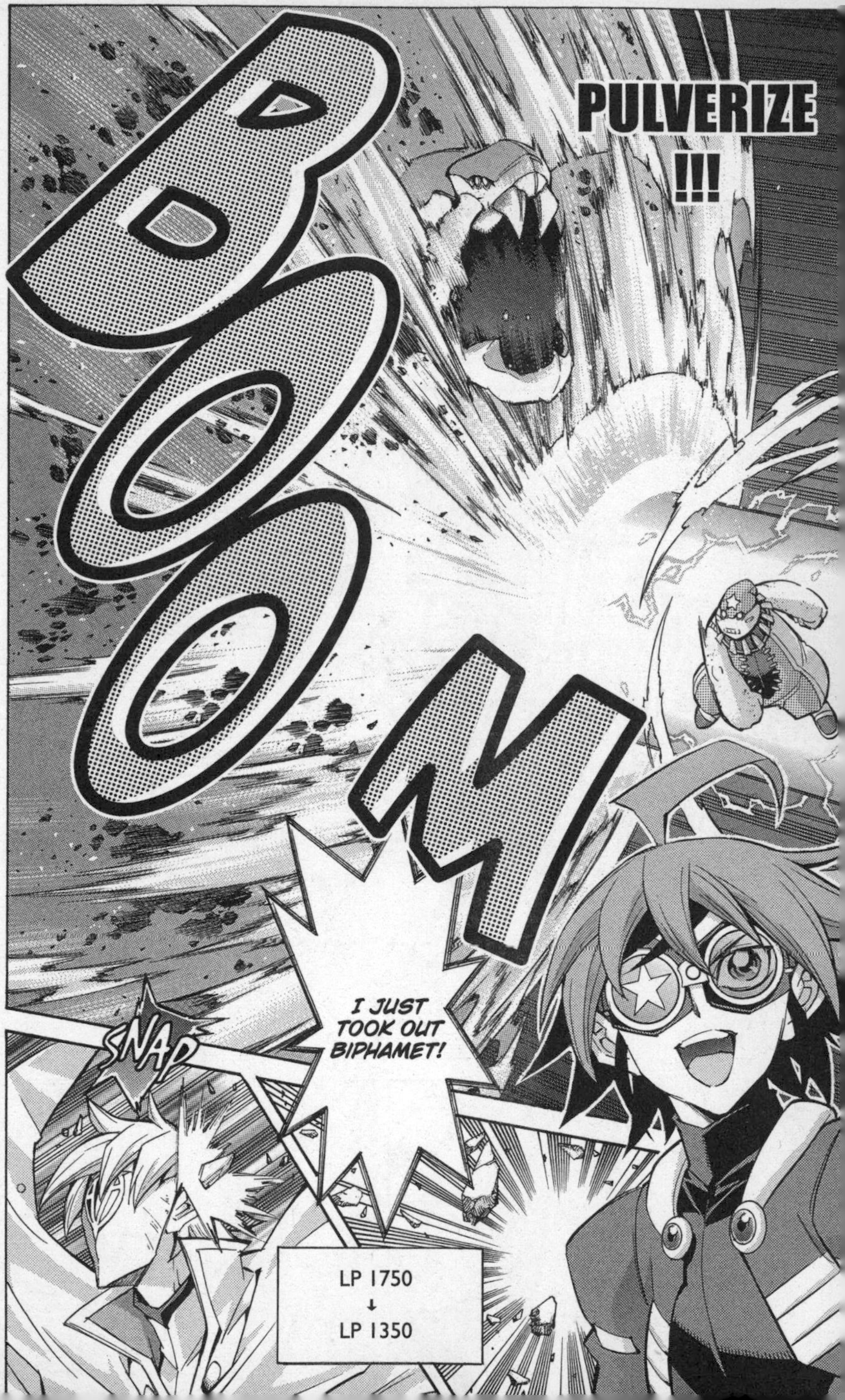
BOOM
PULVERIZE !!!
I JUST TOOK OUT BIPHAMET!
SNAP
LP 1750
↓
LP 1350

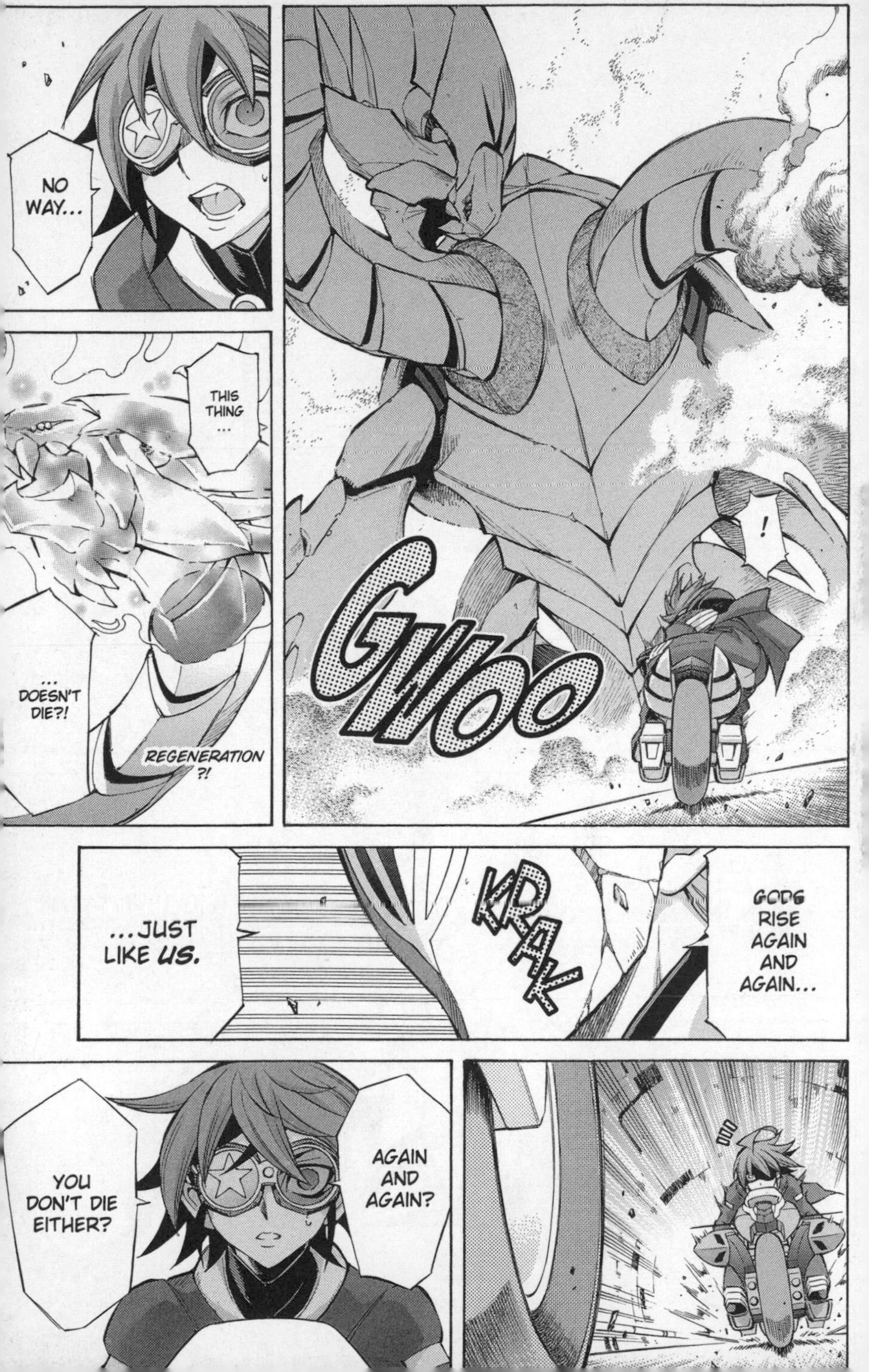
!
GWOO
NO WAY...
THIS THING ...
... DOESN'T DIE?!
REGENERATION ?!
GODS RISE AGAIN AND AGAIN...
KRAK
...JUST LIKE US.
AGAIN AND AGAIN?
YOU DON'T DIE EITHER?

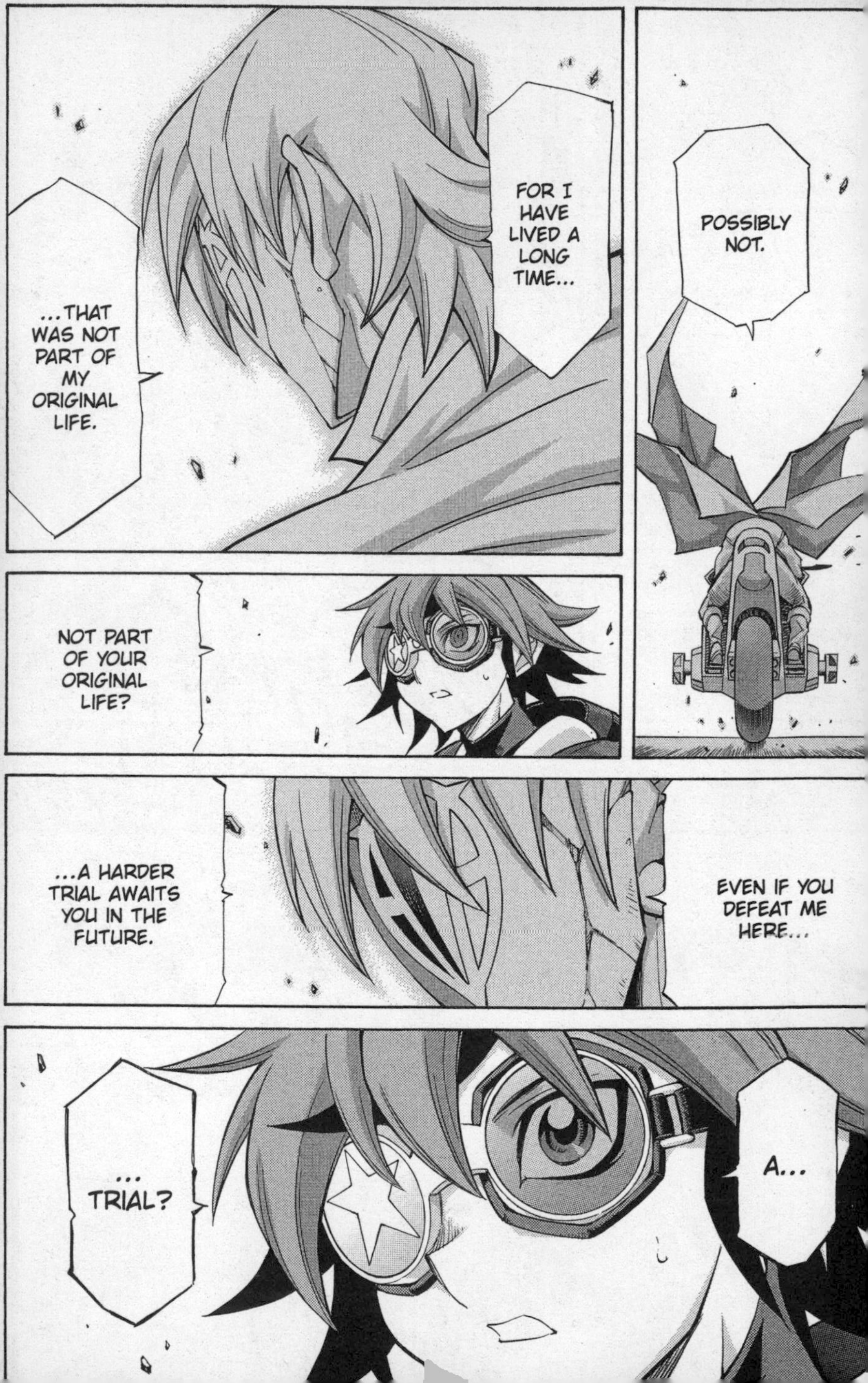
POSSIBLY NOT.
FOR I HAVE LIVED A LONG TIME...
...THAT WAS NOT PART OF MY ORIGINAL LIFE.
NOT PART OF YOUR ORIGINAL LIFE?
EVEN IF YOU DEFEAT ME HERE...
...A HARDER TRIAL AWAITS YOU IN THE FUTURE.
A...
...TRIAL?

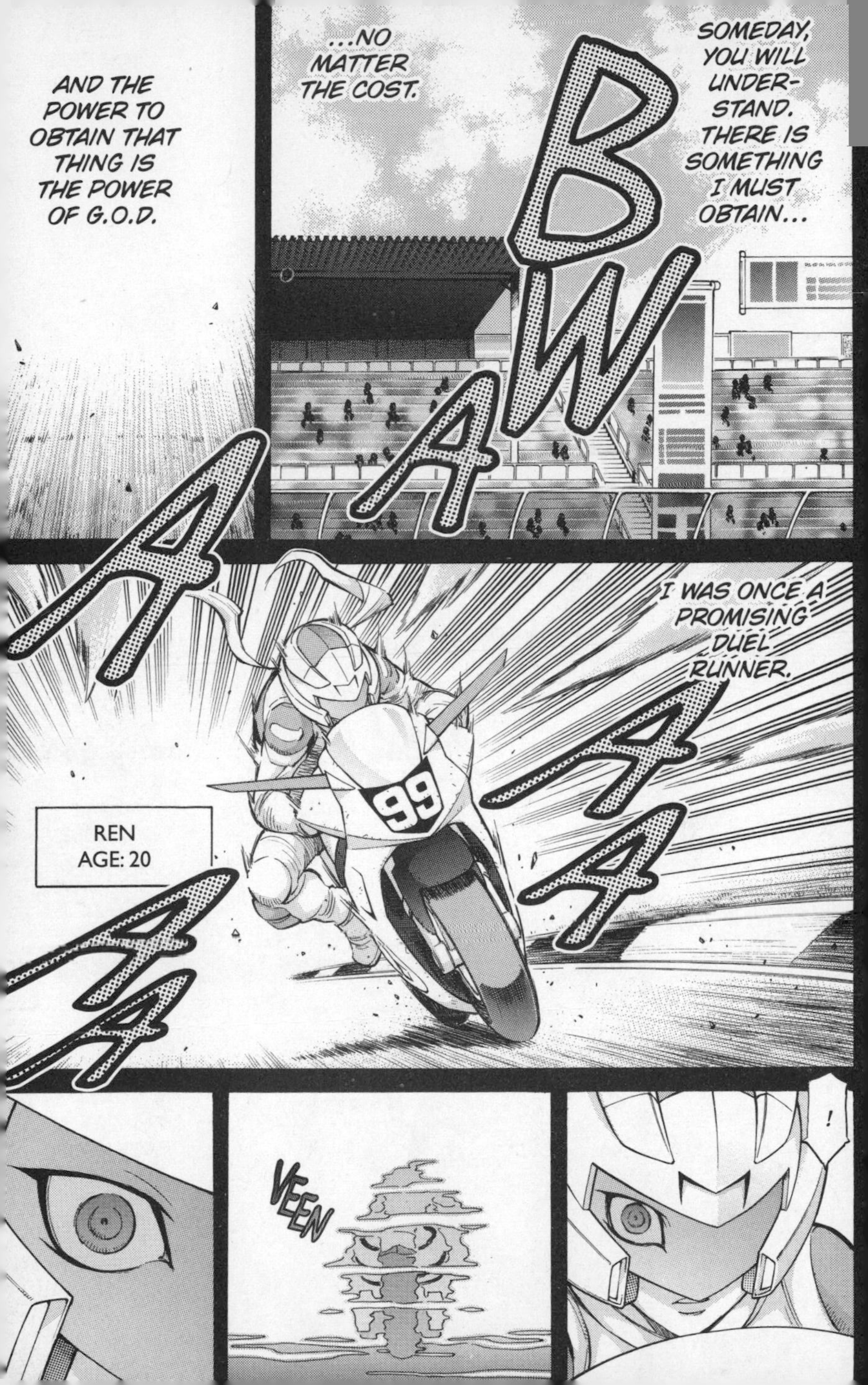
SOMEDAY, YOU WILL UNDER-STAND. THERE IS SOMETHING I MUST OBTAIN...
...NO MATTER THE COST.
BWAAAAAAA
AND THE POWER TO OBTAIN THAT THING IS THE POWER OF G.O.D.
I WAS ONCE A PROMISING DUEL RUNNER.
99
REN
AGE: 20
!
VEEN

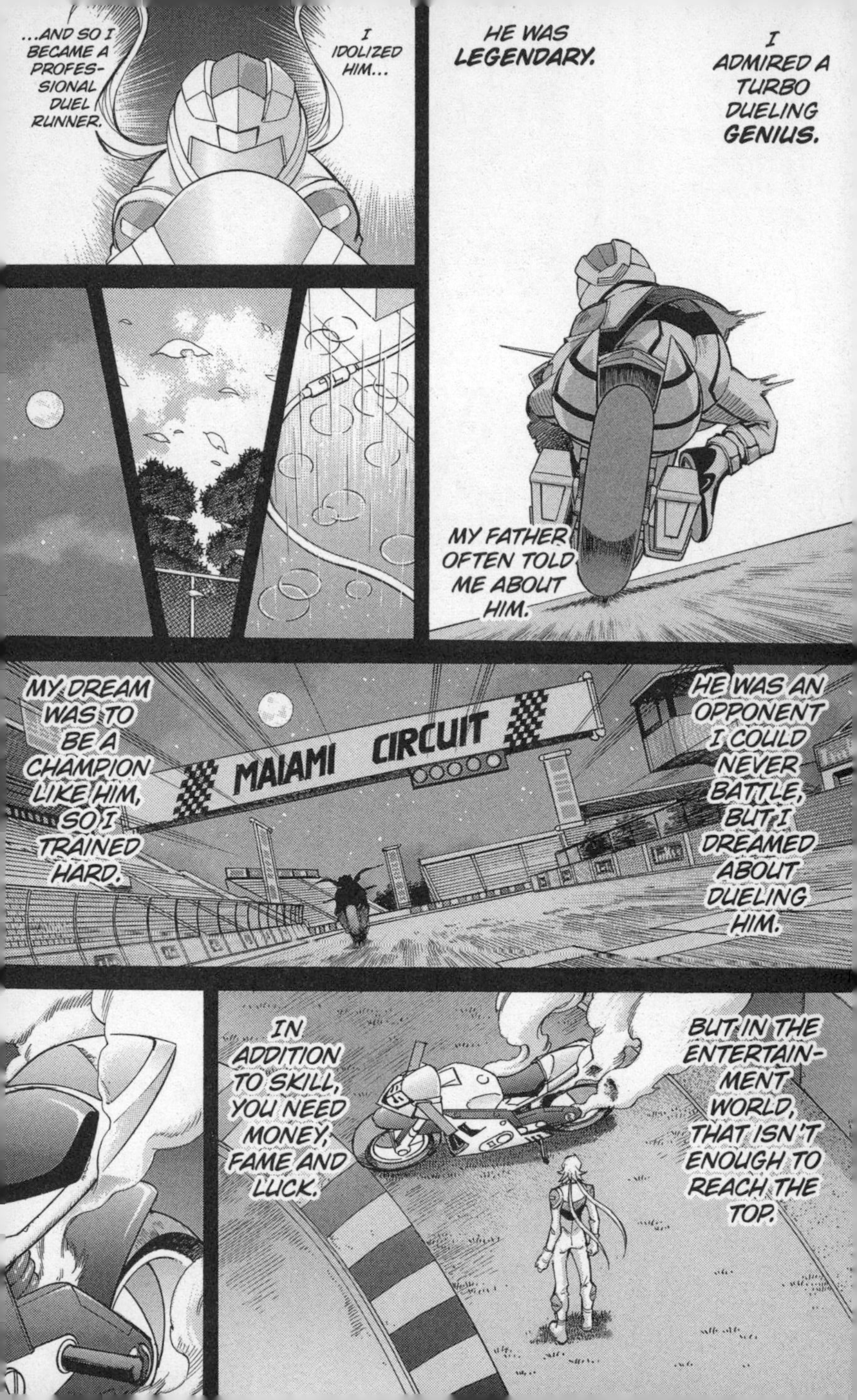
I ADMIRED A TURBO DUELING GENIUS.
HE WAS LEGENDARY.
MY FATHER OFTEN TOLD ME ABOUT HIM.
I IDOLIZED HIM...
...AND SO I BECAME A PROFES-SIONAL DUEL RUNNER.
HE WAS AN OPPONENT I COULD NEVER BATTLE, BUT I DREAMED ABOUT DUELING HIM.
MAIAMI CIRCUIT
MY DREAM WAS TO BE A CHAMPION LIKE HIM, SO I TRAINED HARD.
BUT IN THE ENTERTAIN-MENT WORLD, THAT ISN'T ENOUGH TO REACH THE TOP.
IN ADDITION TO SKILL, YOU NEED MONEY, FAME AND LUCK.

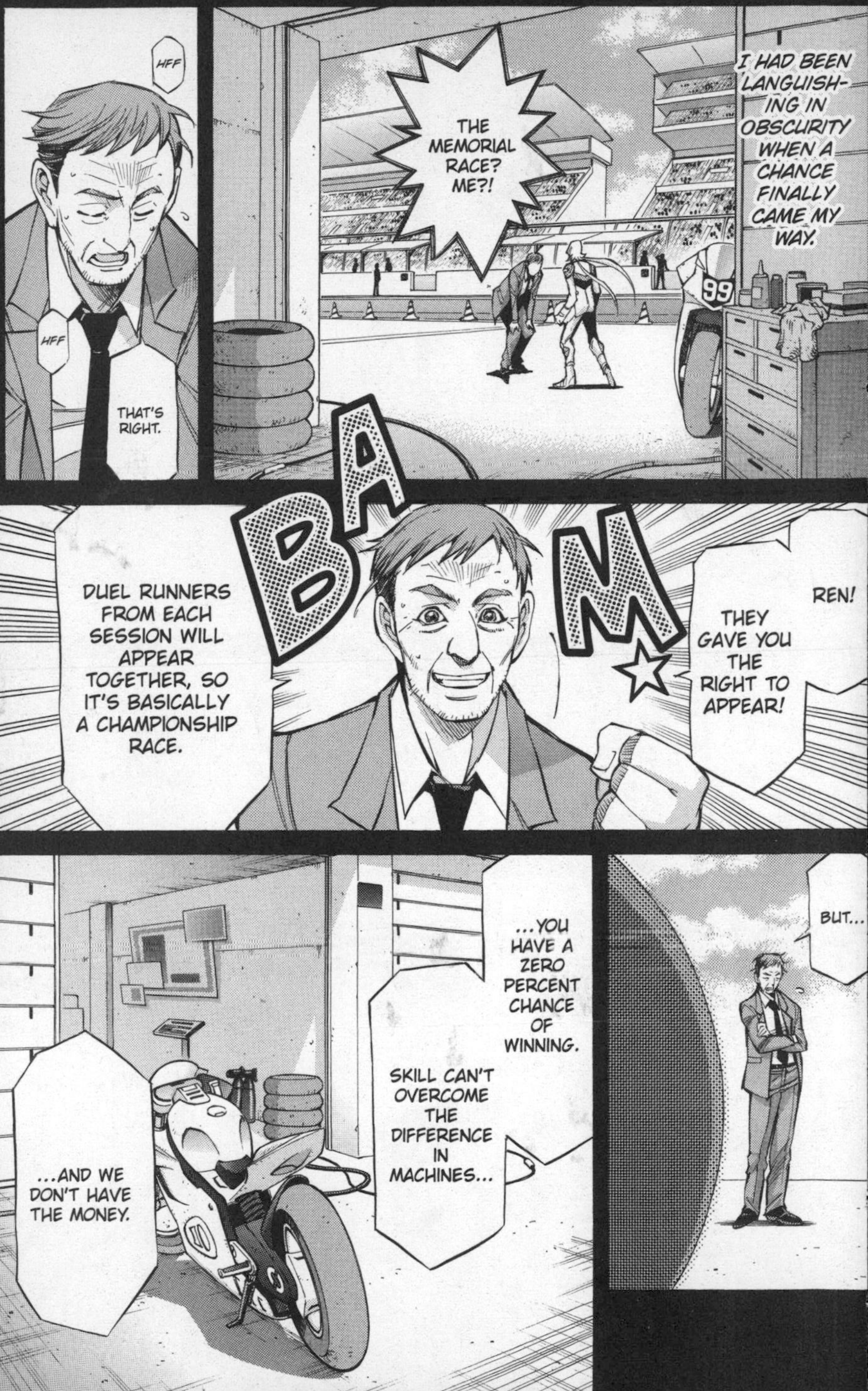
I HAD BEEN LANGUISHING IN OBSCURITY WHEN A CHANCE FINALLY CAME MY WAY.
THE MEMORIAL RACE? ME?!
HFF
HFF
THAT'S RIGHT.
REN!
THEY GAVE YOU THE RIGHT TO APPEAR!
BAM
DUEL RUNNERS FROM EACH SESSION WILL APPEAR TOGETHER, SO IT'S BASICALLY A CHAMPIONSHIP RACE.
BUT...
...YOU HAVE A ZERO PERCENT CHANCE OF WINNING.
SKILL CAN'T OVERCOME THE DIFFERENCE IN MACHINES...
...AND WE DON'T HAVE THE MONEY.

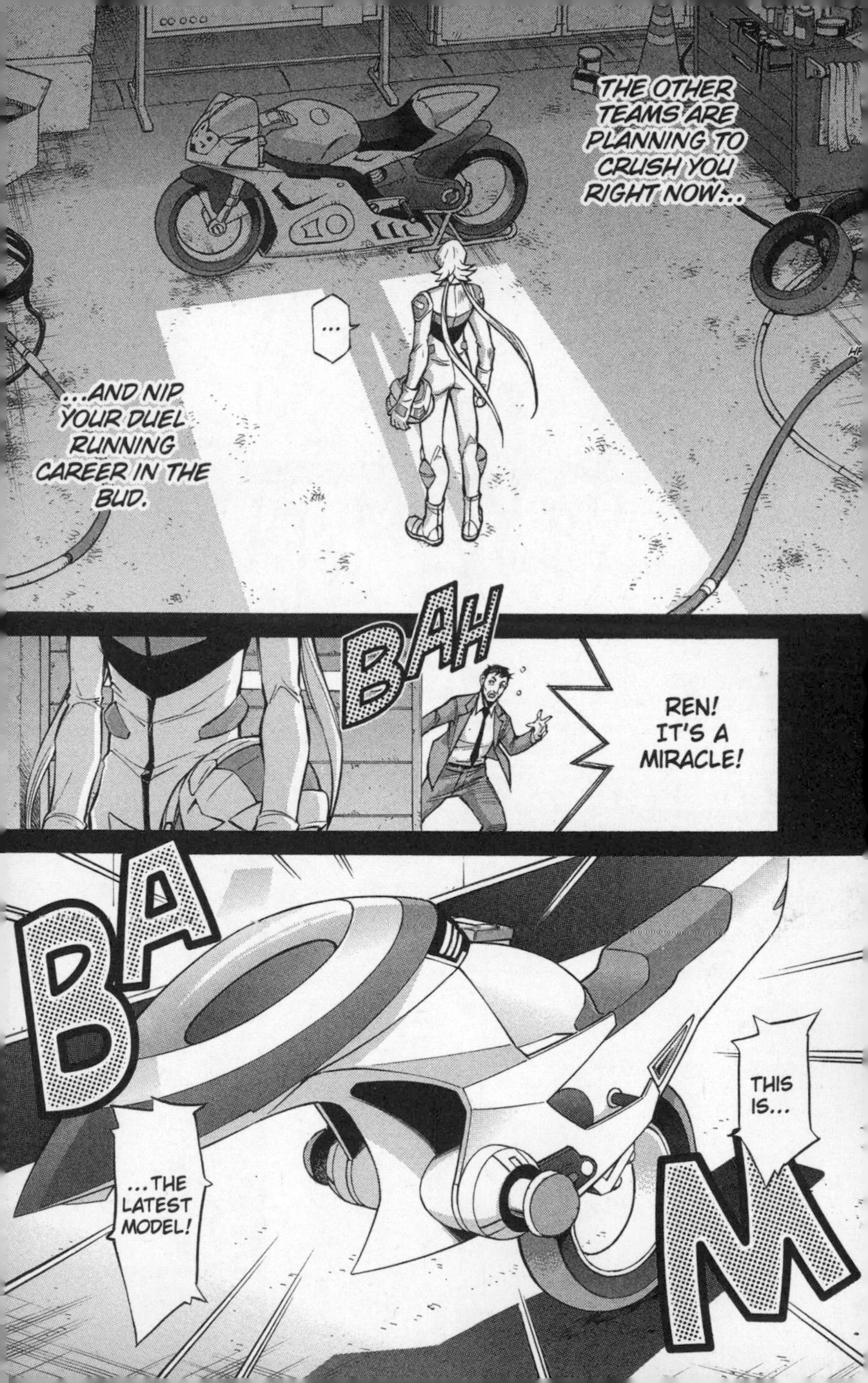
THE OTHER TEAMS ARE PLANNING TO CRUSH YOU RIGHT NOW...
...
...AND NIP YOUR DUEL RUNNING CAREER IN THE BUD.
REN! IT'S A MIRACLE!
BAH
THIS IS...
...THE LATEST MODEL!
BAM

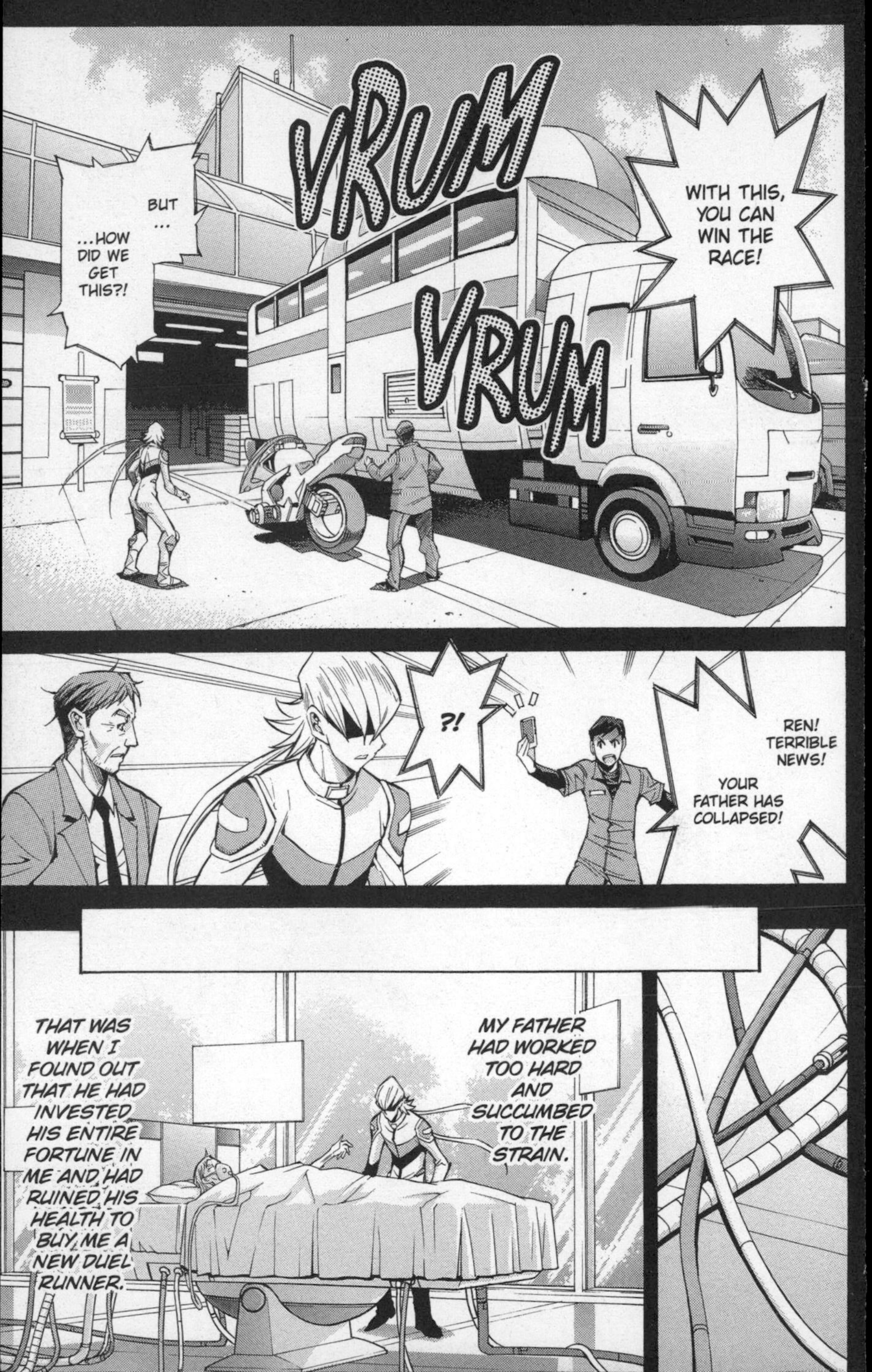
WITH THIS, YOU CAN WIN THE RACE!
VRUM
VRUM
BUT ...
...HOW DID WE GET THIS?!
REN! TERRIBLE NEWS!
YOUR FATHER HAS COLLAPSED!
?!
MY FATHER HAD WORKED TOO HARD AND SUCCUMBED TO THE STRAIN.
THAT WAS WHEN I FOUND OUT THAT HE HAD INVESTED HIS ENTIRE FORTUNE IN ME AND HAD RUINED HIS HEALTH TO BUY ME A NEW DUEL RUNNER.

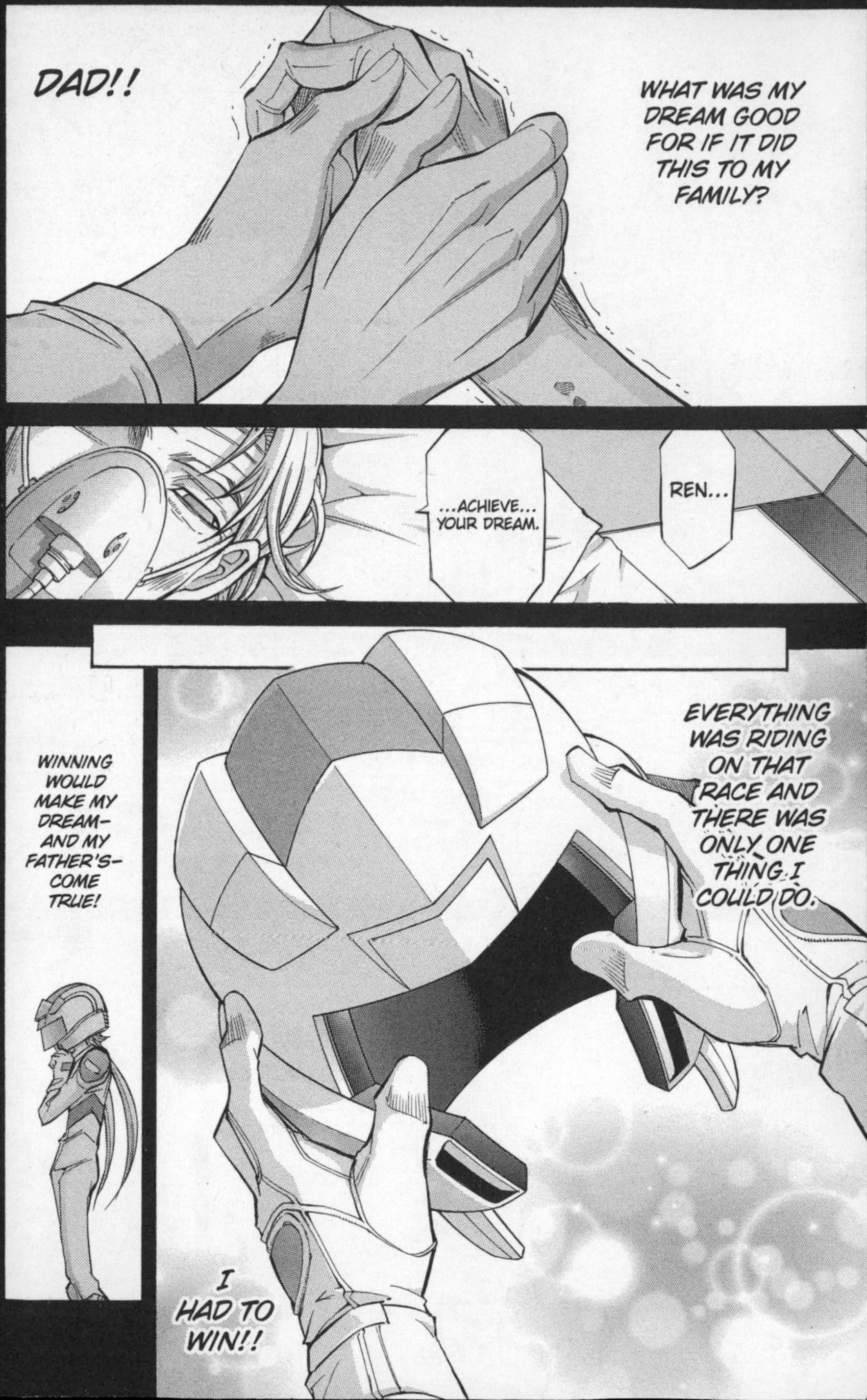
WHAT WAS MY DREAM GOOD FOR IF IT DID THIS TO MY FAMILY?
DAD!!
REN...
...ACHIEVE... YOUR DREAM.
EVERYTHING WAS RIDING ON THAT RACE AND THERE WAS ONLY ONE THING I COULD DO.
I HAD TO WIN!!
WINNING WOULD MAKE MY DREAM- AND MY FATHER'S- COME TRUE!

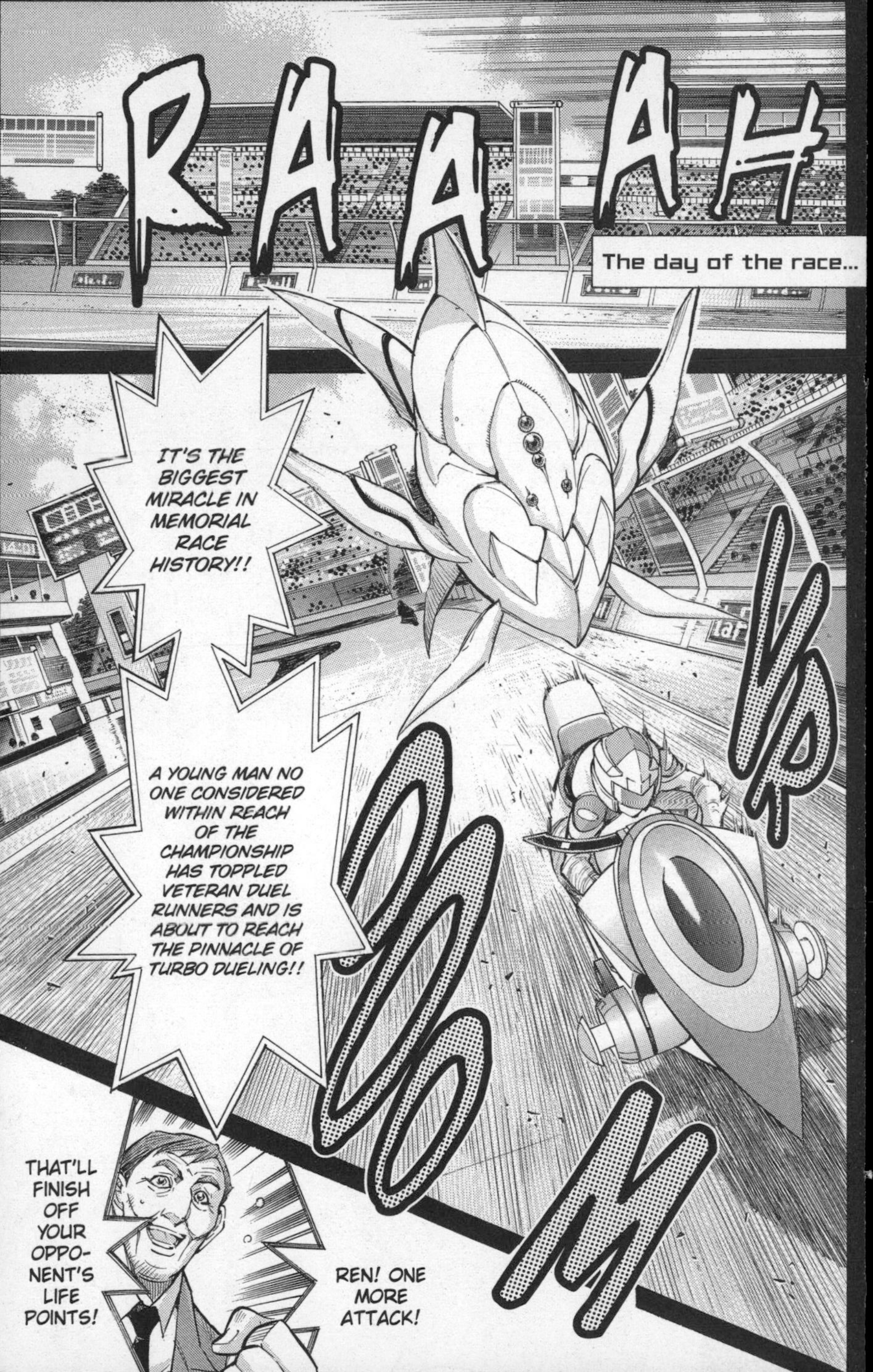
RAAAH
The day of the race...
IT'S THE BIGGEST MIRACLE IN MEMORIAL RACE HISTORY!!
A YOUNG MAN NO ONE CONSIDERED WITHIN REACH OF THE CHAMPIONSHIP HAS TOPPLED VETERAN DUEL RUNNERS AND IS ABOUT TO REACH THE PINNACLE OF TURBO DUELING!!
REN! ONE MORE ATTACK!
THAT'LL FINISH OFF YOUR OPPO-NENT'S LIFE POINTS!

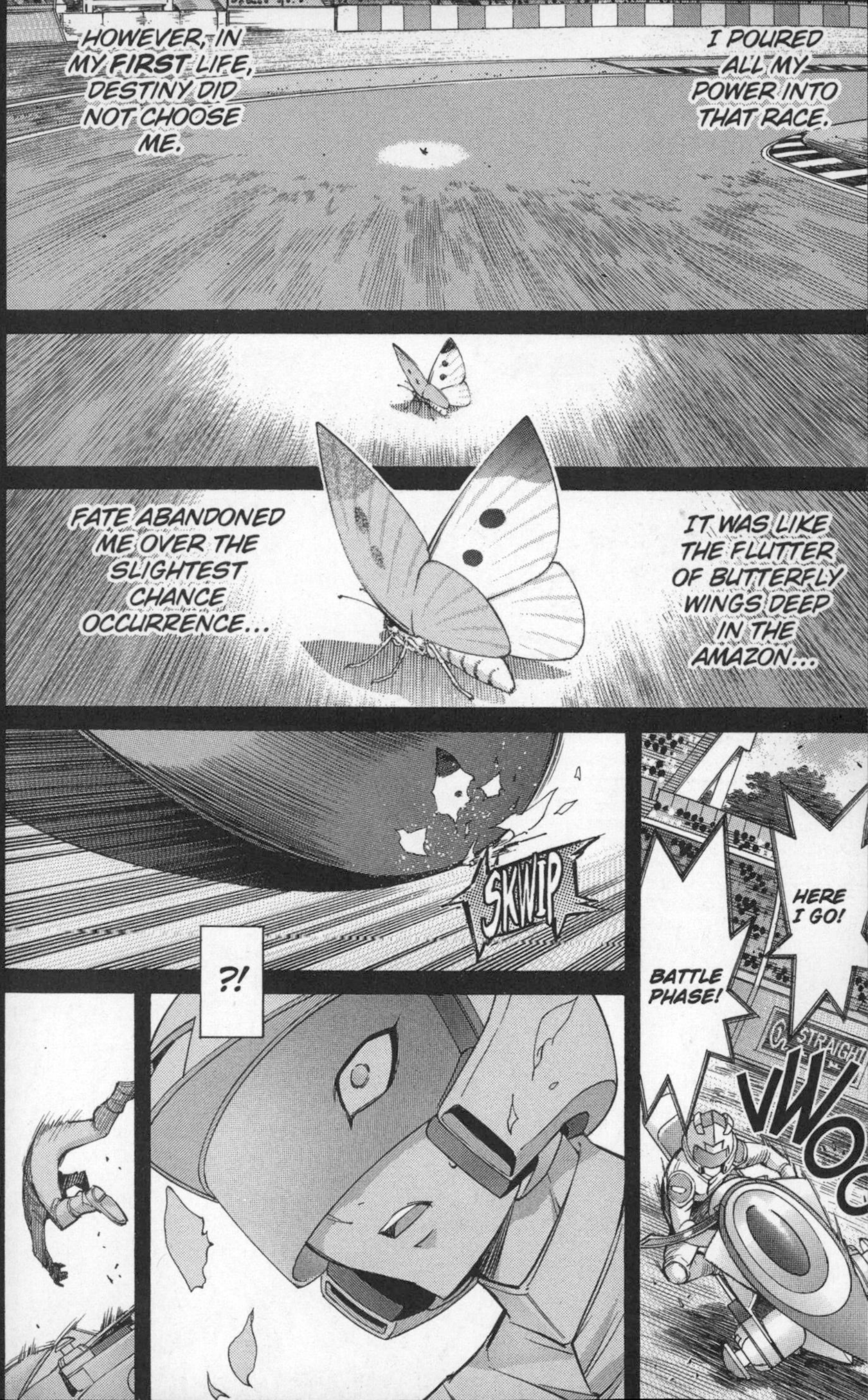
I POURED ALL MY POWER INTO THAT RACE.
HOWEVER, IN MY FIRST LIFE, DESTINY DID NOT CHOOSE ME.
IT WAS LIKE THE FLUTTER OF BUTTERFLY WINGS DEEP IN THE AMAZON...
FATE ABANDONED ME OVER THE SLIGHTEST CHANCE OCCURRENCE...
HERE I GO!
BATTLE PHASE!
STRAIGHT
VWOO
SKWIP
?!

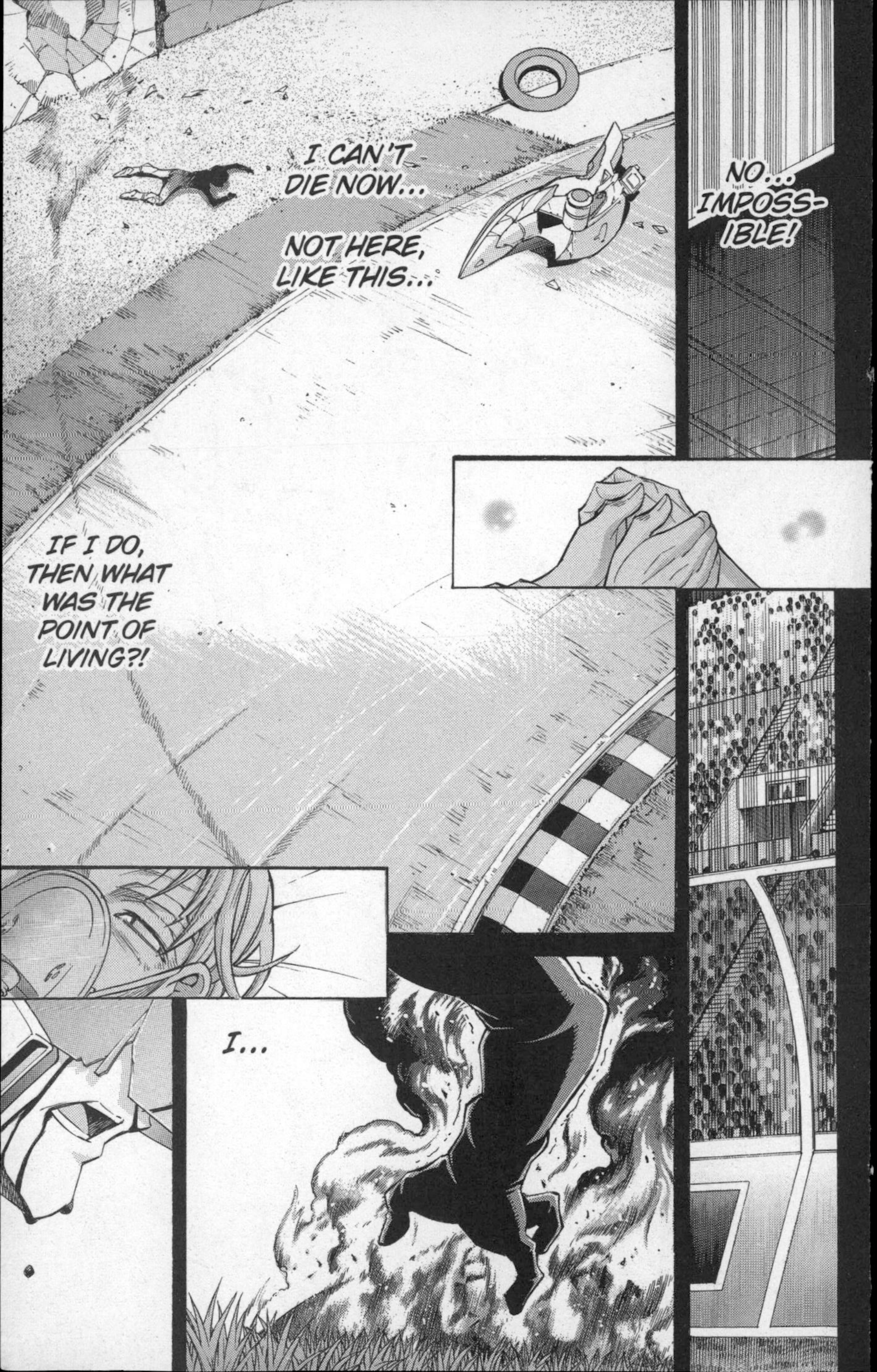
NO... IMPOSSIBLE!
I CAN'T DIE NOW...
NOT HERE, LIKE THIS...
IF I DO, THEN WHAT WAS THE POINT OF LIVING?!
I...

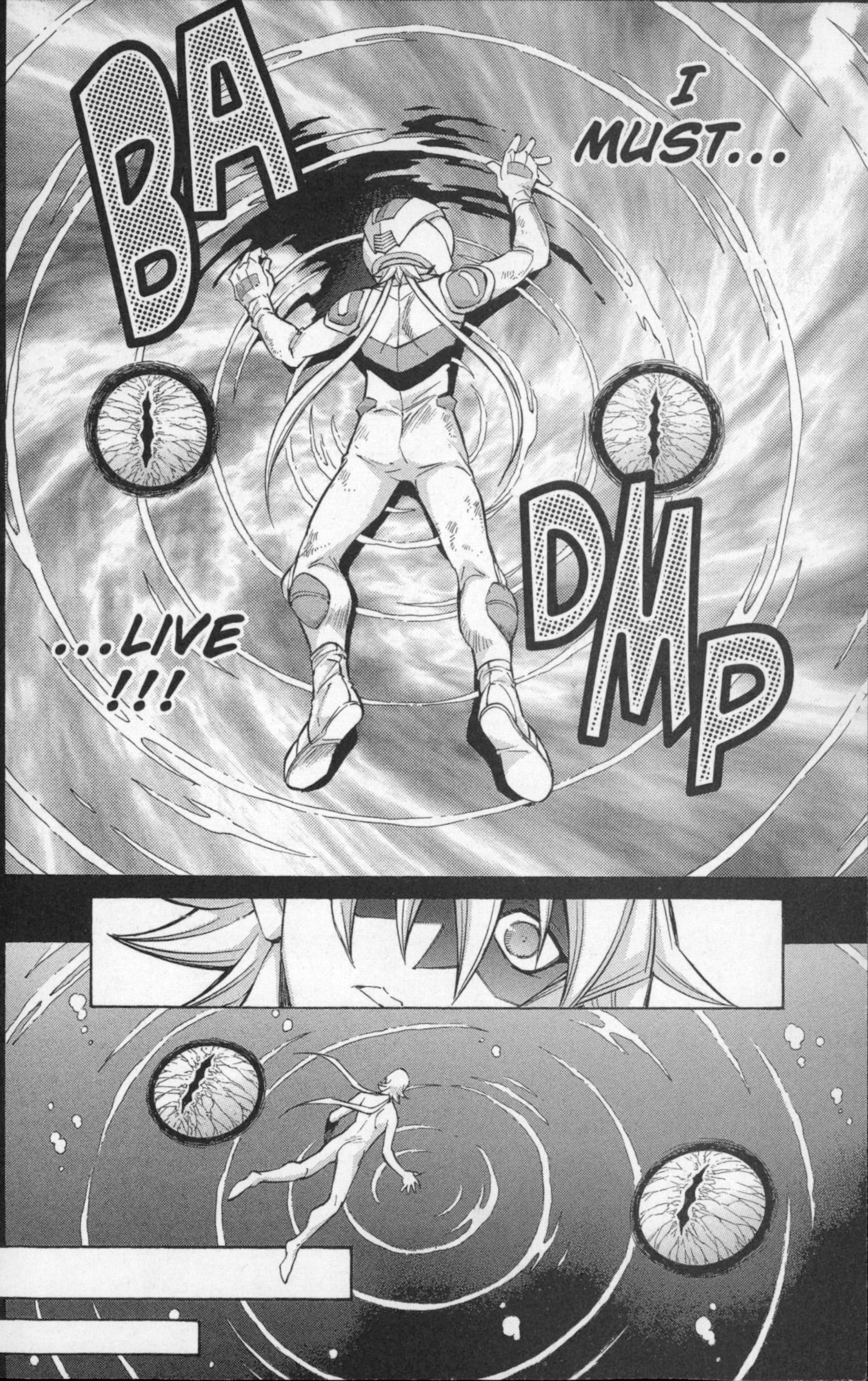
I MUST...
BA
DUMP
...LIVE !!!

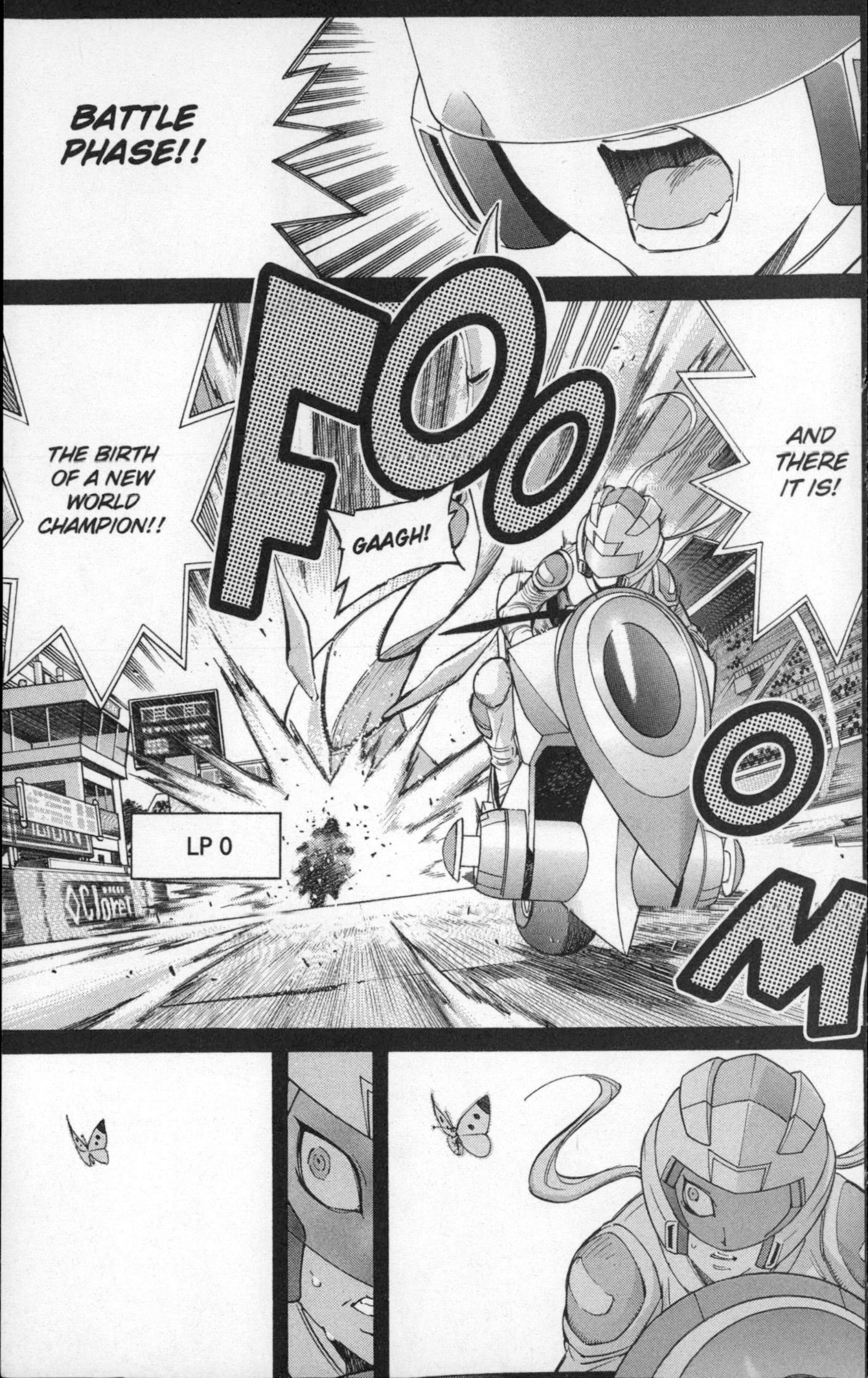
BATTLE PHASE!!
AND THERE IT IS!
FOOOOOM
GAAGH!
THE BIRTH OF A NEW WORLD CHAMPION!!
LP 0

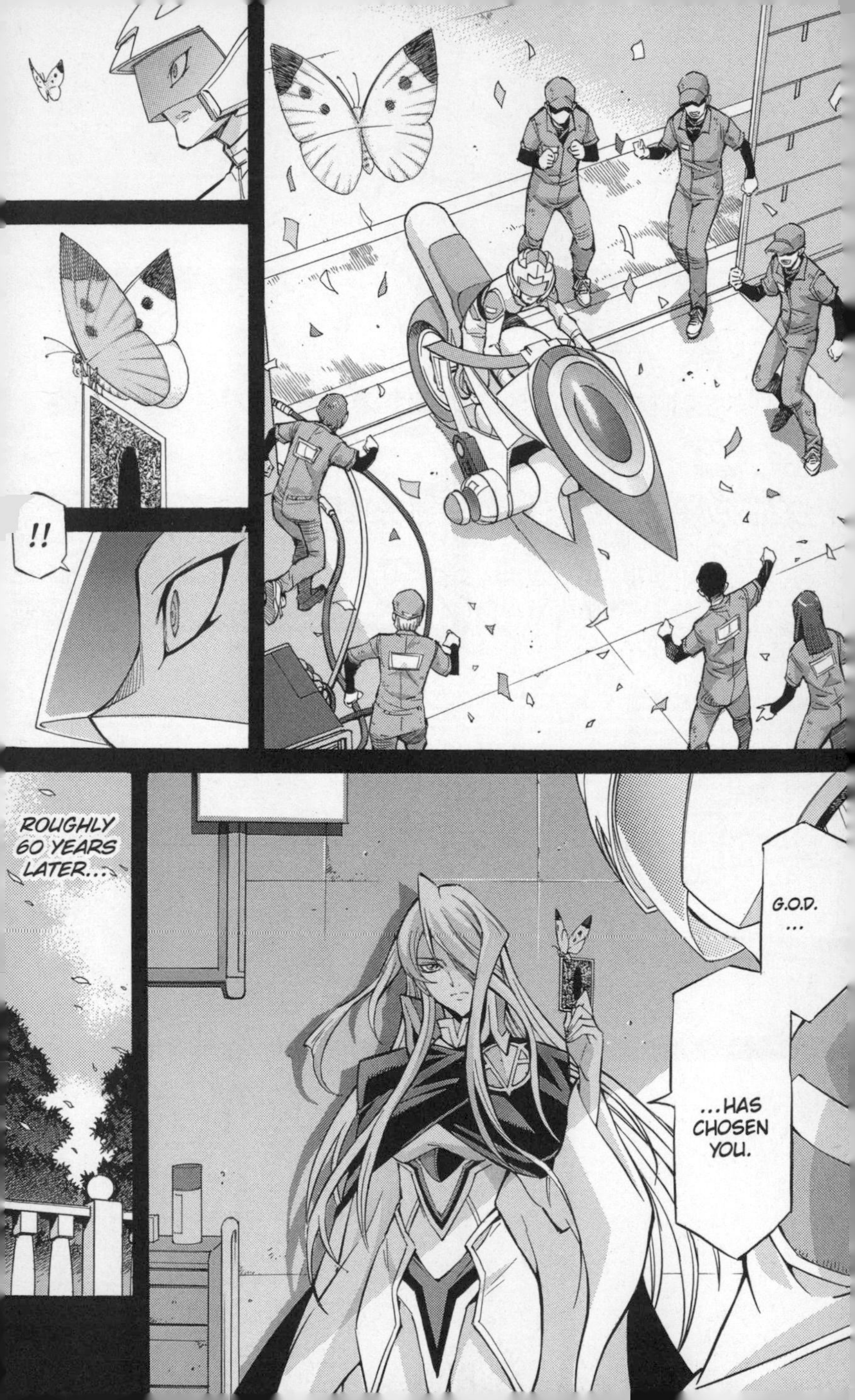
!!
G.O.D. ...
...HAS CHOSEN YOU.
ROUGHLY 60 YEARS LATER...

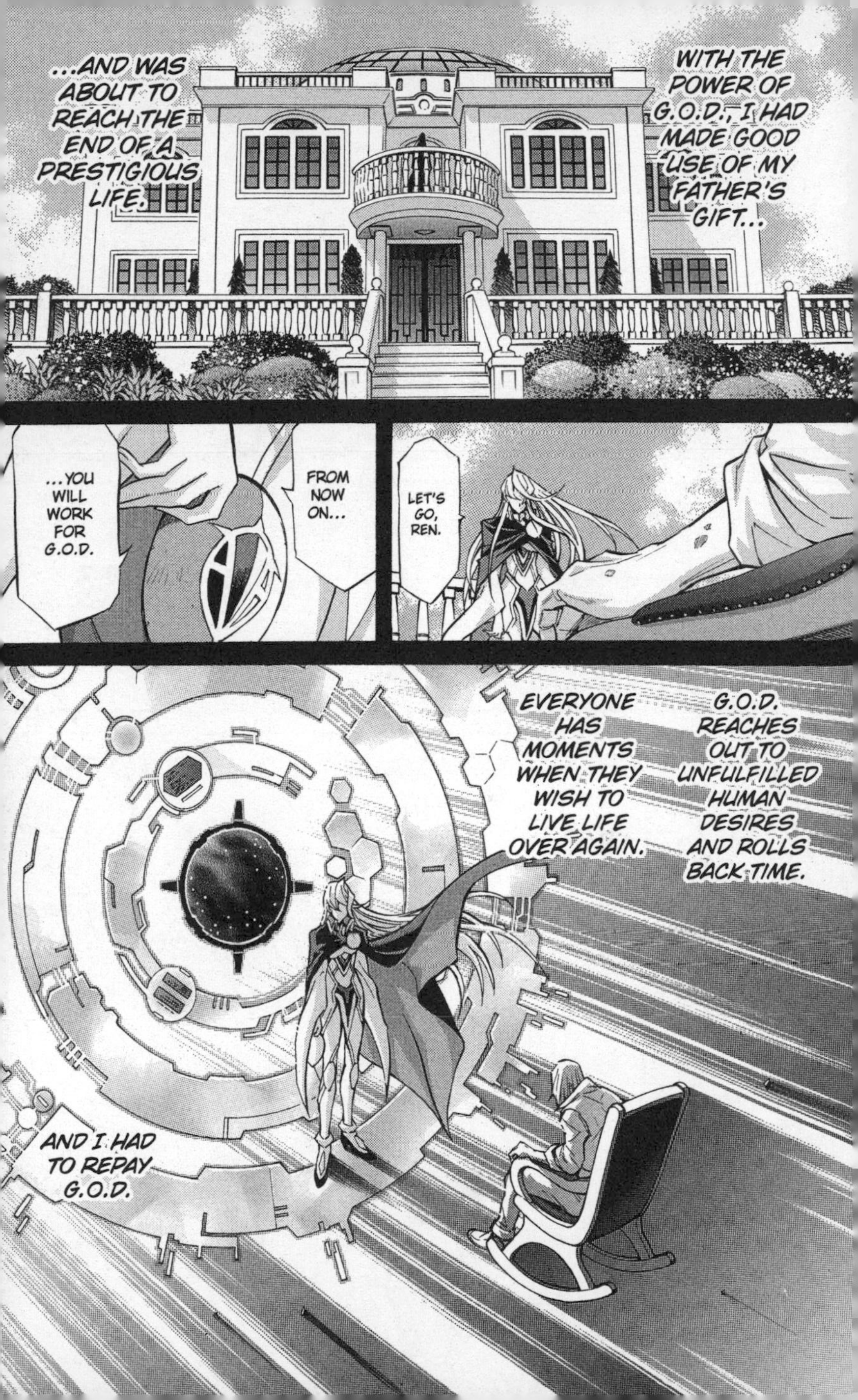
WITH THE POWER OF G.O.D., I HAD MADE GOOD USE OF MY FATHER'S GIFT...
...AND WAS ABOUT TO REACH THE END OF A PRESTIGIOUS LIFE.
LET'S GO, REN.
FROM NOW ON...
...YOU WILL WORK FOR G.O.D.
G.O.D. REACHES OUT TO UNFULFILLED HUMAN DESIRES AND ROLLS BACK TIME.
EVERYONE HAS MOMENTS WHEN THEY WISH TO LIVE LIFE OVER AGAIN.
AND I HAD TO REPAY G.O.D.

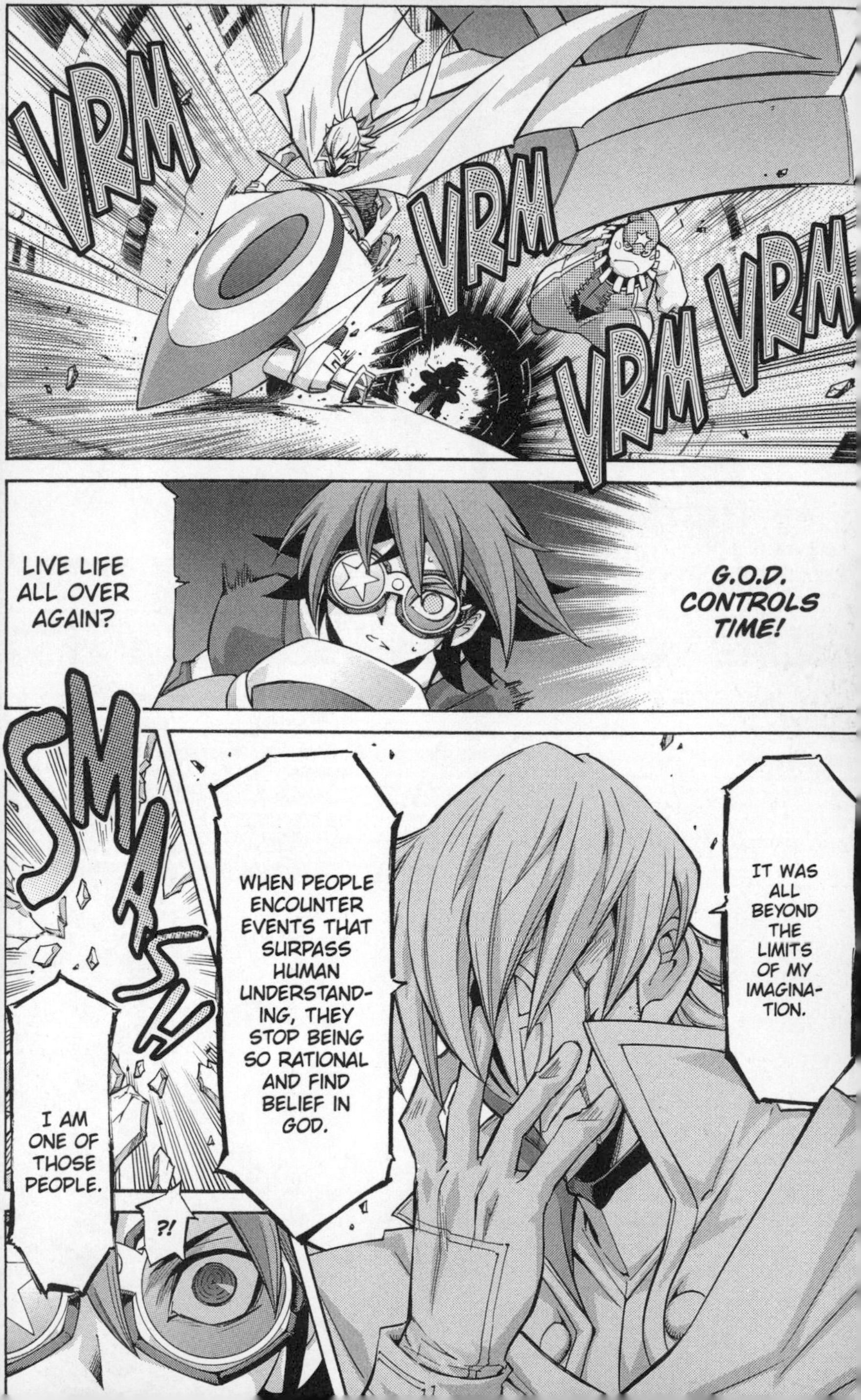
VRM
VRM
VRM
VRM
G.O.D. CONTROLS TIME!
LIVE LIFE ALL OVER AGAIN?
IT WAS ALL BEYOND THE LIMITS OF MY IMAGINATION.
WHEN PEOPLE ENCOUNTER EVENTS THAT SURPASS HUMAN UNDERSTANDING, THEY STOP BEING SO RATIONAL AND FIND BELIEF IN GOD.
SMASH!
I AM ONE OF THOSE PEOPLE.
?!

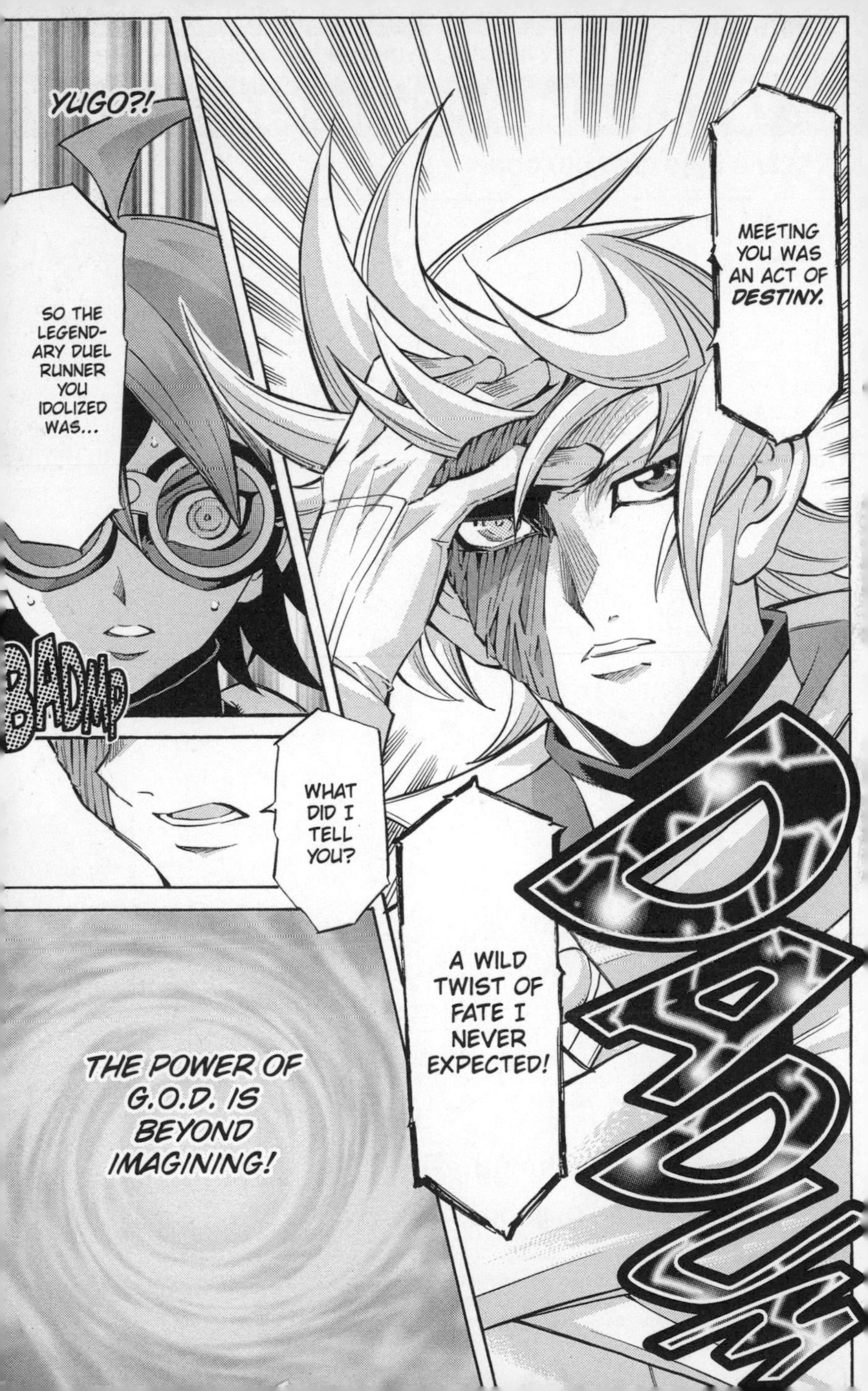
MEETING YOU WAS AN ACT OF DESTINY.
A WILD TWIST OF FATE I NEVER EXPECTED!
DADUM
YUGO?!
SO THE LEGENDARY DUEL RUNNER YOU IDOLIZED WAS...
BADMP
WHAT DID I TELL YOU?
THE POWER OF G.O.D. IS BEYOND IMAGINING!

REVEALING MIYOSHI SENSEI'S EARLY DESIGNS!

scale 17 ARC-V CHARACTER SKETCH

CLEAR WING FAST DRAGON

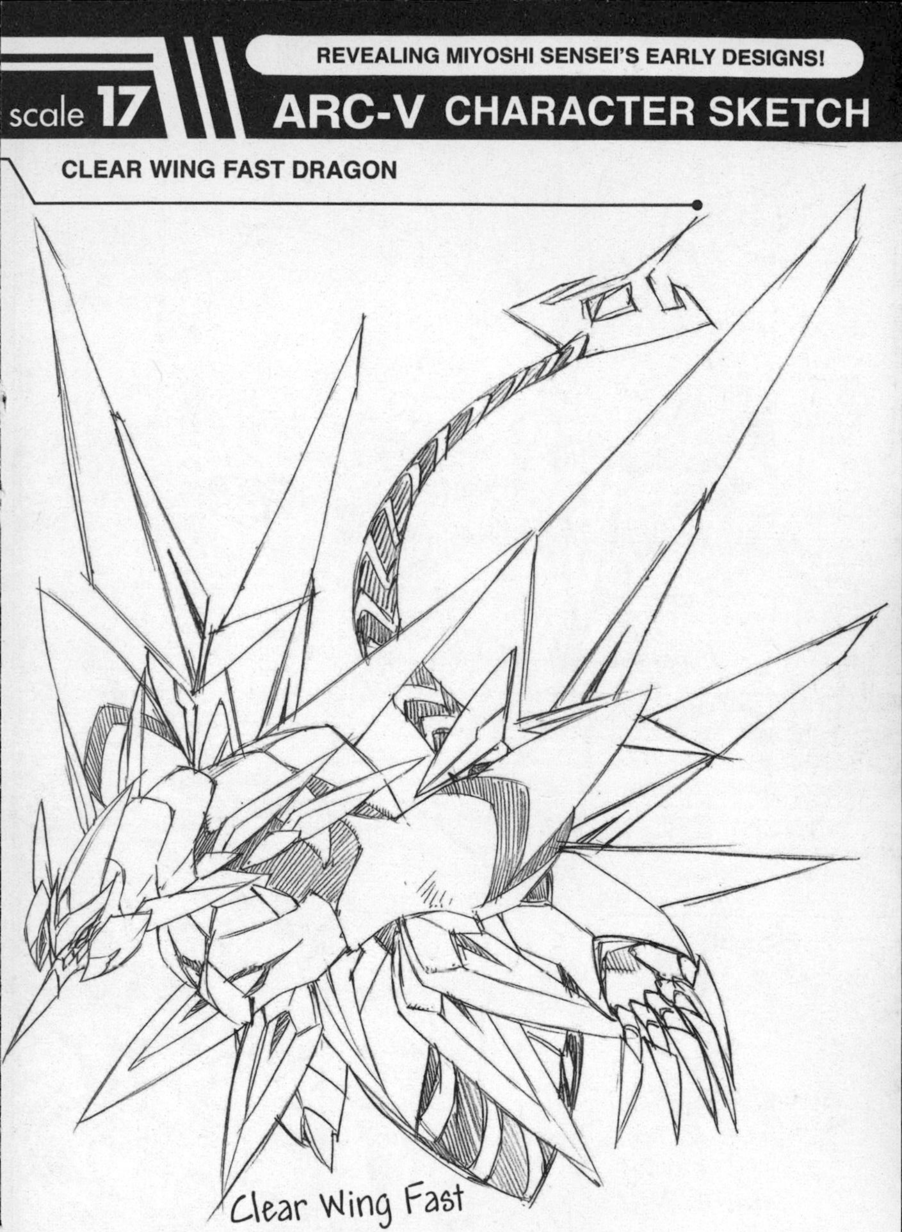
Clear Wing Fast Dragon

This dragon's body is suited to high-speed flight, making it a fitting ace monster for Yugo, a Turbo Duelist. It also has tough effects that render its opponent powerless!

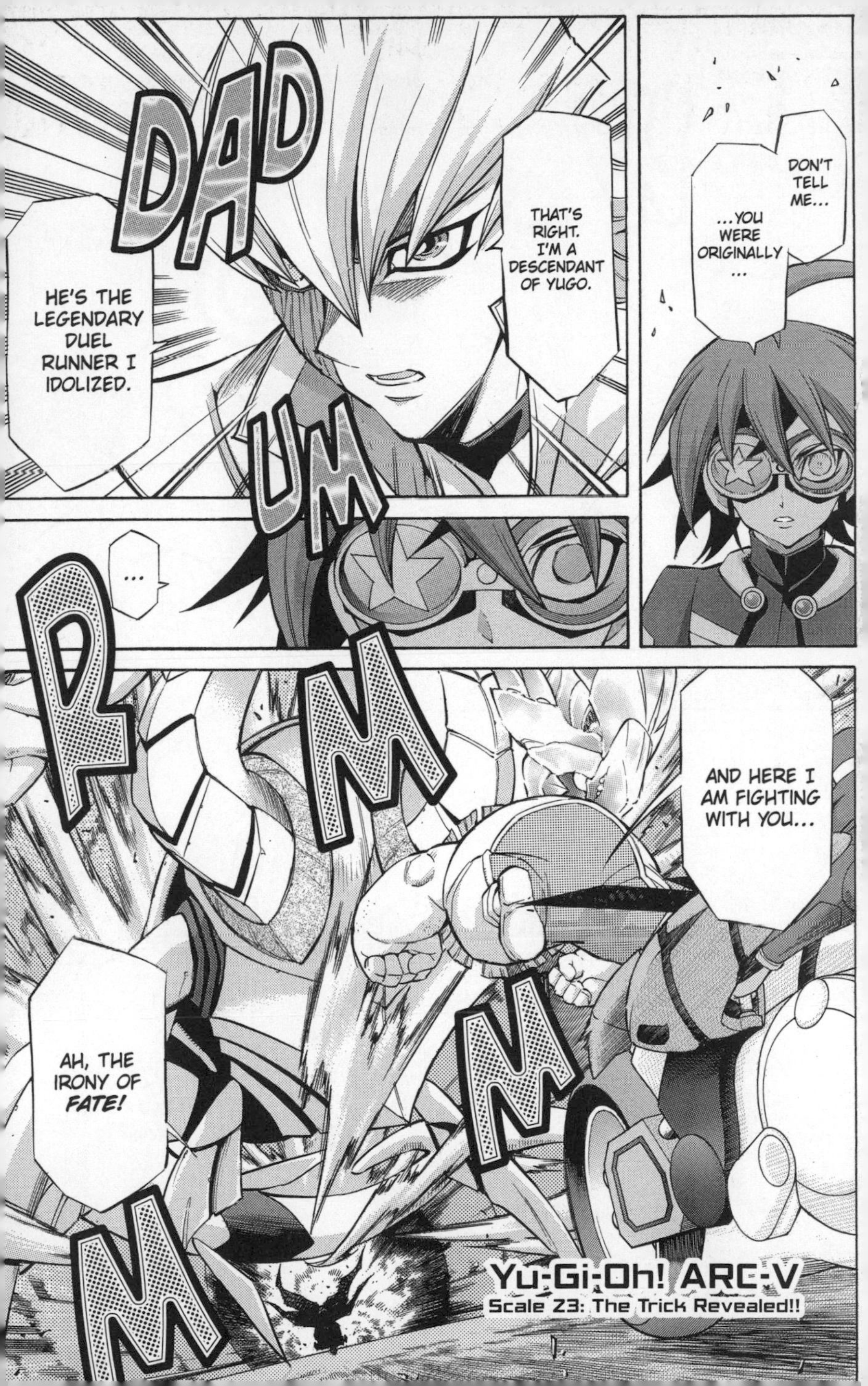
DON'T TELL ME...
...YOU WERE ORIGINALLY...
THAT'S RIGHT. I'M A DESCENDANT OF YUGO.
HE'S THE LEGENDARY DUEL RUNNER I IDOLIZED.
DADUM
...
AND HERE I AM FIGHTING WITH YOU...
AH, THE IRONY OF *FATE!*
Yu-Gi-Oh! ARC-V
Scale 23: The Trick Revealed!!

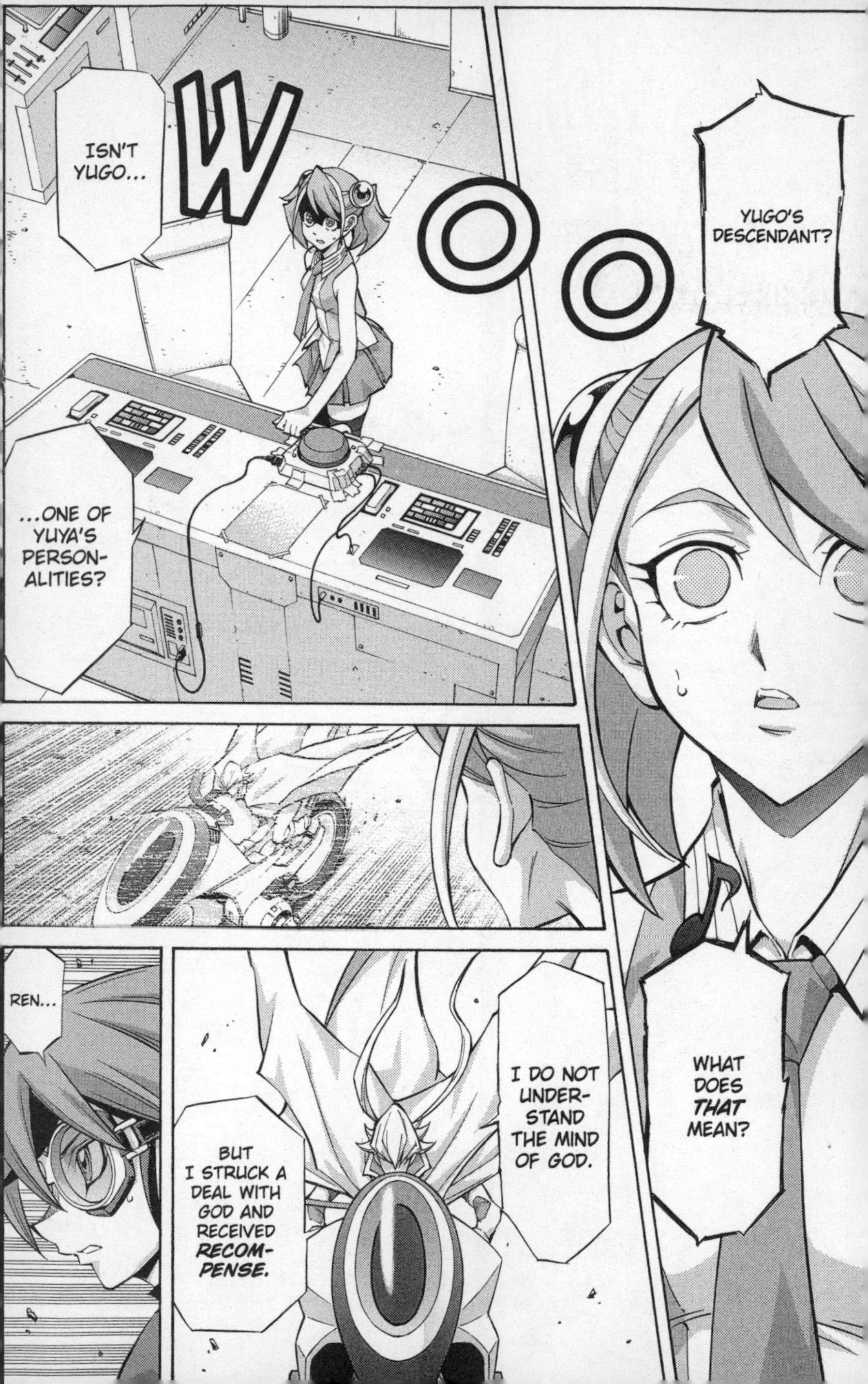
YUGO'S DESCENDANT?
WHAT DOES *THAT* MEAN?
WOOO
ISN'T YUGO...
...ONE OF YUYA'S PERSON-ALITIES?
I DO NOT UNDER-STAND THE MIND OF GOD.
BUT I STRUCK A DEAL WITH GOD AND RECEIVED ***RECOMPENSE.***
REN...

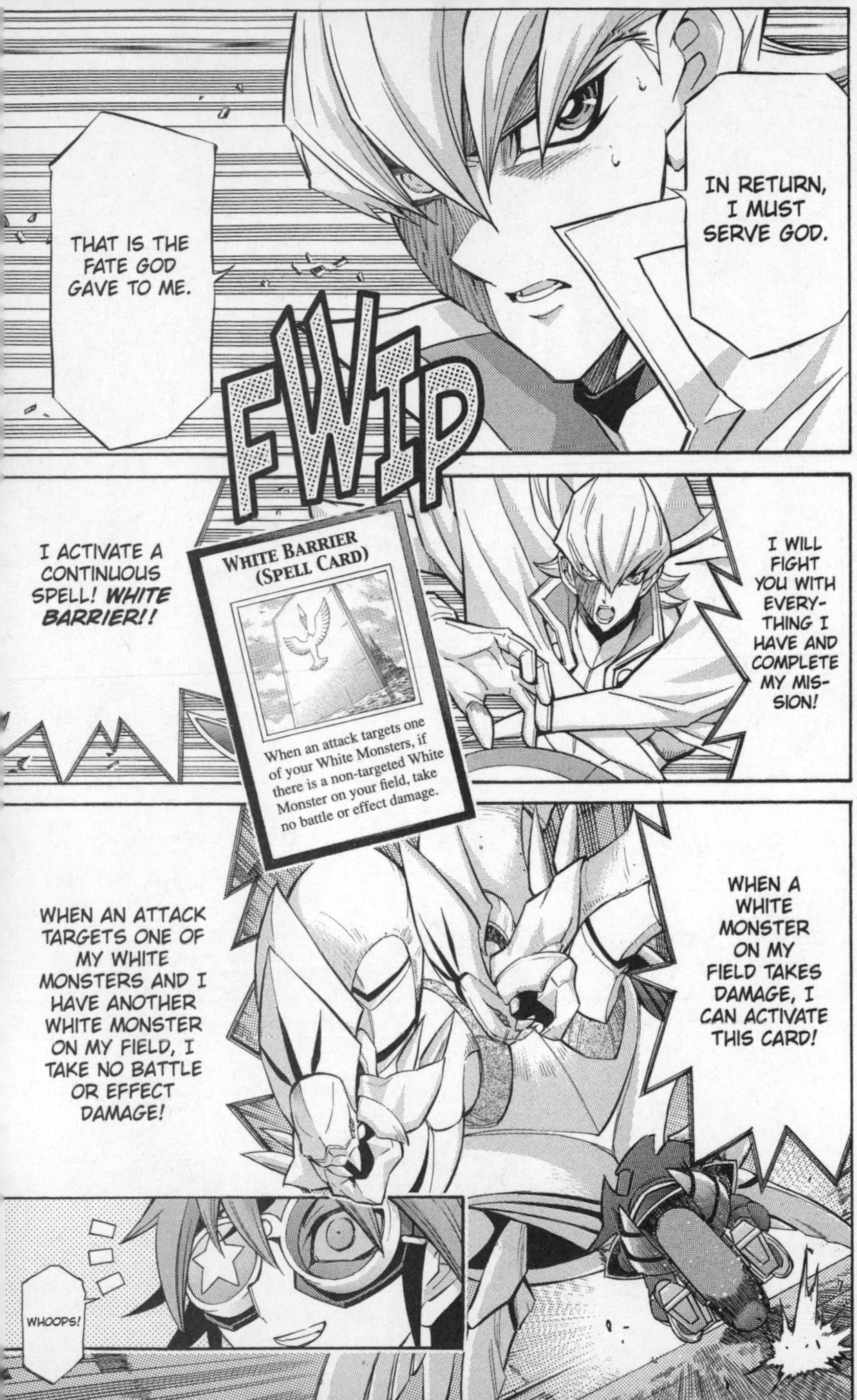

IN RETURN, I MUST SERVE GOD.
THAT IS THE FATE GOD GAVE TO ME.
FWIP
I WILL FIGHT YOU WITH EVERY-THING I HAVE AND COMPLETE MY MIS-SION!
I ACTIVATE A CONTINUOUS SPELL! WHITE BARRIER!!
WHITE BARRIER (SPELL CARD)
When an attack targets one of your White Monsters, if there is a non-targeted White Monster on your field, take no battle or effect damage.
WHEN A WHITE MONSTER ON MY FIELD TAKES DAMAGE, I CAN ACTIVATE THIS CARD!
WHEN AN ATTACK TARGETS ONE OF MY WHITE MONSTERS AND I HAVE ANOTHER WHITE MONSTER ON MY FIELD, I TAKE NO BATTLE OR EFFECT DAMAGE!
WHOOPS!

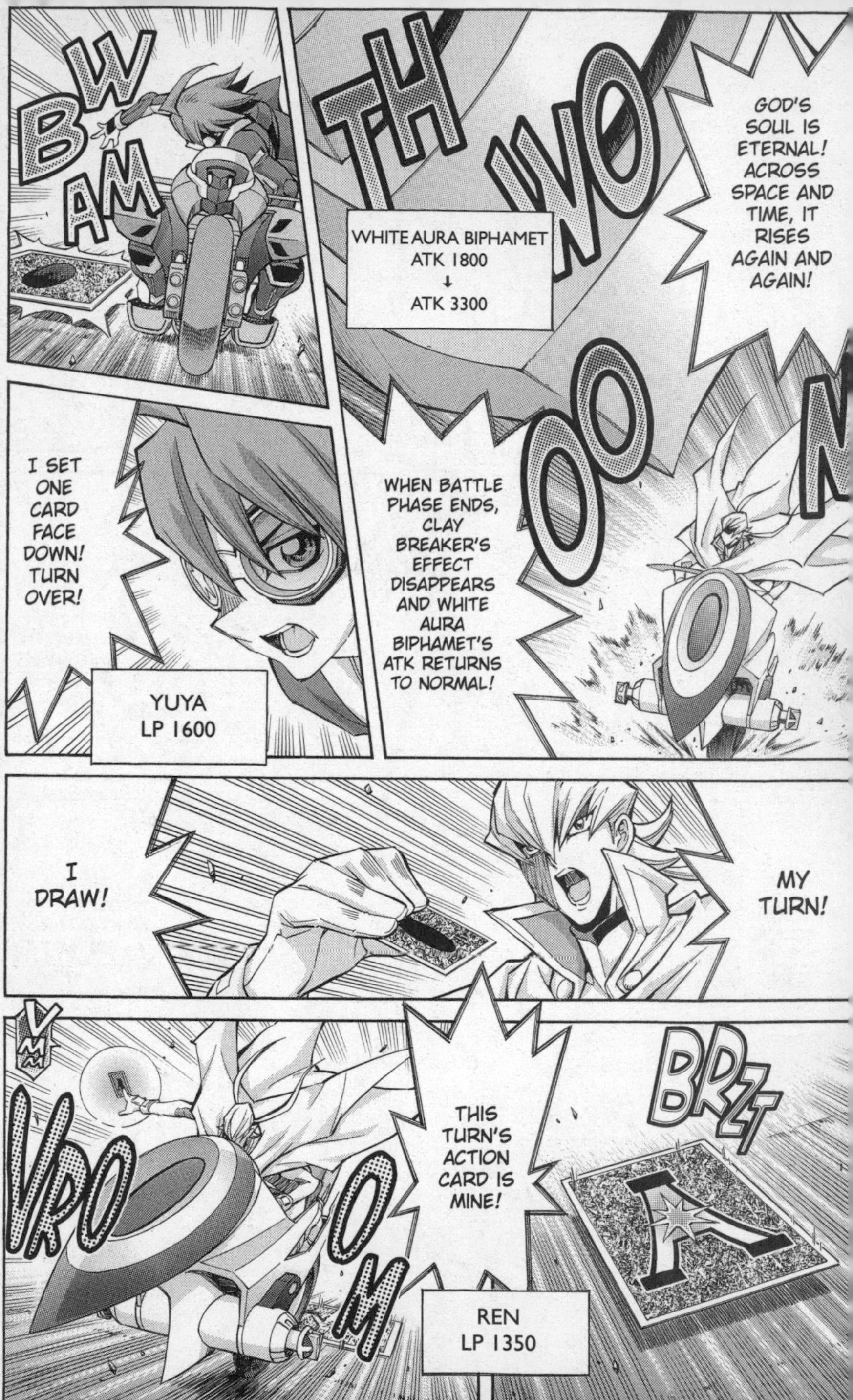
THWOOOOM
GOD'S SOUL IS ETERNAL! ACROSS SPACE AND TIME, IT RISES AGAIN AND AGAIN!
WHITE AURA BIPHAMET
ATK 1800
↓
ATK 3300
WHEN BATTLE PHASE ENDS, CLAY BREAKER'S EFFECT DISAPPEARS AND WHITE AURA BIPHAMET'S ATK RETURNS TO NORMAL!
BWAM
I SET ONE CARD FACE DOWN! TURN OVER!
YUYA
LP 1600
MY TURN!
I DRAW!
BRZZT
REN
LP 1350
THIS TURN'S ACTION CARD IS MINE!
VROOOM
VMM

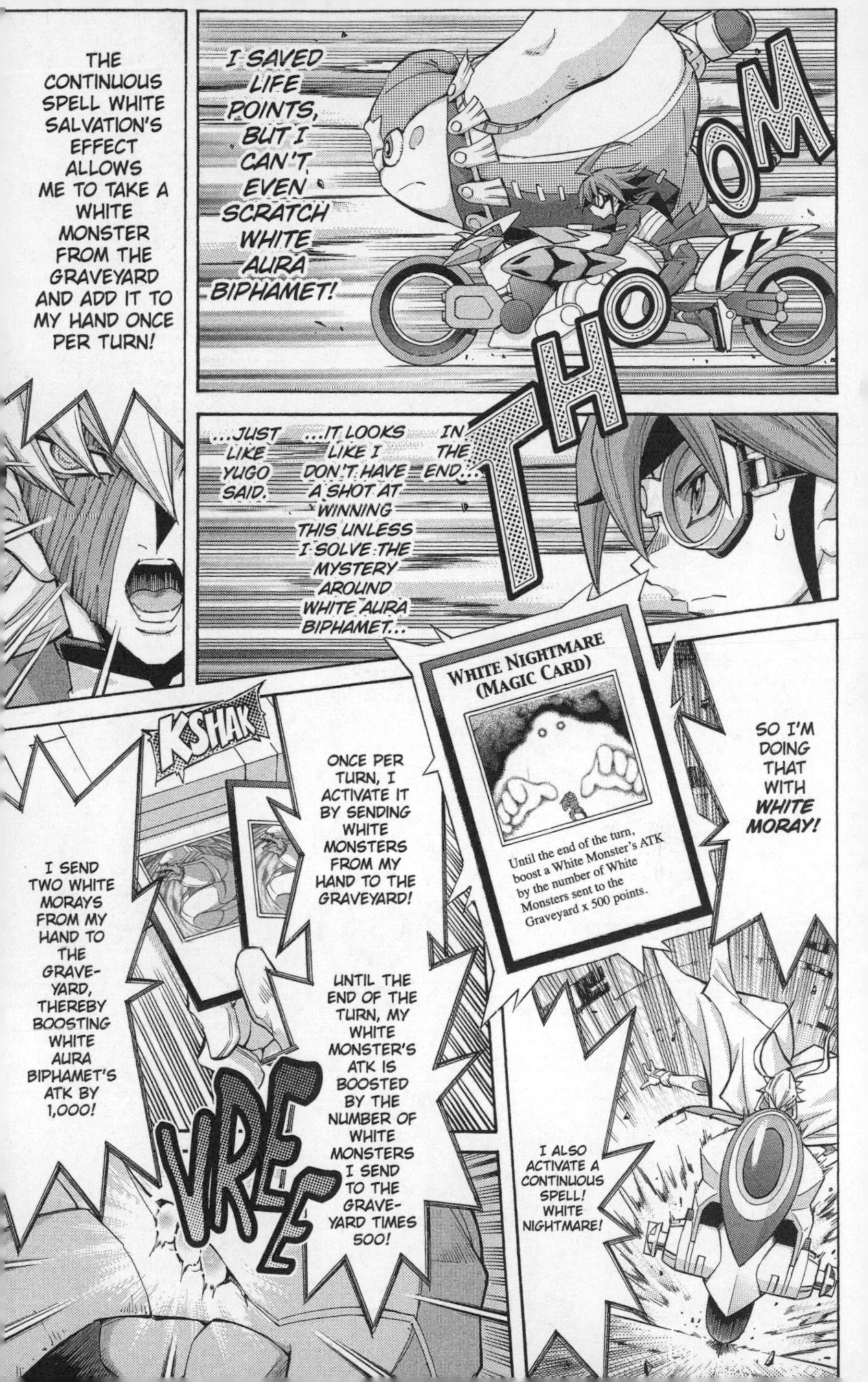
I SAVED LIFE POINTS, BUT I CAN'T EVEN SCRATCH WHITE AURA BIPHAMET!
THOOOM
IN THE END...
...IT LOOKS LIKE I DON'T HAVE A SHOT AT WINNING THIS UNLESS I SOLVE THE MYSTERY AROUND WHITE AURA BIPHAMET...
...JUST LIKE YUGO SAID.
THE CONTINUOUS SPELL WHITE SALVATION'S EFFECT ALLOWS ME TO TAKE A WHITE MONSTER FROM THE GRAVEYARD AND ADD IT TO MY HAND ONCE PER TURN!
I ALSO ACTIVATE A CONTINUOUS SPELL! WHITE NIGHTMARE!
WHITE NIGHTMARE (MAGIC CARD)
Until the end of the turn, boost a White Monster's ATK by the number of White Monsters sent to the Graveyard x 500 points.
ONCE PER TURN, I ACTIVATE IT BY SENDING WHITE MONSTERS FROM MY HAND TO THE GRAVEYARD!
UNTIL THE END OF THE TURN, MY WHITE MONSTER'S ATK IS BOOSTED BY THE NUMBER OF WHITE MONSTERS I SEND TO THE GRAVEYARD TIMES 500!
SO I'M DOING THAT WITH WHITE MORAY!
KSHAK
I SEND TWO WHITE MORAYS FROM MY HAND TO THE GRAVEYARD, THEREBY BOOSTING WHITE AURA BIPHAMET'S ATK BY 1,000!
VREEE

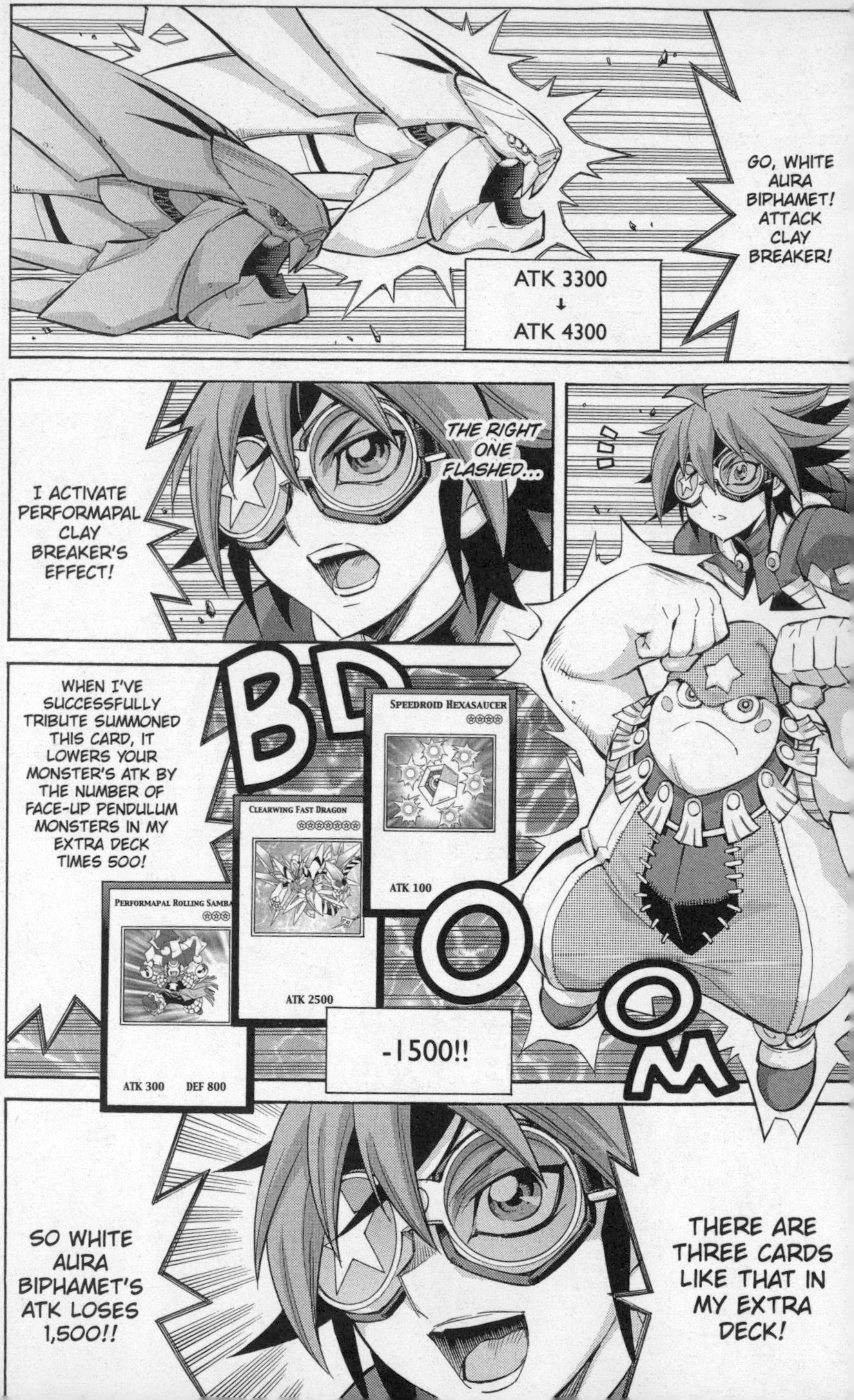

GO, WHITE AURA BIPHAMET! ATTACK CLAY BREAKER!
ATK 3300
↓
ATK 4300
THE RIGHT ONE FLASHED...
I ACTIVATE PERFORMAPAL CLAY BREAKER'S EFFECT!
WHEN I'VE SUCCESSFULLY TRIBUTE SUMMONED THIS CARD, IT LOWERS YOUR MONSTER'S ATK BY THE NUMBER OF FACE-UP PENDULUM MONSTERS IN MY EXTRA DECK TIMES 500!
BDOOM
SPEEDROID HEXASAUCER
ATK 100
CLEARWING FAST DRAGON
ATK 2500
PERFORMAPAL ROLLING SAMBA
ATK 300 DEF 800
-1500!!
THERE ARE THREE CARDS LIKE THAT IN MY EXTRA DECK!
SO WHITE AURA BIPHAMET'S ATK LOSES 1,500!!

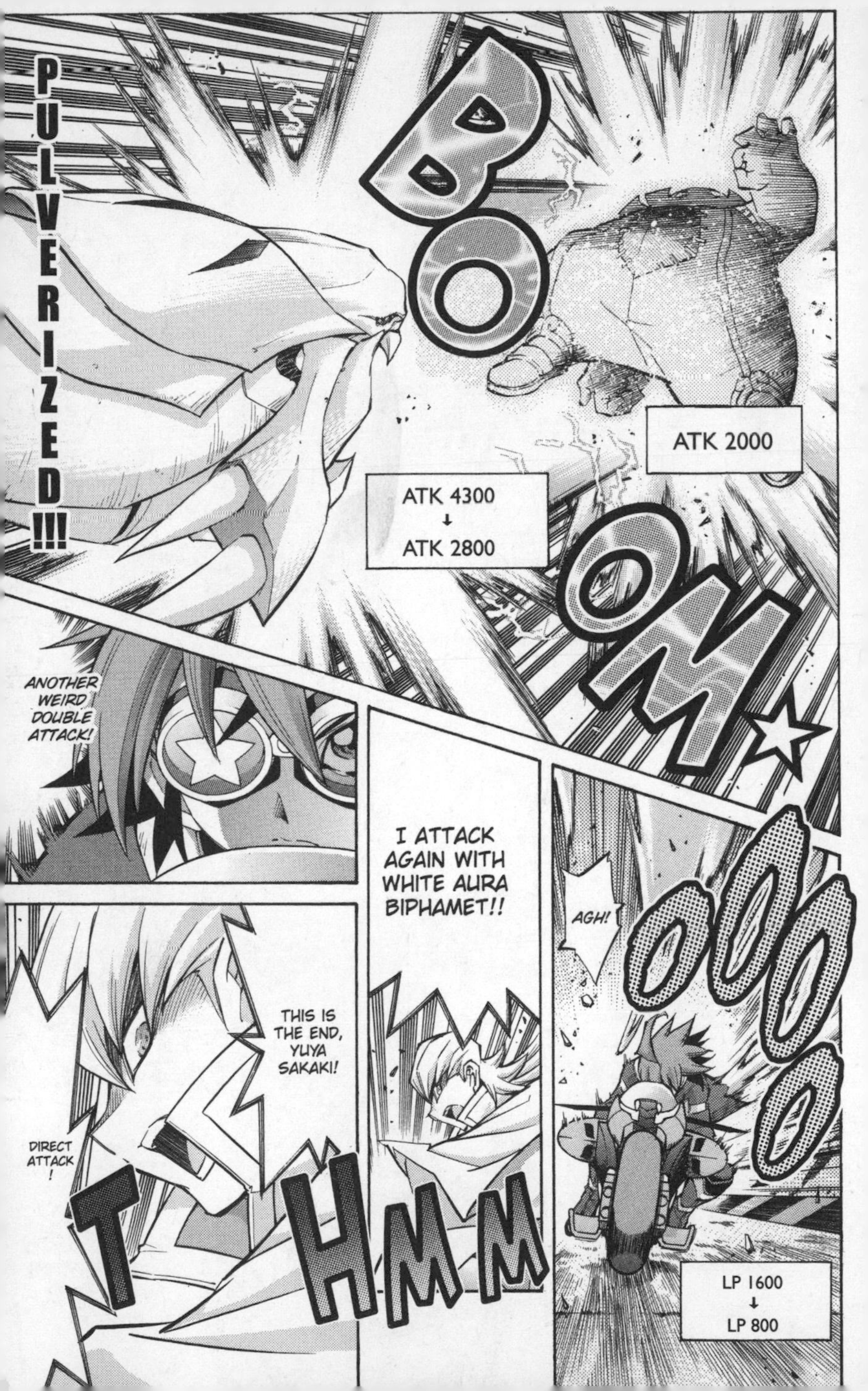
BOOM
ATK 2000
ATK 4300
↓
ATK 2800
PULVERIZED!!!
I ATTACK AGAIN WITH WHITE AURA BIPHAMET!!
ANOTHER WEIRD DOUBLE ATTACK!
THIS IS THE END, YUYA SAKAKI!
DIRECT ATTACK!
THMM
AGH!
OOOOO
LP 1600
↓
LP 800

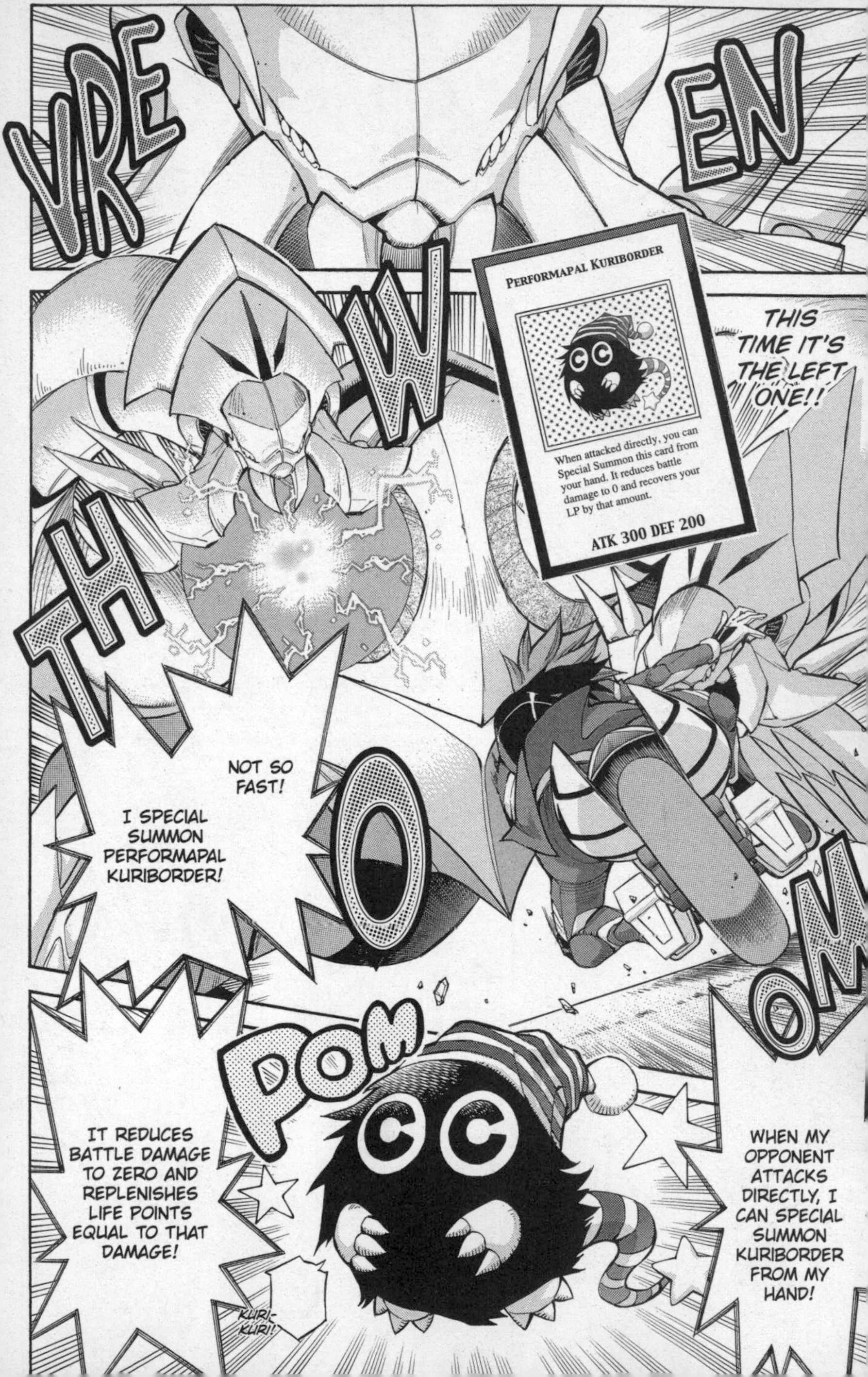
VRE
EN
Performapal Kuriborder
When attacked directly, you can Special Summon this card from your hand. It reduces battle damage to 0 and recovers your LP by that amount.
ATK 300 DEF 200
THIS TIME IT'S THE LEFT ONE!!
NOT SO FAST!
I SPECIAL SUMMON PERFORMAPAL KURIBORDER!
TH
W
O
OM
POM
WHEN MY OPPONENT ATTACKS DIRECTLY, I CAN SPECIAL SUMMON KURIBORDER FROM MY HAND!
IT REDUCES BATTLE DAMAGE TO ZERO AND REPLENISHES LIFE POINTS EQUAL TO THAT DAMAGE!
KURI-KURI!

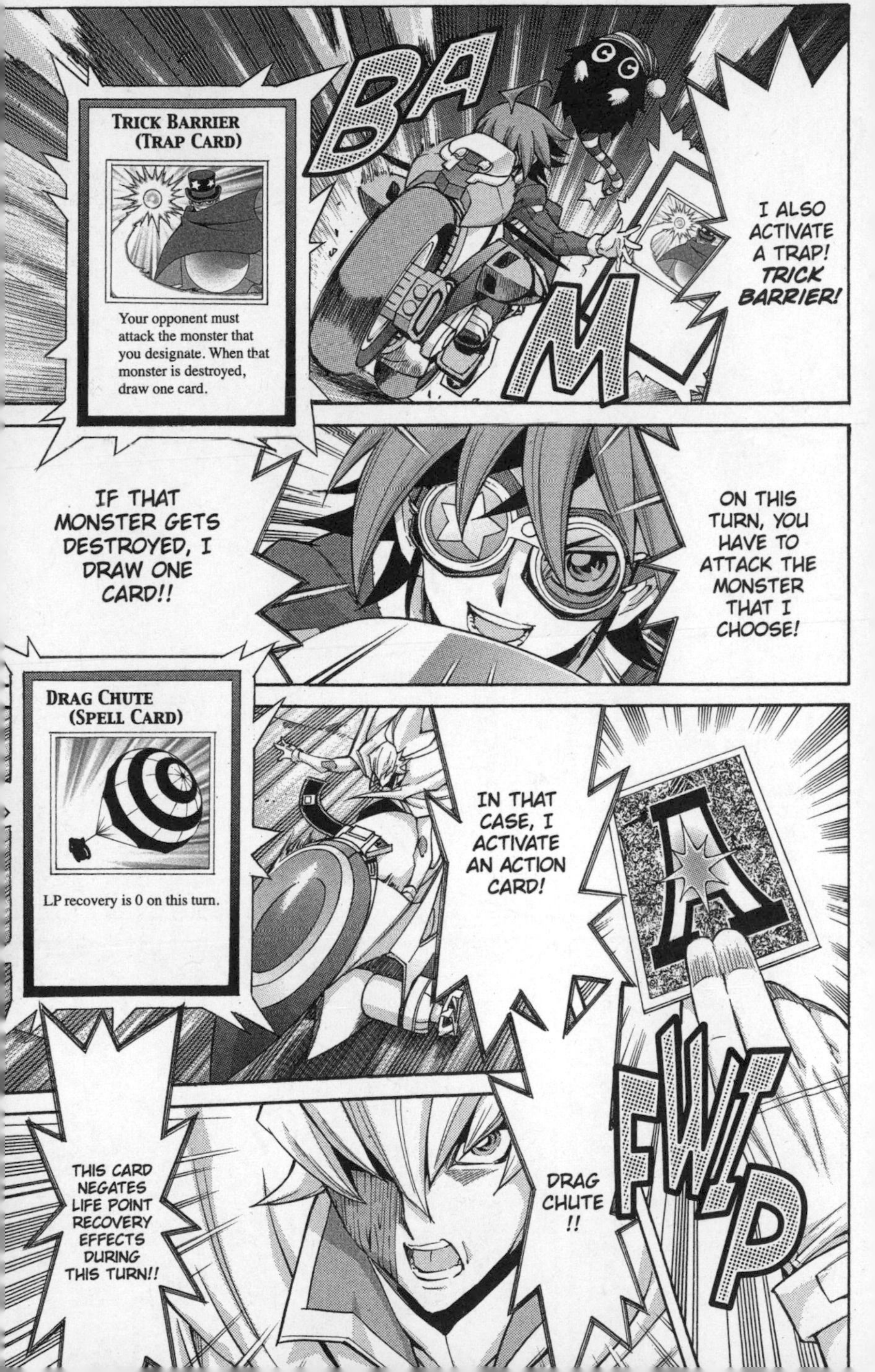
I ALSO ACTIVATE A TRAP! TRICK BARRIER!
BAM
TRICK BARRIER (TRAP CARD)
Your opponent must attack the monster that you designate. When that monster is destroyed, draw one card.
ON THIS TURN, YOU HAVE TO ATTACK THE MONSTER THAT I CHOOSE!
IF THAT MONSTER GETS DESTROYED, I DRAW ONE CARD!!
IN THAT CASE, I ACTIVATE AN ACTION CARD!
A
DRAG CHUTE (SPELL CARD)
LP recovery is 0 on this turn.
FWIP
DRAG CHUTE !!
THIS CARD NEGATES LIFE POINT RECOVERY EFFECTS DURING THIS TURN!!

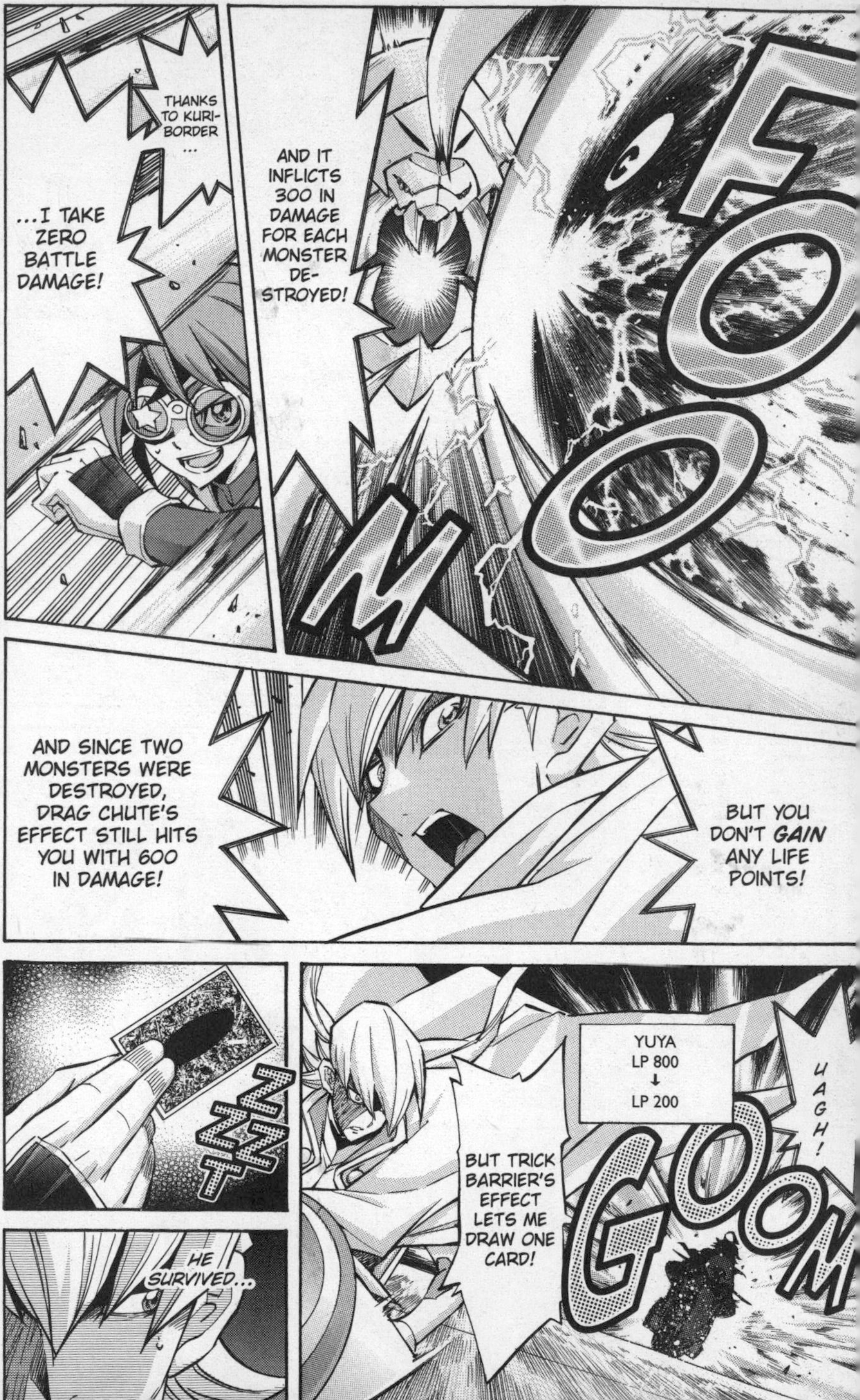

AND IT INFLICTS 300 IN DAMAGE FOR EACH MONSTER DE-STROYED!
FOOM
M
THANKS TO KURI-BORDER ...
...I TAKE ZERO BATTLE DAMAGE!
BUT YOU DON'T ***GAIN*** ANY LIFE POINTS!
AND SINCE TWO MONSTERS WERE DESTROYED, DRAG CHUTE'S EFFECT STILL HITS YOU WITH 600 IN DAMAGE!
YUYA LP 800 ↓ LP 200
UAGH!
GOOOM
BUT TRICK BARRIER'S EFFECT LETS ME DRAW ONE CARD!
ZZZT
HE SURVIVED...

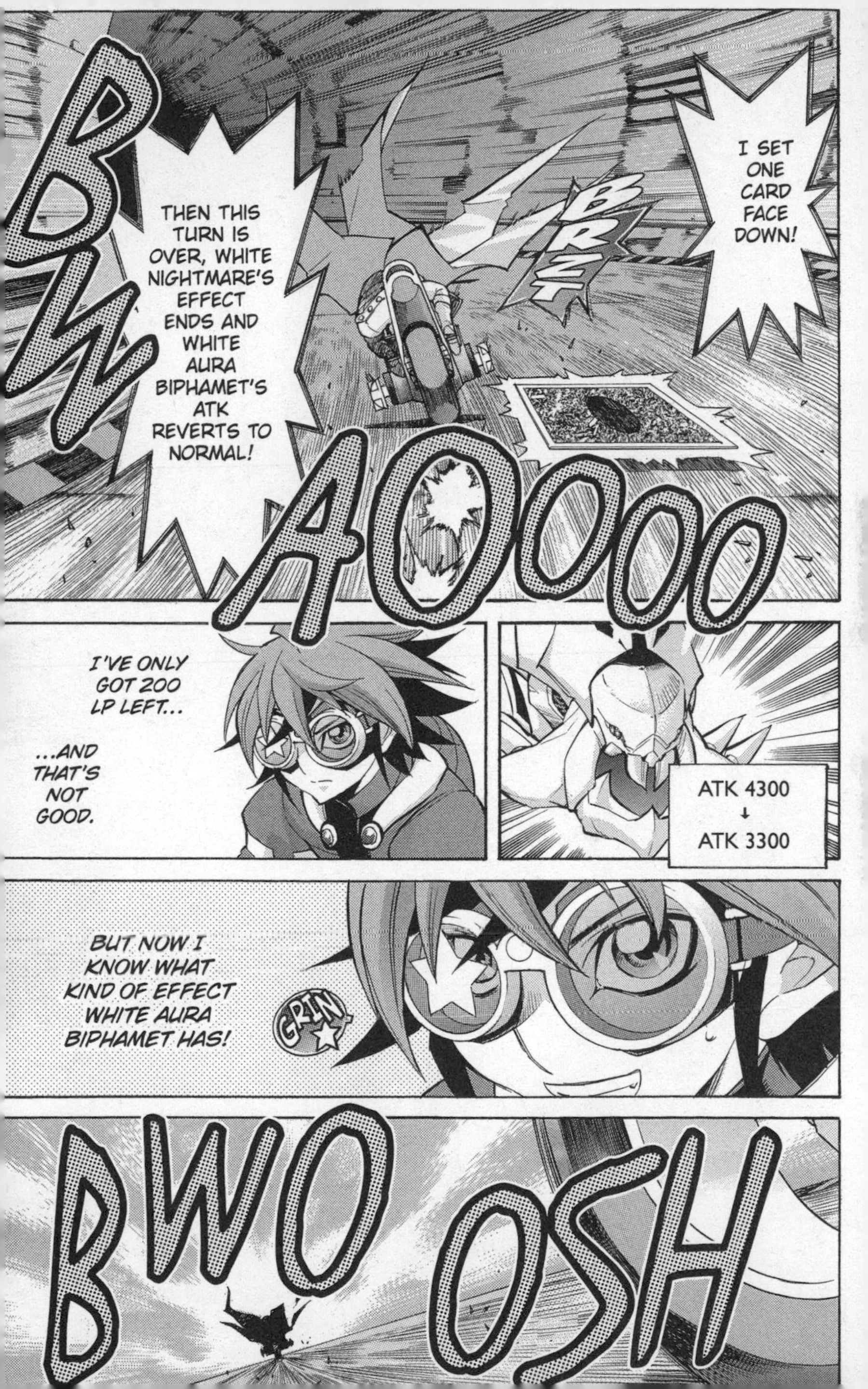
I SET ONE CARD FACE DOWN!
BRZT
THEN THIS TURN IS OVER, WHITE NIGHTMARE'S EFFECT ENDS AND WHITE AURA BIPHAMET'S ATK REVERTS TO NORMAL!
BWAOOOO
ATK 4300 ↓ ATK 3300
I'VE ONLY GOT 200 LP LEFT...
...AND THAT'S NOT GOOD.
GRIN
BUT NOW I KNOW WHAT KIND OF EFFECT WHITE AURA BIPHAMET HAS!
BWOOSH

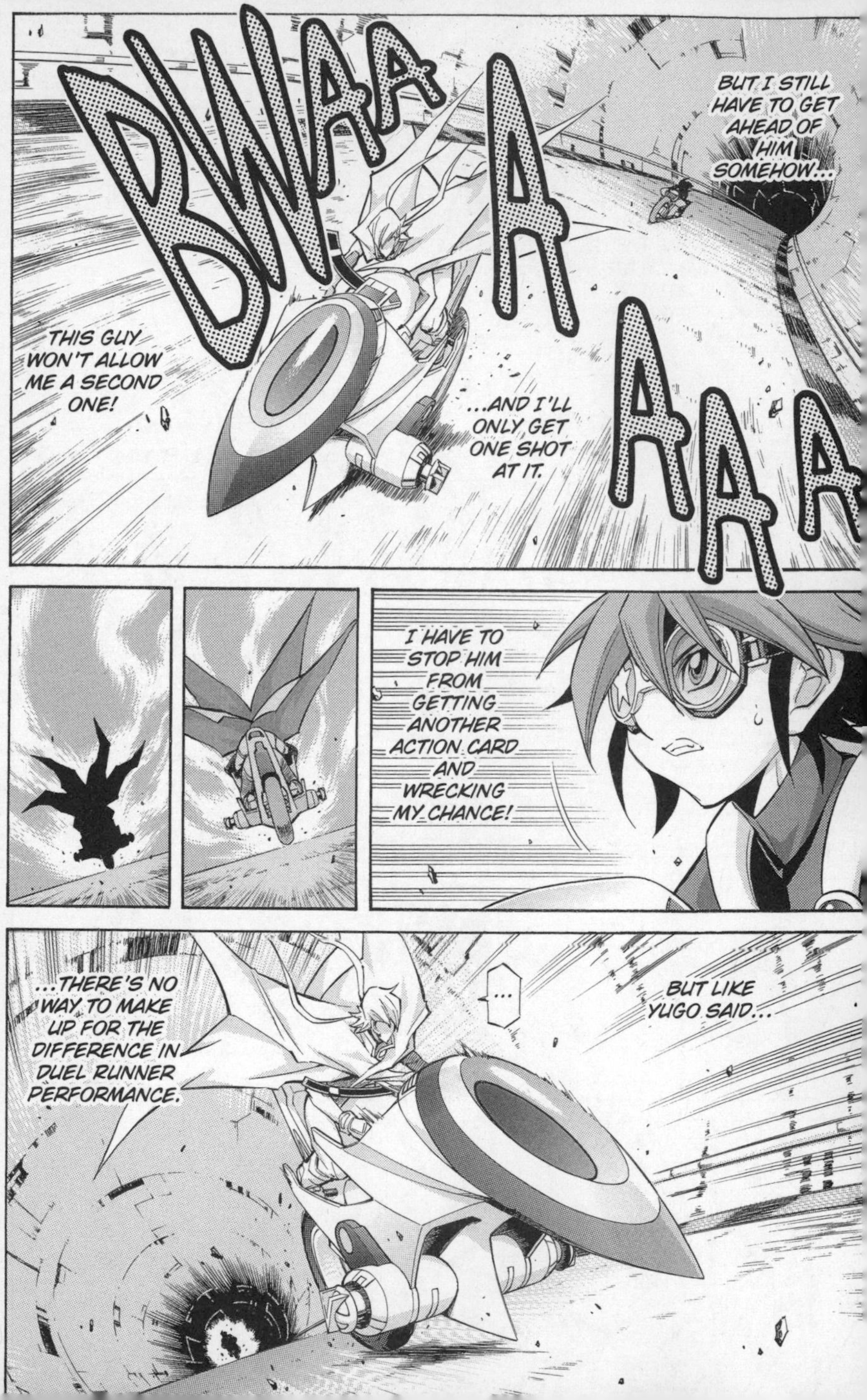
BUT I STILL HAVE TO GET AHEAD OF HIM SOMEHOW...
BWAAAAAAA
...AND I'LL ONLY GET ONE SHOT AT IT.
THIS GUY WON'T ALLOW ME A SECOND ONE!
I HAVE TO STOP HIM FROM GETTING ANOTHER ACTION CARD AND WRECKING MY CHANCE!
BUT LIKE YUGO SAID...
...
...THERE'S NO WAY TO MAKE UP FOR THE DIFFERENCE IN DUEL RUNNER PERFORMANCE.

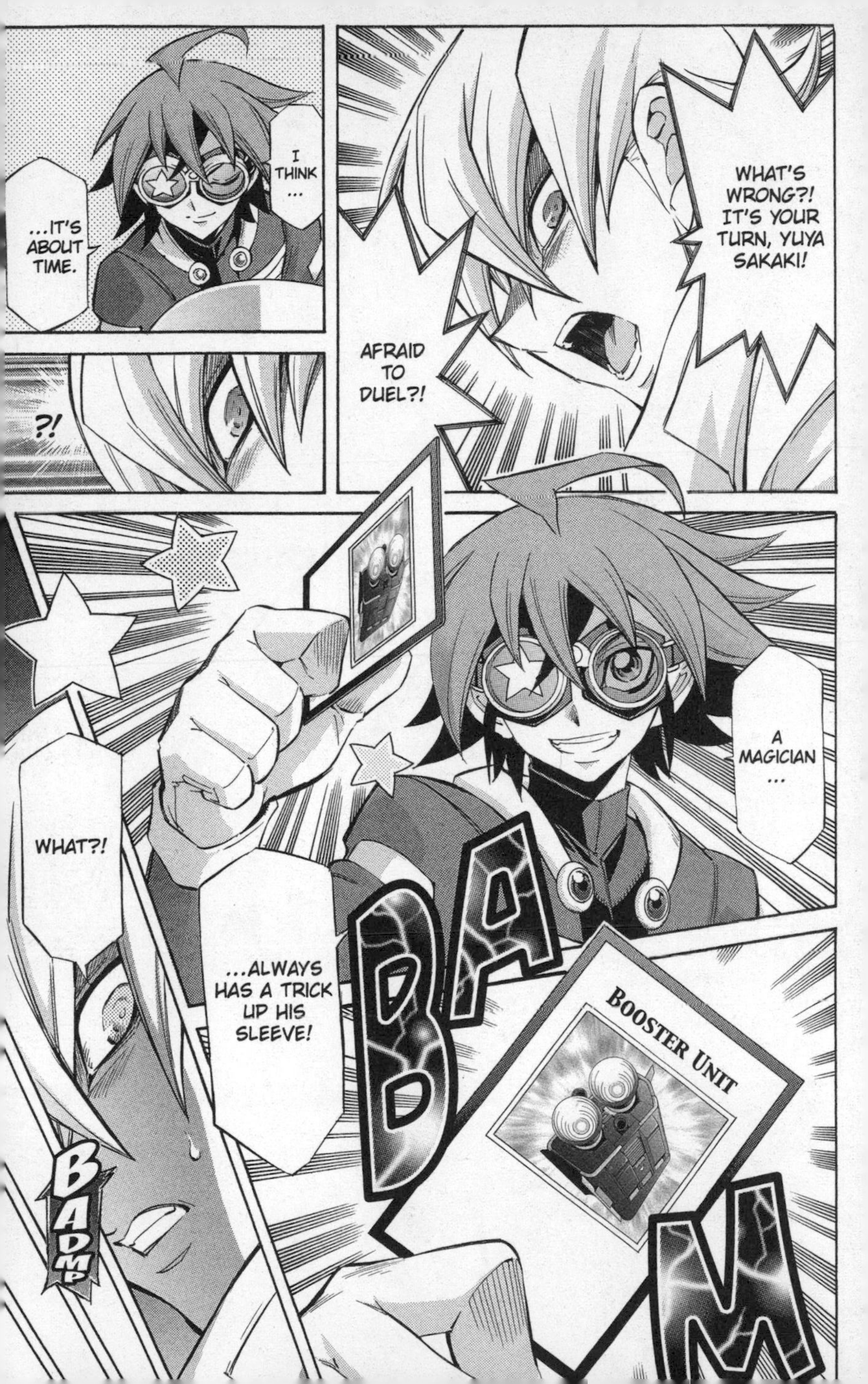
WHAT'S WRONG?! IT'S YOUR TURN, YUYA SAKAKI!
AFRAID TO DUEL?!
I THINK ...
...IT'S ABOUT TIME.
?!
A MAGICIAN ...
...ALWAYS HAS A TRICK UP HIS SLEEVE!
WHAT?!
BAM
BOOSTER UNIT
BADMP

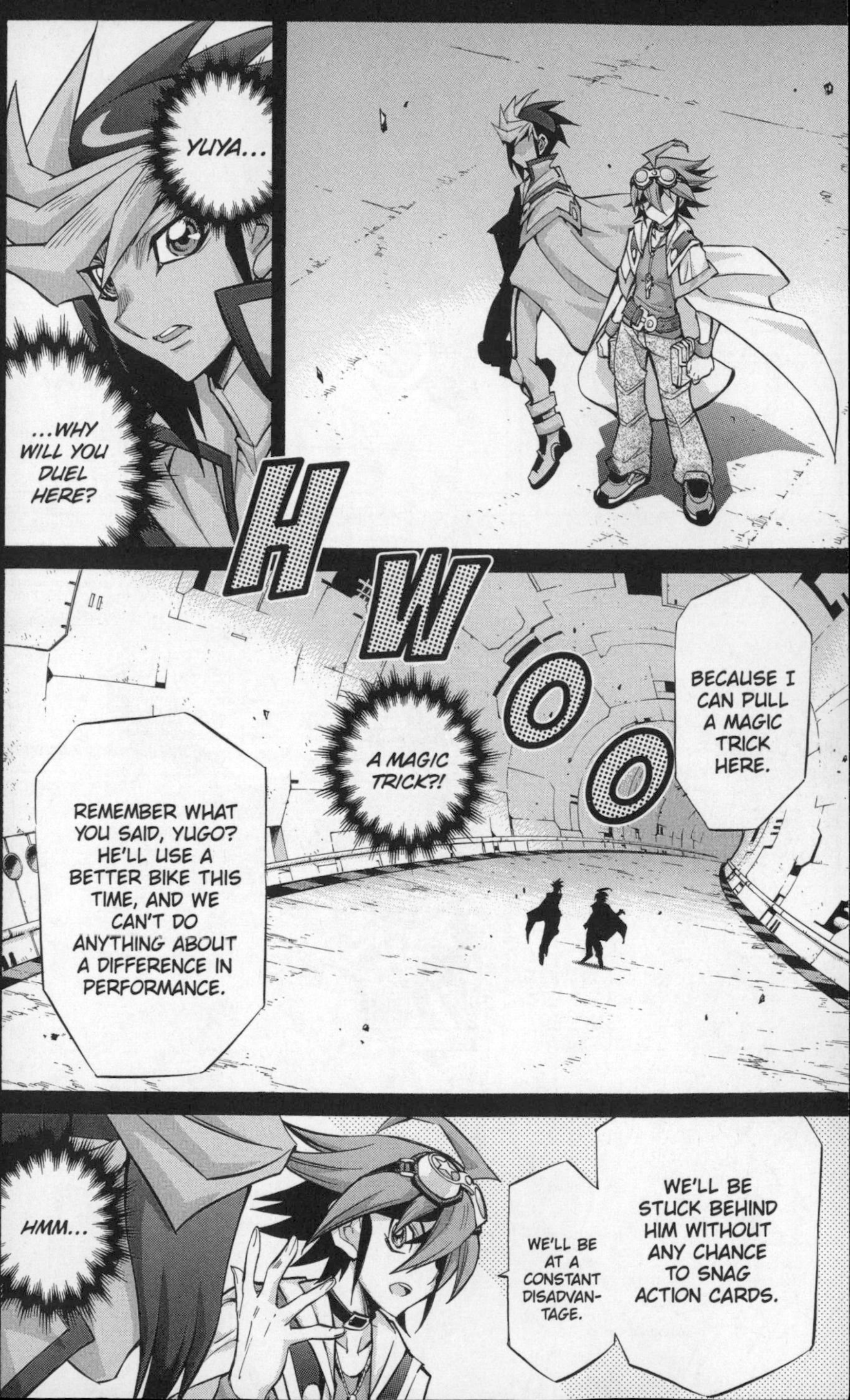
YUYA...
...WHY WILL YOU DUEL HERE?
HWOOO
BECAUSE I CAN PULL A MAGIC TRICK HERE.
A MAGIC TRICK?!
REMEMBER WHAT YOU SAID, YUGO? HE'LL USE A BETTER BIKE THIS TIME, AND WE CAN'T DO ANYTHING ABOUT A DIFFERENCE IN PERFORMANCE.
WE'LL BE STUCK BEHIND HIM WITHOUT ANY CHANCE TO SNAG ACTION CARDS.
WE'LL BE AT A CONSTANT DISADVAN-TAGE.
HMM...

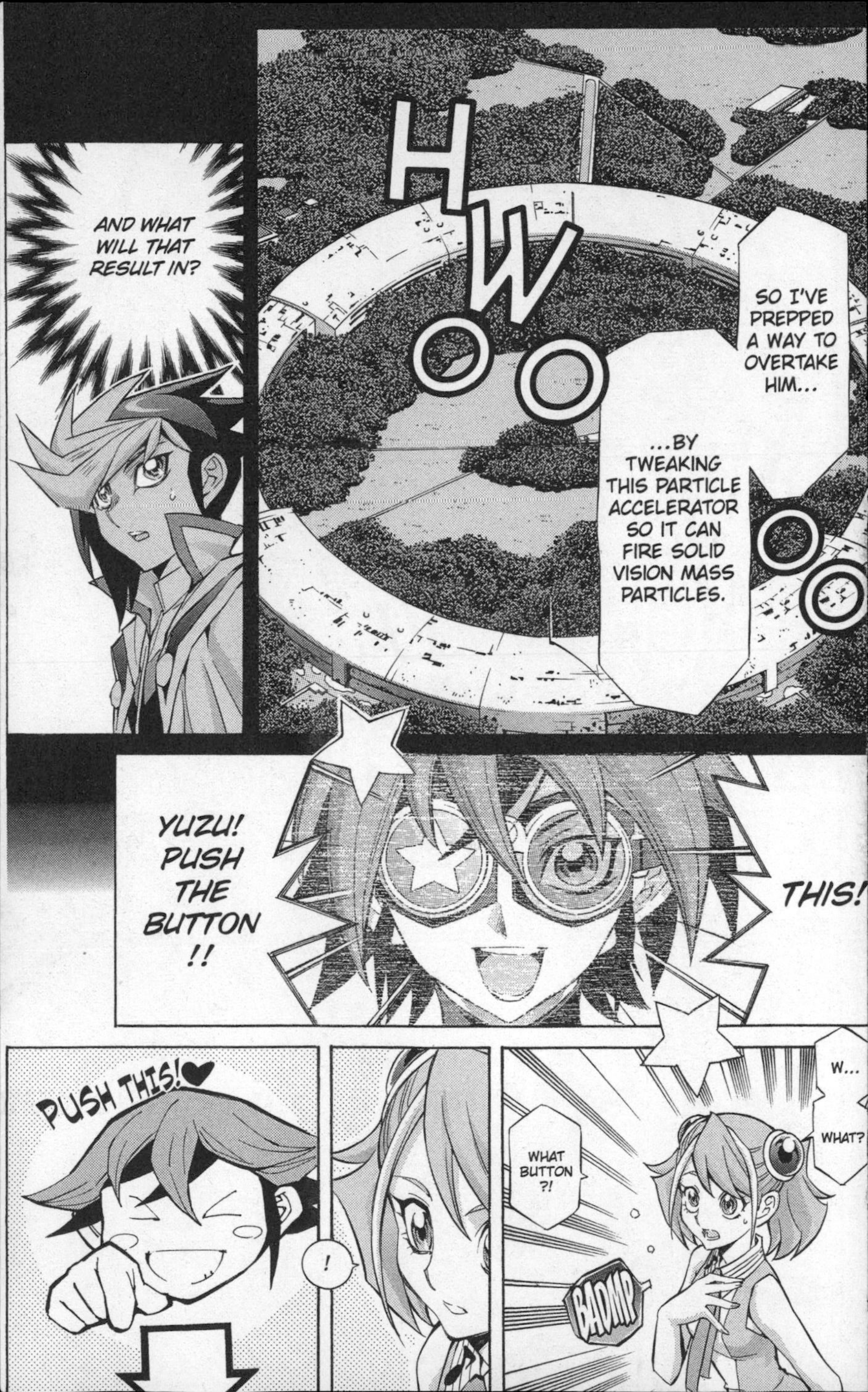
SO I'VE PREPPED A WAY TO OVERTAKE HIM...
HWOOO
...BY TWEAKING THIS PARTICLE ACCELERATOR SO IT CAN FIRE SOLID VISION MASS PARTICLES.
AND WHAT WILL THAT RESULT IN?
THIS!
YUZU! PUSH THE BUTTON!!
W... WHAT?
WHAT BUTTON?!
BADMP
!
PUSH THIS!♥

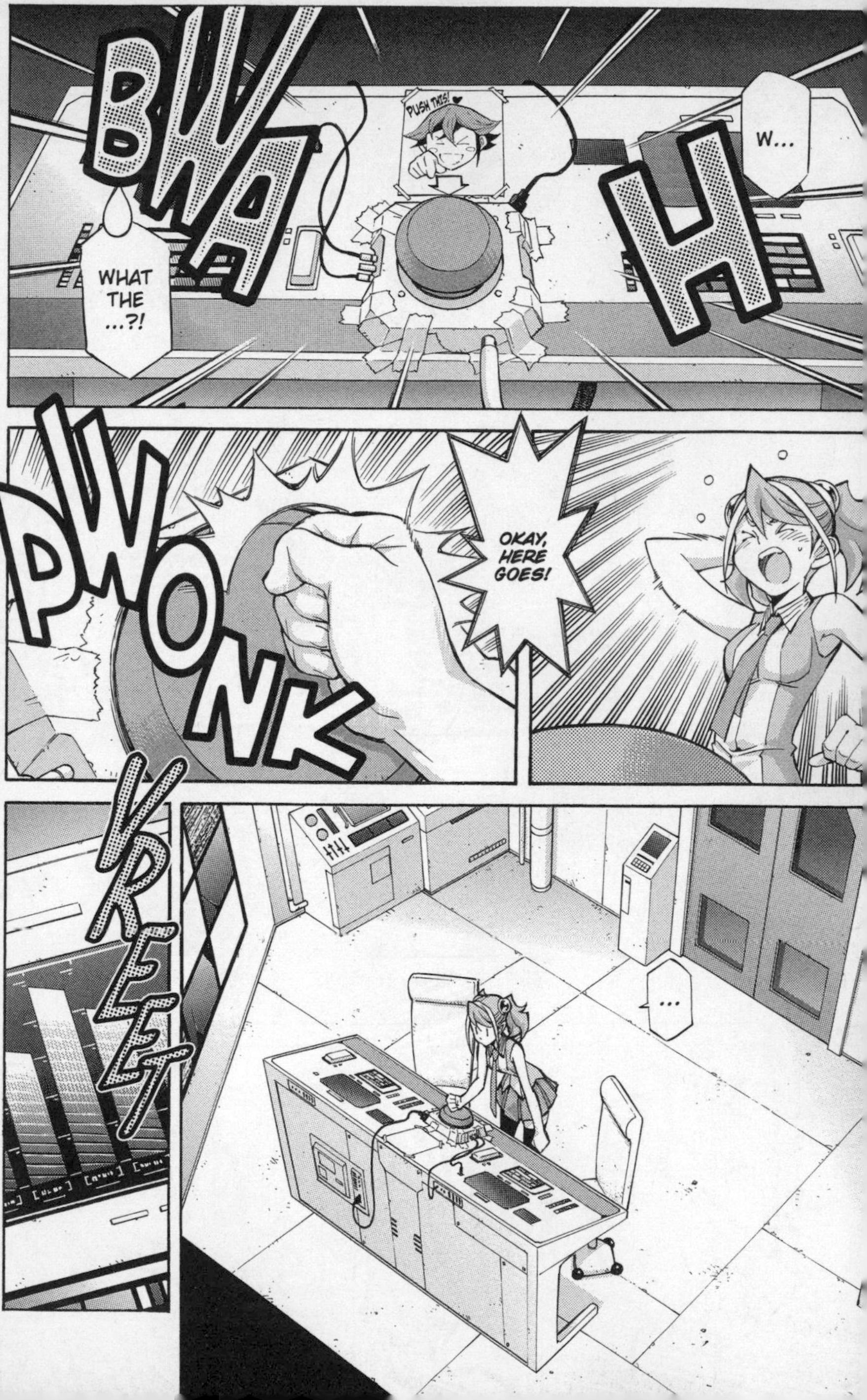
W...
BWAH
PUSH THIS!
WHAT THE ...?!
OKAY, HERE GOES!
PWONK
...
VREET

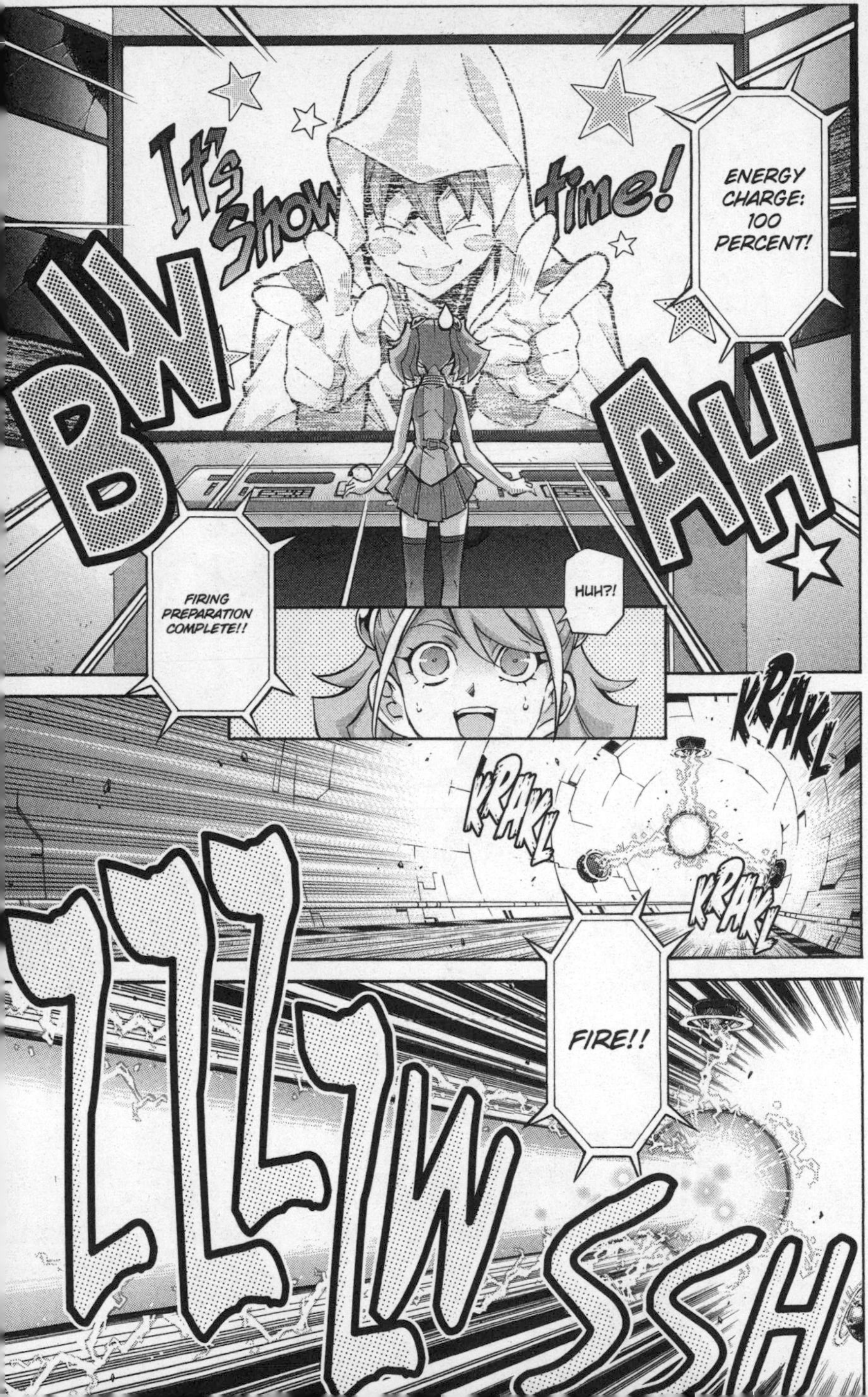
ENERGY CHARGE: 100 PERCENT!
It's Showtime!
BWAH
HUH?!
FIRING PREPARATION COMPLETE!!
KRAKL
KRAKL
KRAKL
FIRE!!
ZZZWSSH

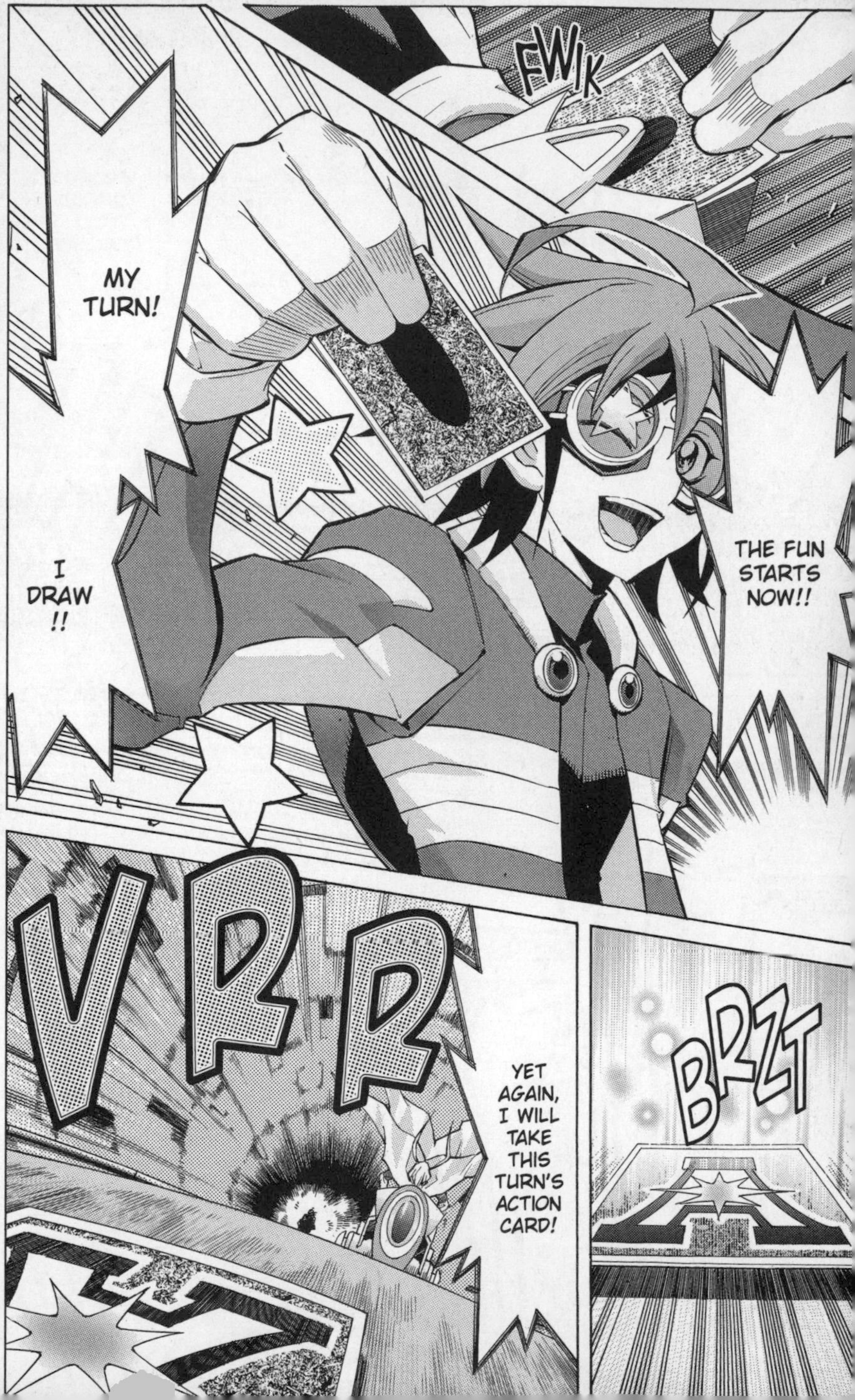
FWIK
MY TURN!
I DRAW!!
THE FUN STARTS NOW!!
BRZT
VRR
YET AGAIN, I WILL TAKE THIS TURN'S ACTION CARD!

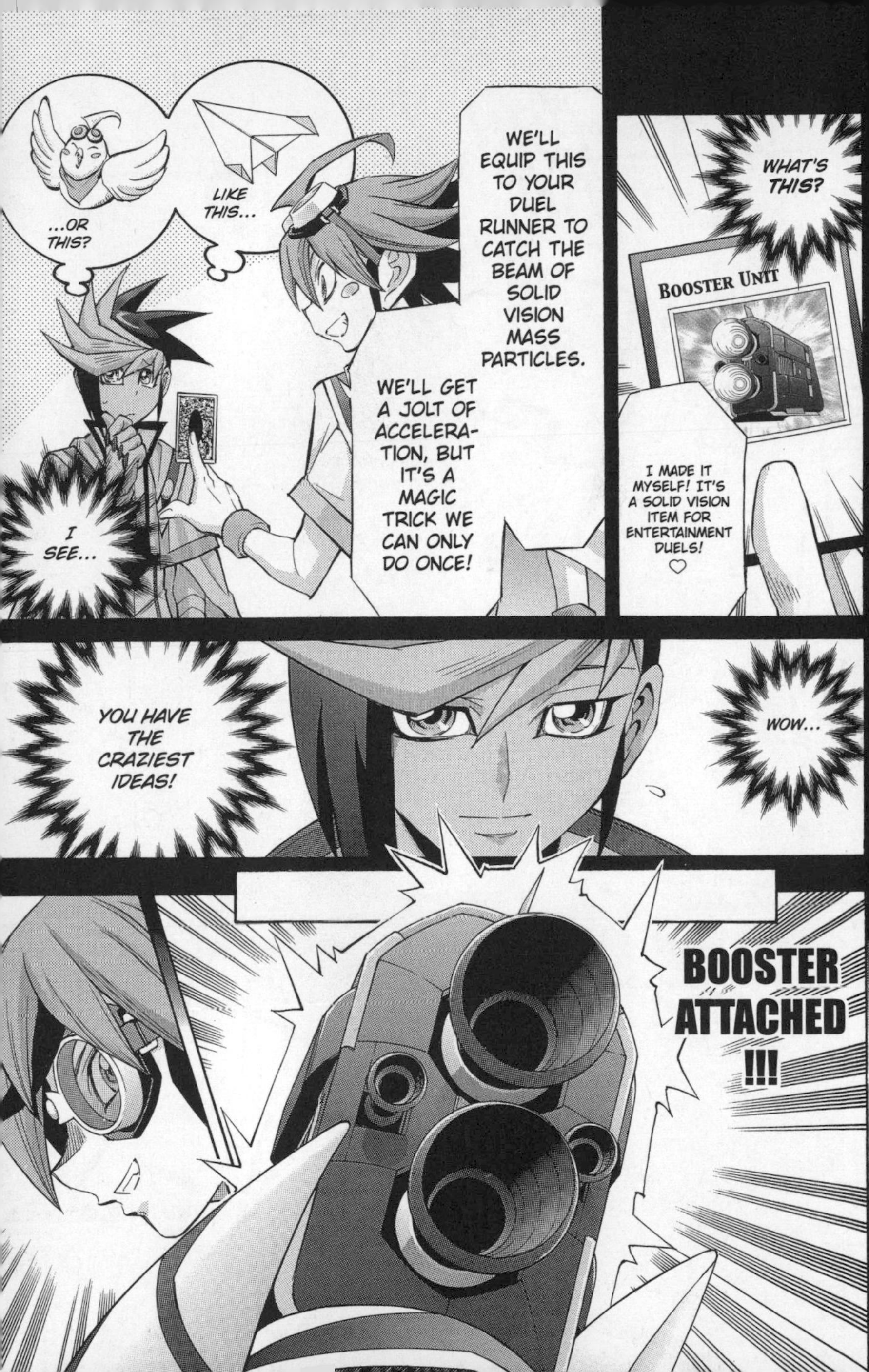
WHAT'S THIS?
BOOSTER UNIT
I MADE IT MYSELF! IT'S A SOLID VISION ITEM FOR ENTERTAINMENT DUELS! ♡
WE'LL EQUIP THIS TO YOUR DUEL RUNNER TO CATCH THE BEAM OF SOLID VISION MASS PARTICLES.
LIKE THIS...
...OR THIS?
WE'LL GET A JOLT OF ACCELERA-TION, BUT IT'S A MAGIC TRICK WE CAN ONLY DO ONCE!
I SEE...
WOW...
YOU HAVE THE CRAZIEST IDEAS!
BOOSTER ATTACHED!!!

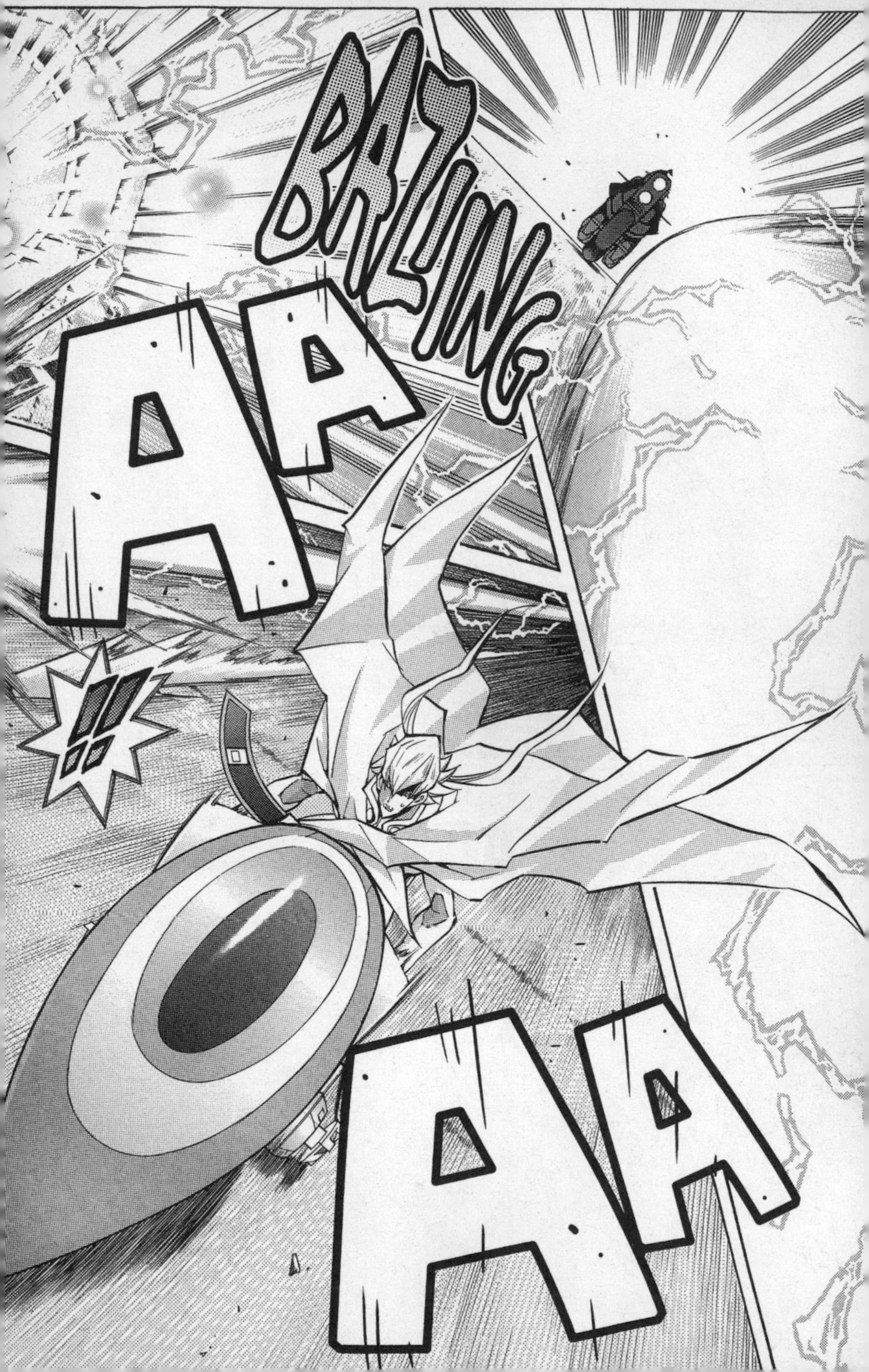
BAZING
AA
!!
AA

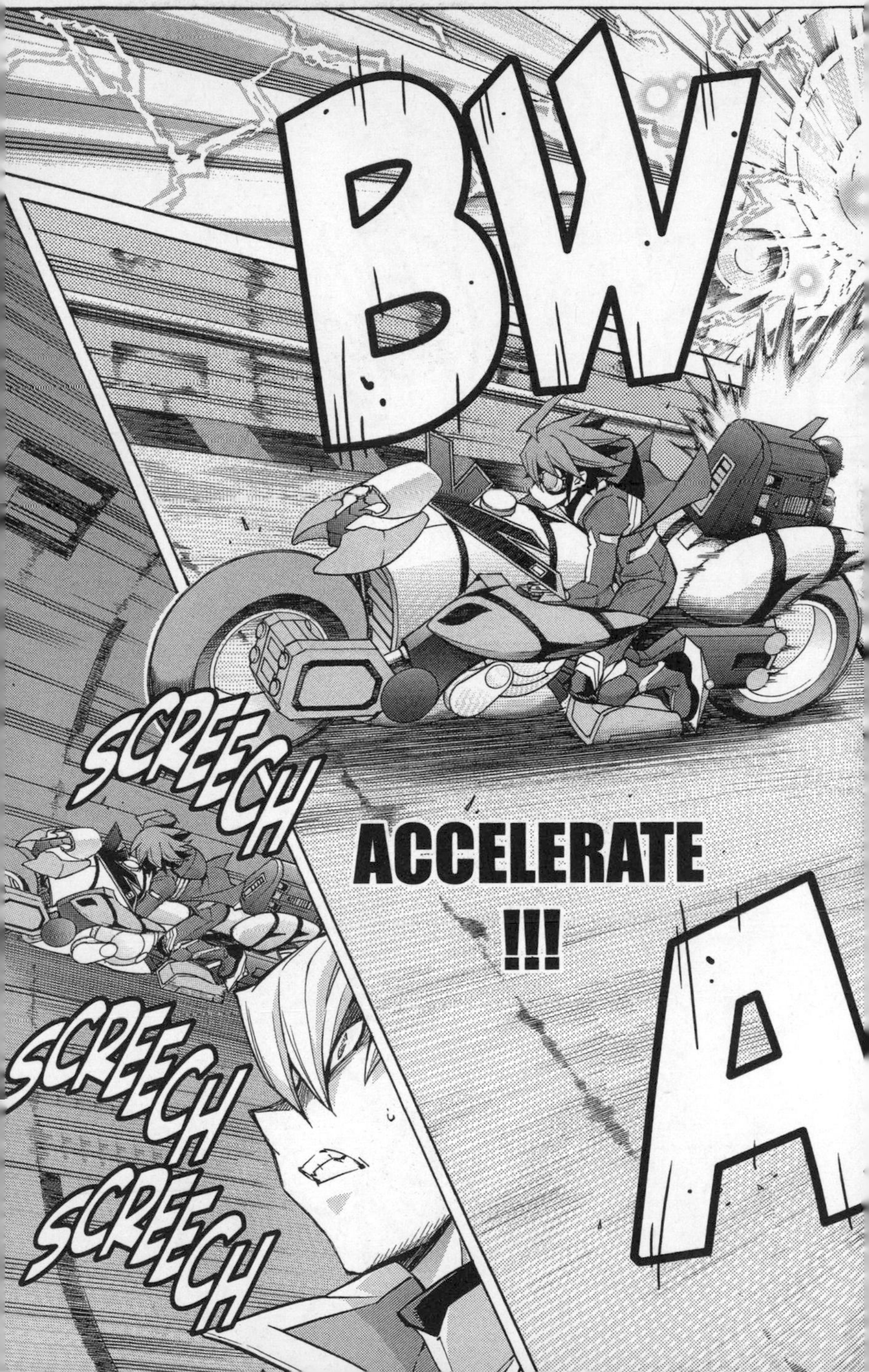
BW
A
ACCELERATE !!!
SCREECH
SCREECH
SCREECH
SCREECH

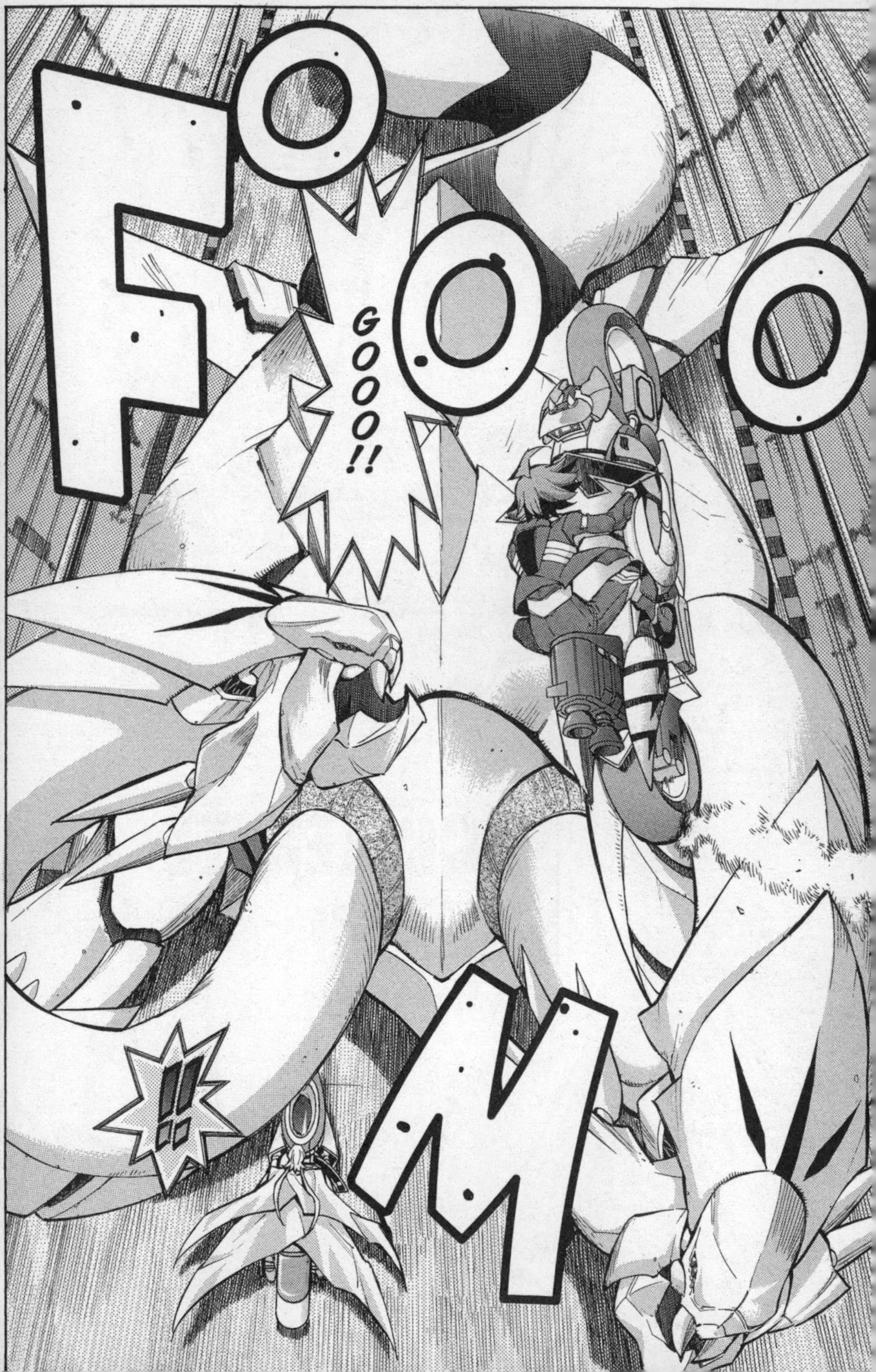
FOOOOM
GOOOO!!
!!

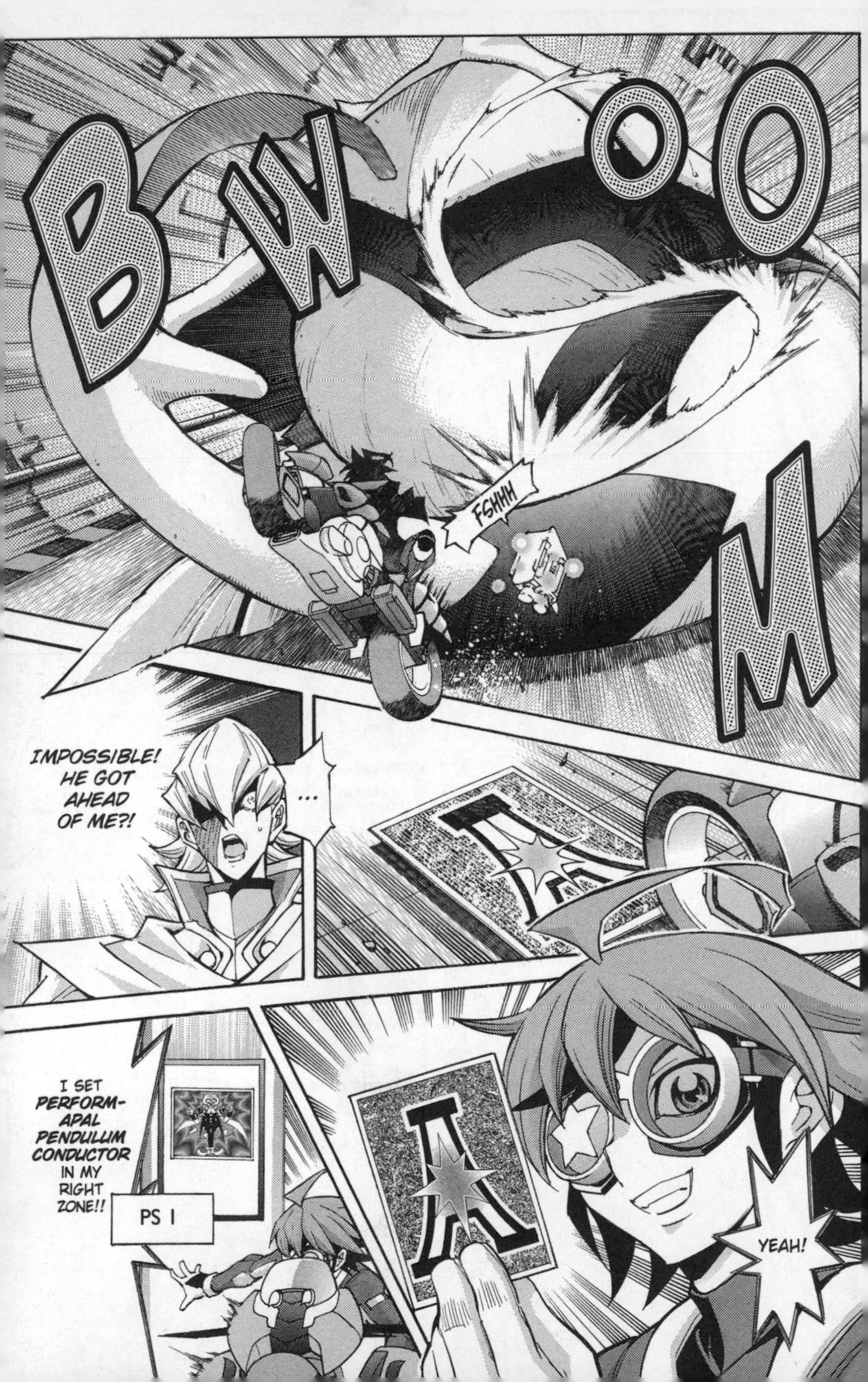
BWOOOM
FSHHH
...
IMPOSSIBLE! HE GOT AHEAD OF ME?!
YEAH!
I SET PERFORM-APAL PENDULUM CONDUCTOR IN MY RIGHT ZONE!!
PS 1

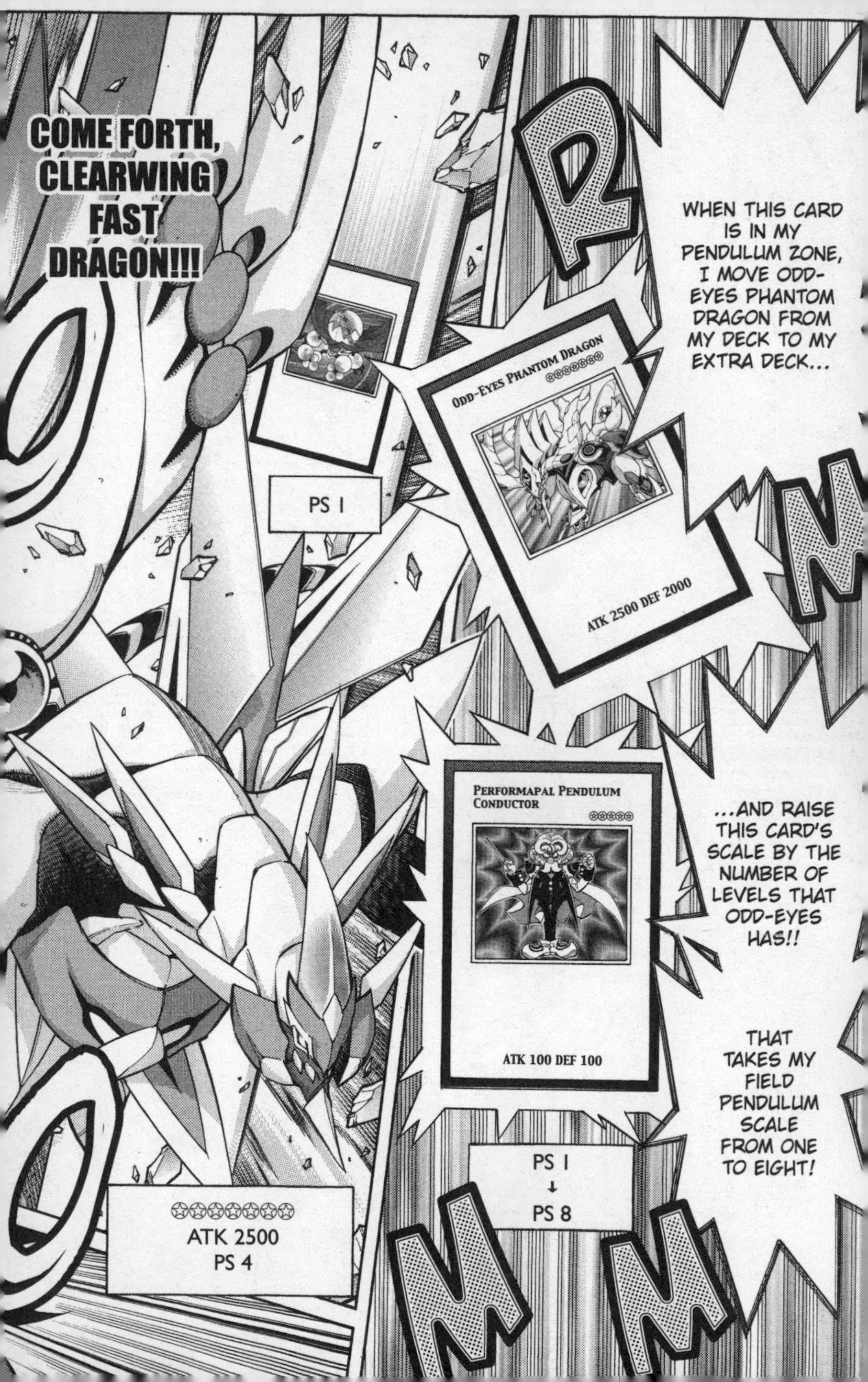

WHEN THIS CARD IS IN MY PENDULUM ZONE, I MOVE ODD-EYES PHANTOM DRAGON FROM MY DECK TO MY EXTRA DECK...
ODD-EYES PHANTOM DRAGON
ATK 2500 DEF 2000
...AND RAISE THIS CARD'S SCALE BY THE NUMBER OF LEVELS THAT ODD-EYES HAS!!
PERFORMAPAL PENDULUM CONDUCTOR
ATK 100 DEF 100
THAT TAKES MY FIELD PENDULUM SCALE FROM ONE TO EIGHT!
PS 1
↓
PS 8
COME FORTH, CLEARWING FAST DRAGON!!!
PS 1
ATK 2500
PS 4

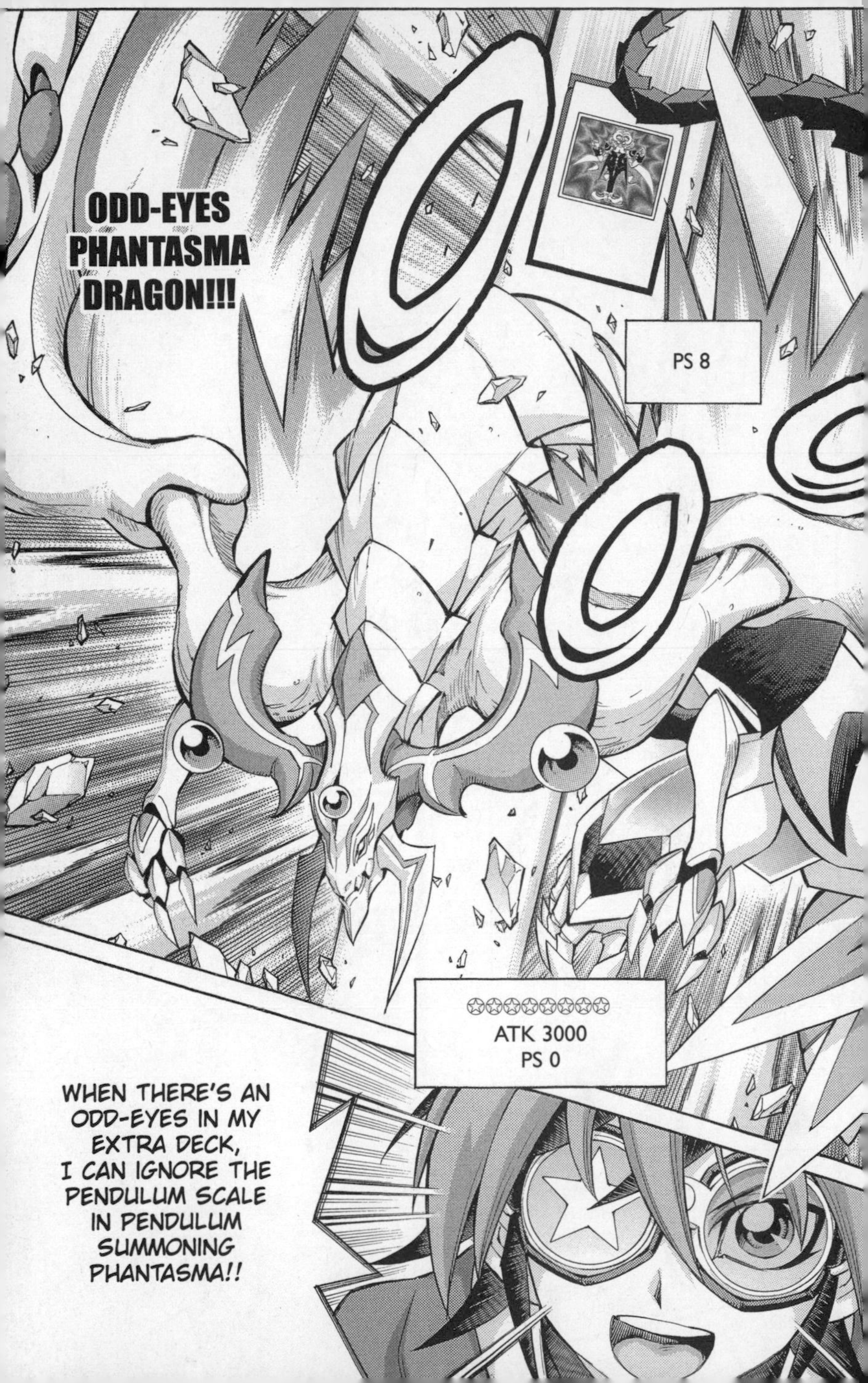
ODD-EYES PHANTASMA DRAGON!!!
PS 8
ATK 3000
PS 0
WHEN THERE'S AN ODD-EYES IN MY EXTRA DECK, I CAN IGNORE THE PENDULUM SCALE IN PENDULUM SUMMONING PHANTASMA!!

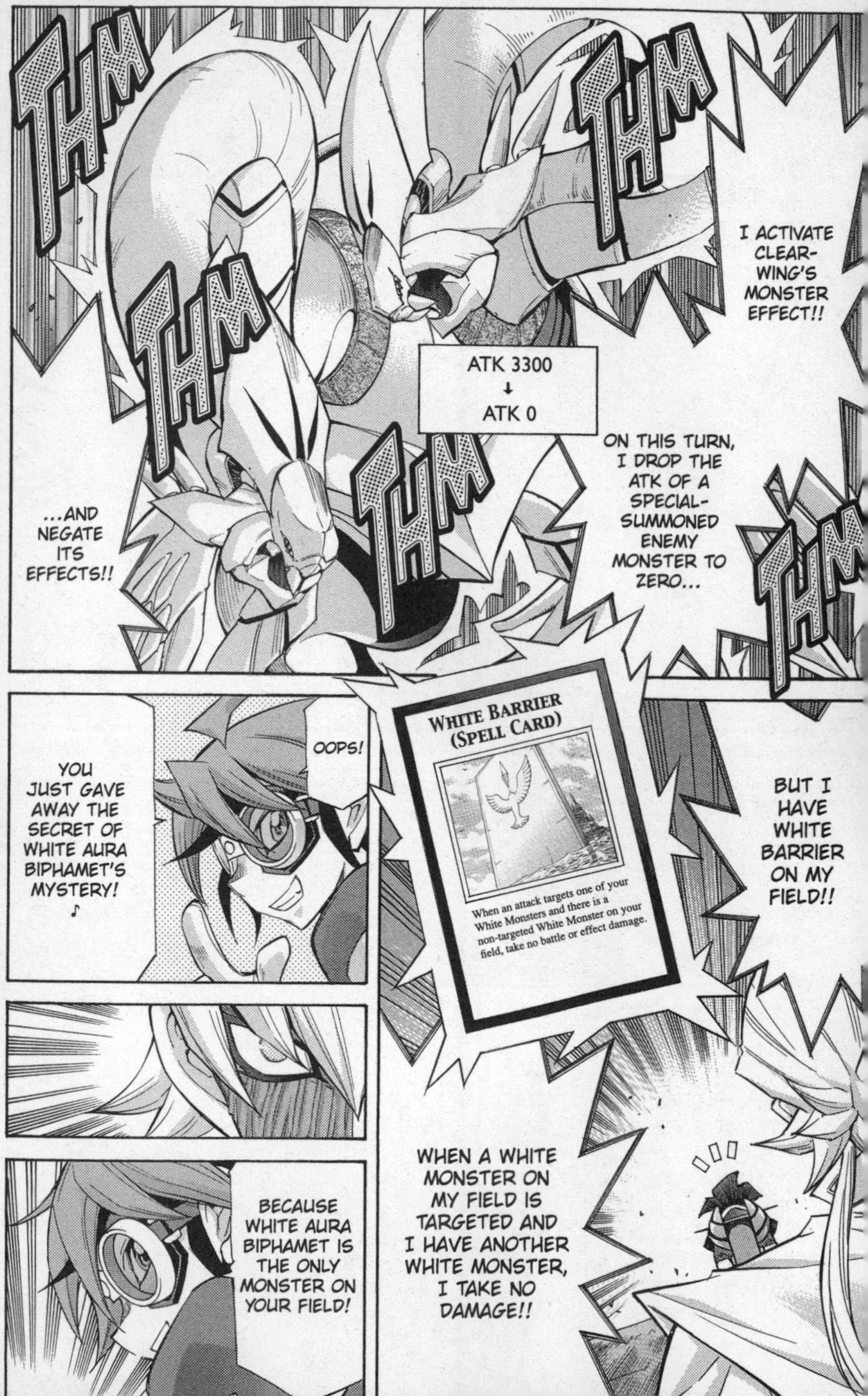
THM
THM
I ACTIVATE CLEAR-WING'S MONSTER EFFECT!!
THM
THM
ATK 3300 → ATK 0
ON THIS TURN, I DROP THE ATK OF A SPECIAL-SUMMONED ENEMY MONSTER TO ZERO...
...AND NEGATE ITS EFFECTS!!
THM
BUT I HAVE WHITE BARRIER ON MY FIELD!!
WHITE BARRIER (SPELL CARD)
When an attack targets one of your White Monsters and there is a non-targeted White Monster on your field, take no battle or effect damage.
WHEN A WHITE MONSTER ON MY FIELD IS TARGETED AND I HAVE ANOTHER WHITE MONSTER, I TAKE NO DAMAGE!!
OOPS!
YOU JUST GAVE AWAY THE SECRET OF WHITE AURA BIPHAMET'S MYSTERY! ♪
BECAUSE WHITE AURA BIPHAMET IS THE ONLY MONSTER ON YOUR FIELD!

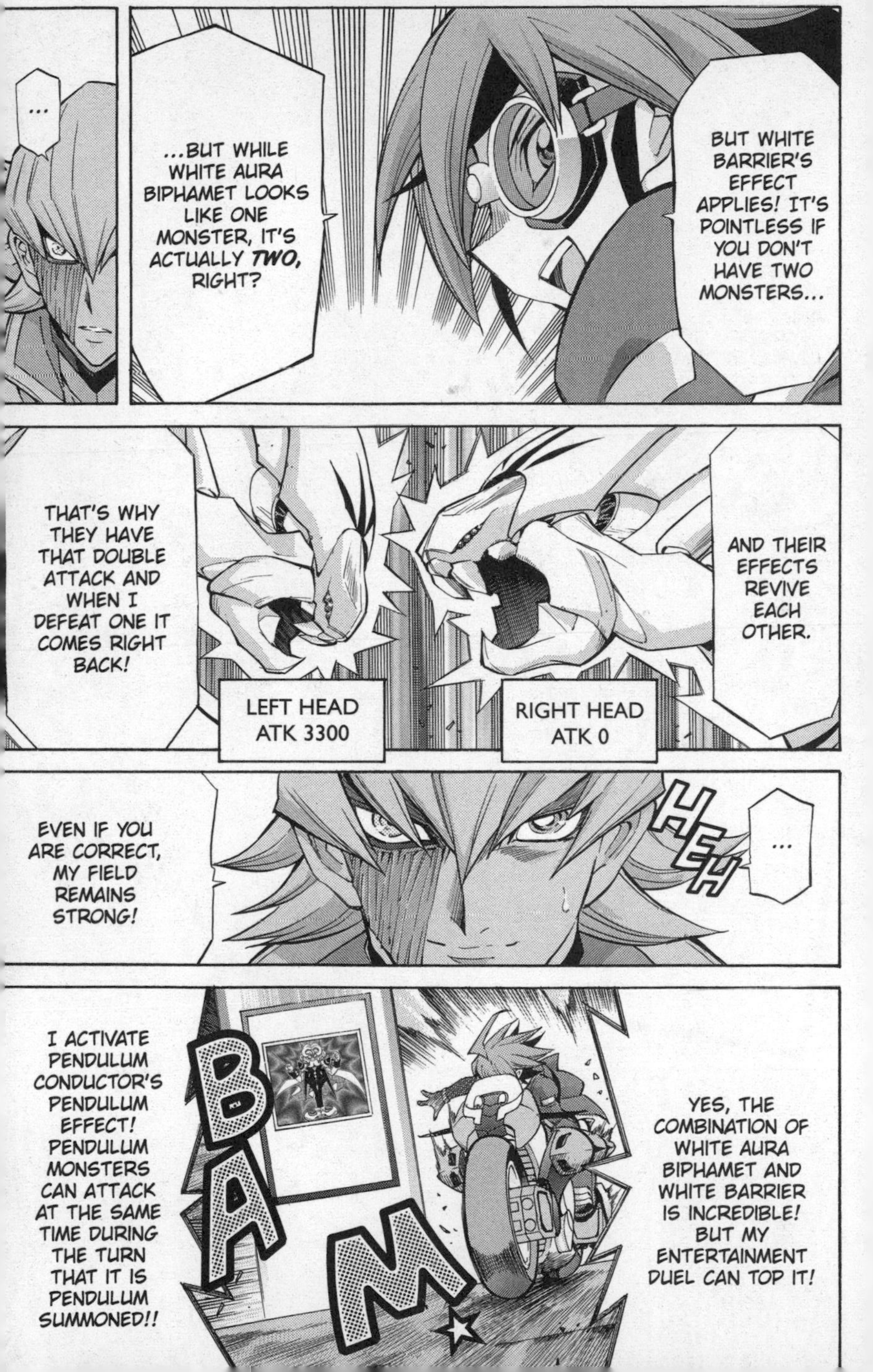
BUT WHITE BARRIER'S EFFECT APPLIES! IT'S POINTLESS IF YOU DON'T HAVE TWO MONSTERS...
...BUT WHILE WHITE AURA BIPHAMET LOOKS LIKE ONE MONSTER, IT'S ACTUALLY ***TWO,*** RIGHT?
...
THAT'S WHY THEY HAVE THAT DOUBLE ATTACK AND WHEN I DEFEAT ONE IT COMES RIGHT BACK!
AND THEIR EFFECTS REVIVE EACH OTHER.
RIGHT HEAD ATK 0
LEFT HEAD ATK 3300
HEH
...
EVEN IF YOU ARE CORRECT, MY FIELD REMAINS STRONG!
YES, THE COMBINATION OF WHITE AURA BIPHAMET AND WHITE BARRIER IS INCREDIBLE! BUT MY ENTERTAINMENT DUEL CAN TOP IT!
BAM
I ACTIVATE PENDULUM CONDUCTOR'S PENDULUM EFFECT! PENDULUM MONSTERS CAN ATTACK AT THE SAME TIME DURING THE TURN THAT IT IS PENDULUM SUMMONED!!

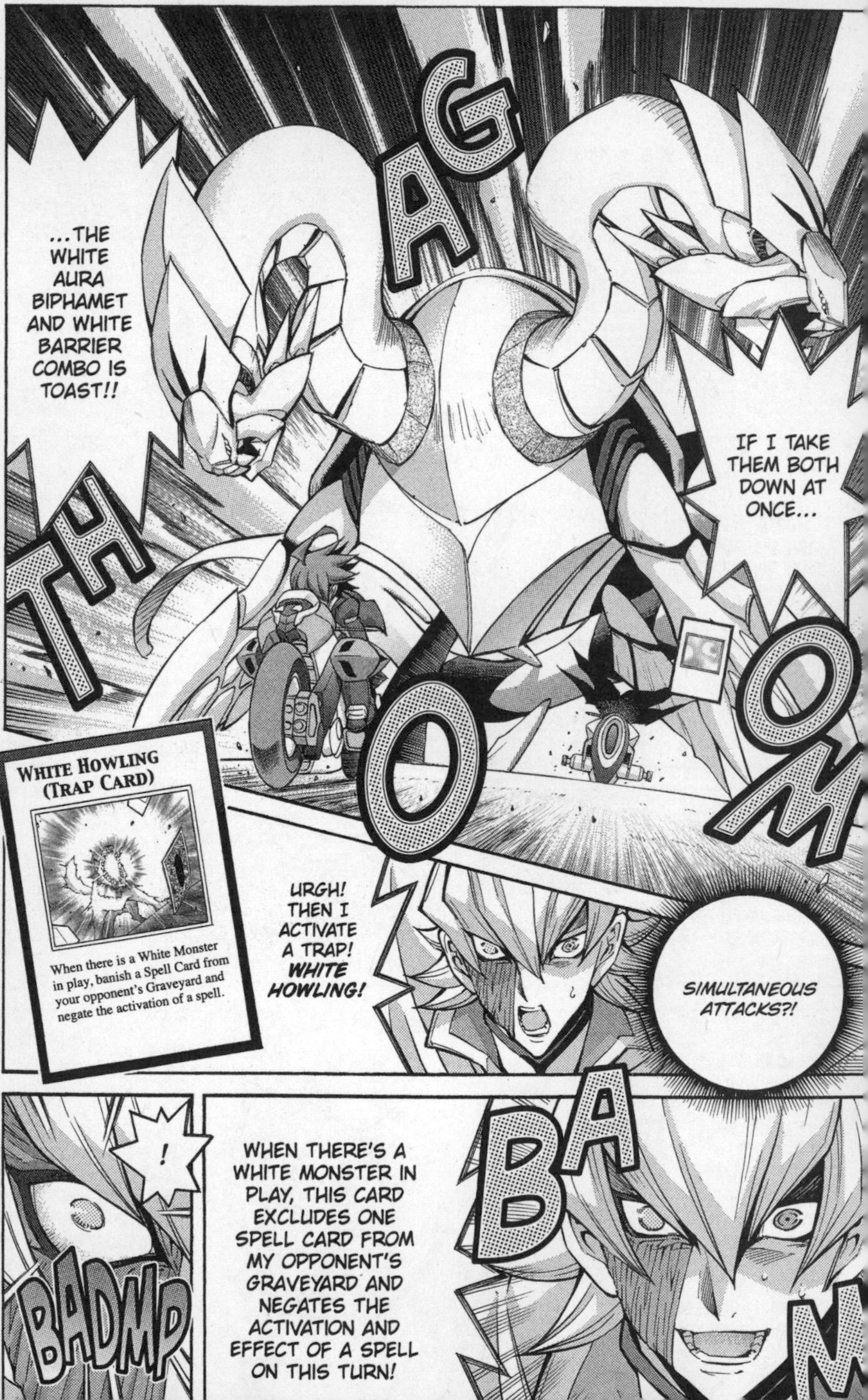
IF I TAKE THEM BOTH DOWN AT ONCE...
...THE WHITE AURA BIPHAMET AND WHITE BARRIER COMBO IS TOAST!!
THOOOM
SIMULTANEOUS ATTACKS?!
URGH! THEN I ACTIVATE A TRAP! *WHITE HOWLING!*
WHITE HOWLING (TRAP CARD)
When there is a White Monster in play, banish a Spell Card from your opponent's Graveyard and negate the activation of a spell.
BA
WHEN THERE'S A WHITE MONSTER IN PLAY, THIS CARD EXCLUDES ONE SPELL CARD FROM MY OPPONENT'S GRAVEYARD AND NEGATES THE ACTIVATION AND EFFECT OF A SPELL ON THIS TURN!
!
BADMP

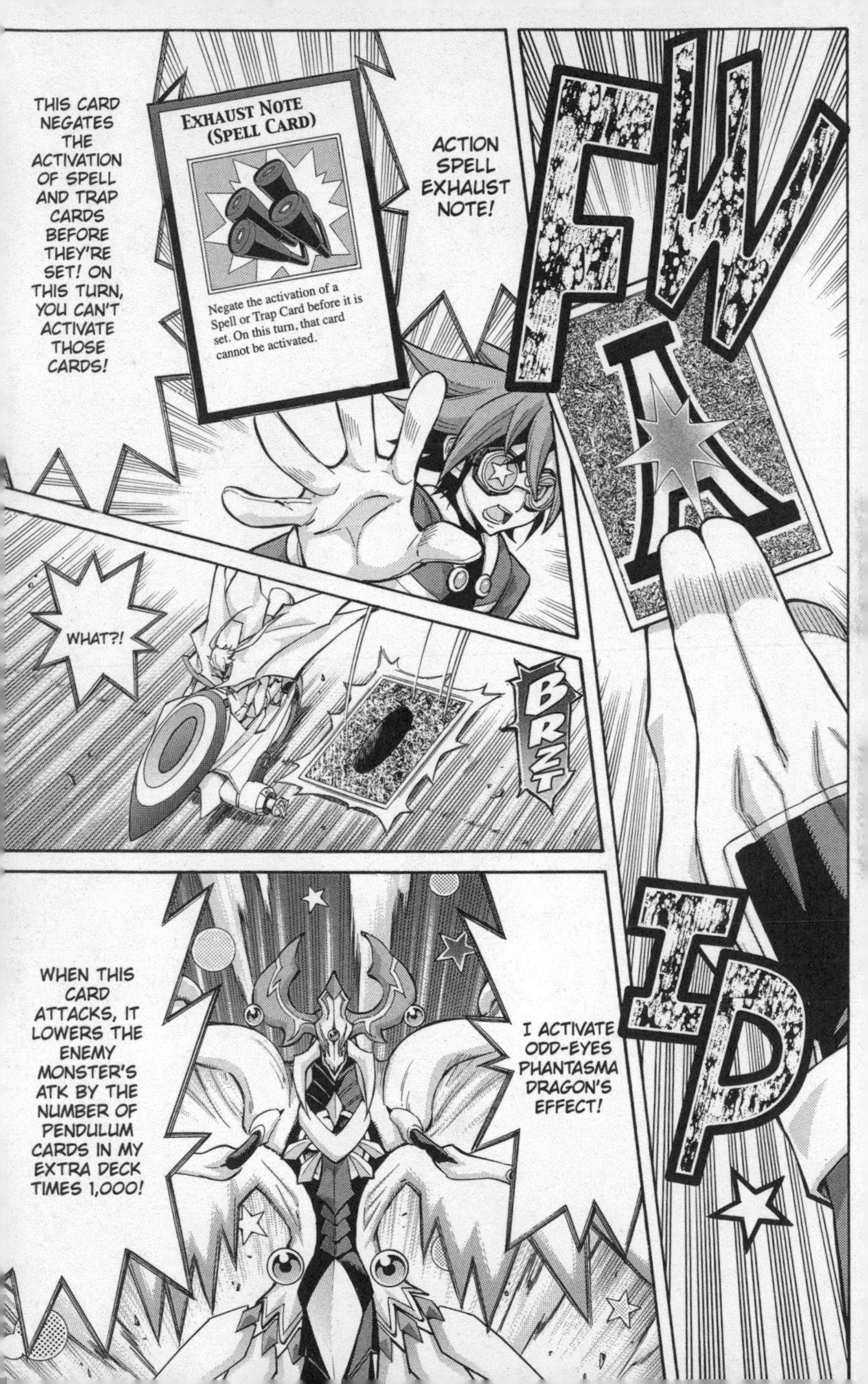
FWA
FWIP
ACTION SPELL EXHAUST NOTE!
EXHAUST NOTE (SPELL CARD)
Negate the activation of a Spell or Trap Card before it is set. On this turn, that card cannot be activated.
THIS CARD NEGATES THE ACTIVATION OF SPELL AND TRAP CARDS BEFORE THEY'RE SET! ON THIS TURN, YOU CAN'T ACTIVATE THOSE CARDS!
BRZT
WHAT?!
I ACTIVATE ODD-EYES PHANTASMA DRAGON'S EFFECT!
WHEN THIS CARD ATTACKS, IT LOWERS THE ENEMY MONSTER'S ATK BY THE NUMBER OF PENDULUM CARDS IN MY EXTRA DECK TIMES 1,000!

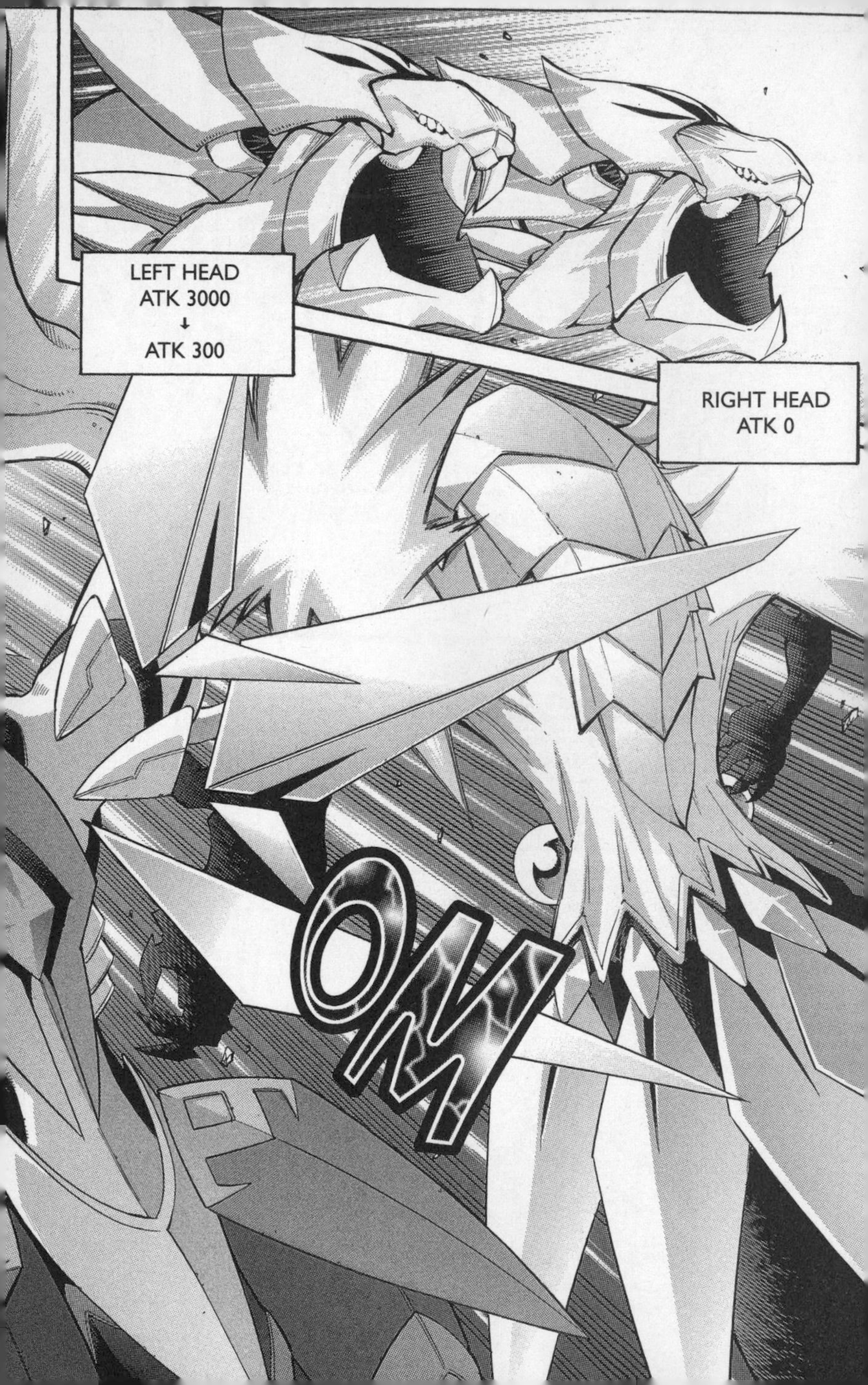
RIGHT HEAD
ATK 0
LEFT HEAD
ATK 3000
↓
ATK 300
OM

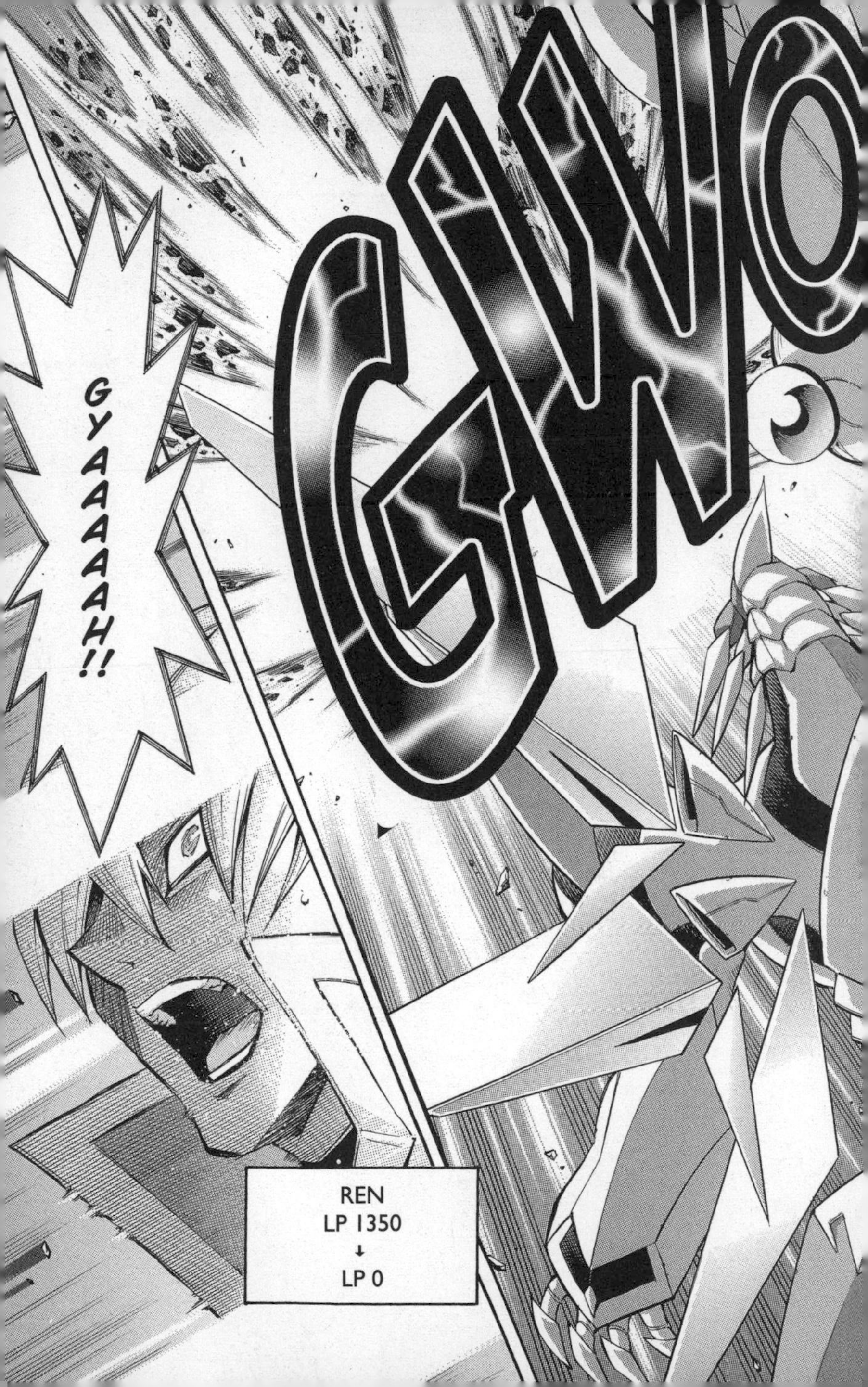
GWO
GYAAAAAAH!!
REN
LP 1350
↓
LP 0

STARVING VENEMY DRAGON

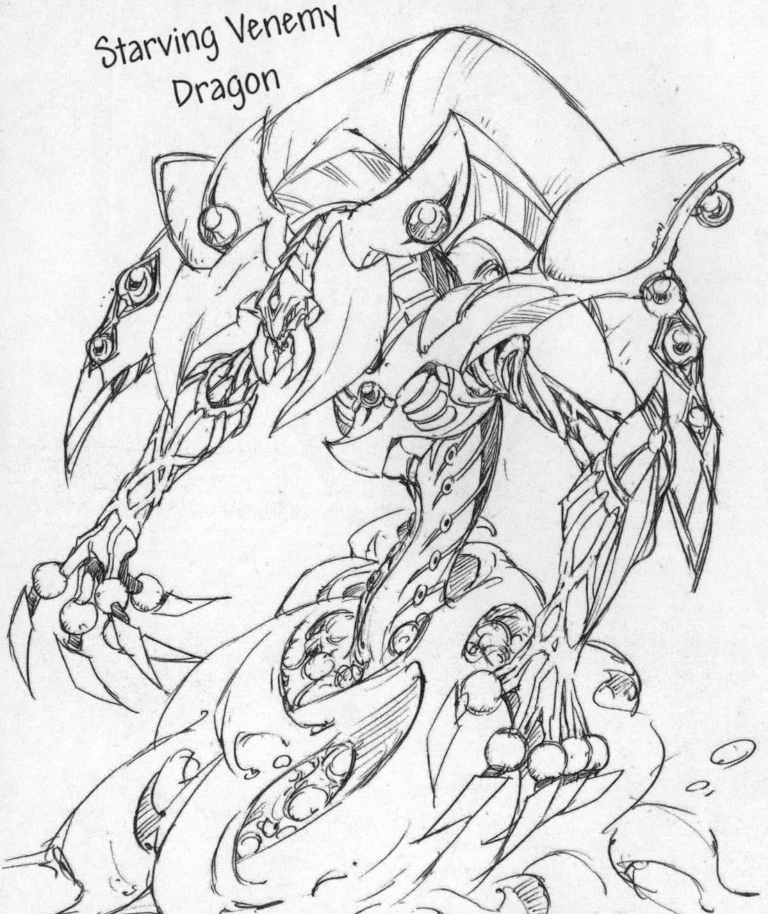
Starving Venemy Dragon

Yuri's ace monster Venemy gets its name from the words "venom" and "enemy." Its distinctive design resembles plant roots.

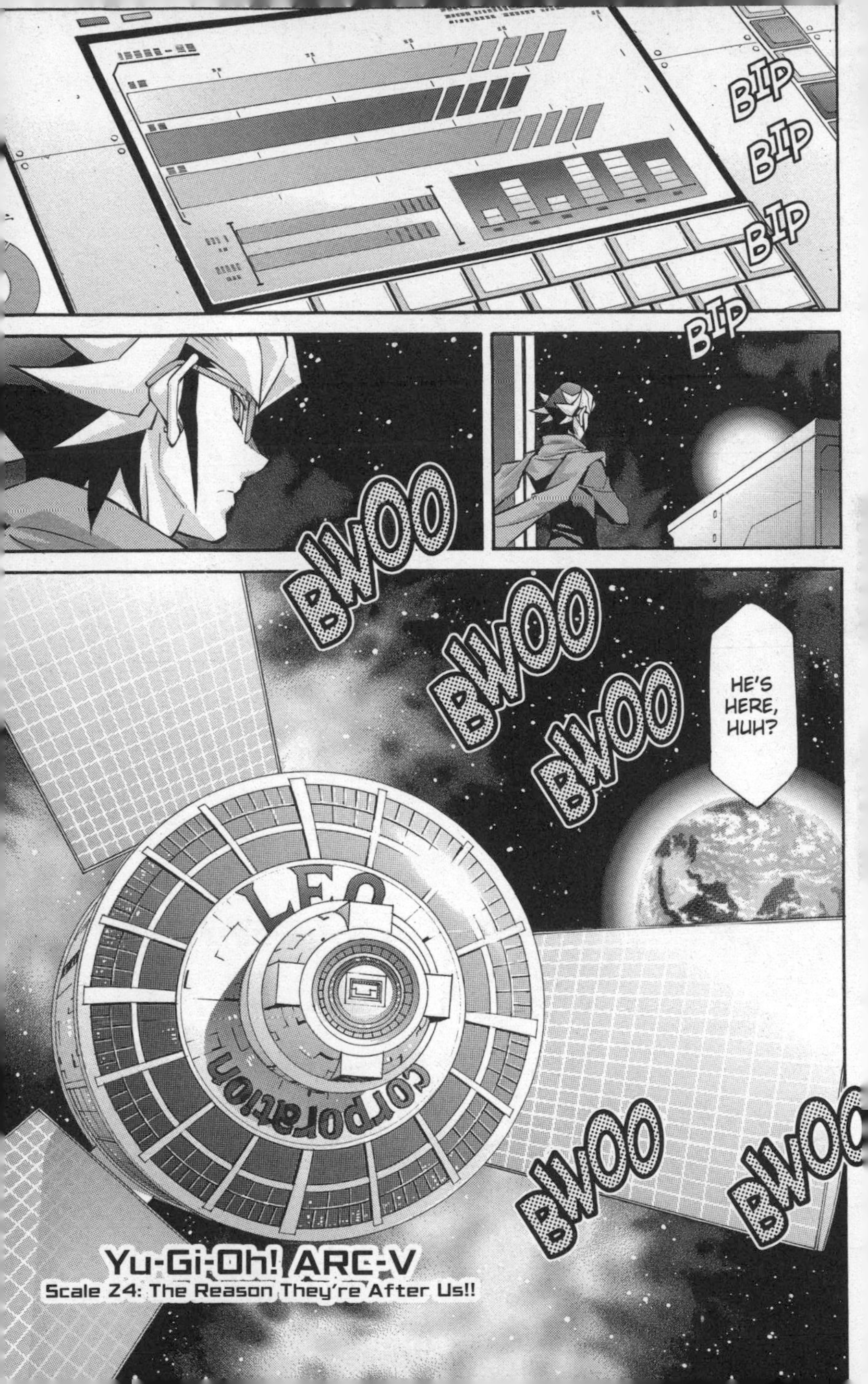

BIP
BIP
BIP
BIP
BWOO
BWOO
BWOO
HE'S HERE, HUH?
LEO
corporation
BWOO
BWOO
Yu-Gi-Oh! ARC-V
Scale 24: The Reason They're After Us!!

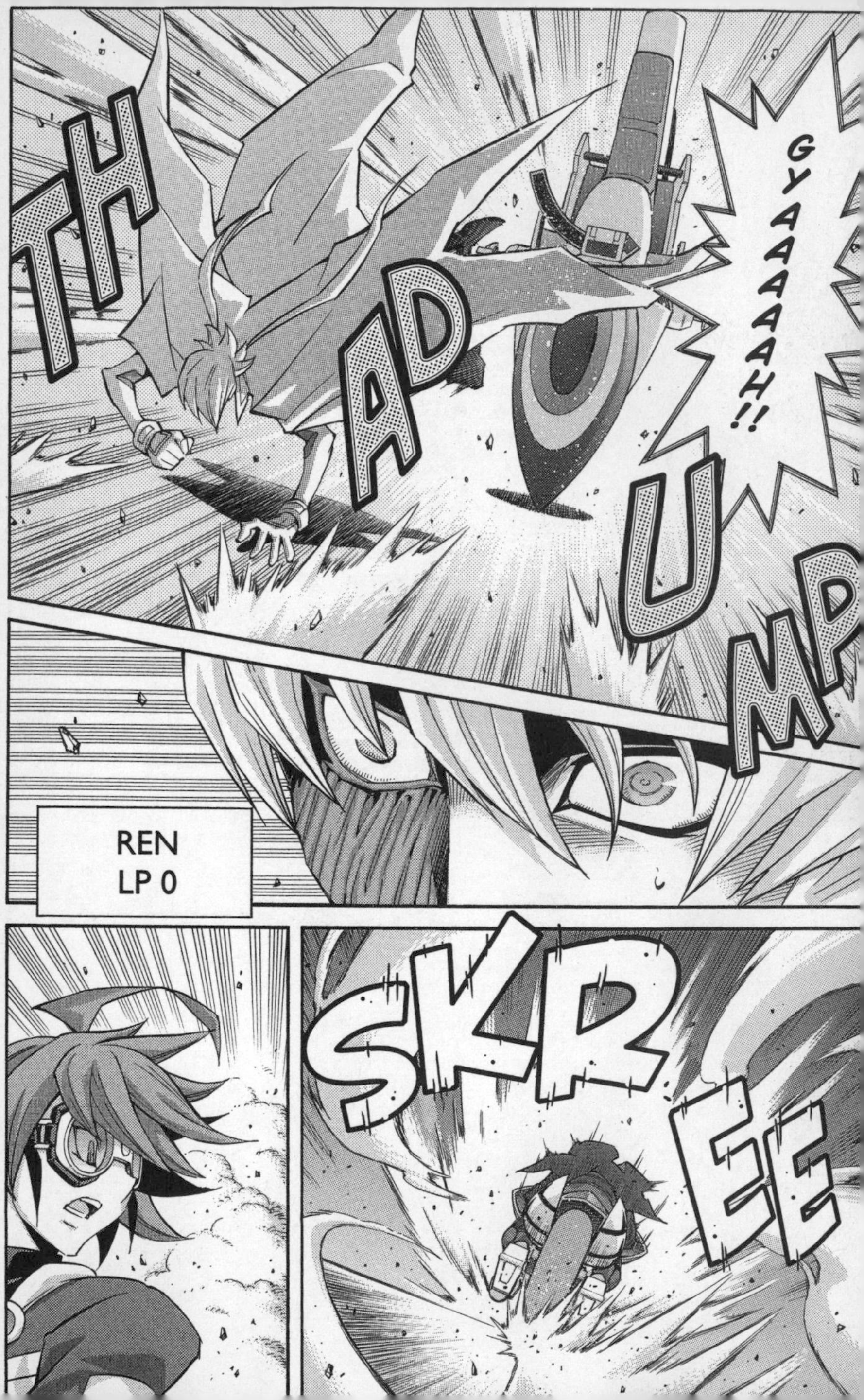
GYAAAAAAH!!
THADUMP
REN
LP 0
SKREE

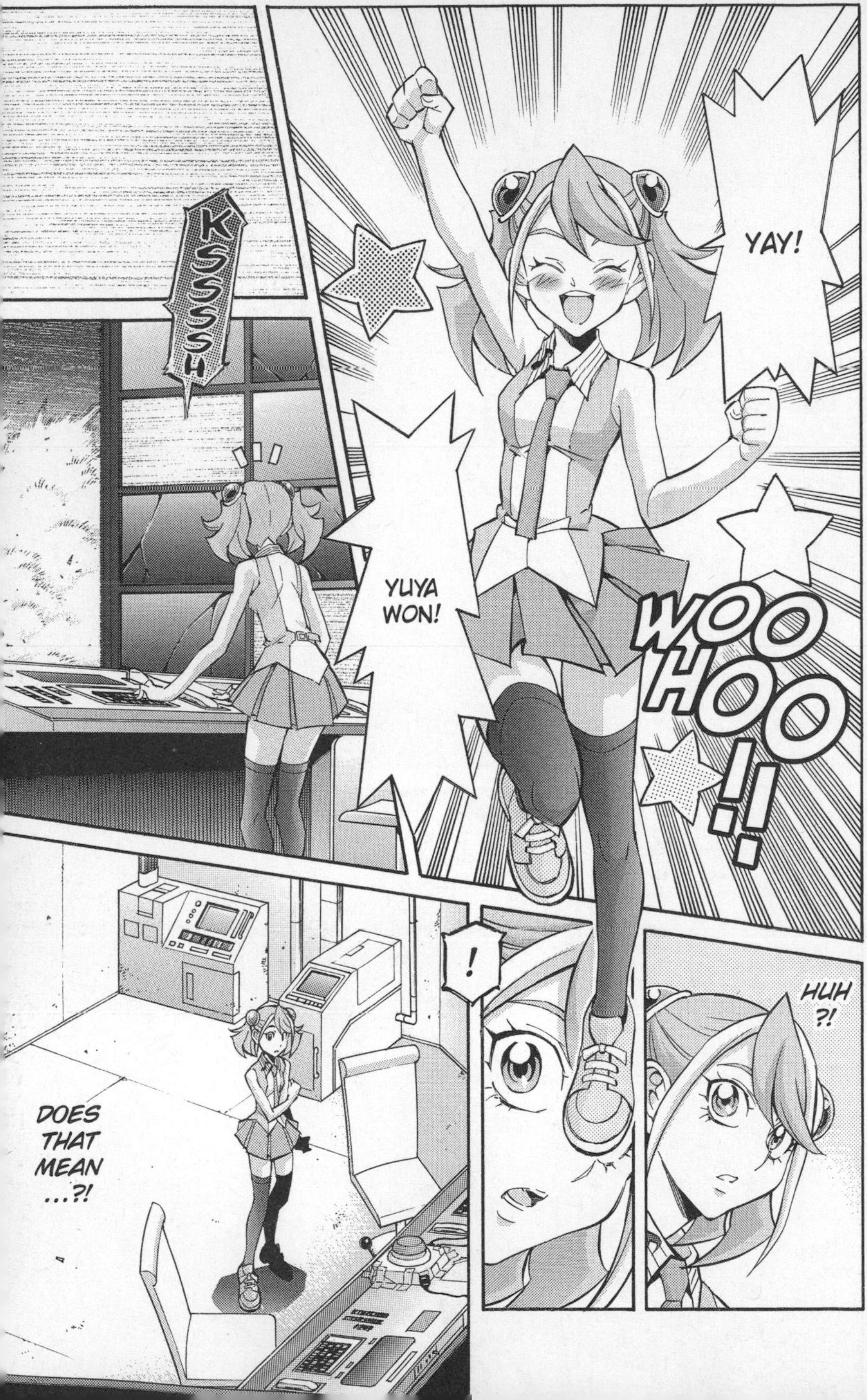
YAY!
YUYA WON!
WOO HOO!!
KSSSSSH
HUH?!
!
DOES THAT MEAN...?!

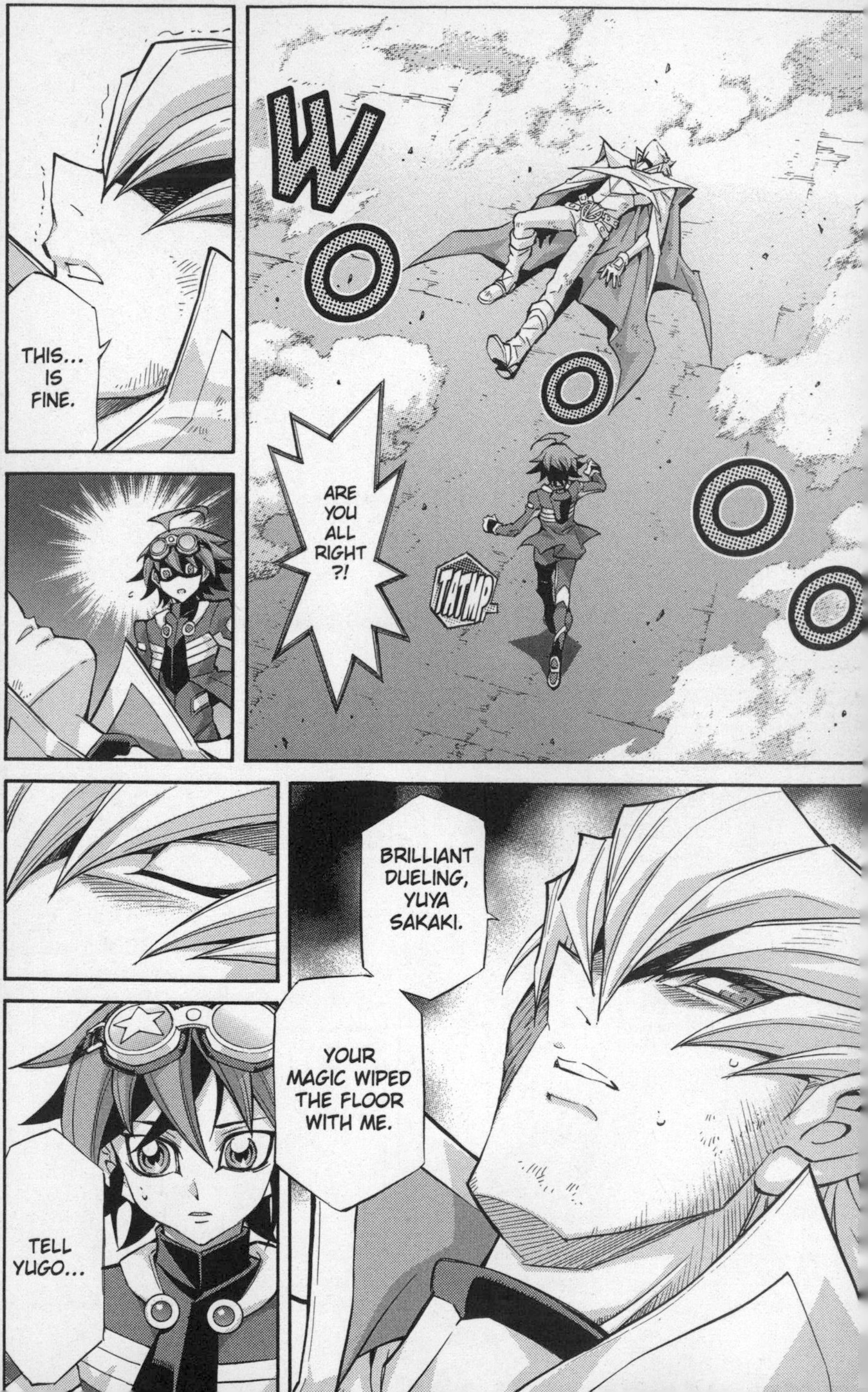
WOOOO
ARE YOU ALL RIGHT?!
TATMP
THIS... IS FINE.
BRILLIANT DUELING, YUYA SAKAKI.
YOUR MAGIC WIPED THE FLOOR WITH ME.
TELL YUGO...

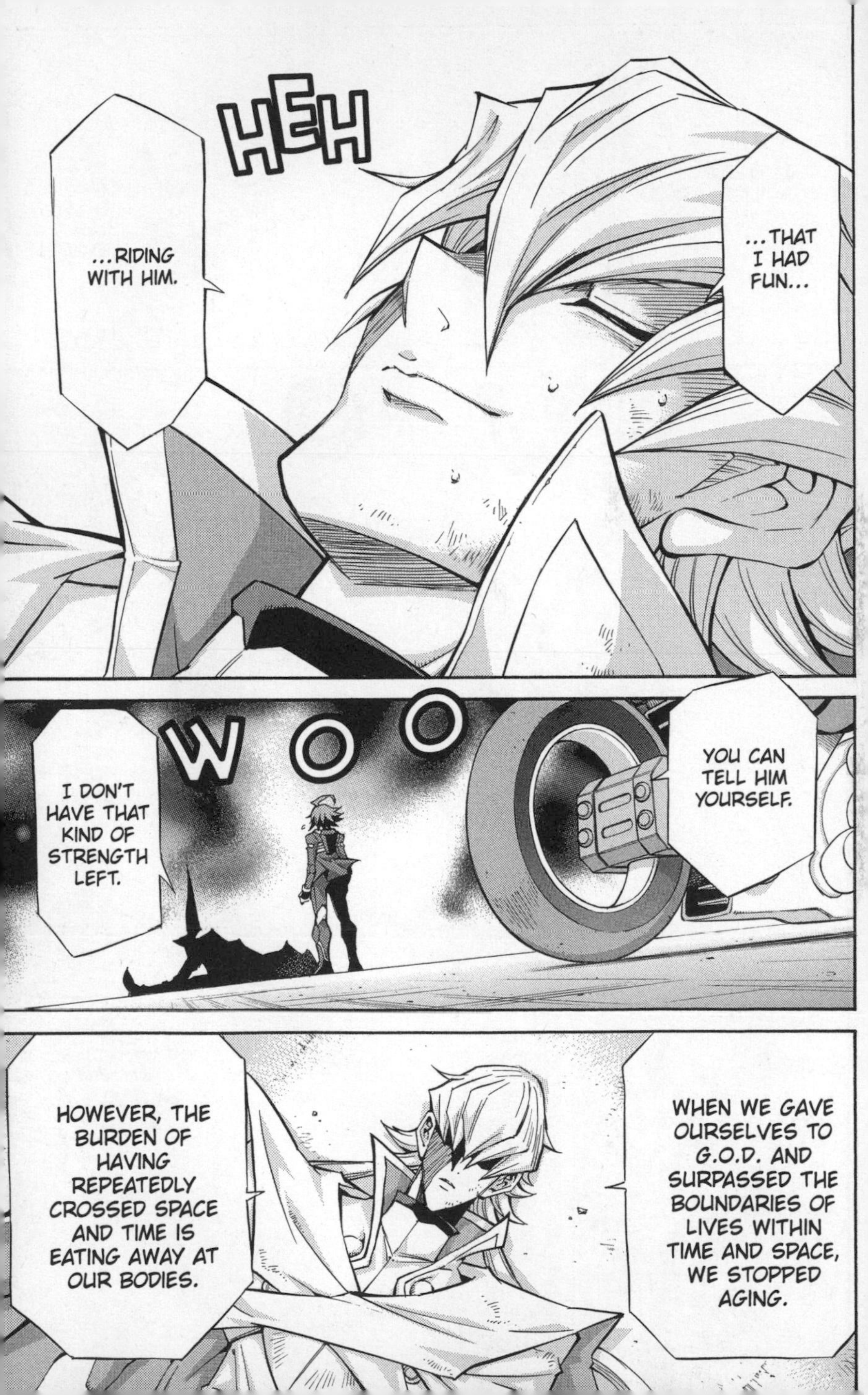
...THAT I HAD FUN...
HEH
...RIDING WITH HIM.
YOU CAN TELL HIM YOURSELF.
WOOO
I DON'T HAVE THAT KIND OF STRENGTH LEFT.
WHEN WE GAVE OURSELVES TO G.O.D. AND SURPASSED THE BOUNDARIES OF LIVES WITHIN TIME AND SPACE, WE STOPPED AGING.
HOWEVER, THE BURDEN OF HAVING REPEATEDLY CROSSED SPACE AND TIME IS EATING AWAY AT OUR BODIES.

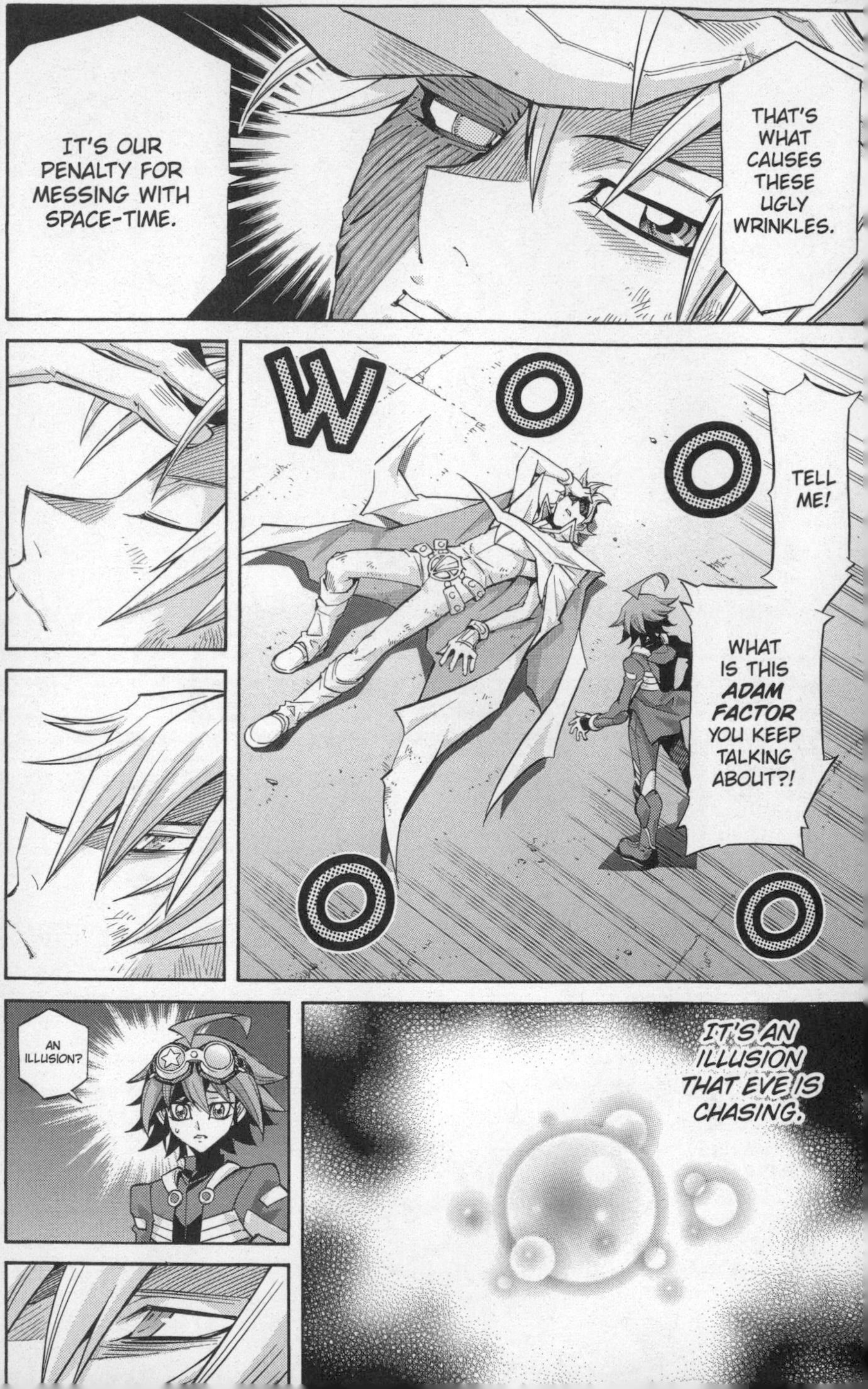
THAT'S WHAT CAUSES THESE UGLY WRINKLES.
IT'S OUR PENALTY FOR MESSING WITH SPACE-TIME.
TELL ME!
WHAT IS THIS ADAM FACTOR YOU KEEP TALKING ABOUT?!
WOOOO
IT'S AN ILLUSION THAT EVE IS CHASING.
AN ILLUSION?

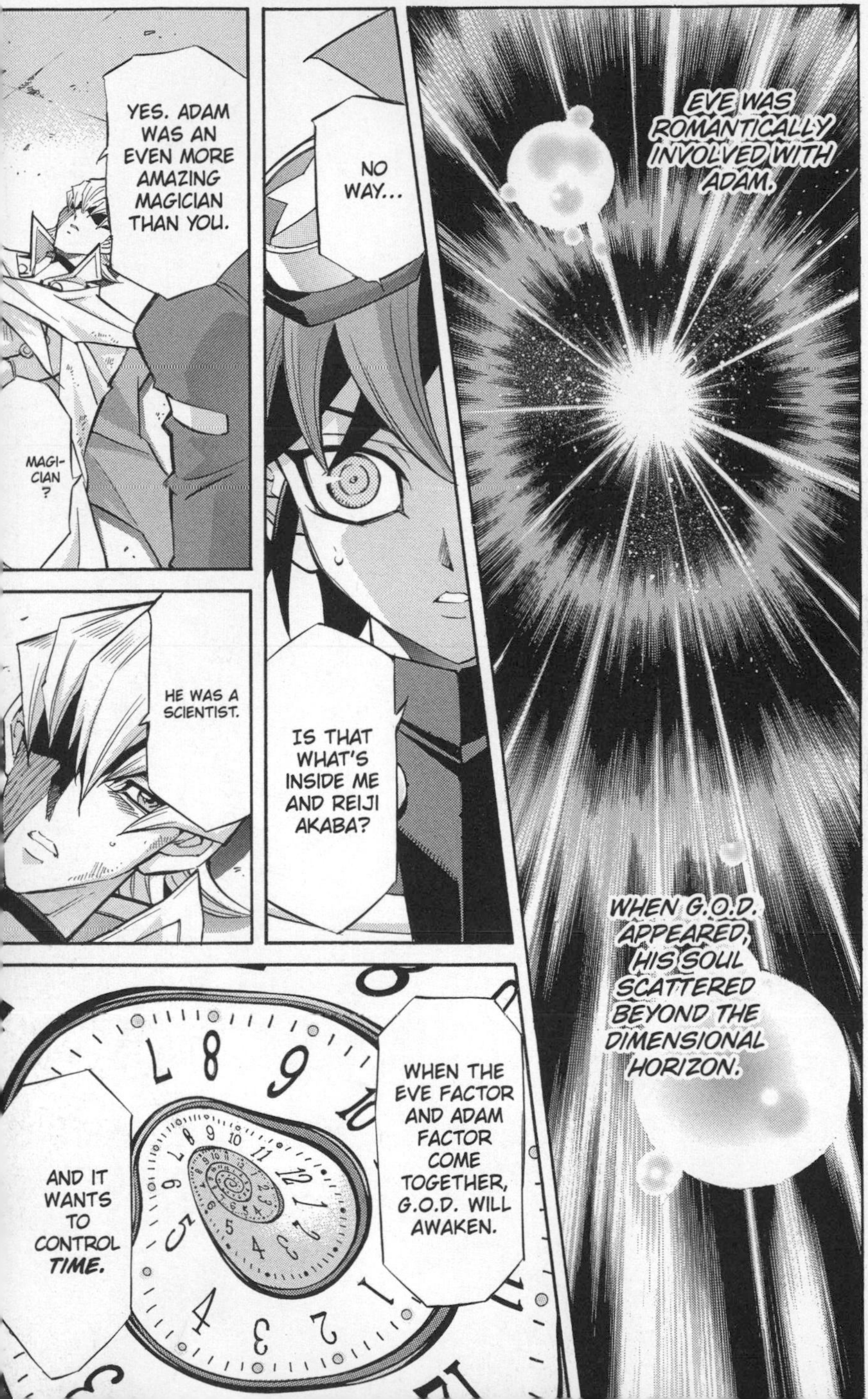
EVE WAS ROMANTICALLY INVOLVED WITH ADAM.
WHEN G.O.D. APPEARED, HIS SOUL SCATTERED BEYOND THE DIMENSIONAL HORIZON.
NO WAY...
IS THAT WHAT'S INSIDE ME AND REIJI AKABA?
YES. ADAM WAS AN EVEN MORE AMAZING MAGICIAN THAN YOU.
MAGICIAN?
HE WAS A SCIENTIST.
WHEN THE EVE FACTOR AND ADAM FACTOR COME TOGETHER, G.O.D. WILL AWAKEN.
AND IT WANTS TO CONTROL *TIME.*

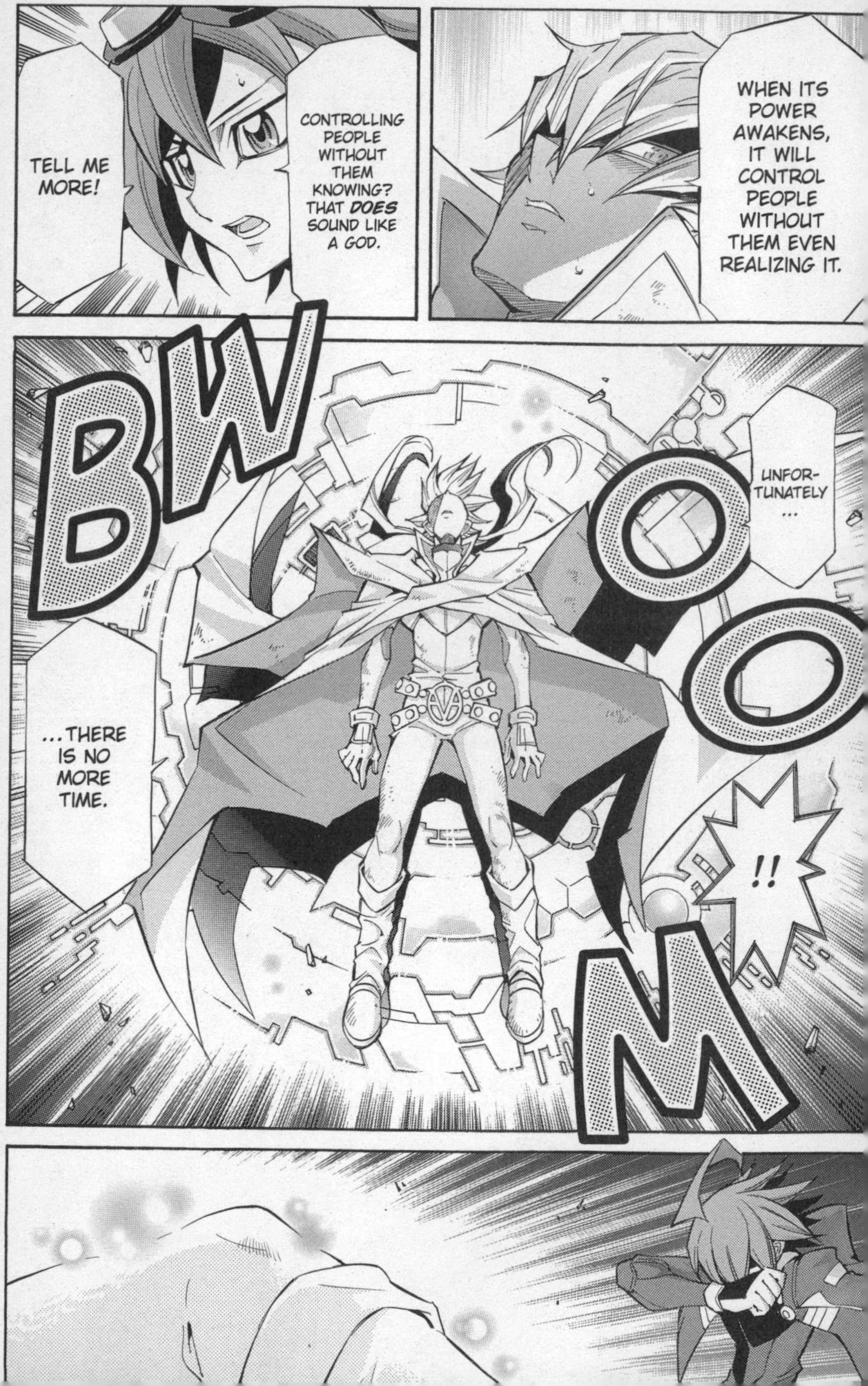
WHEN ITS POWER AWAKENS, IT WILL CONTROL PEOPLE WITHOUT THEM EVEN REALIZING IT.
CONTROLLING PEOPLE WITHOUT THEM KNOWING? THAT *DOES* SOUND LIKE A GOD.
TELL ME MORE!
BWOOOM
UNFOR-TUNATELY ...
...THERE IS NO MORE TIME.
!!

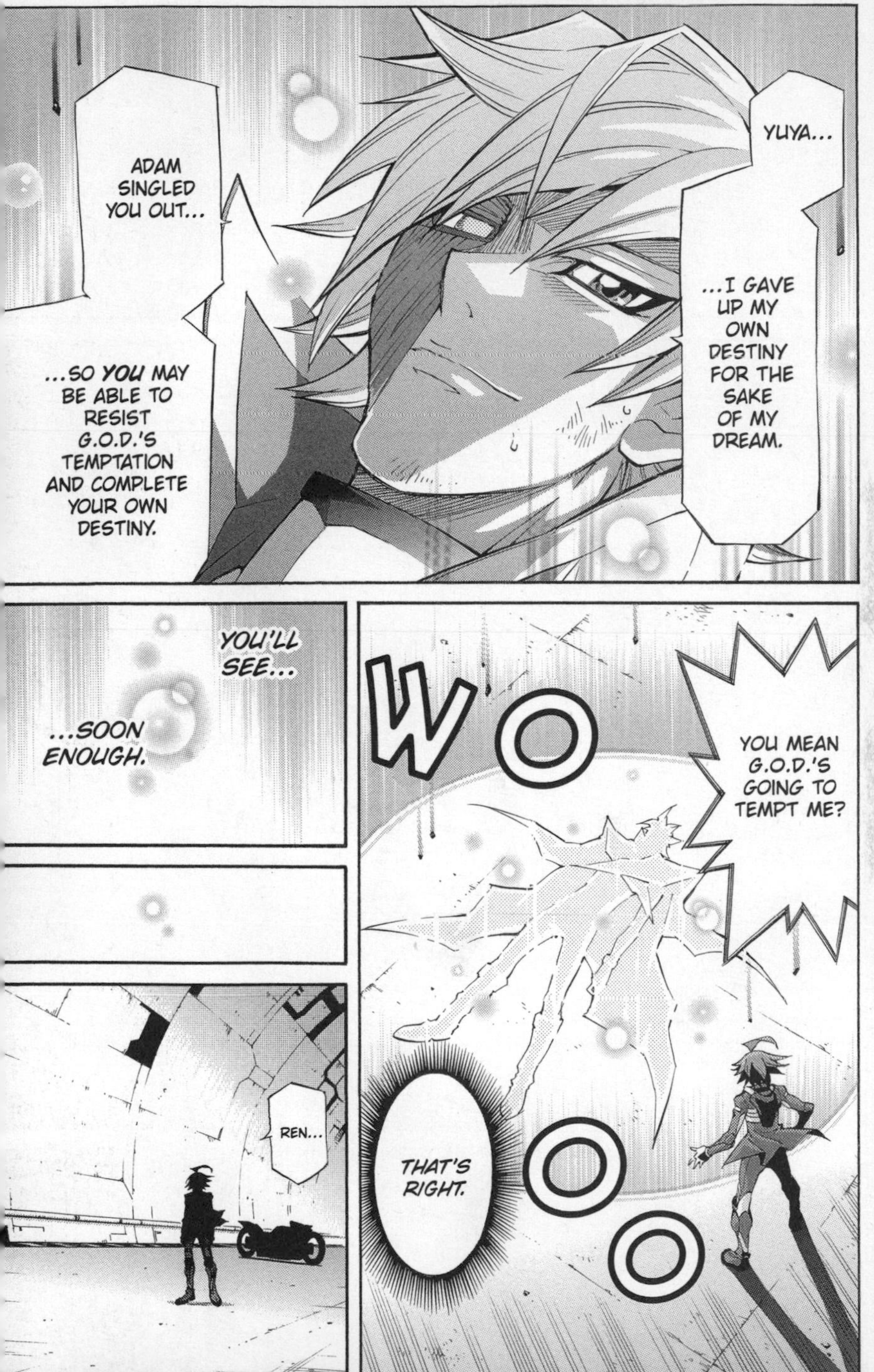
YUYA...
...I GAVE UP MY OWN DESTINY FOR THE SAKE OF MY DREAM.
ADAM SINGLED YOU OUT...
...SO *YOU* MAY BE ABLE TO RESIST G.O.D.'S TEMPTATION AND COMPLETE YOUR OWN DESTINY.
YOU MEAN G.O.D.'S GOING TO TEMPT ME?
WOOO
THAT'S RIGHT.
YOU'LL SEE...
...SOON ENOUGH.
REN...

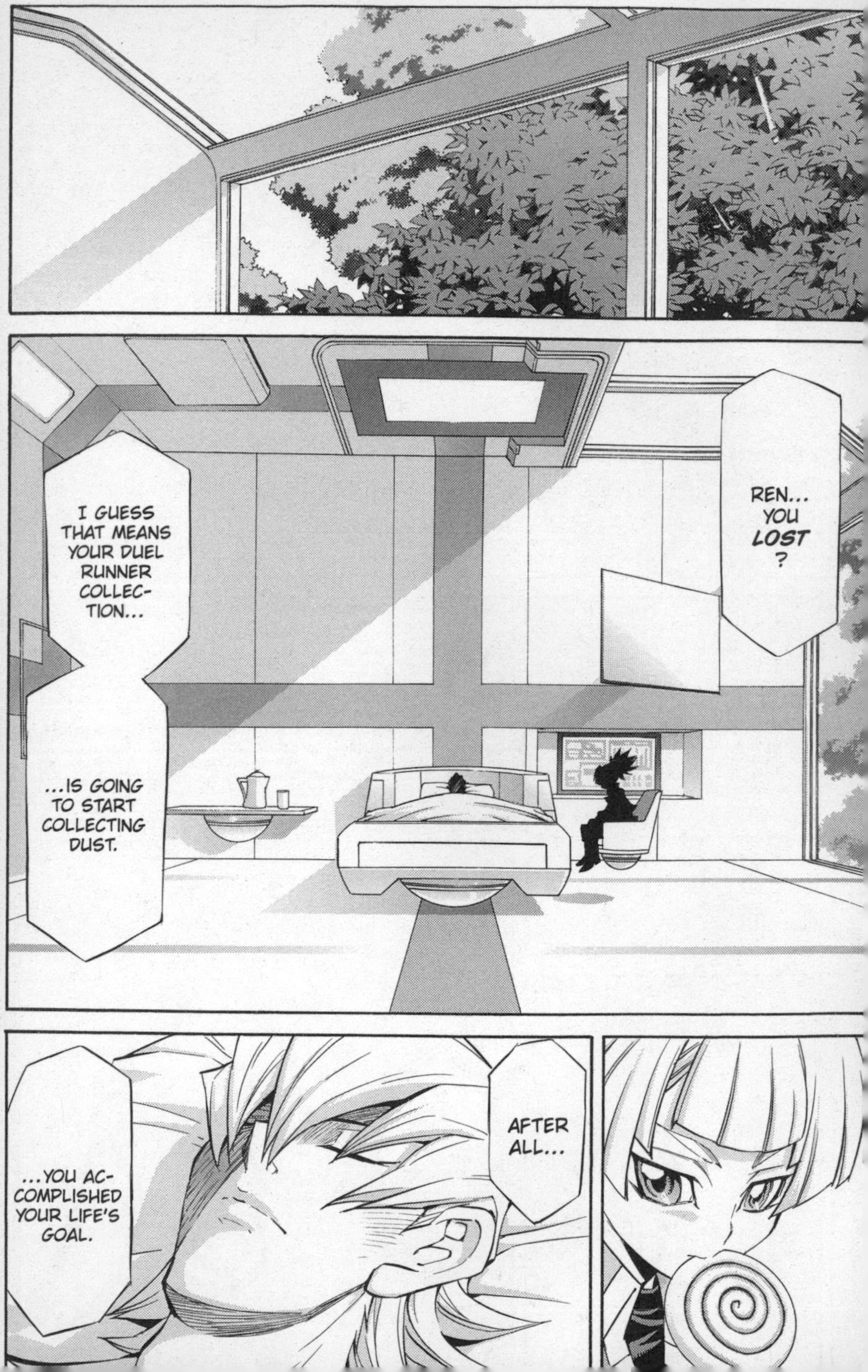
REN... YOU LOST?
I GUESS THAT MEANS YOUR DUEL RUNNER COLLECTION...
...IS GOING TO START COLLECTING DUST.
AFTER ALL...
...YOU ACCOMPLISHED YOUR LIFE'S GOAL.

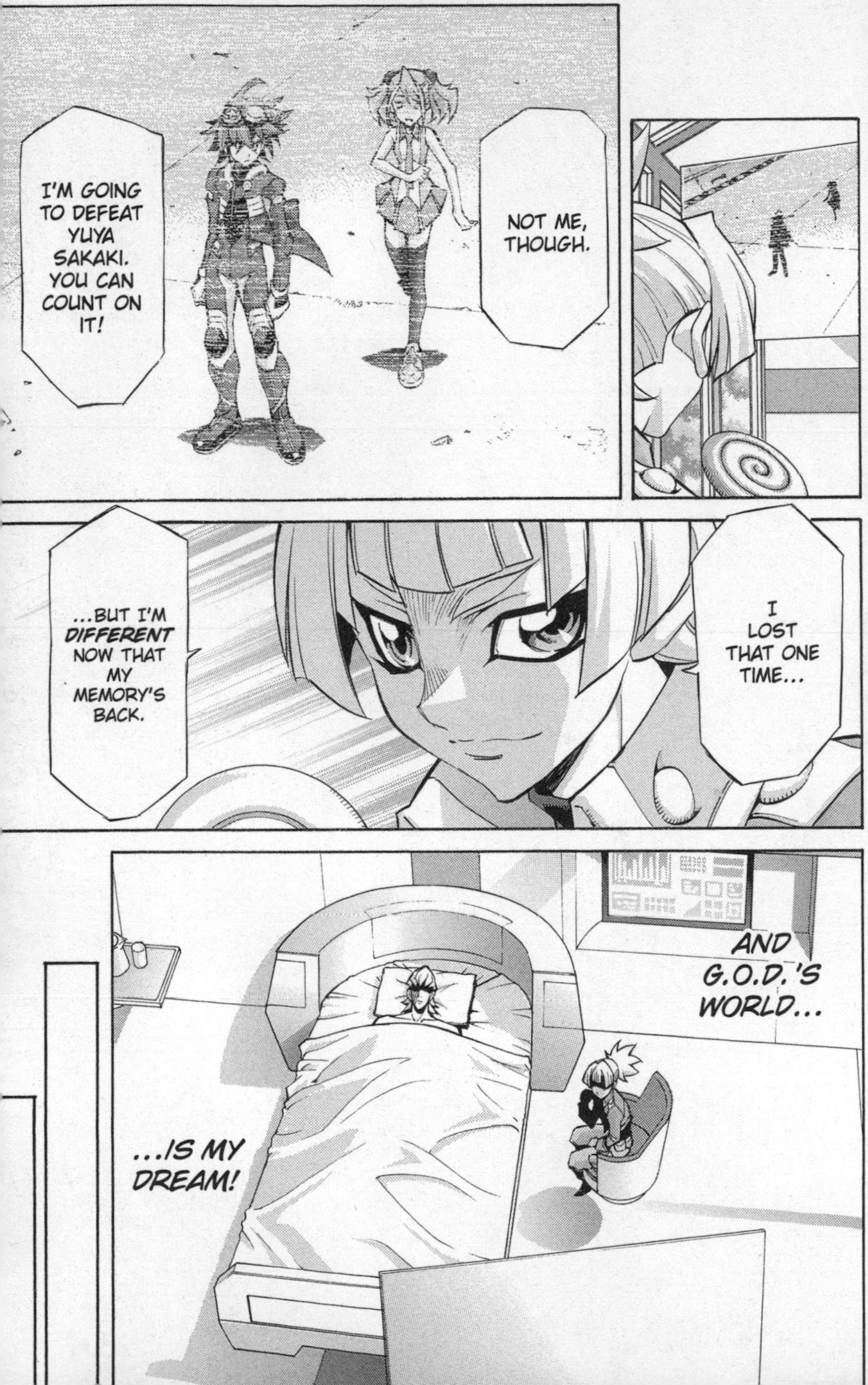
NOT ME, THOUGH.
I'M GOING TO DEFEAT YUYA SAKAKI. YOU CAN COUNT ON IT!
I LOST THAT ONE TIME...
...BUT I'M *DIFFERENT* NOW THAT MY MEMORY'S BACK.
AND G.O.D.'S WORLD...
...IS MY DREAM!

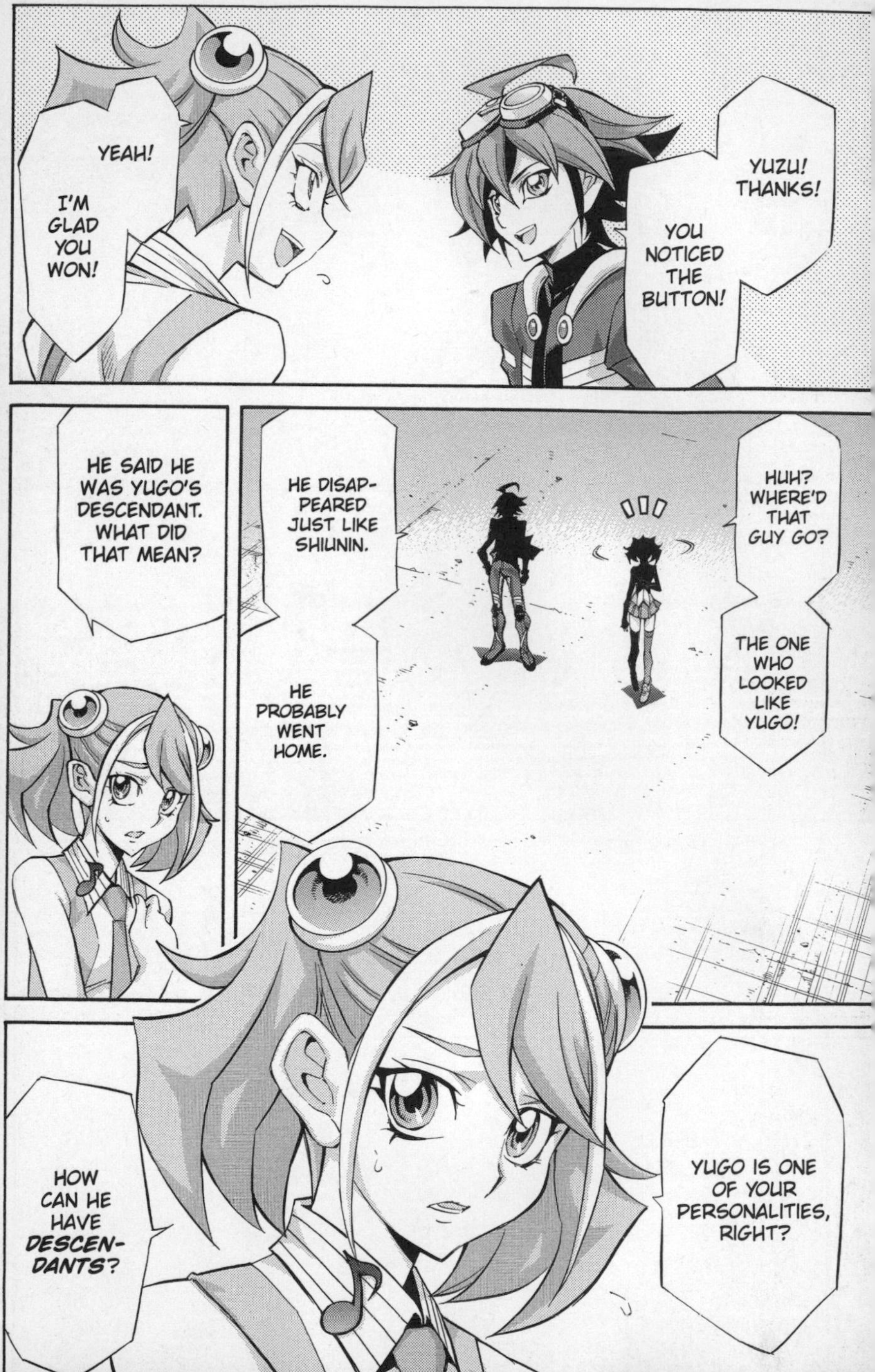
YUZU! THANKS!
YOU NOTICED THE BUTTON!
YEAH!
I'M GLAD YOU WON!
HUH? WHERE'D THAT GUY GO?
THE ONE WHO LOOKED LIKE YUGO!
HE DISAP-PEARED JUST LIKE SHIUNIN.
HE PROBABLY WENT HOME.
HE SAID HE WAS YUGO'S DESCENDANT. WHAT DID THAT MEAN?
YUGO IS ONE OF YOUR PERSONALITIES, RIGHT?
HOW CAN HE HAVE *DESCEN-DANTS*?

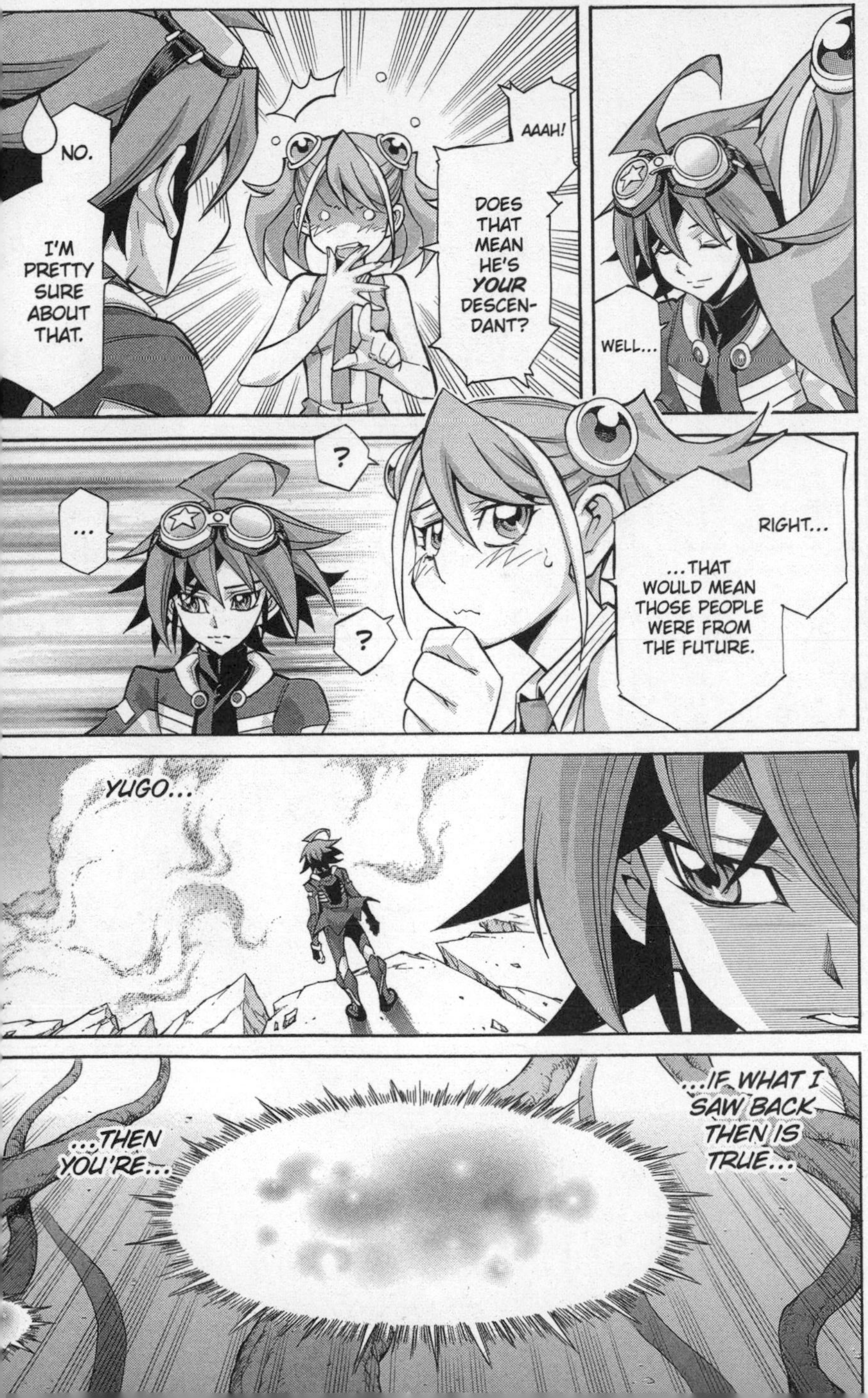
WELL...
AAAH!
DOES THAT MEAN HE'S ***YOUR*** DESCENDANT?
NO.
I'M PRETTY SURE ABOUT THAT.
RIGHT...
...THAT WOULD MEAN THOSE PEOPLE WERE FROM THE FUTURE.
?
...
?
YUGO...
...IF WHAT I SAW BACK THEN IS TRUE...
...THEN YOU'RE...

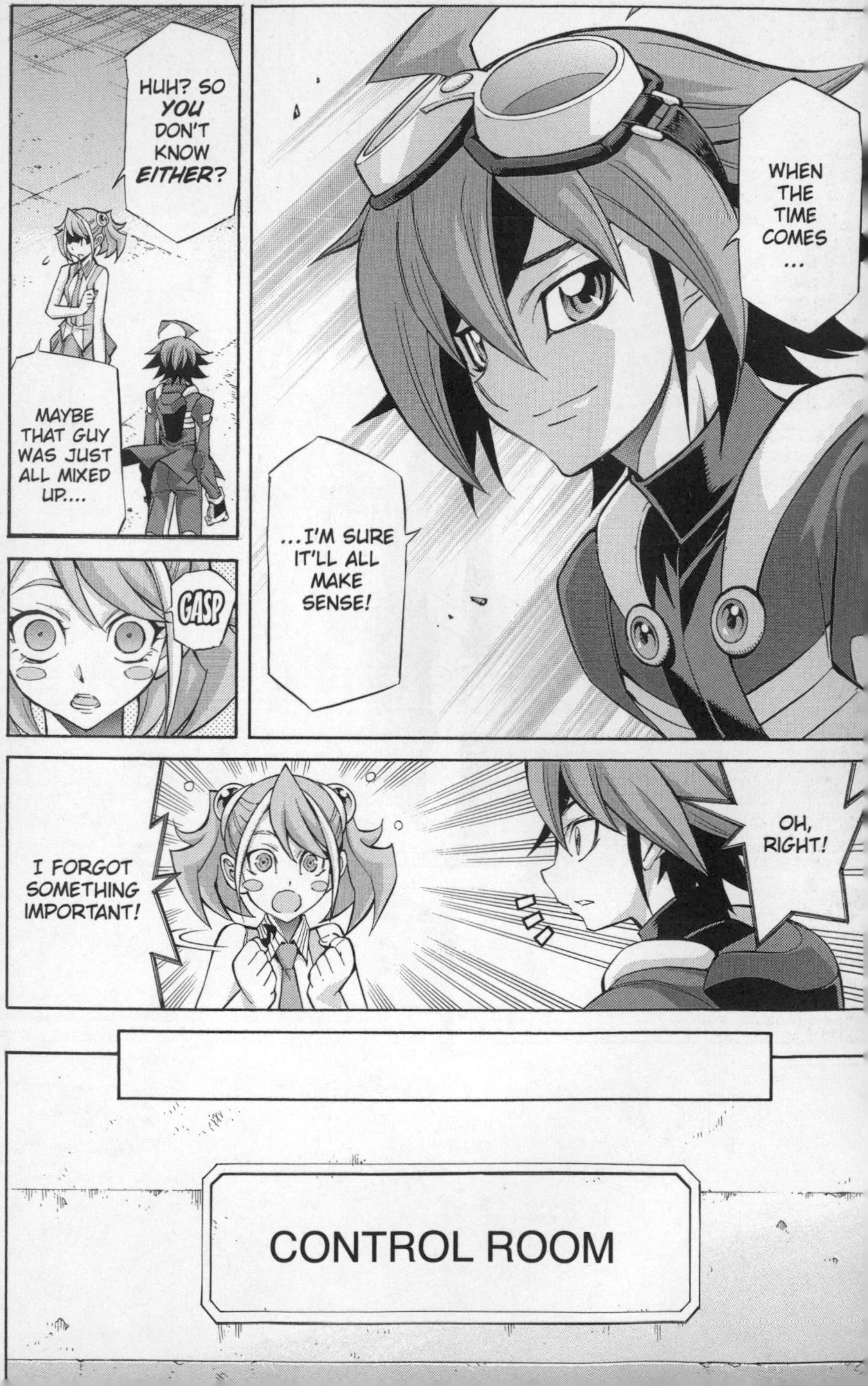
WHEN THE TIME COMES ...
...I'M SURE IT'LL ALL MAKE SENSE!
HUH? SO YOU DON'T KNOW EITHER?
MAYBE THAT GUY WAS JUST ALL MIXED UP....
GASP
OH, RIGHT!
I FORGOT SOMETHING IMPORTANT!
CONTROL ROOM

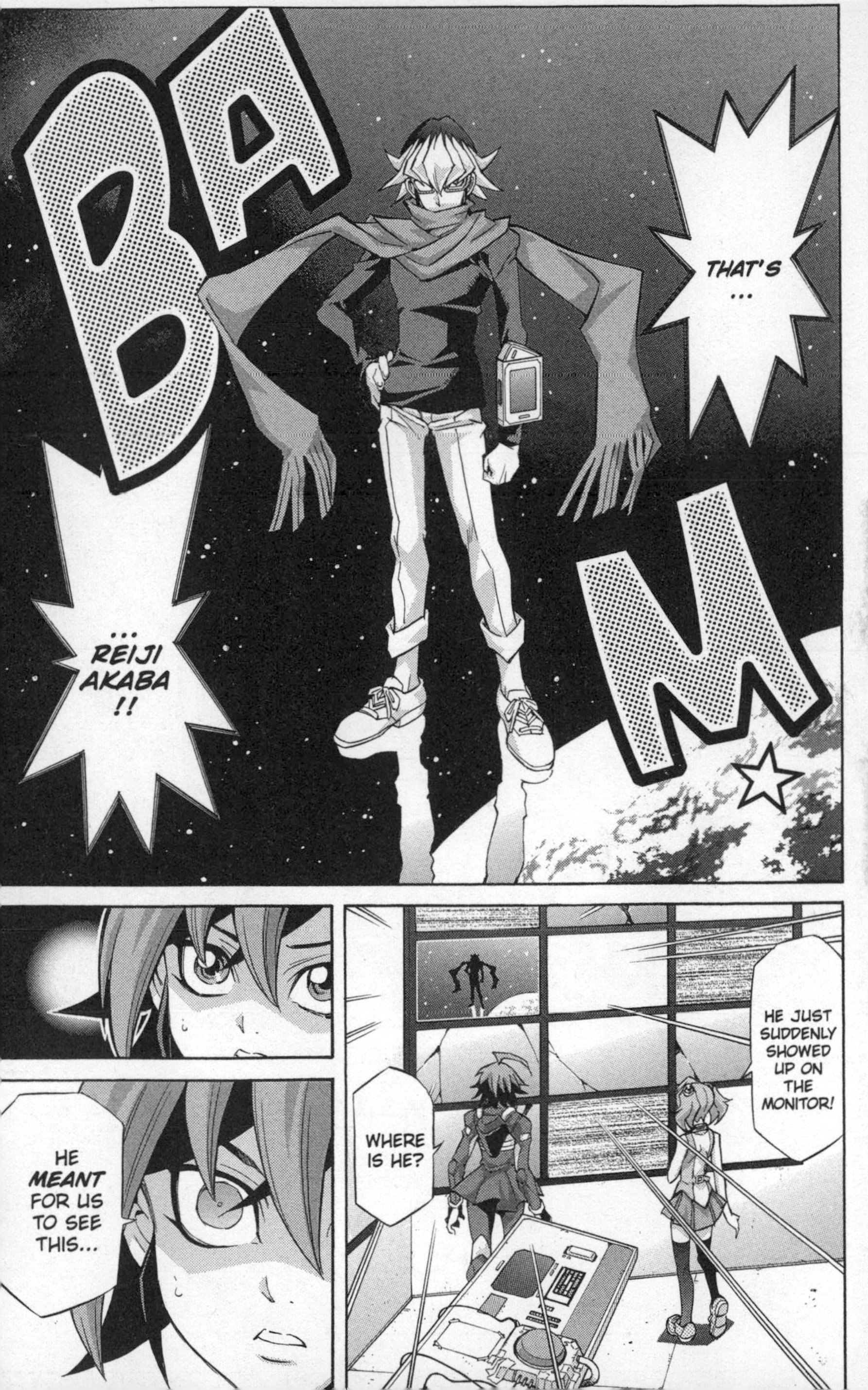
THAT'S ...
BAM
... REIJI AKABA !!
HE JUST SUDDENLY SHOWED UP ON THE MONITOR!
WHERE IS HE?
HE *MEANT* FOR US TO SEE THIS...

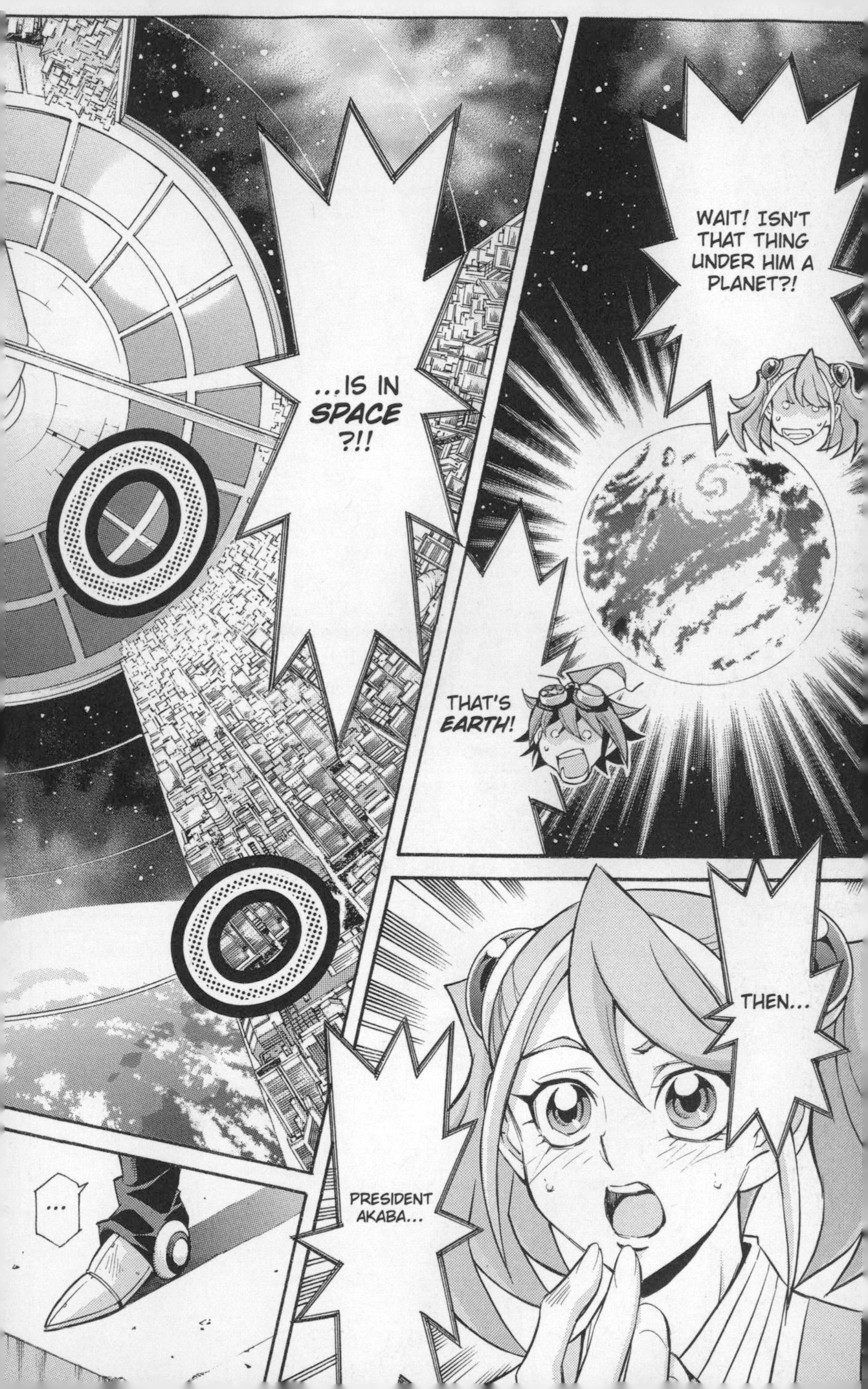
WAIT! ISN'T THAT THING UNDER HIM A PLANET?!
THAT'S *EARTH*!
THEN...
PRESIDENT AKABA...
...IS IN *SPACE* ?!!
...

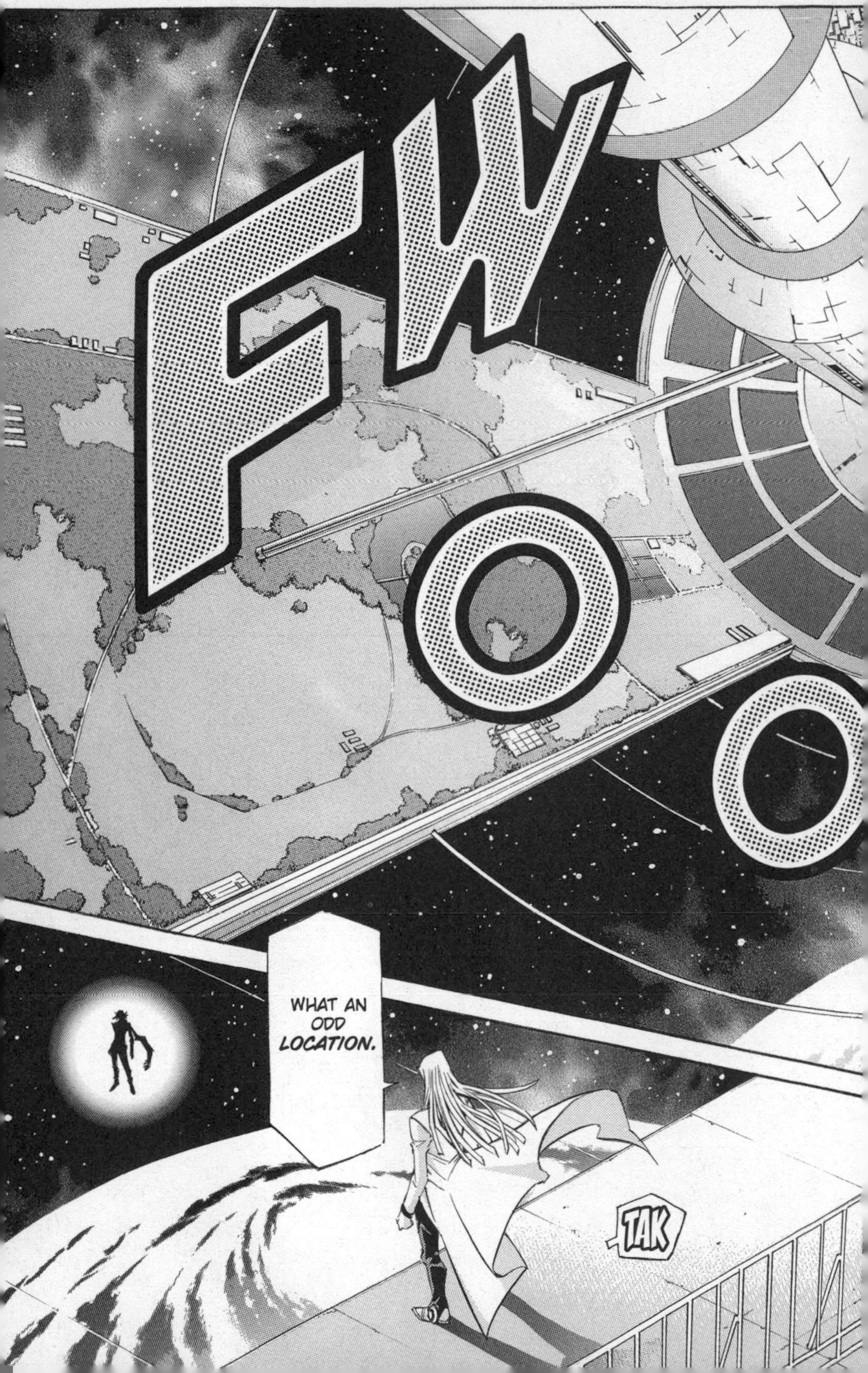
FWOOO
WHAT AN ODD LOCATION.
TAK

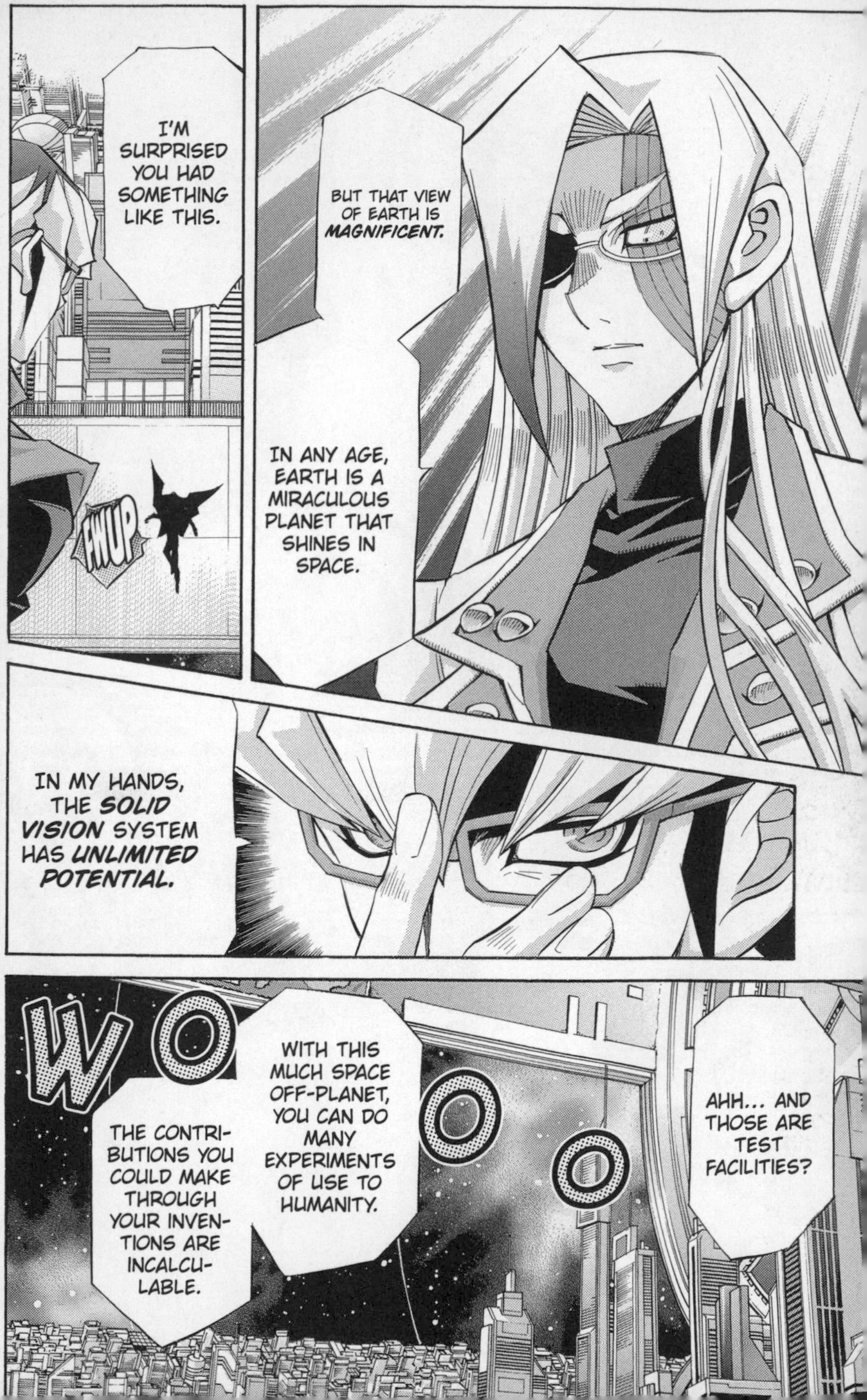
BUT THAT VIEW OF EARTH IS *MAGNIFICENT.*
IN ANY AGE, EARTH IS A MIRACULOUS PLANET THAT SHINES IN SPACE.
I'M SURPRISED YOU HAD SOMETHING LIKE THIS.
FWUP
IN MY HANDS, THE ***SOLID VISION*** SYSTEM HAS ***UNLIMITED POTENTIAL.***
AHH... AND THOSE ARE TEST FACILITIES?
WITH THIS MUCH SPACE OFF-PLANET, YOU CAN DO MANY EXPERIMENTS OF USE TO HUMANITY.
THE CONTRIBUTIONS YOU COULD MAKE THROUGH YOUR INVENTIONS ARE INCALCULABLE.
WOOOO

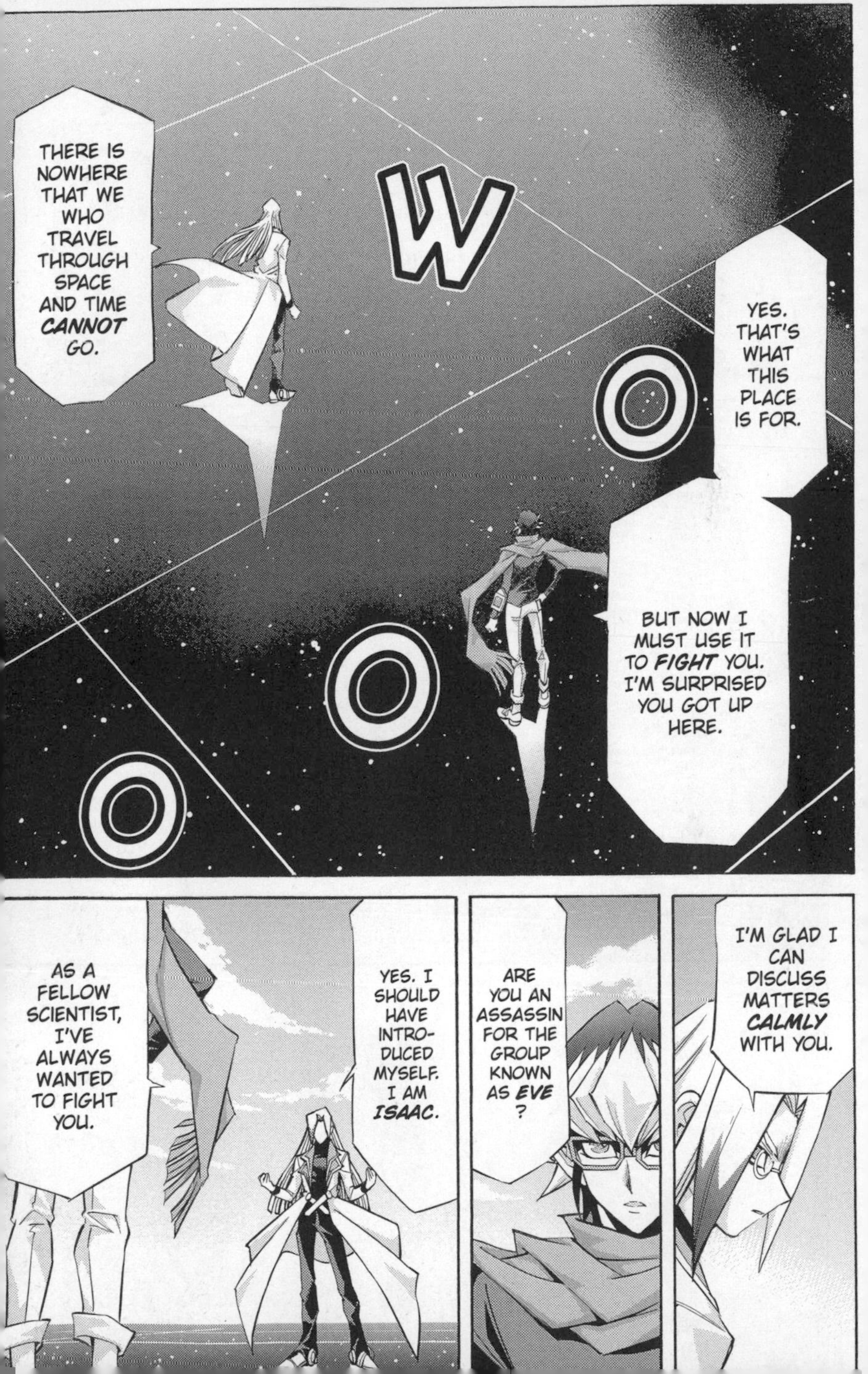
THERE IS NOWHERE THAT WE WHO TRAVEL THROUGH SPACE AND TIME *CANNOT* GO.
W
YES. THAT'S WHAT THIS PLACE IS FOR.
BUT NOW I MUST USE IT TO *FIGHT* YOU. I'M SURPRISED YOU GOT UP HERE.
I'M GLAD I CAN DISCUSS MATTERS *CALMLY* WITH YOU.
ARE YOU AN ASSASSIN FOR THE GROUP KNOWN AS *EVE* ?
YES. I SHOULD HAVE INTRO-DUCED MYSELF. I AM *ISAAC*.
AS A FELLOW SCIENTIST, I'VE ALWAYS WANTED TO FIGHT YOU.

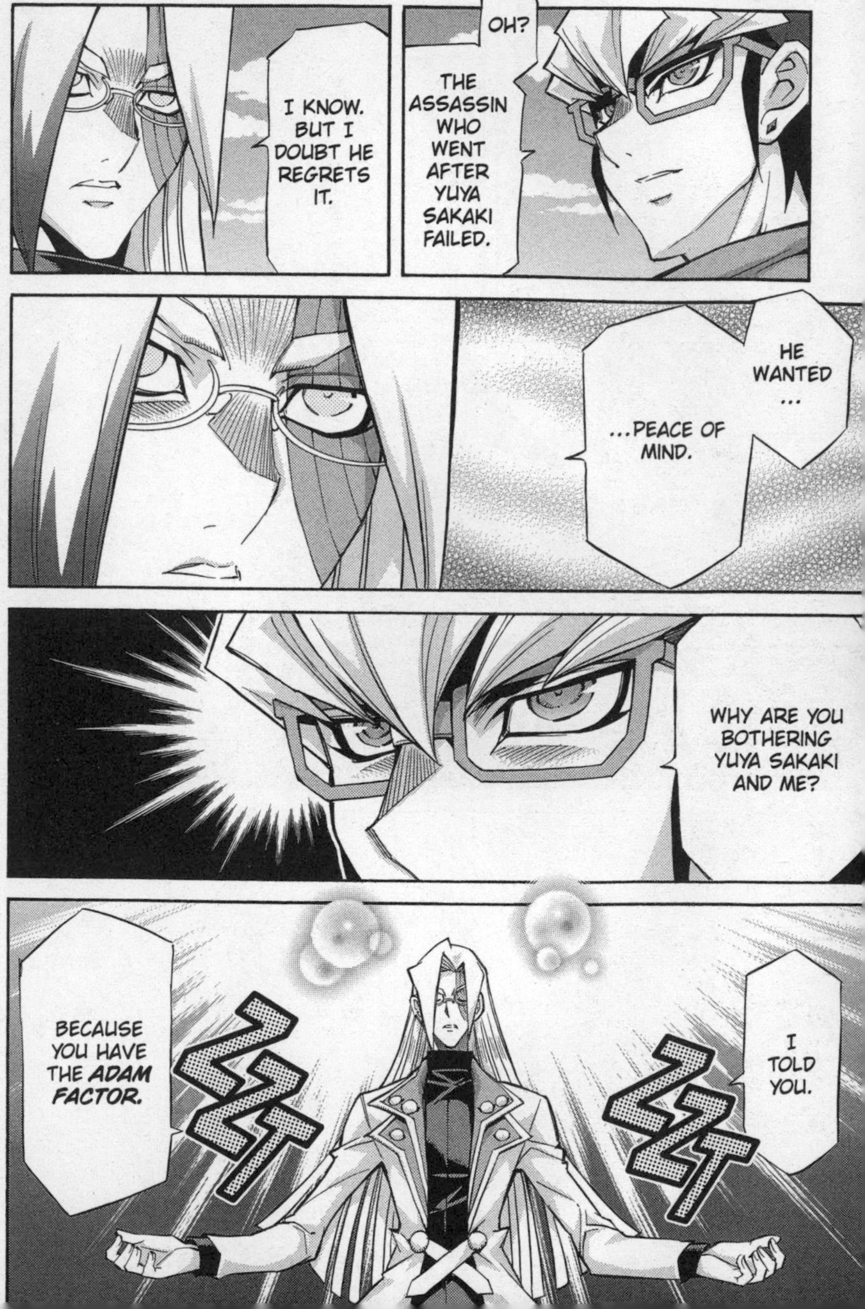
OH?
THE ASSASSIN WHO WENT AFTER YUYA SAKAKI FAILED.
I KNOW. BUT I DOUBT HE REGRETS IT.
HE WANTED...
...PEACE OF MIND.
WHY ARE YOU BOTHERING YUYA SAKAKI AND ME?
I TOLD YOU.
ZZT
ZZT
BECAUSE YOU HAVE THE *ADAM FACTOR.*

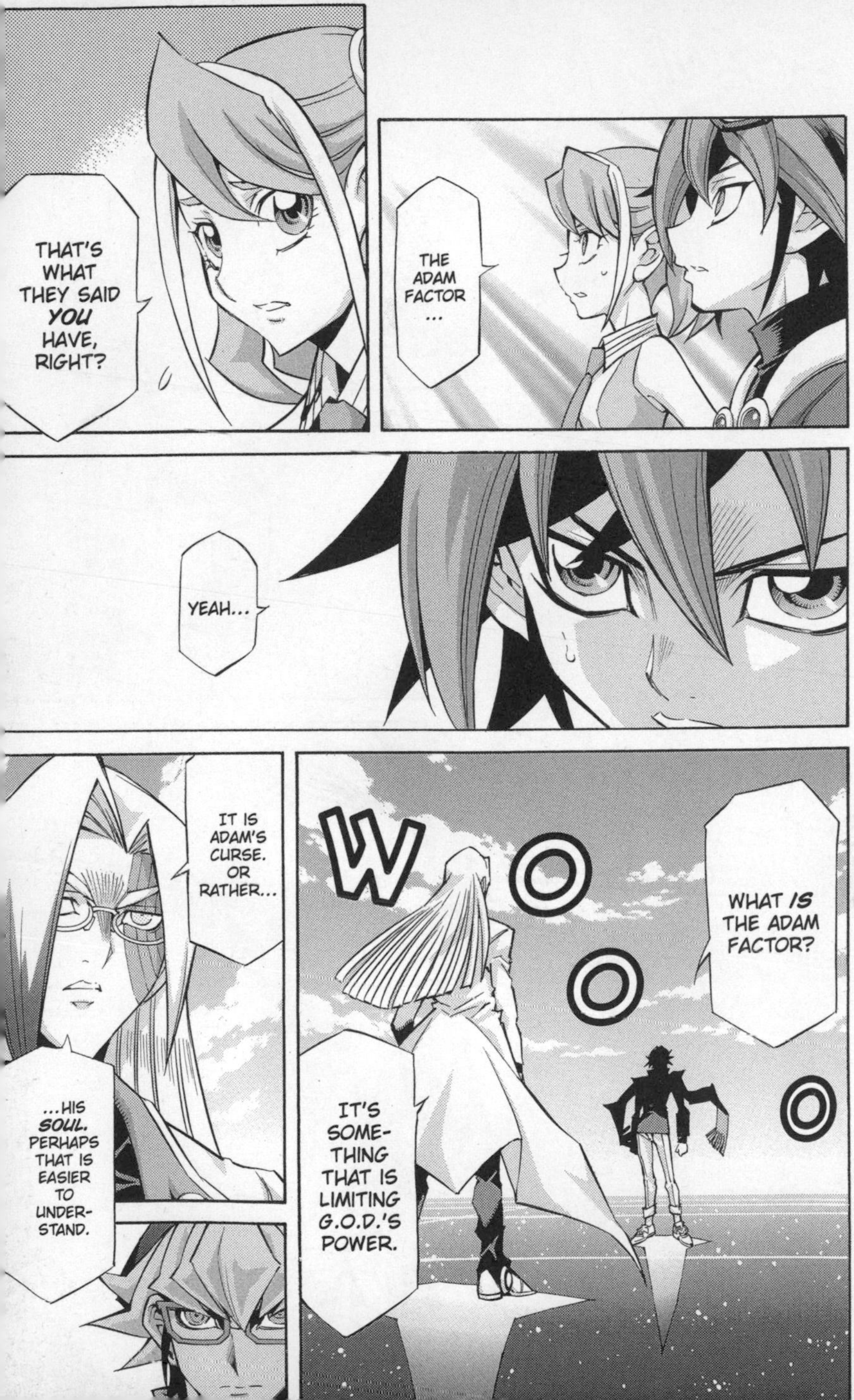
THE ADAM FACTOR ...
THAT'S WHAT THEY SAID *YOU* HAVE, RIGHT?
YEAH...
WHAT *IS* THE ADAM FACTOR?
WOOO
IT'S SOME-THING THAT IS LIMITING G.O.D.'S POWER.
IT IS ADAM'S CURSE. OR RATHER...
...HIS *SOUL.* PERHAPS THAT IS EASIER TO UNDER-STAND.

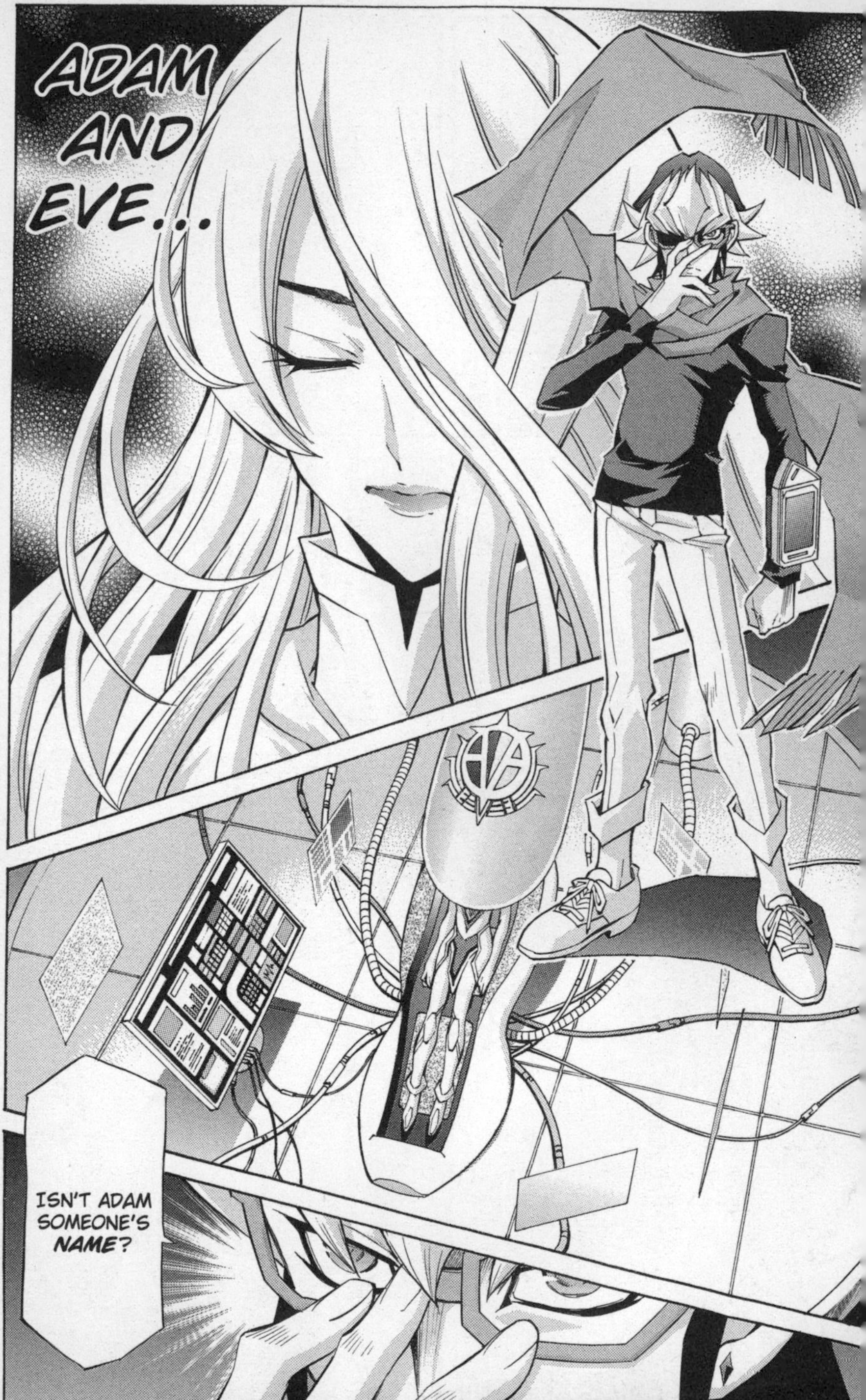
ADAM AND EVE...
ISN'T ADAM SOMEONE'S *NAME*?

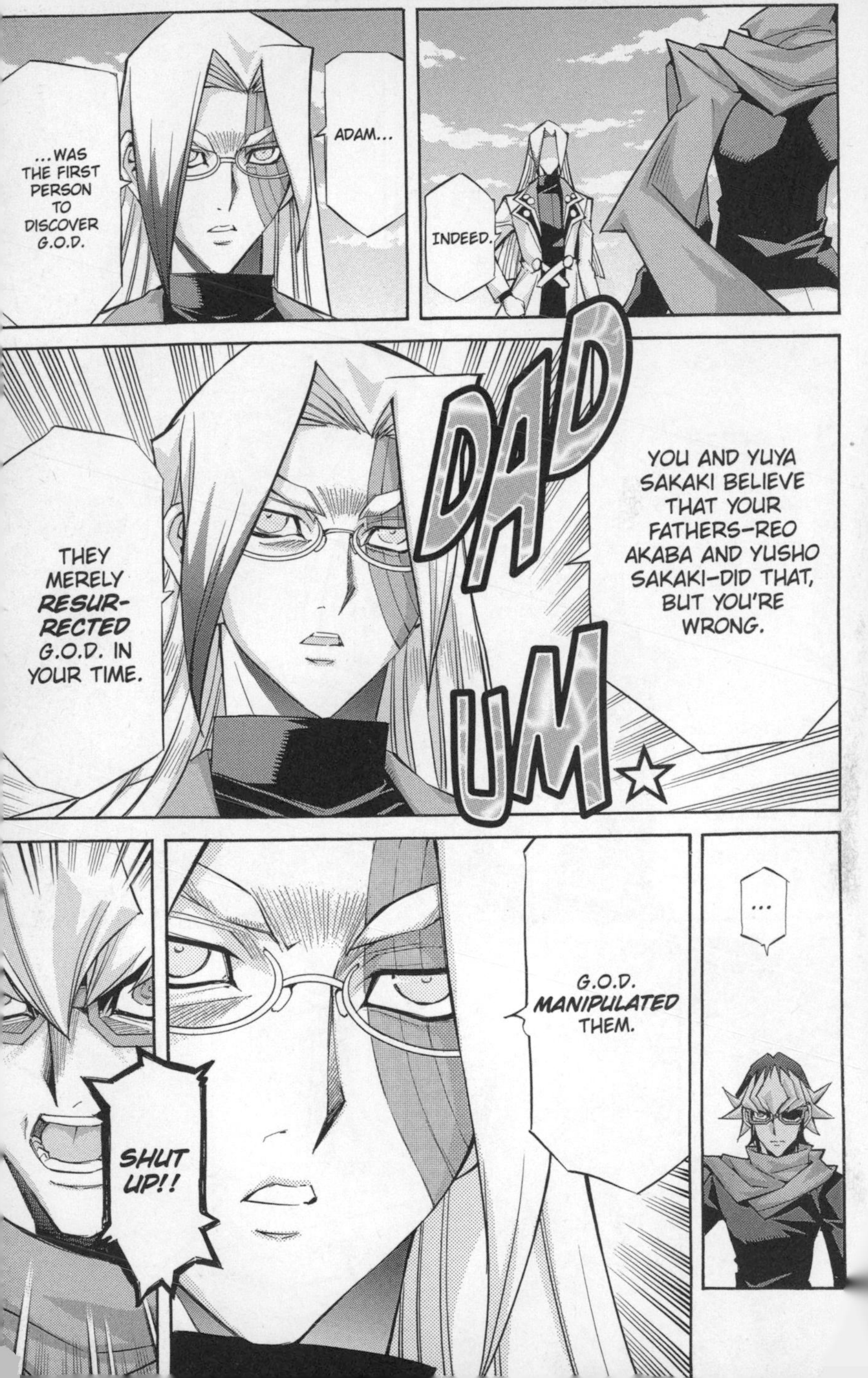
INDEED.
ADAM...
...WAS THE FIRST PERSON TO DISCOVER G.O.D.
YOU AND YUYA SAKAKI BELIEVE THAT YOUR FATHERS–REO AKABA AND YUSHO SAKAKI–DID THAT, BUT YOU'RE WRONG.
DADUM☆
THEY MERELY *RESURRECTED* G.O.D. IN YOUR TIME.
...
G.O.D. *MANIPULATED* THEM.
SHUT UP!!

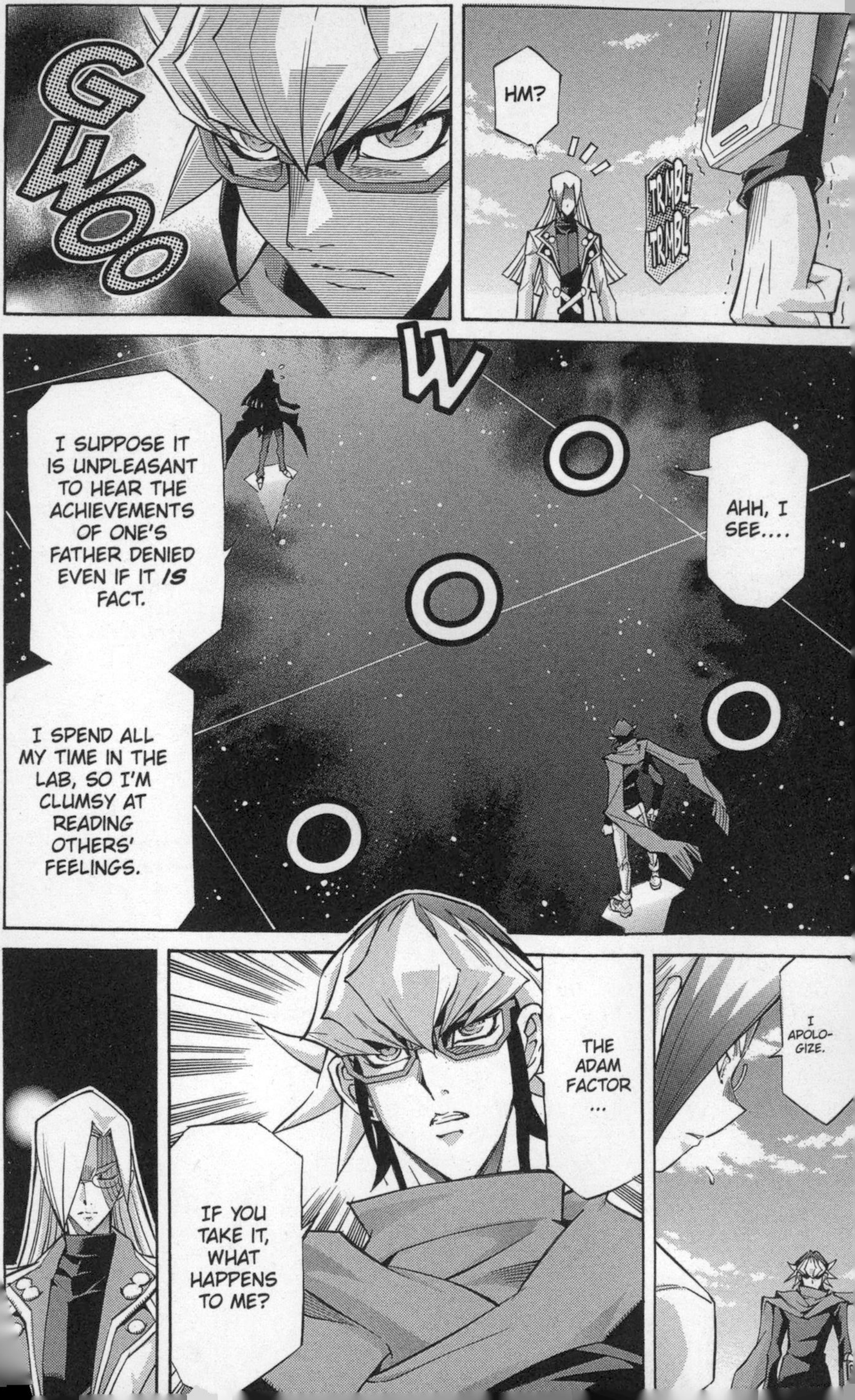
HM?
TRMBL TRMBL
GWOO
WOOOO
AHH, I SEE....
I SUPPOSE IT IS UNPLEASANT TO HEAR THE ACHIEVEMENTS OF ONE'S FATHER DENIED EVEN IF IT *IS* FACT.
I SPEND ALL MY TIME IN THE LAB, SO I'M CLUMSY AT READING OTHERS' FEELINGS.
I APOLOGIZE.
THE ADAM FACTOR ...
IF YOU TAKE IT, WHAT HAPPENS TO ME?

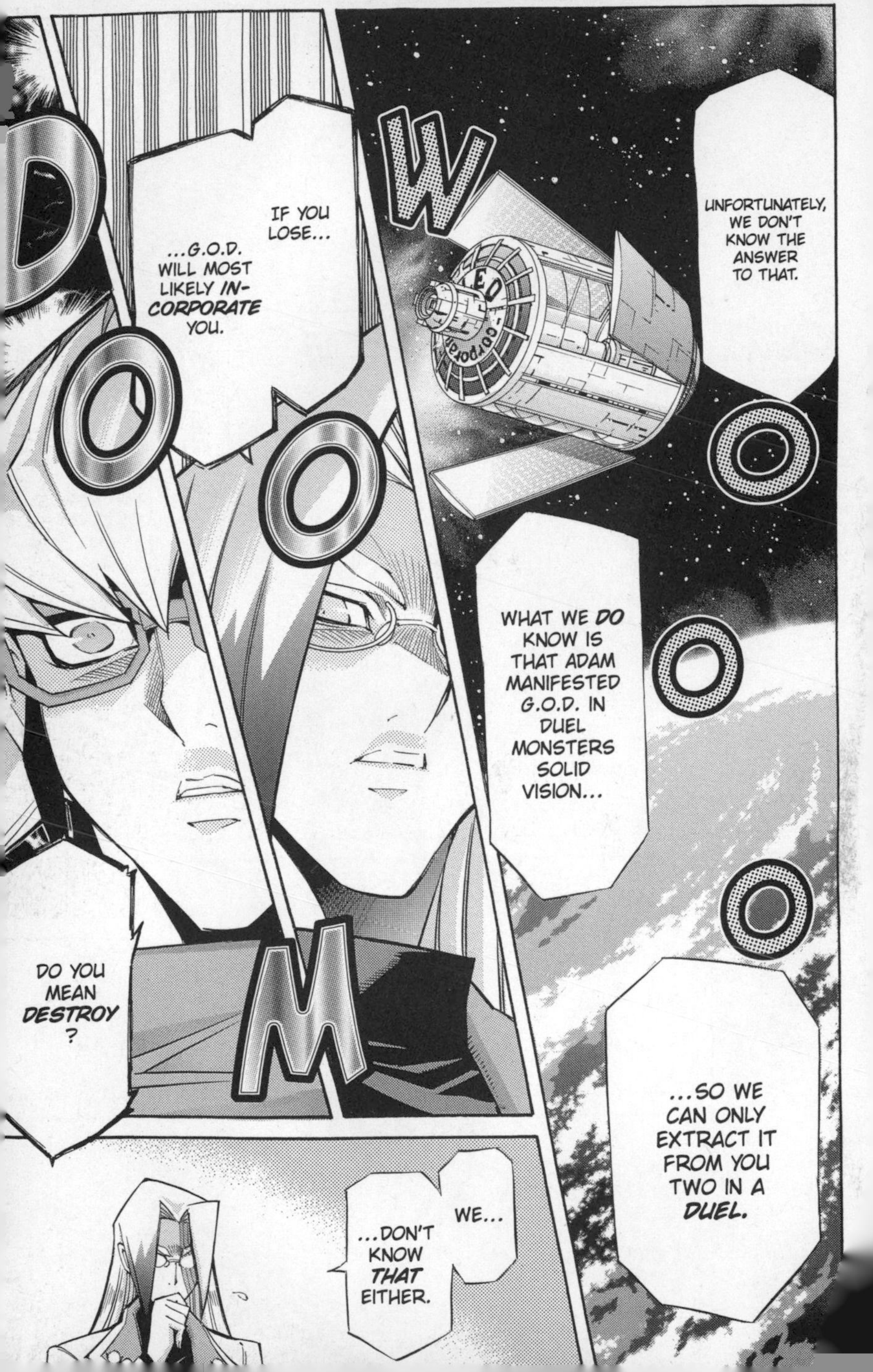
UNFORTUNATELY, WE DON'T KNOW THE ANSWER TO THAT.
WHAT WE *DO* KNOW IS THAT ADAM MANIFESTED G.O.D. IN DUEL MONSTERS SOLID VISION...
...SO WE CAN ONLY EXTRACT IT FROM YOU TWO IN A **DUEL.**
DOOWOOOM
IF YOU LOSE...
...G.O.D. WILL MOST LIKELY ***IN-CORPORATE*** YOU.
DO YOU MEAN ***DESTROY*** ?
WE...
...DON'T KNOW ***THAT*** EITHER.

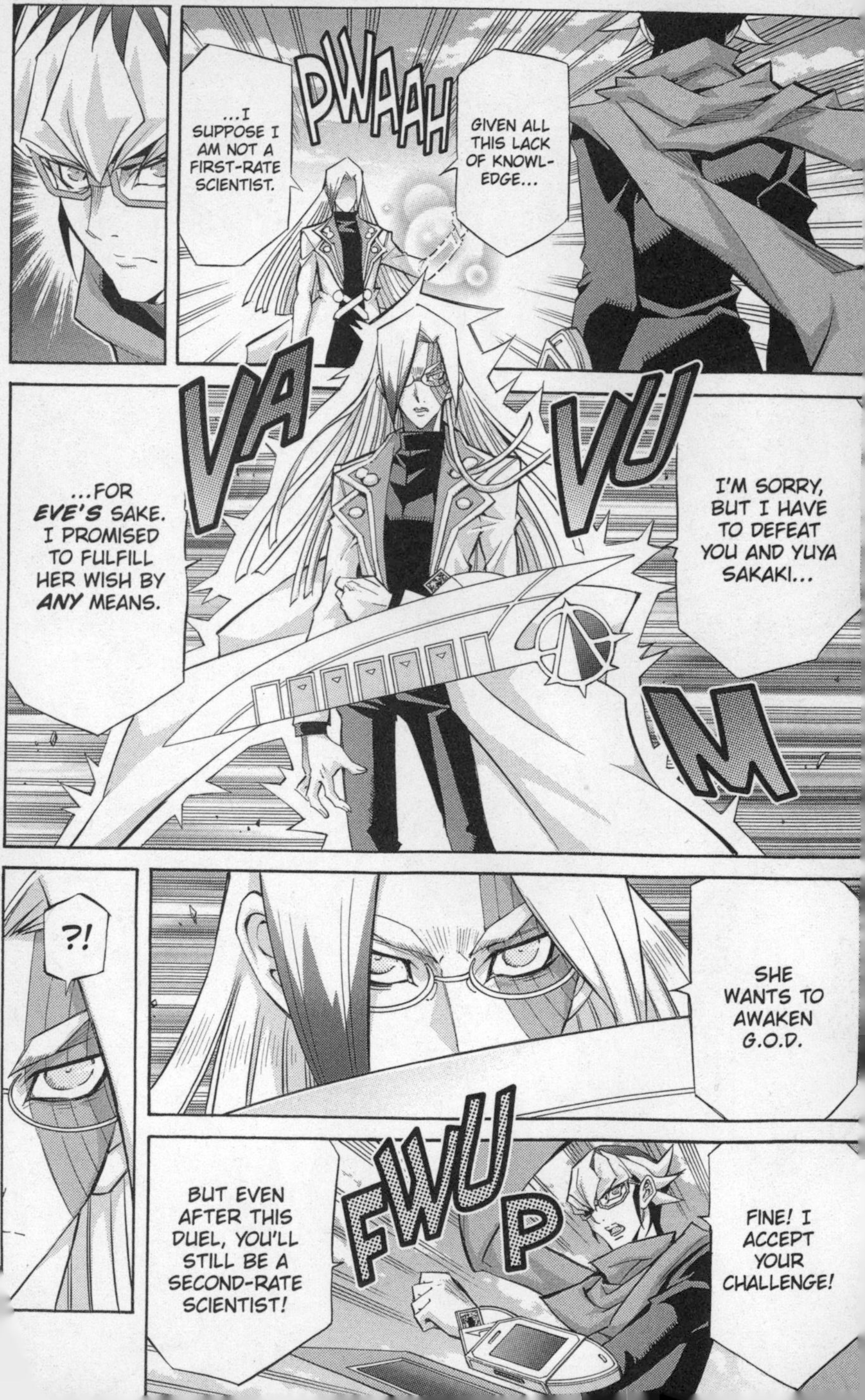
GIVEN ALL THIS LACK OF KNOWL-EDGE...
PWAAH
...I SUPPOSE I AM NOT A FIRST-RATE SCIENTIST.
I'M SORRY, BUT I HAVE TO DEFEAT YOU AND YUYA SAKAKI...
VA VU M
...FOR ***EVE'S*** SAKE. I PROMISED TO FULFILL HER WISH BY ***ANY*** MEANS.
SHE WANTS TO AWAKEN G.O.D.
FINE! I ACCEPT YOUR CHALLENGE!
FWUP
BUT EVEN AFTER THIS DUEL, YOU'LL STILL BE A SECOND-RATE SCIENTIST!
?!

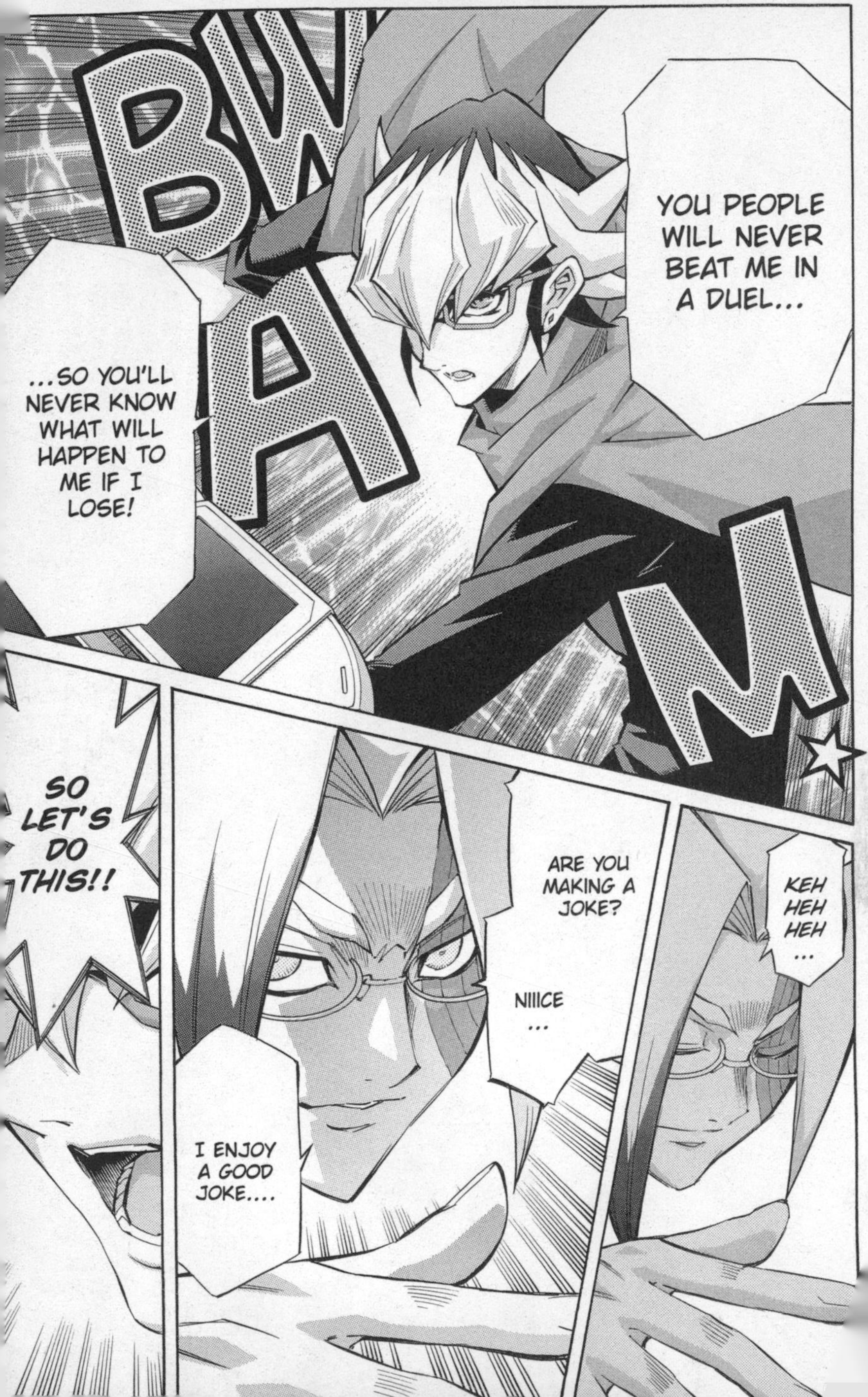
YOU PEOPLE WILL NEVER BEAT ME IN A DUEL...
BWAM
...SO YOU'LL NEVER KNOW WHAT WILL HAPPEN TO ME IF I LOSE!
KEH HEH HEH ...
ARE YOU MAKING A JOKE?
NIIICE ...
I ENJOY A GOOD JOKE....
SO LET'S DO THIS!!

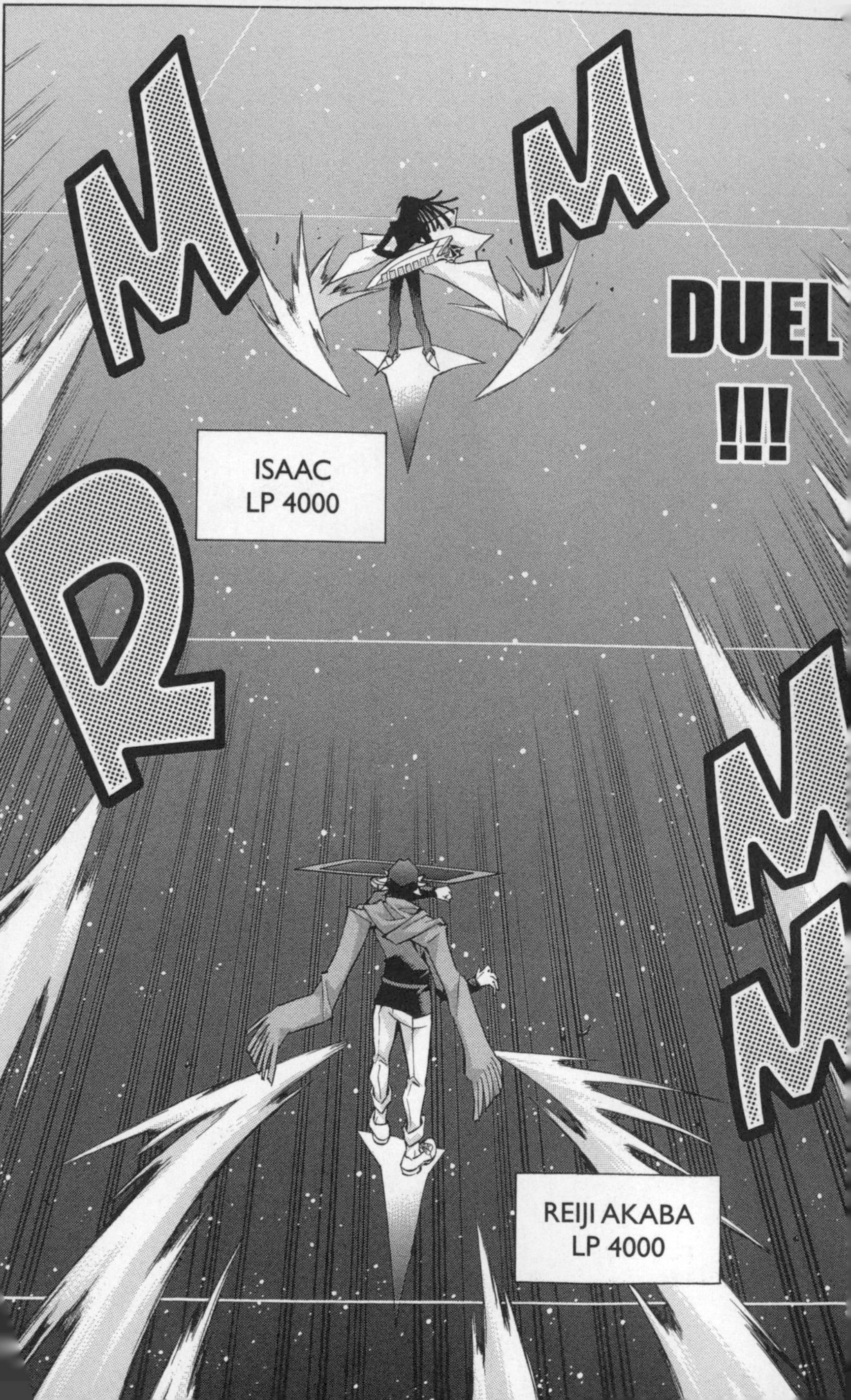
DUEL!!!
ISAAC
LP 4000
REIJI AKABA
LP 4000

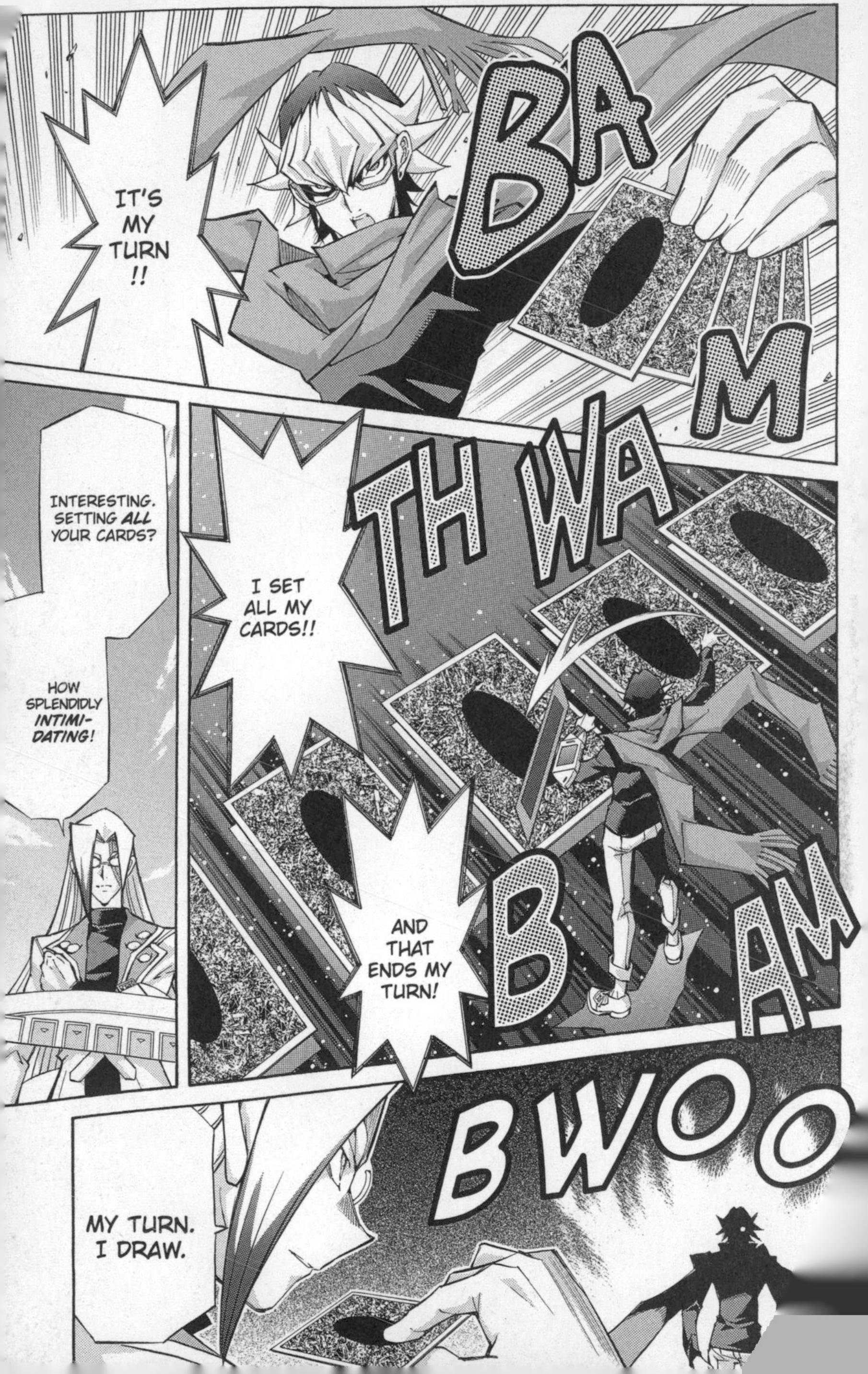
IT'S MY TURN!!
BA M
I SET ALL MY CARDS!!
TH WA
B AM
AND THAT ENDS MY TURN!
INTERESTING. SETTING *ALL* YOUR CARDS?
HOW SPLENDIDLY *INTIMIDATING!*
BWOO
MY TURN. I DRAW.

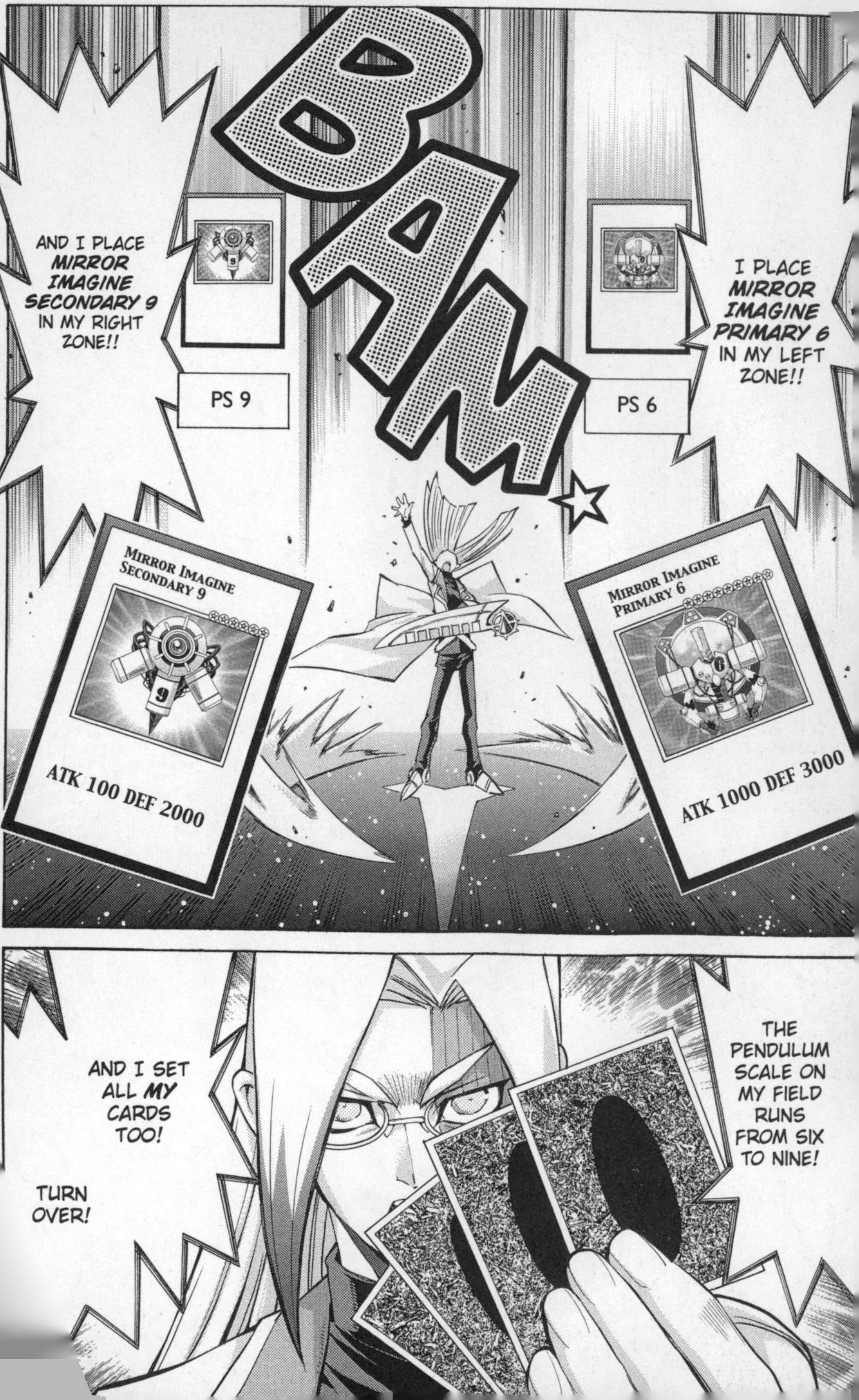
I PLACE MIRROR IMAGINE PRIMARY 6 IN MY LEFT ZONE!!
PS 6
BAM
AND I PLACE MIRROR IMAGINE SECONDARY 9 IN MY RIGHT ZONE!!
PS 9
Mirror Imagine Primary 6
ATK 1000 DEF 3000
Mirror Imagine Secondary 9
ATK 100 DEF 2000
THE PENDULUM SCALE ON MY FIELD RUNS FROM SIX TO NINE!
AND I SET ALL MY CARDS TOO!
TURN OVER!

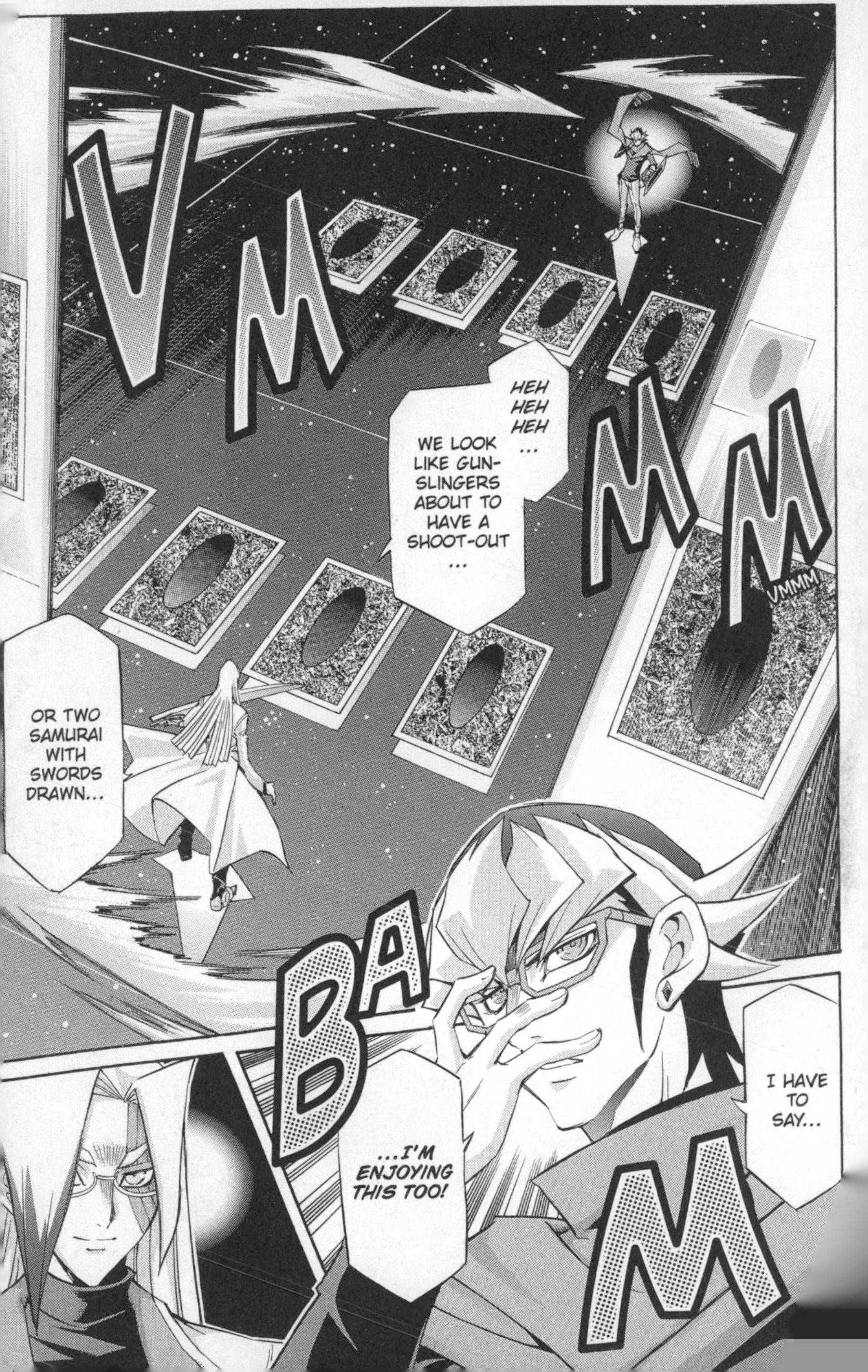
VMMMMM
HEH HEH HEH...
WE LOOK LIKE GUN-SLINGERS ABOUT TO HAVE A SHOOT-OUT...
VMMM
OR TWO SAMURAI WITH SWORDS DRAWN...
I HAVE TO SAY...
...I'M ENJOYING THIS TOO!
BAMM

Yu-Gi-Oh! ARC-V

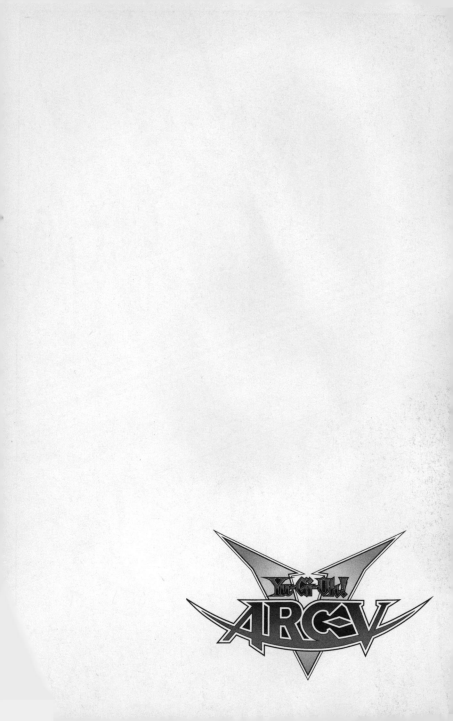

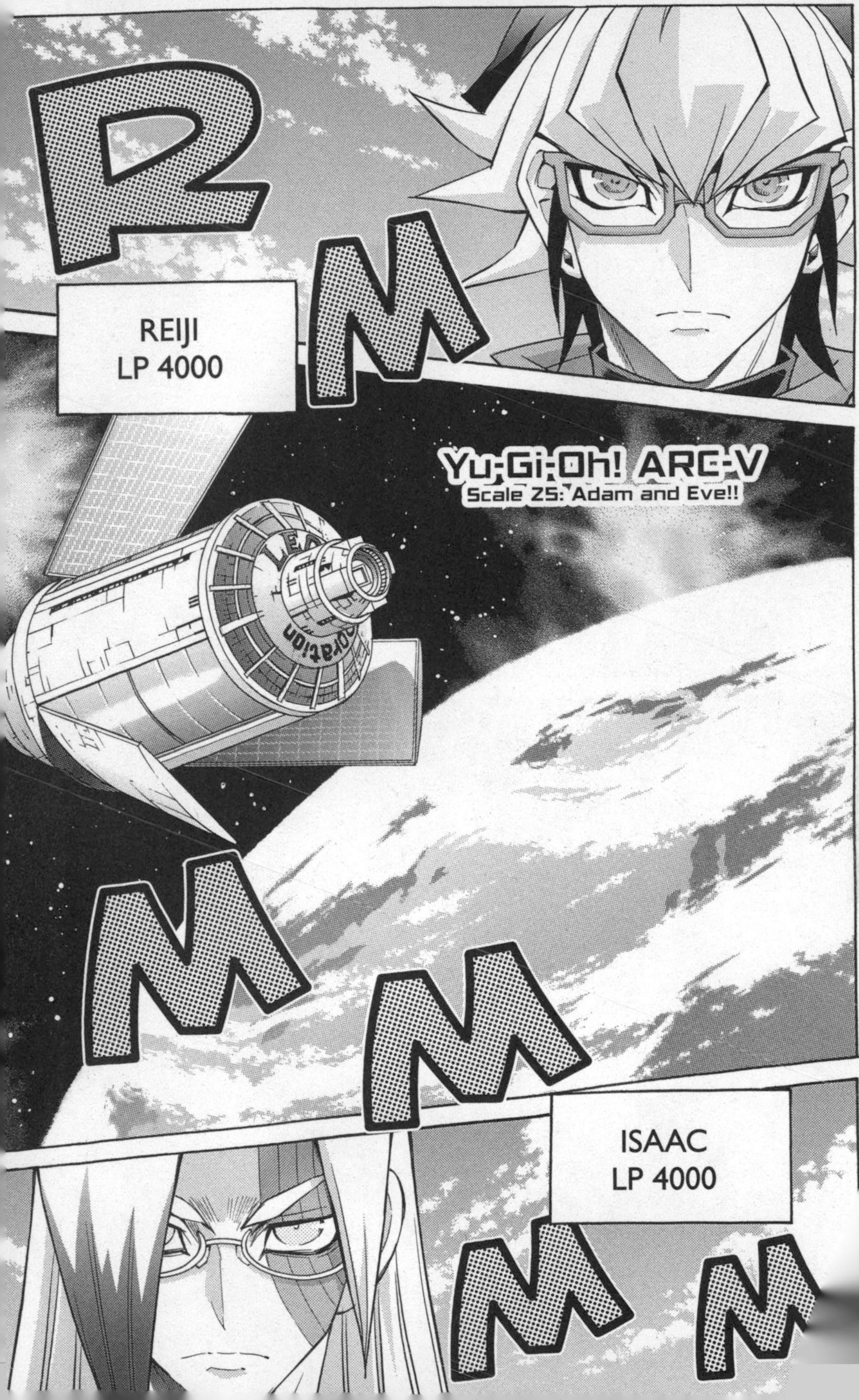
RMMMMMM
REIJI
LP 4000
Yu-Gi-Oh! ARC-V
Scale 25: Adam and Eve!!
ISAAC
LP 4000

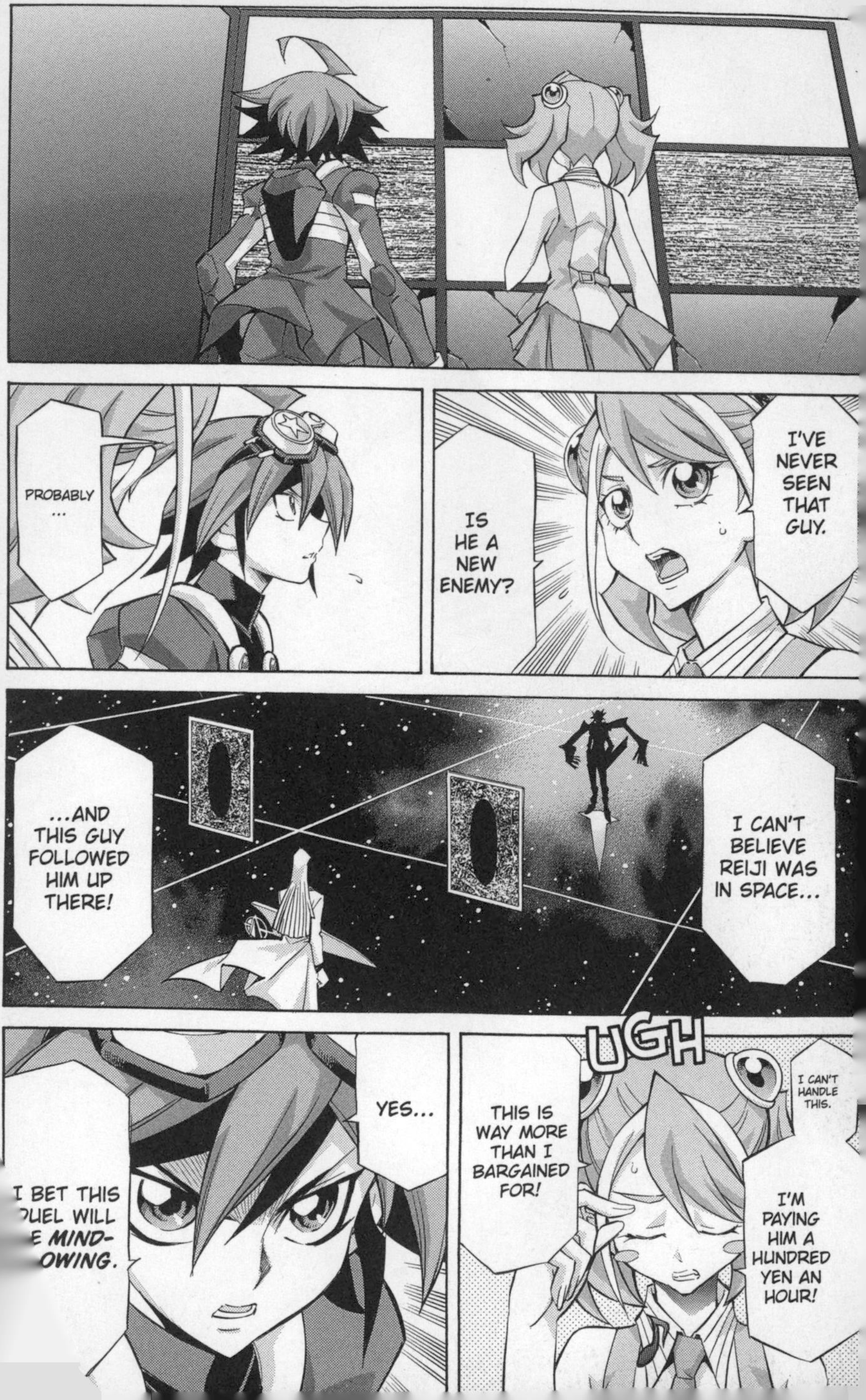
I'VE NEVER SEEN THAT GUY.
IS HE A NEW ENEMY?
PROBABLY...
I CAN'T BELIEVE REIJI WAS IN SPACE...
...AND THIS GUY FOLLOWED HIM UP THERE!
UGH
I CAN'T HANDLE THIS.
I'M PAYING HIM A HUNDRED YEN AN HOUR!
THIS IS WAY MORE THAN I BARGAINED FOR!
YES...
I BET THIS UEL WILL E MIND-OWING.

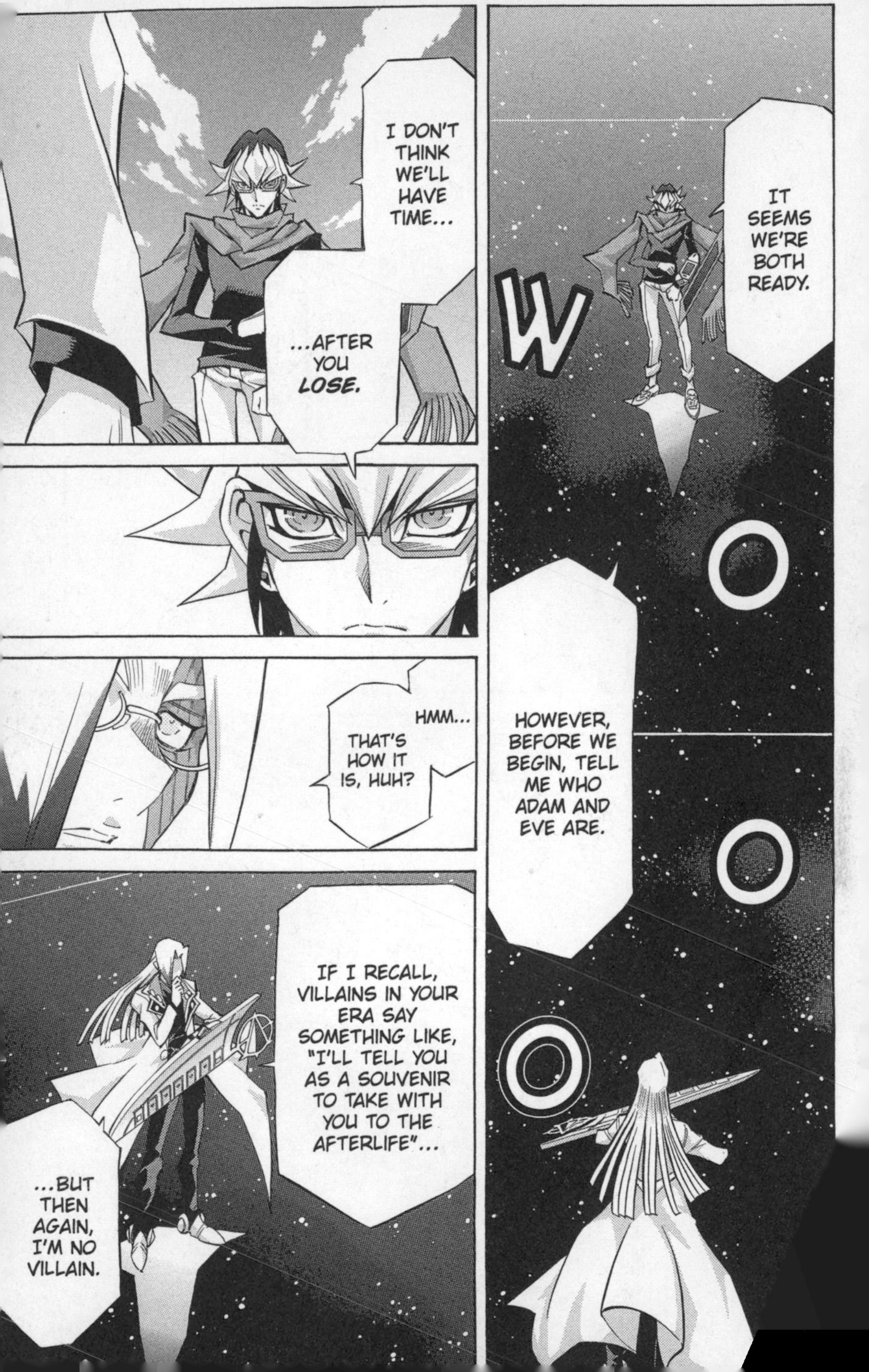

IT SEEMS WE'RE BOTH READY.
W
HOWEVER, BEFORE WE BEGIN, TELL ME WHO ADAM AND EVE ARE.
I DON'T THINK WE'LL HAVE TIME...
...AFTER YOU **LOSE.**
HMM...
THAT'S HOW IT IS, HUH?
IF I RECALL, VILLAINS IN YOUR ERA SAY SOMETHING LIKE, "I'LL TELL YOU AS A SOUVENIR TO TAKE WITH YOU TO THE AFTERLIFE"...
...BUT THEN AGAIN, I'M NO VILLAIN.

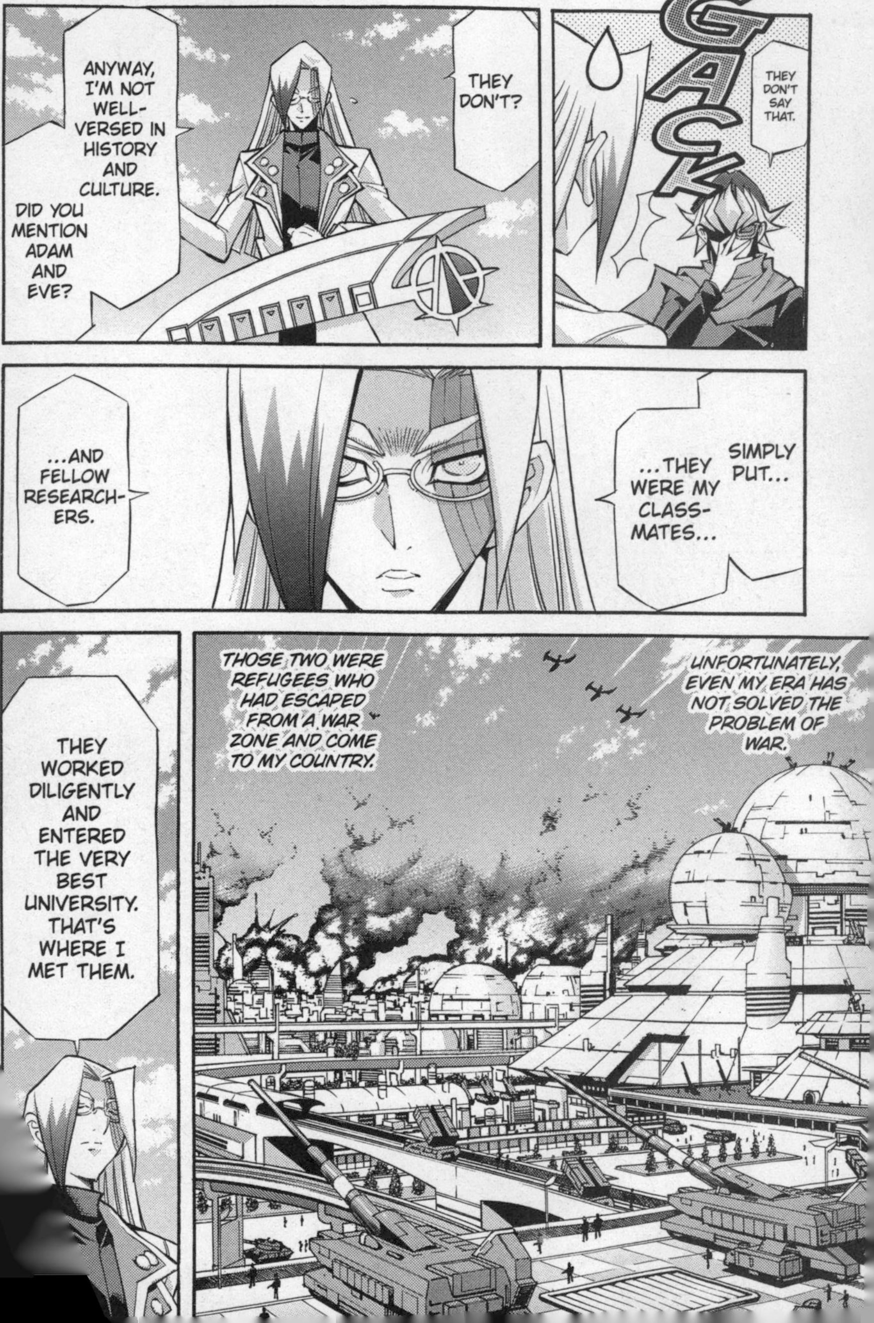
THEY DON'T SAY THAT.
GACK
THEY DON'T?
ANYWAY, I'M NOT WELL-VERSED IN HISTORY AND CULTURE.
DID YOU MENTION ADAM AND EVE?
SIMPLY PUT...
...THEY WERE MY CLASSMATES...
...AND FELLOW RESEARCHERS.
UNFORTUNATELY, EVEN MY ERA HAS NOT SOLVED THE PROBLEM OF WAR.
THOSE TWO WERE REFUGEES WHO HAD ESCAPED FROM A WAR ZONE AND COME TO MY COUNTRY.
THEY WORKED DILIGENTLY AND ENTERED THE VERY BEST UNIVERSITY. THAT'S WHERE I MET THEM.

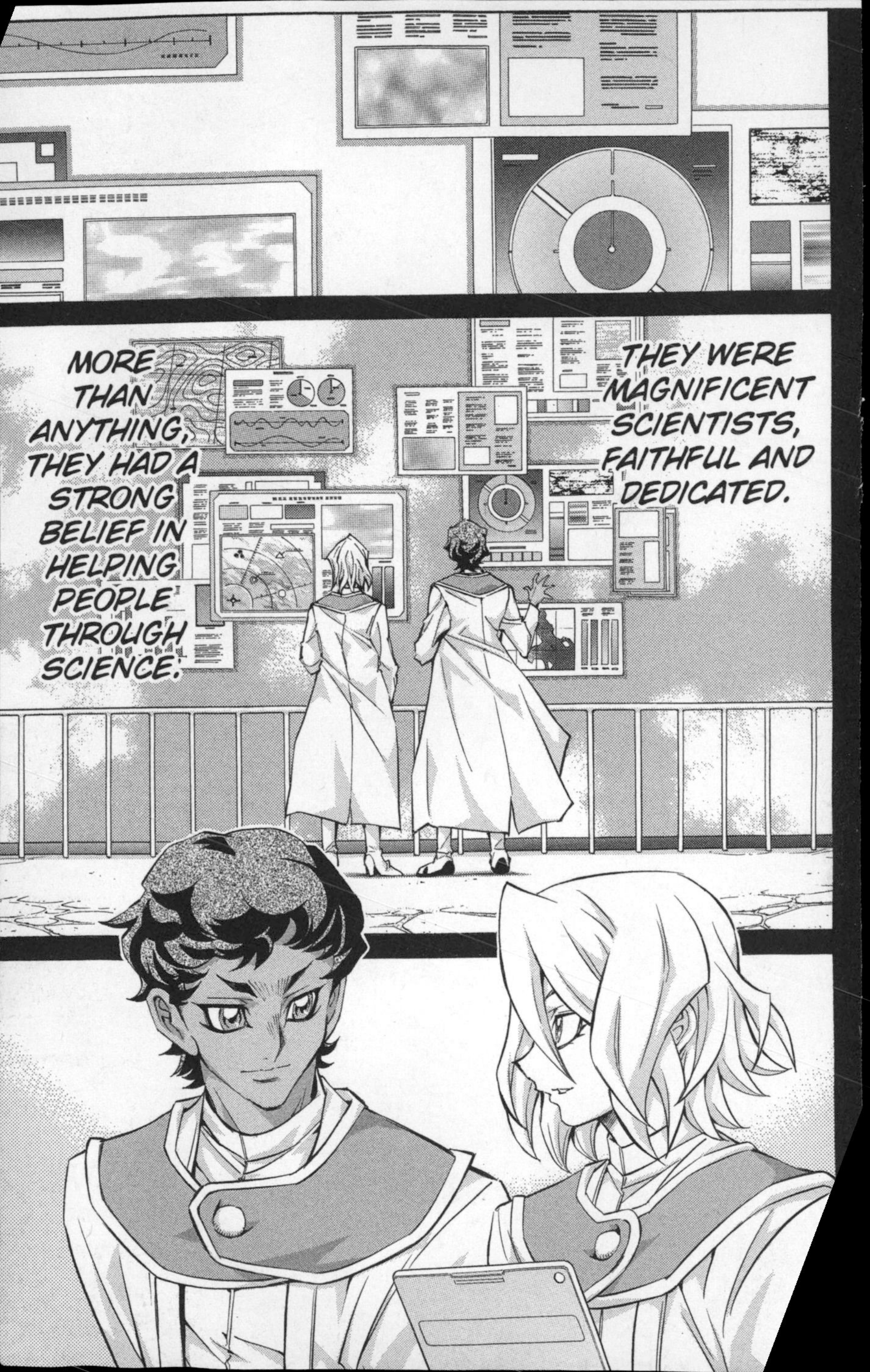
THEY WERE MAGNIFICENT SCIENTISTS, FAITHFUL AND DEDICATED.
MORE THAN ANYTHING, THEY HAD A STRONG BELIEF IN HELPING PEOPLE THROUGH SCIENCE.

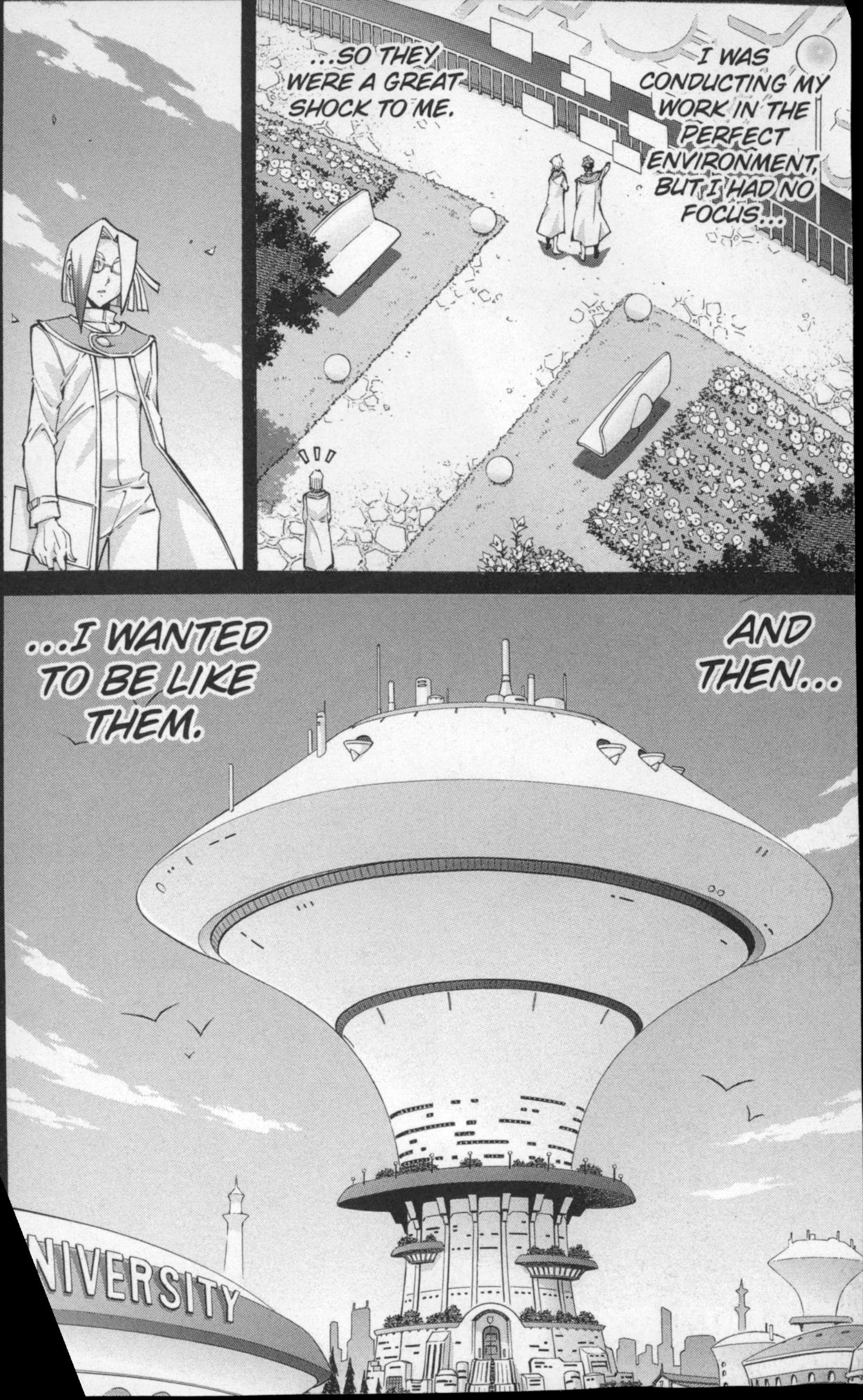
I WAS CONDUCTING MY WORK IN THE PERFECT ENVIRONMENT, BUT I HAD NO FOCUS...
...SO THEY WERE A GREAT SHOCK TO ME.
AND THEN...
...I WANTED TO BE LIKE THEM.
NIVERSITY

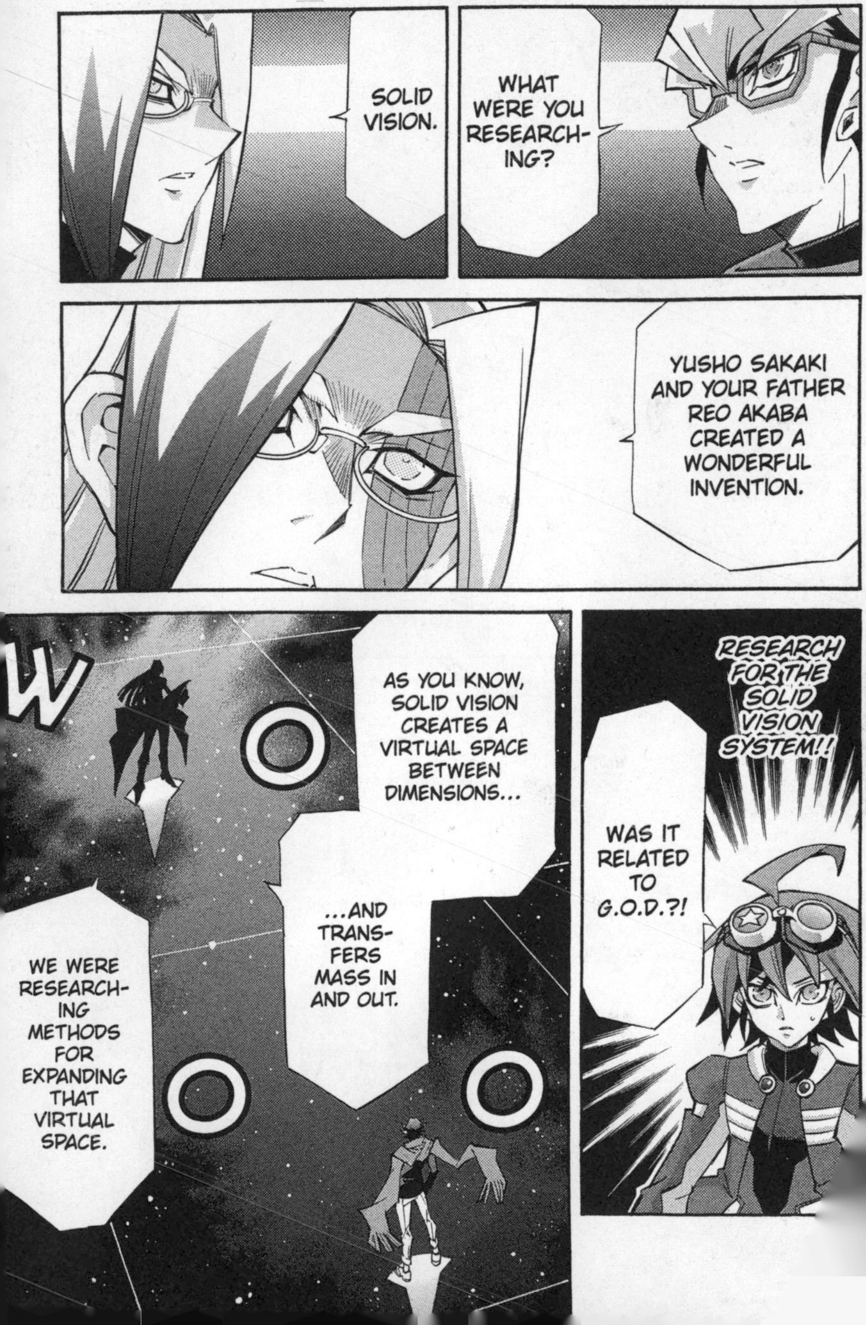
WHAT WERE YOU RESEARCHING?
SOLID VISION.
YUSHO SAKAKI AND YOUR FATHER REO AKABA CREATED A WONDERFUL INVENTION.
RESEARCH FOR THE SOLID VISION SYSTEM!!
WAS IT RELATED TO G.O.D.?!
AS YOU KNOW, SOLID VISION CREATES A VIRTUAL SPACE BETWEEN DIMENSIONS...
...AND TRANSFERS MASS IN AND OUT.
WE WERE RESEARCHING METHODS FOR EXPANDING THAT VIRTUAL SPACE.

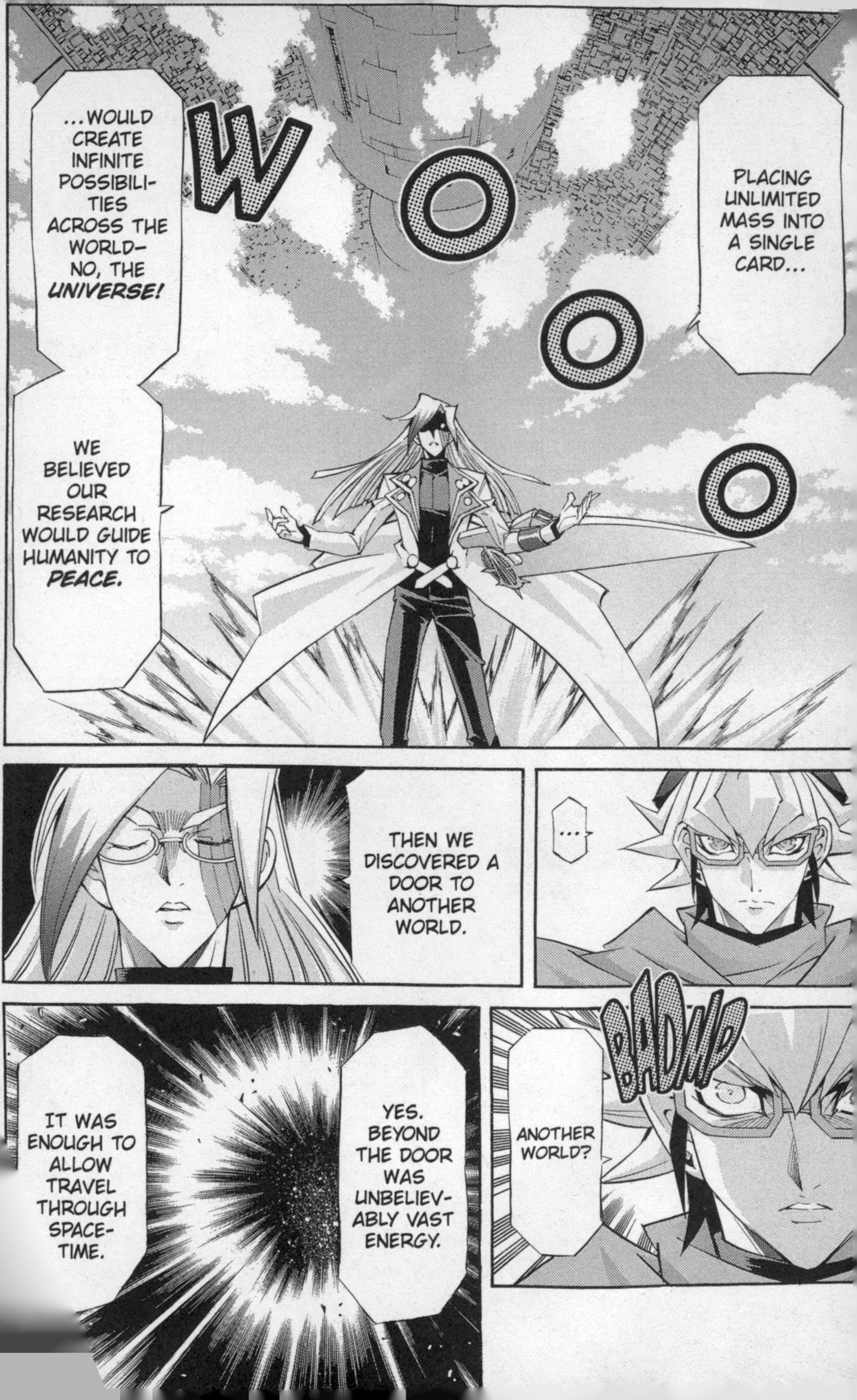
PLACING UNLIMITED MASS INTO A SINGLE CARD...
WOOO
...WOULD CREATE INFINITE POSSIBILI-TIES ACROSS THE WORLD— NO, THE *UNIVERSE!*
WE BELIEVED OUR RESEARCH WOULD GUIDE HUMANITY TO *PEACE.*
...
THEN WE DISCOVERED A DOOR TO ANOTHER WORLD.
BADMP
ANOTHER WORLD?
YES. BEYOND THE DOOR WAS UNBELIEV-ABLY VAST ENERGY.
IT WAS ENOUGH TO ALLOW TRAVEL THROUGH SPACE-TIME.

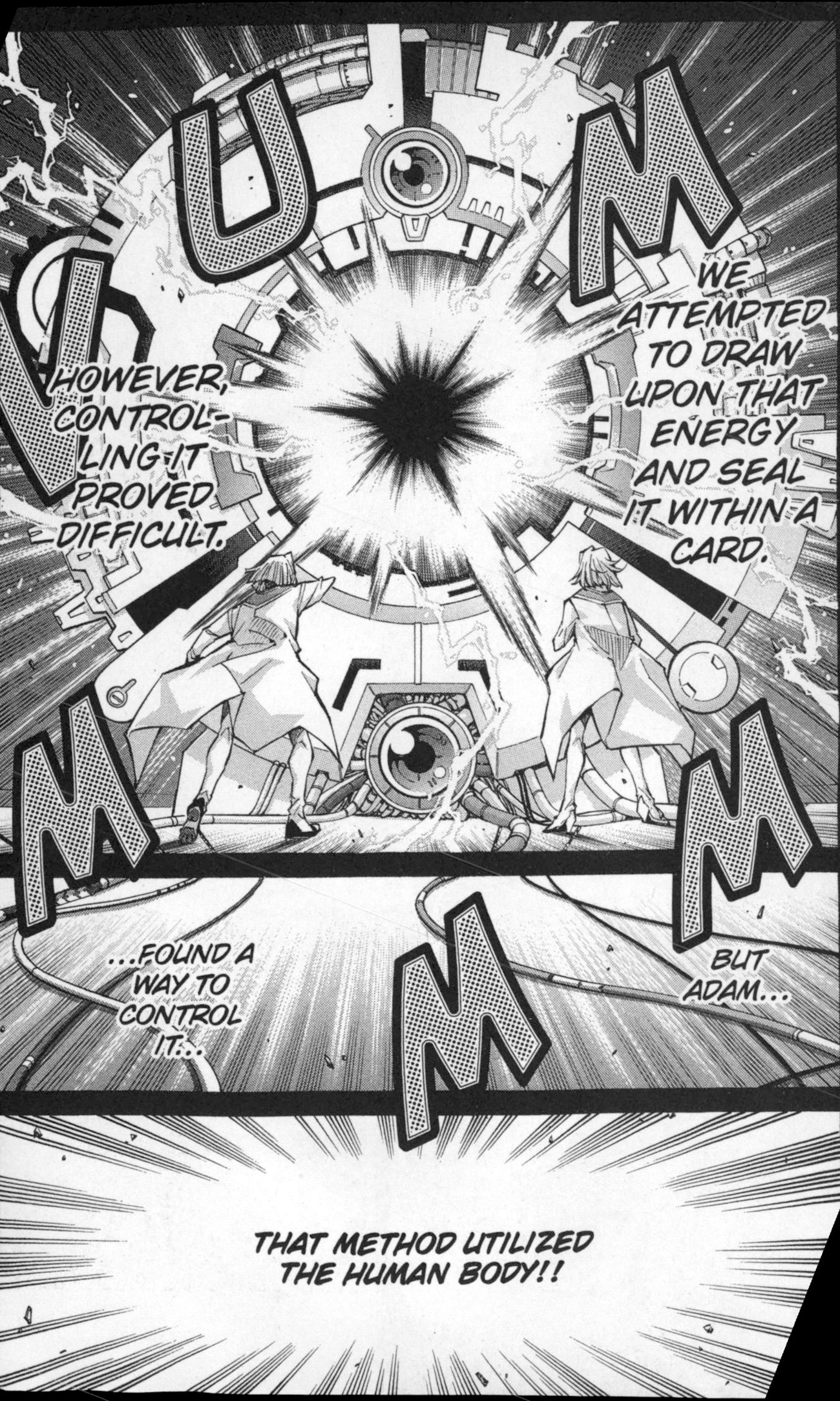
WE ATTEMPTED TO DRAW UPON THAT ENERGY AND SEAL IT WITHIN A CARD.
HOWEVER, CONTROL-LING IT PROVED DIFFICULT.
VUMMMM
BUT ADAM...
...FOUND A WAY TO CONTROL IT...
THAT METHOD UTILIZED THE HUMAN BODY!!

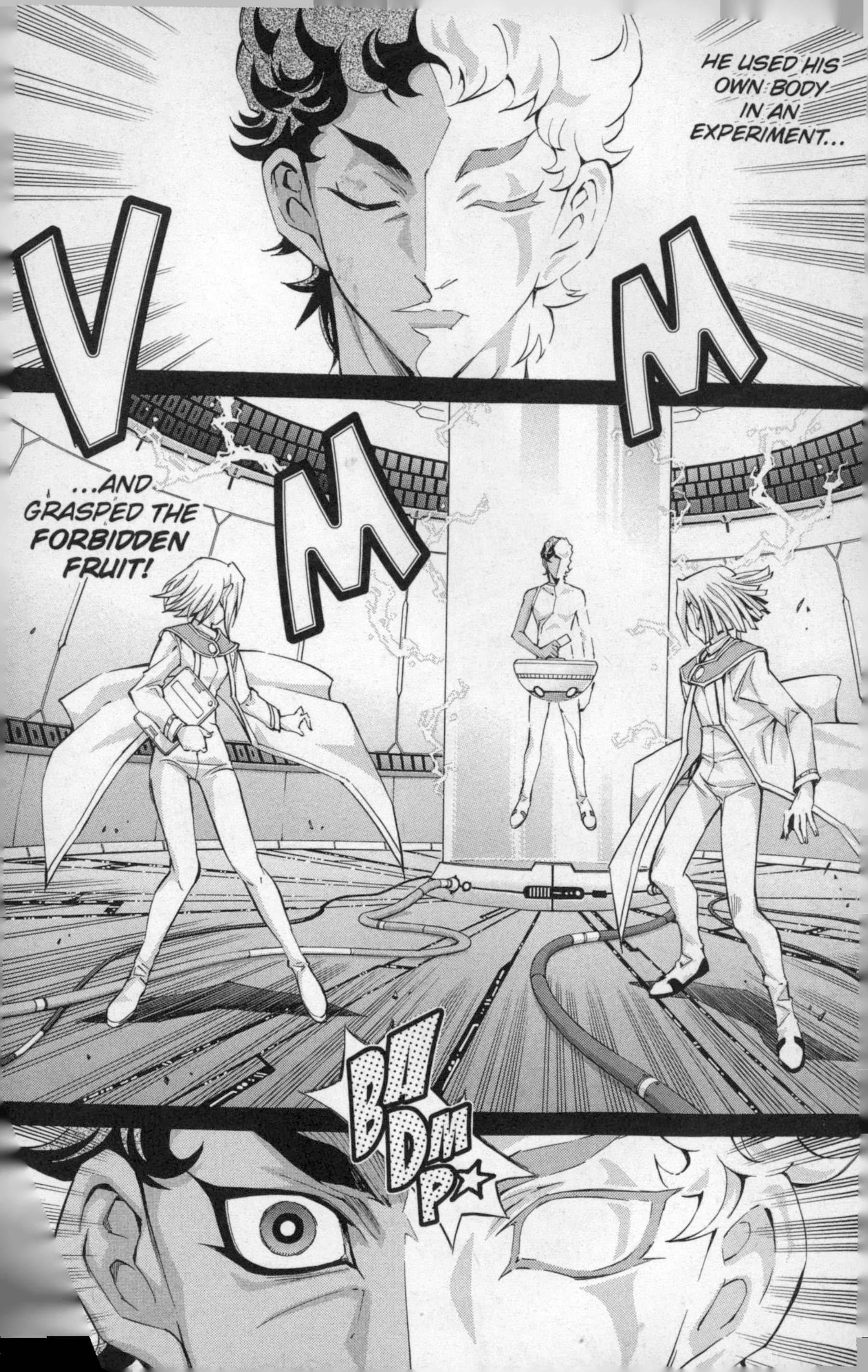
HE USED HIS OWN BODY IN AN EXPERIMENT...
VMM
...AND GRASPED THE FORBIDDEN FRUIT!
BADMP

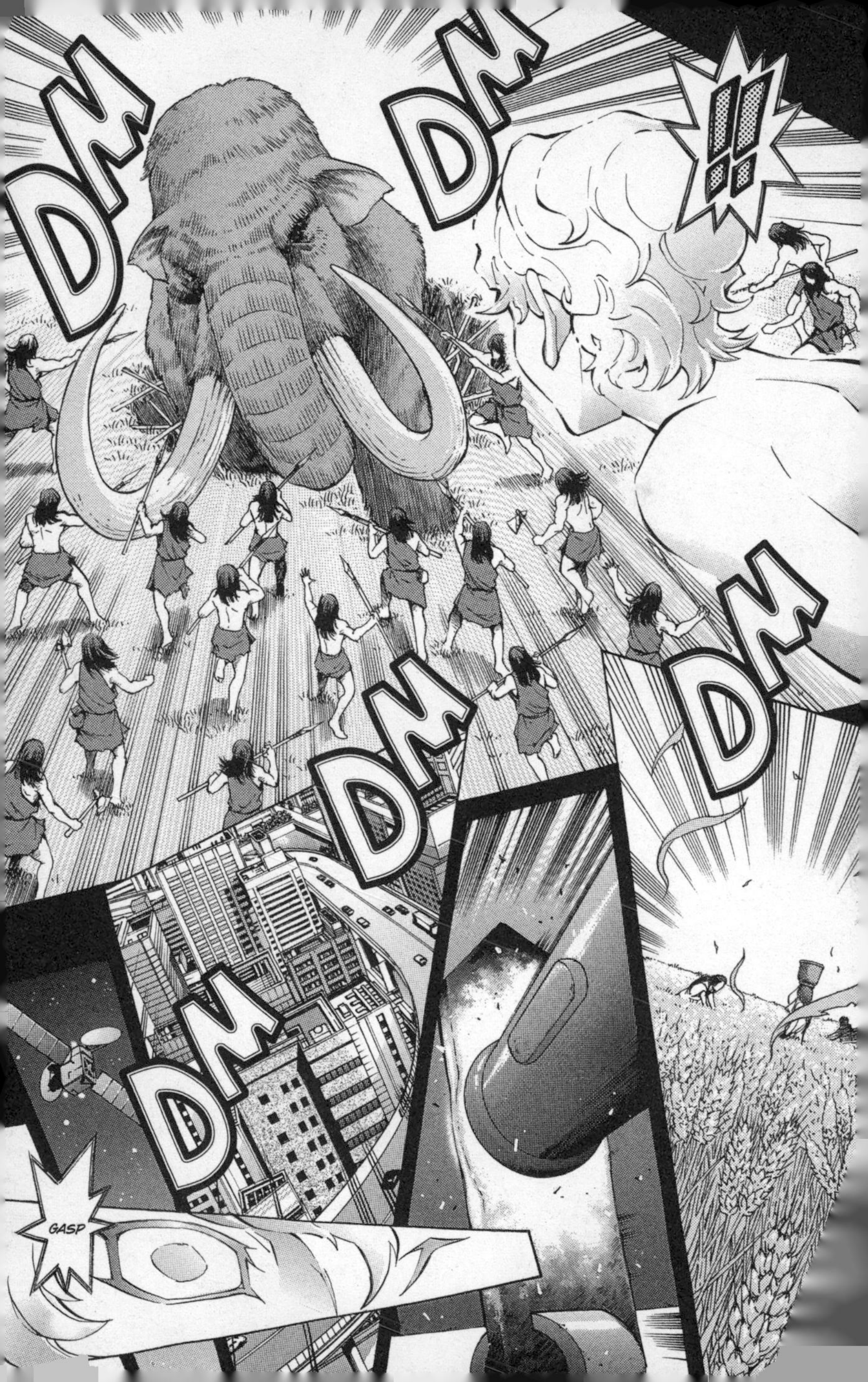
!!
DM
DM
DM
DM
DM
GASP

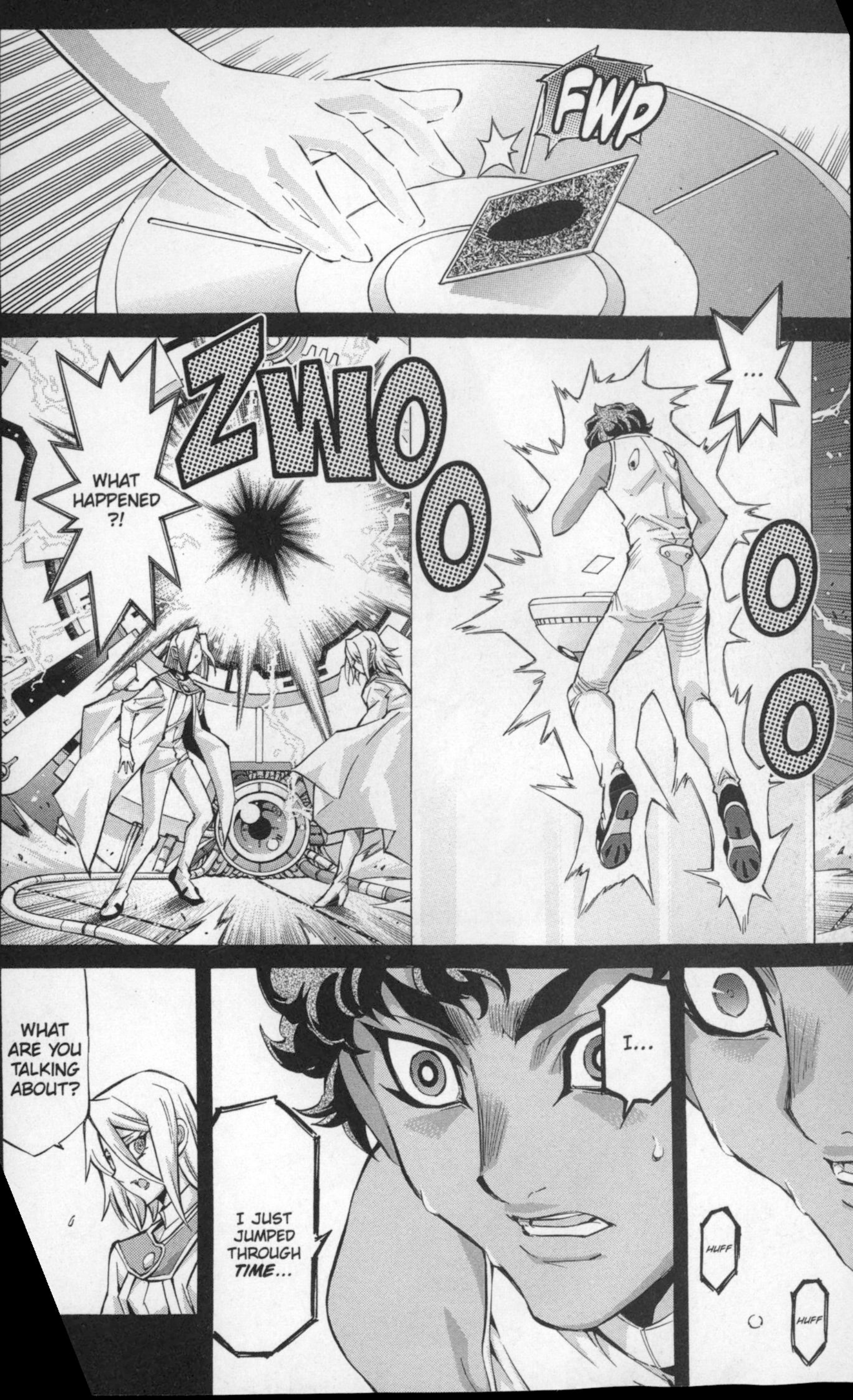
FWP
...
ZWOOOOO
WHAT HAPPENED ?!
HUFF
HUFF
I...
I JUST JUMPED THROUGH *TIME*...
WHAT ARE YOU TALKING ABOUT?

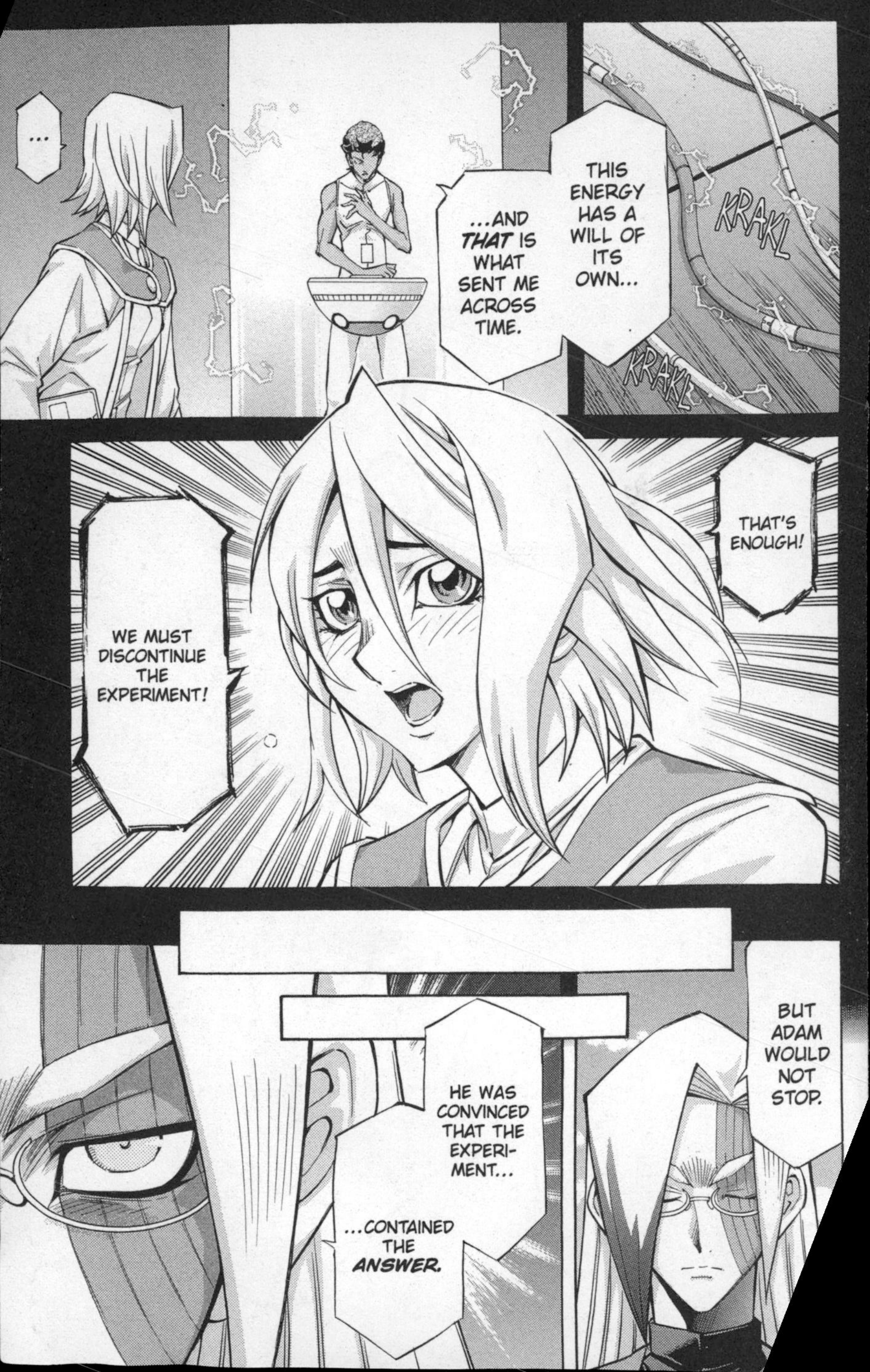
KRAKL
KRAKL
THIS ENERGY HAS A WILL OF ITS OWN...
...AND *THAT* IS WHAT SENT ME ACROSS TIME.
...
THAT'S ENOUGH!
WE MUST DISCONTINUE THE EXPERIMENT!
BUT ADAM WOULD NOT STOP.
HE WAS CONVINCED THAT THE EXPERI-MENT...
...CONTAINED THE ***ANSWER.***

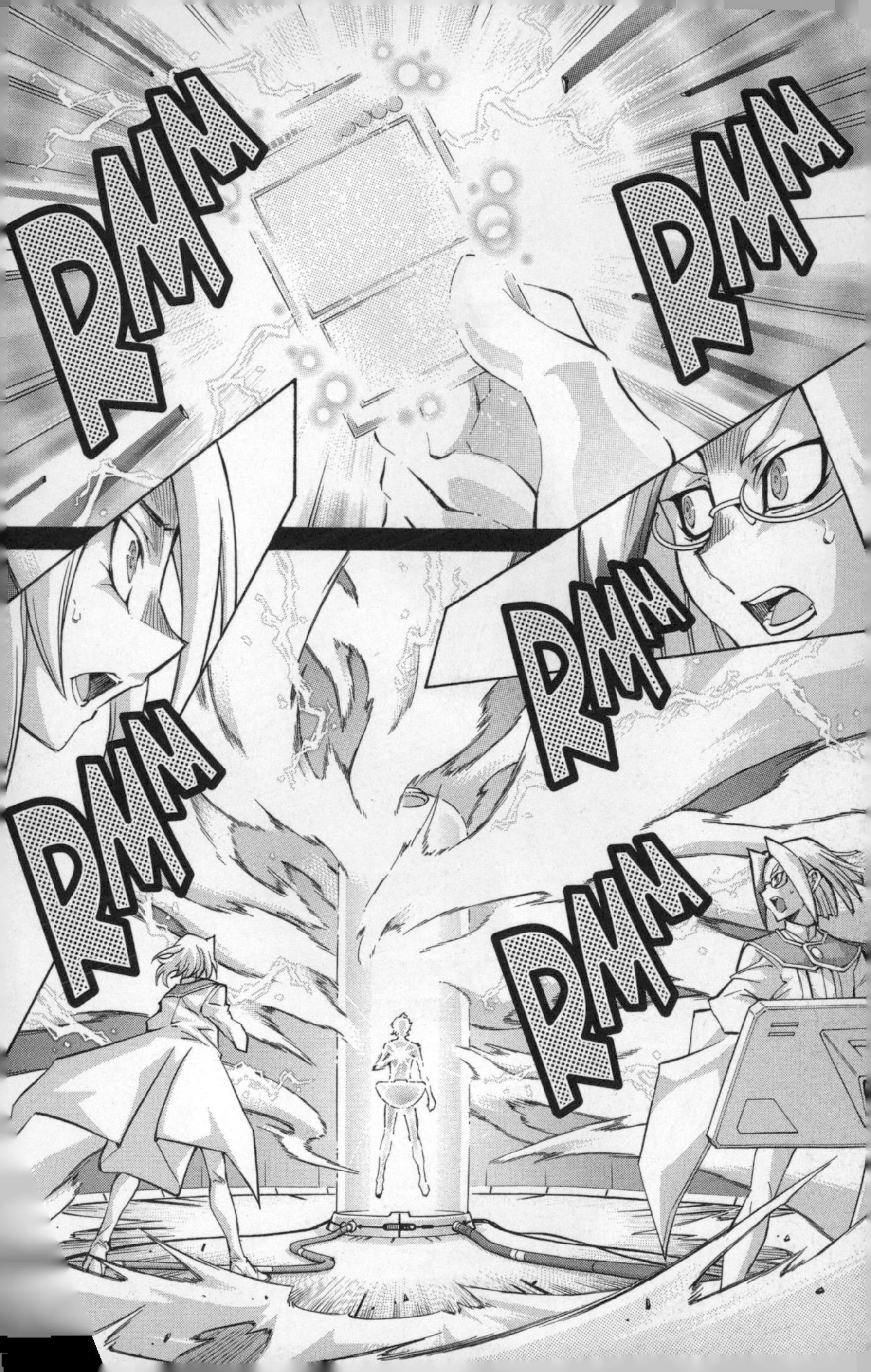
RMM
RMM
RMM
RMM
RMM
RMM

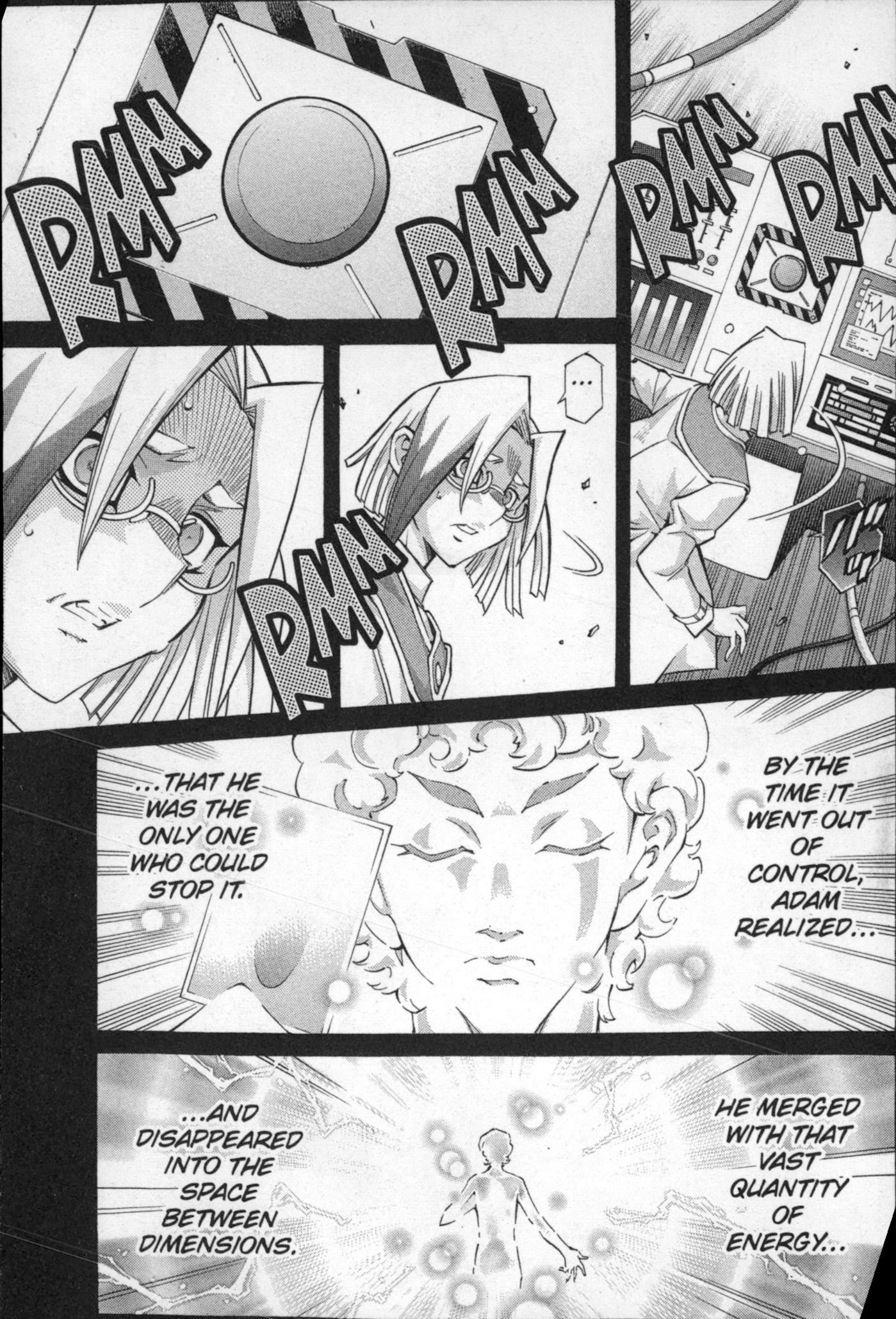
RMM
RMM
RMM
RMM
...
RMM
BY THE TIME IT WENT OUT OF CONTROL, ADAM REALIZED...
...THAT HE WAS THE ONLY ONE WHO COULD STOP IT.
HE MERGED WITH THAT VAST QUANTITY OF ENERGY...
...AND DISAPPEARED INTO THE SPACE BETWEEN DIMENSIONS.

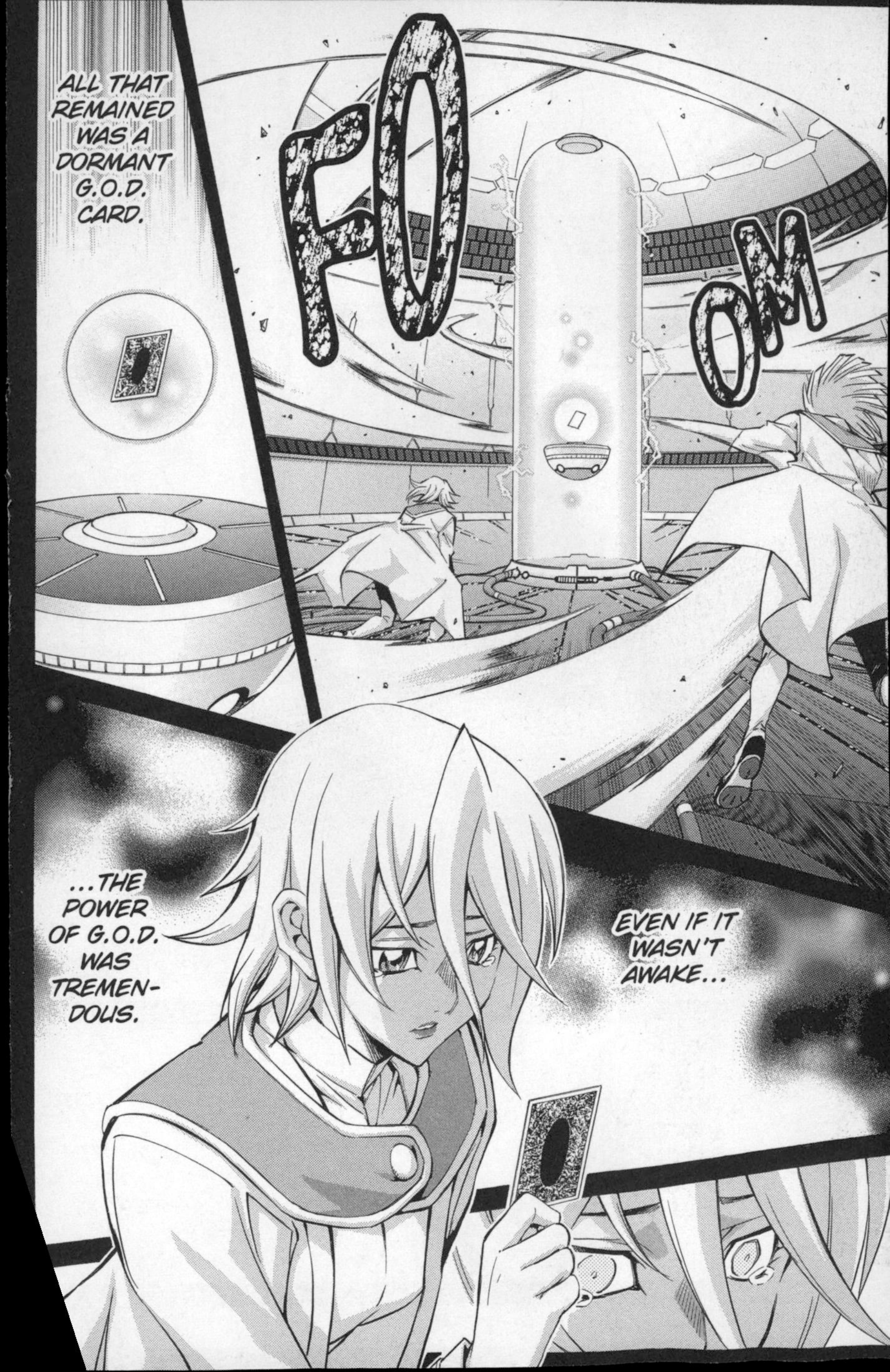
FOOM
ALL THAT REMAINED WAS A DORMANT G.O.D. CARD.
EVEN IF IT WASN'T AWAKE...
...THE POWER OF G.O.D. WAS TREMENDOUS.

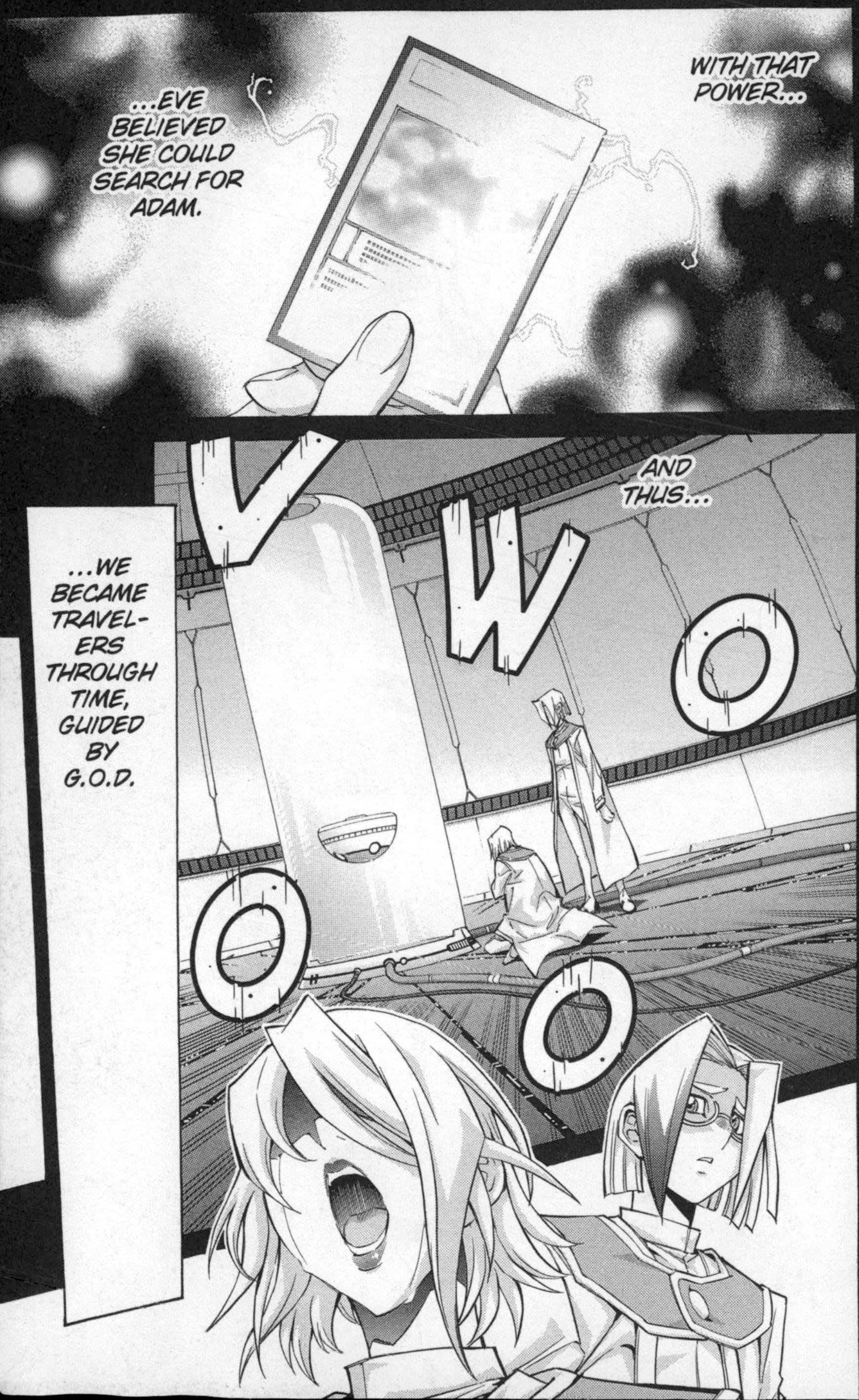
WITH THAT POWER...
...EVE BELIEVED SHE COULD SEARCH FOR ADAM.
AND THUS...
...WE BECAME TRAVEL-ERS THROUGH TIME, GUIDED BY G.O.D.
VWOOO

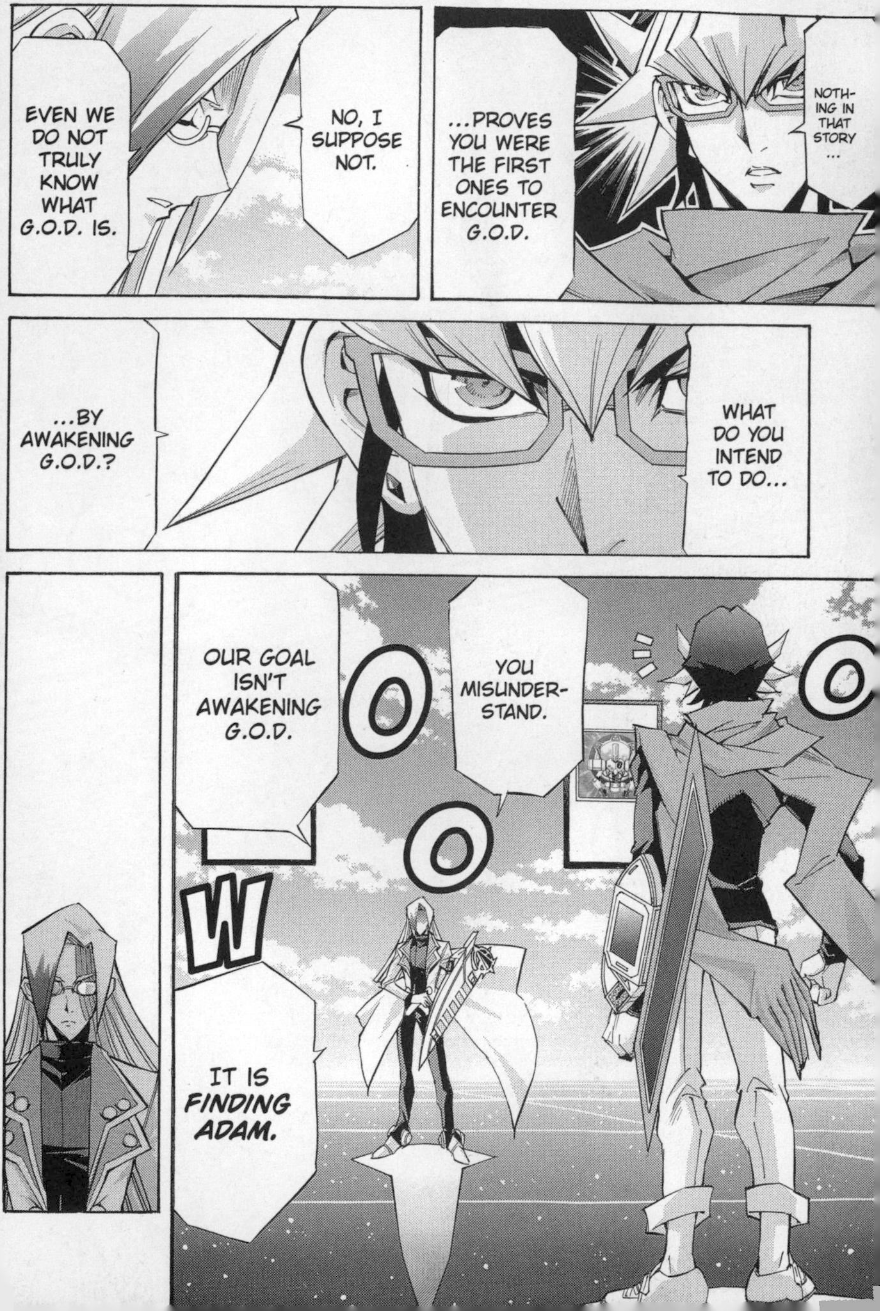
NOTH-ING IN THAT STORY ...
...PROVES YOU WERE THE FIRST ONES TO ENCOUNTER G.O.D.
NO, I SUPPOSE NOT.
EVEN WE DO NOT TRULY KNOW WHAT G.O.D. IS.
WHAT DO YOU INTEND TO DO...
...BY AWAKENING G.O.D.?
YOU MISUNDER-STAND.
OUR GOAL ISN'T AWAKENING G.O.D.
WOOO
IT IS *FINDING* ADAM.

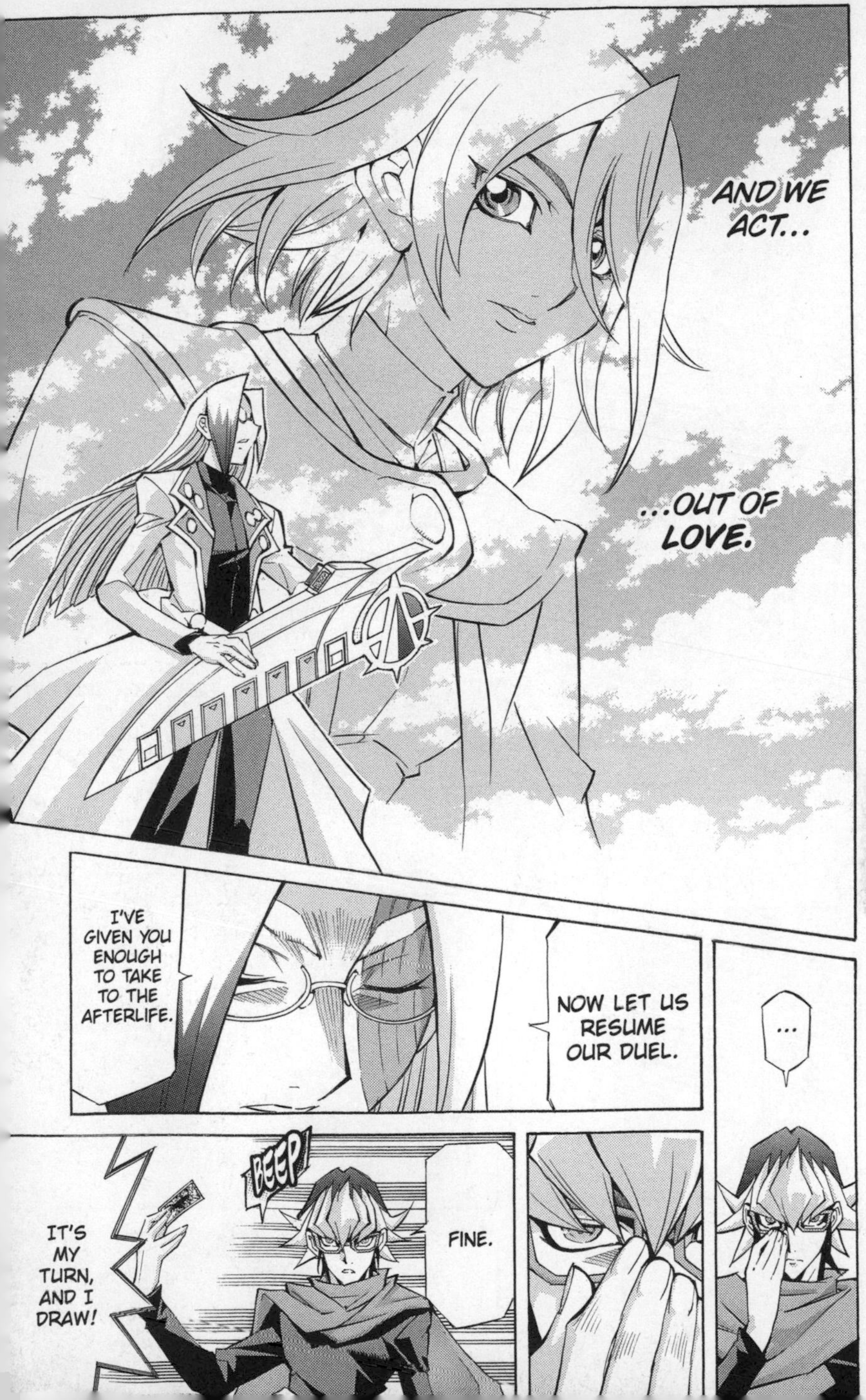
AND WE ACT...
...OUT OF LOVE.
...
I'VE GIVEN YOU ENOUGH TO TAKE TO THE AFTERLIFE.
NOW LET US RESUME OUR DUEL.
BEEP
FINE.
IT'S MY TURN, AND I DRAW!

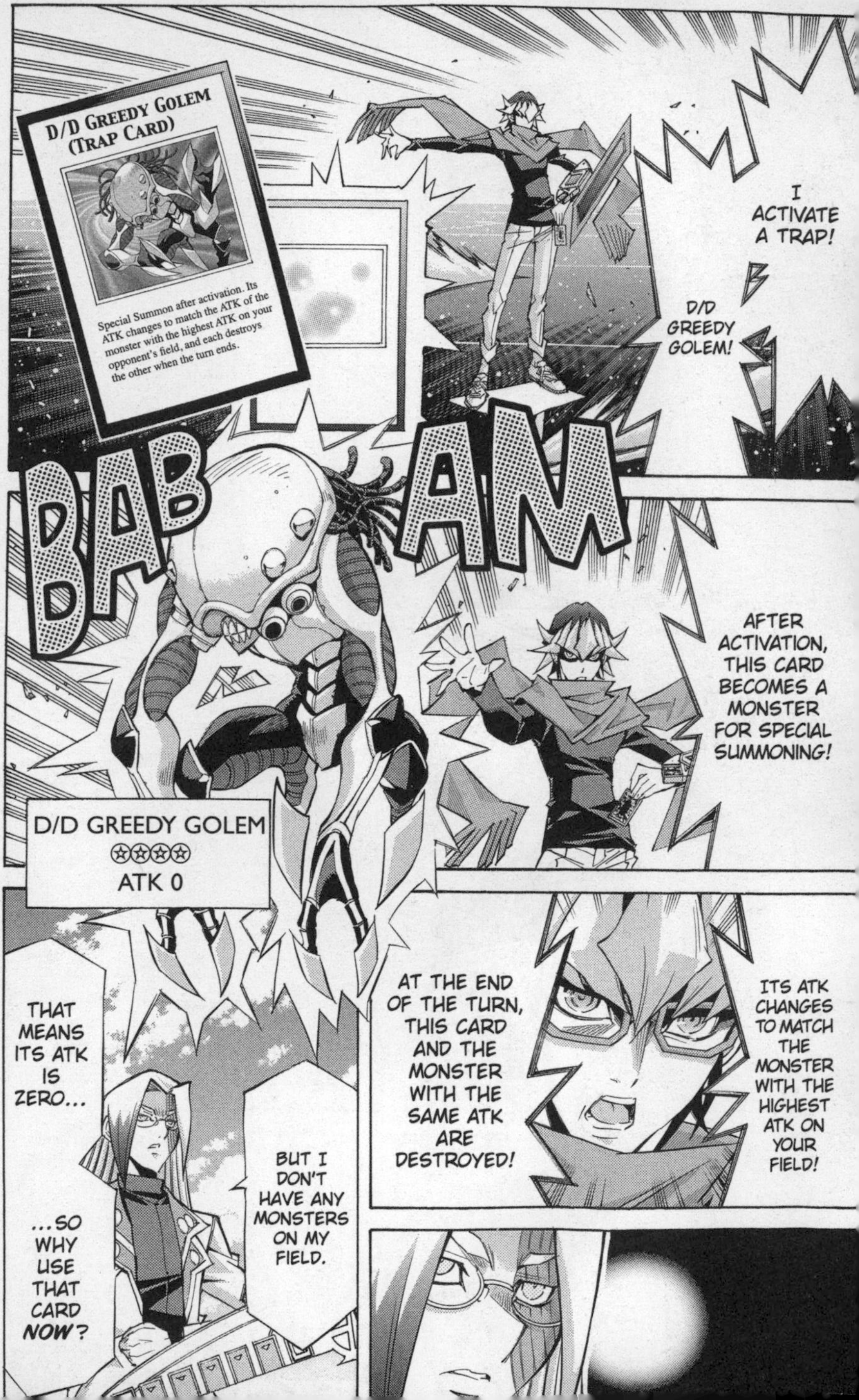
I ACTIVATE A TRAP!
D/D GREEDY GOLEM!
D/D GREEDY GOLEM (TRAP CARD)
Special Summon after activation. Its ATK changes to match the ATK of the monster with the highest ATK on your opponent's field, and each destroys the other when the turn ends.
BABAM
AFTER ACTIVATION, THIS CARD BECOMES A MONSTER FOR SPECIAL SUMMONING!
D/D GREEDY GOLEM
ATK 0
ITS ATK CHANGES TO MATCH THE MONSTER WITH THE HIGHEST ATK ON YOUR FIELD!
AT THE END OF THE TURN, THIS CARD AND THE MONSTER WITH THE SAME ATK ARE DESTROYED!
THAT MEANS ITS ATK IS ZERO...
BUT I DON'T HAVE ANY MONSTERS ON MY FIELD.
...SO WHY USE THAT CARD NOW?

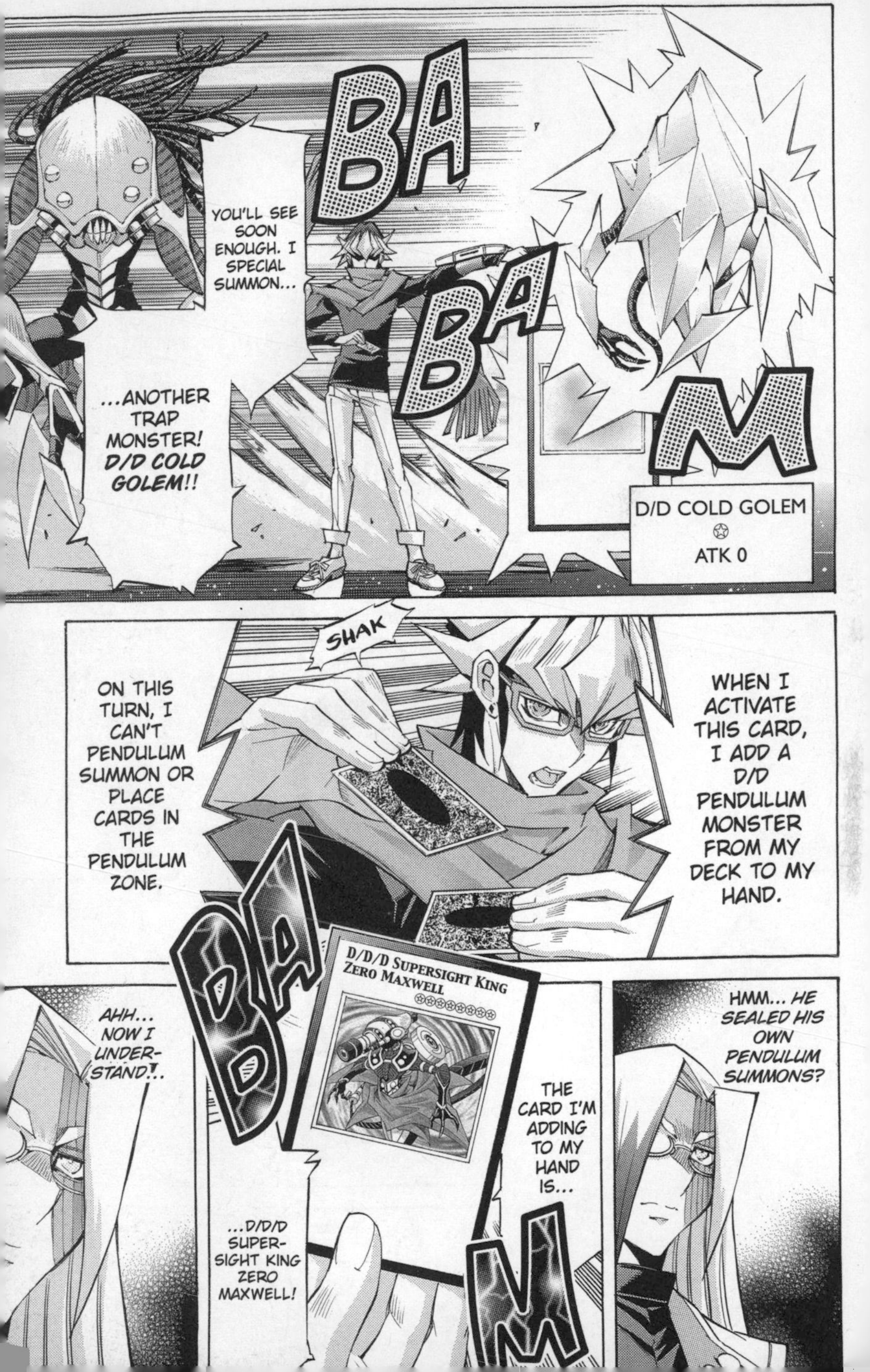
BA
BA
M
D/D COLD GOLEM
ATK 0
YOU'LL SEE SOON ENOUGH. I SPECIAL SUMMON...
...ANOTHER TRAP MONSTER! D/D COLD GOLEM!!
SHAK
WHEN I ACTIVATE THIS CARD, I ADD A D/D PENDULUM MONSTER FROM MY DECK TO MY HAND.
ON THIS TURN, I CAN'T PENDULUM SUMMON OR PLACE CARDS IN THE PENDULUM ZONE.
HMM... HE SEALED HIS OWN PENDULUM SUMMONS?
THE CARD I'M ADDING TO MY HAND IS...
...D/D/D SUPER-SIGHT KING ZERO MAXWELL!
D/D/D SUPERSIGHT KING ZERO MAXWELL
BA
M
AHH... NOW I UNDER-STAND...

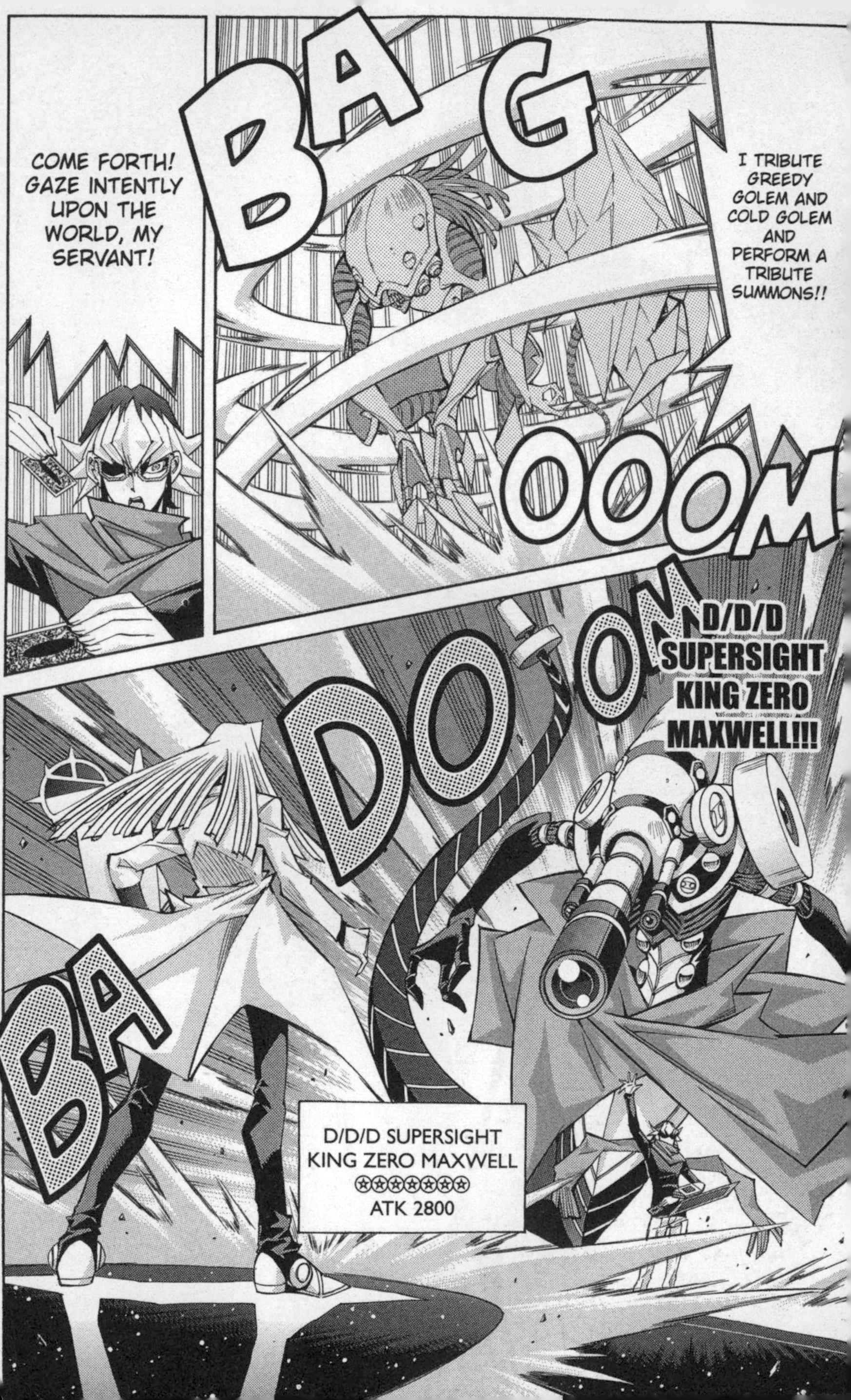
BAG
I TRIBUTE GREEDY GOLEM AND COLD GOLEM AND PERFORM A TRIBUTE SUMMONS!!
OOOOM
COME FORTH! GAZE INTENTLY UPON THE WORLD, MY SERVANT!
D/D/D SUPERSIGHT KING ZERO MAXWELL!!!
DOOOM
BA
D/D/D SUPERSIGHT KING ZERO MAXWELL
✪✪✪✪✪✪✪
ATK 2800

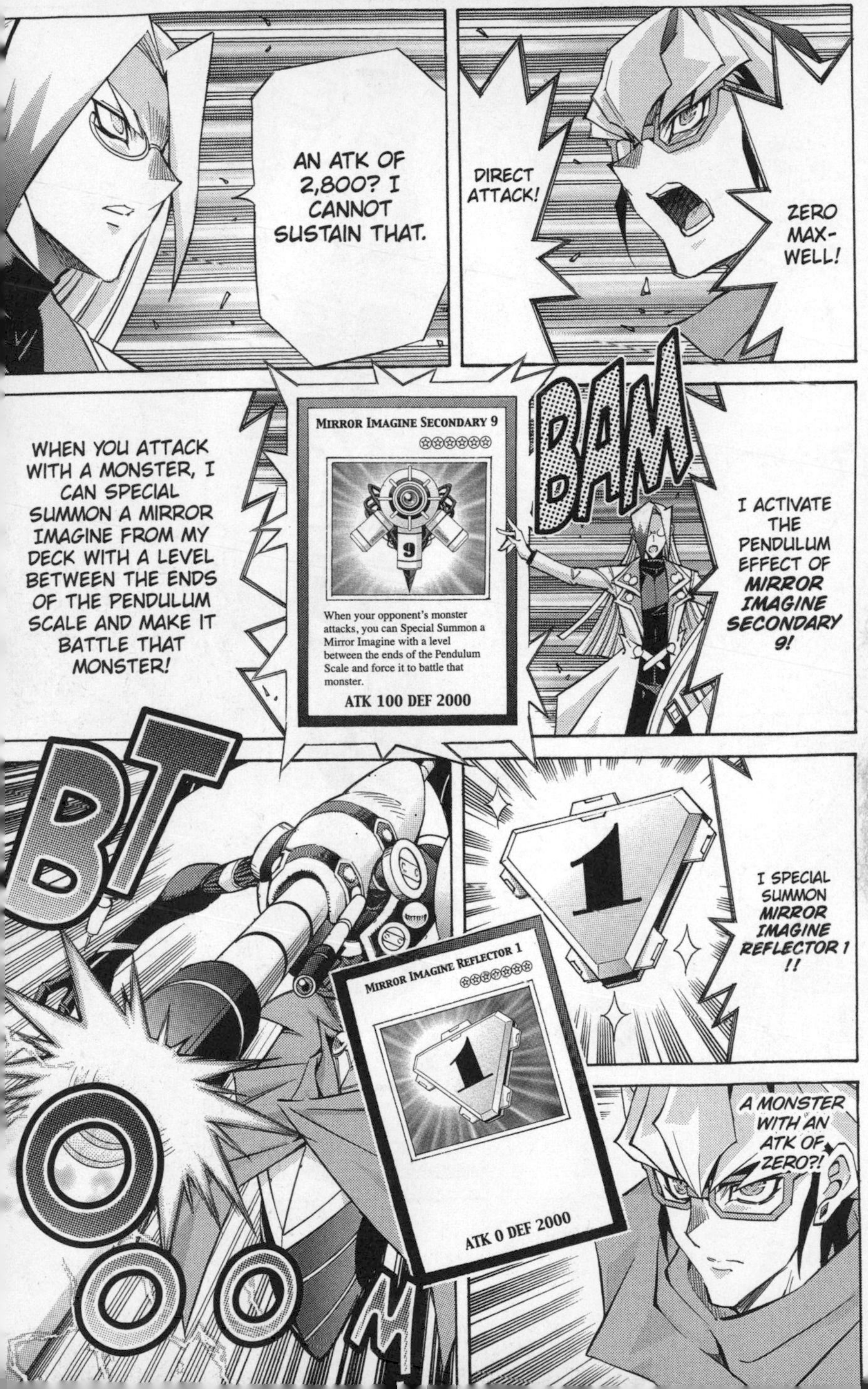
ZERO MAX-WELL!
DIRECT ATTACK!
AN ATK OF 2,800? I CANNOT SUSTAIN THAT.
BAM
I ACTIVATE THE PENDULUM EFFECT OF MIRROR IMAGINE SECONDARY 9!
MIRROR IMAGINE SECONDARY 9
When your opponent's monster attacks, you can Special Summon a Mirror Imagine with a level between the ends of the Pendulum Scale and force it to battle that monster.
ATK 100 DEF 2000
WHEN YOU ATTACK WITH A MONSTER, I CAN SPECIAL SUMMON A MIRROR IMAGINE FROM MY DECK WITH A LEVEL BETWEEN THE ENDS OF THE PENDULUM SCALE AND MAKE IT BATTLE THAT MONSTER!
I SPECIAL SUMMON MIRROR IMAGINE REFLECTOR 1 !!
MIRROR IMAGINE REFLECTOR 1
ATK 0 DEF 2000
A MONSTER WITH AN ATK OF ZERO?!
BT
OOOM

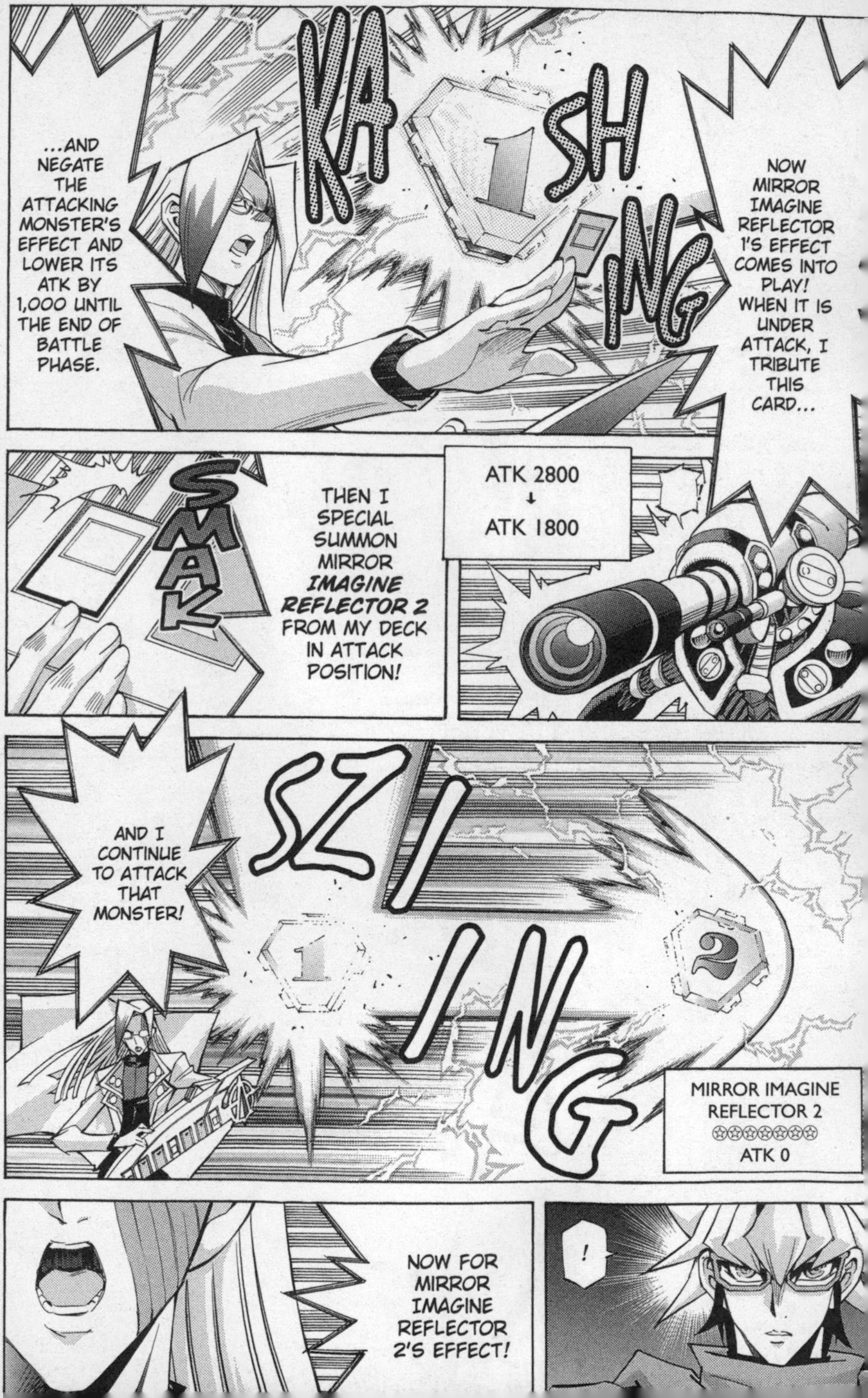
NOW MIRROR IMAGINE REFLECTOR 1'S EFFECT COMES INTO PLAY! WHEN IT IS UNDER ATTACK, I TRIBUTE THIS CARD...
KA SH ING
...AND NEGATE THE ATTACKING MONSTER'S EFFECT AND LOWER ITS ATK BY 1,000 UNTIL THE END OF BATTLE PHASE.
ATK 2800 ↓ ATK 1800
!
THEN I SPECIAL SUMMON MIRROR IMAGINE REFLECTOR 2 FROM MY DECK IN ATTACK POSITION!
SMAK
SZ I ING
MIRROR IMAGINE REFLECTOR 2 ✩✩✩✩✩✩✩ ATK 0
AND I CONTINUE TO ATTACK THAT MONSTER!
!
NOW FOR MIRROR IMAGINE REFLECTOR 2'S EFFECT!

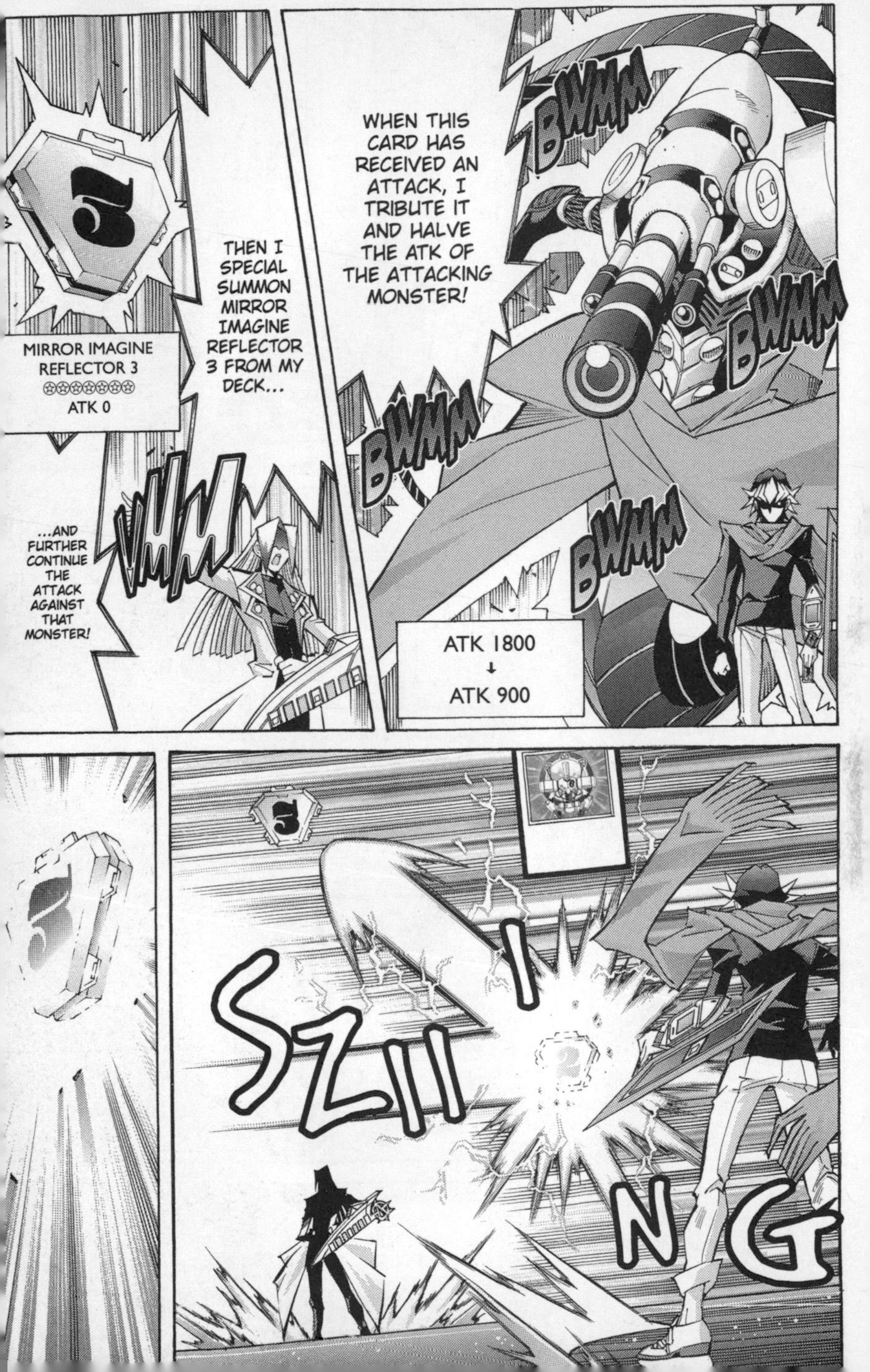
WHEN THIS CARD HAS RECEIVED AN ATTACK, I TRIBUTE IT AND HALVE THE ATK OF THE ATTACKING MONSTER!
BWMM
ATK 1800 ↓ ATK 900
MIRROR IMAGINE REFLECTOR 3 ATK 0
THEN I SPECIAL SUMMON MIRROR IMAGINE REFLECTOR 3 FROM MY DECK...
VMM
...AND FURTHER CONTINUE THE ATTACK AGAINST THAT MONSTER!
SZIIING

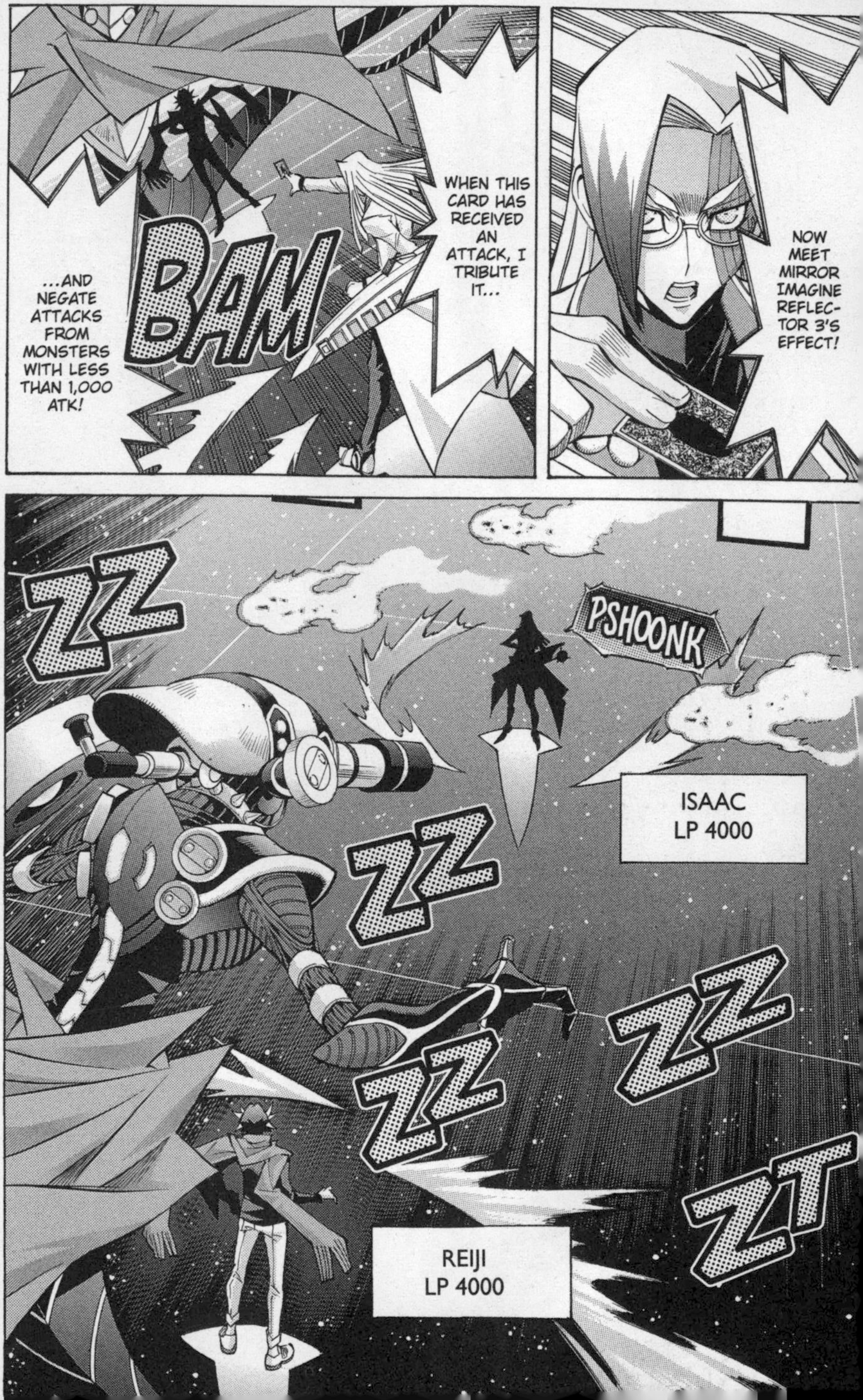
NOW MEET MIRROR IMAGINE REFLECTOR 3'S EFFECT!
WHEN THIS CARD HAS RECEIVED AN ATTACK, I TRIBUTE IT...
BAM
...AND NEGATE ATTACKS FROM MONSTERS WITH LESS THAN 1,000 ATK!
ISAAC
LP 4000
PSHOONK
ZZ
ZZ
ZZ
ZZ
ZZT
REIJI
LP 4000

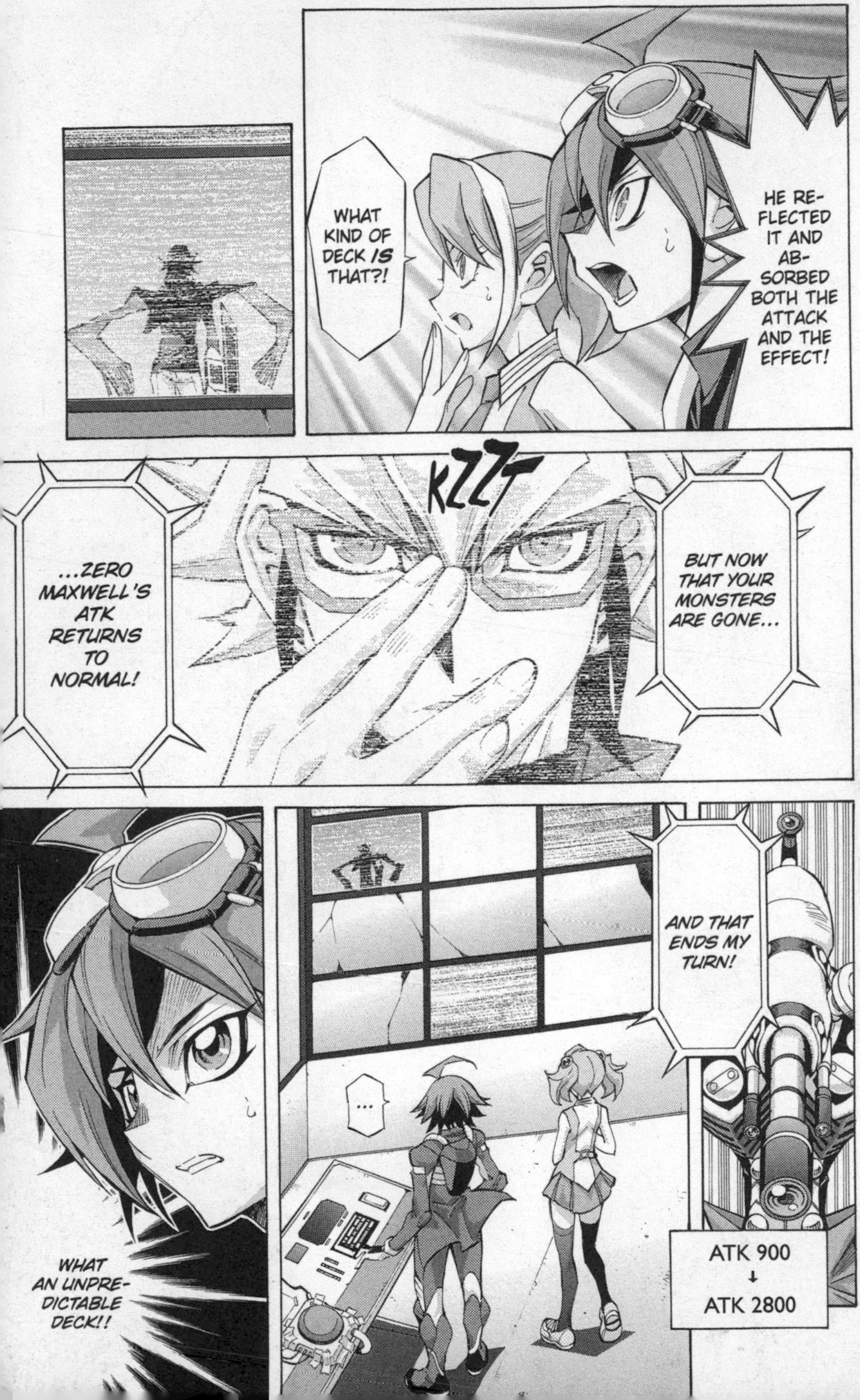
HE RE-FLECTED IT AND AB-SORBED BOTH THE ATTACK AND THE EFFECT!
WHAT KIND OF DECK *IS* THAT?!
BUT NOW THAT YOUR MONSTERS ARE GONE...
KZZT
...ZERO MAXWELL'S ATK RETURNS TO NORMAL!
AND THAT ENDS MY TURN!
...
ATK 900
↓
ATK 2800
WHAT AN UNPRE-DICTABLE DECK!!

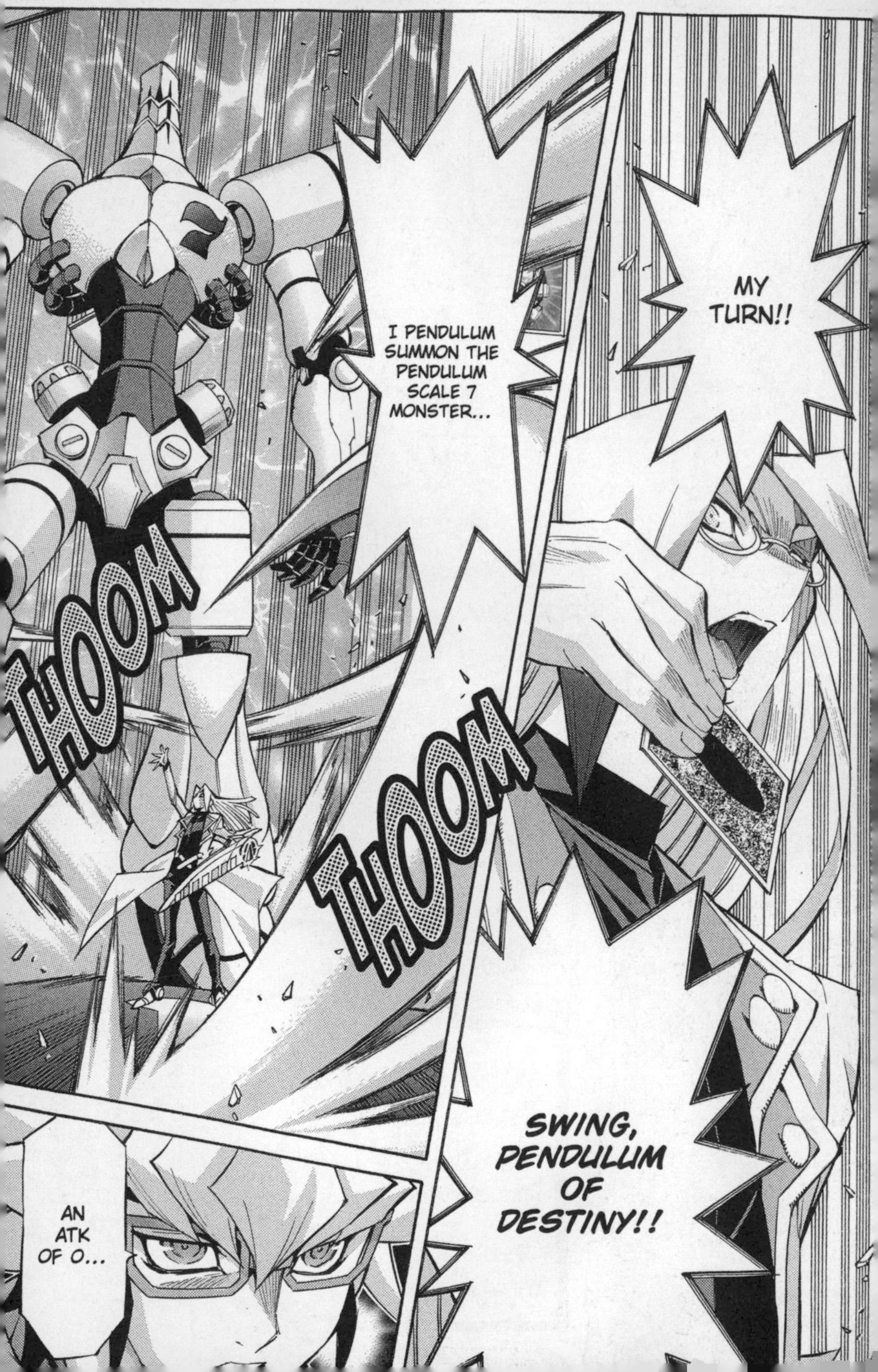
MY TURN!!
I PENDULUM SUMMON THE PENDULUM SCALE 7 MONSTER...
THOOM
THOOM
SWING, PENDULUM OF DESTINY!!
AN ATK OF 0...

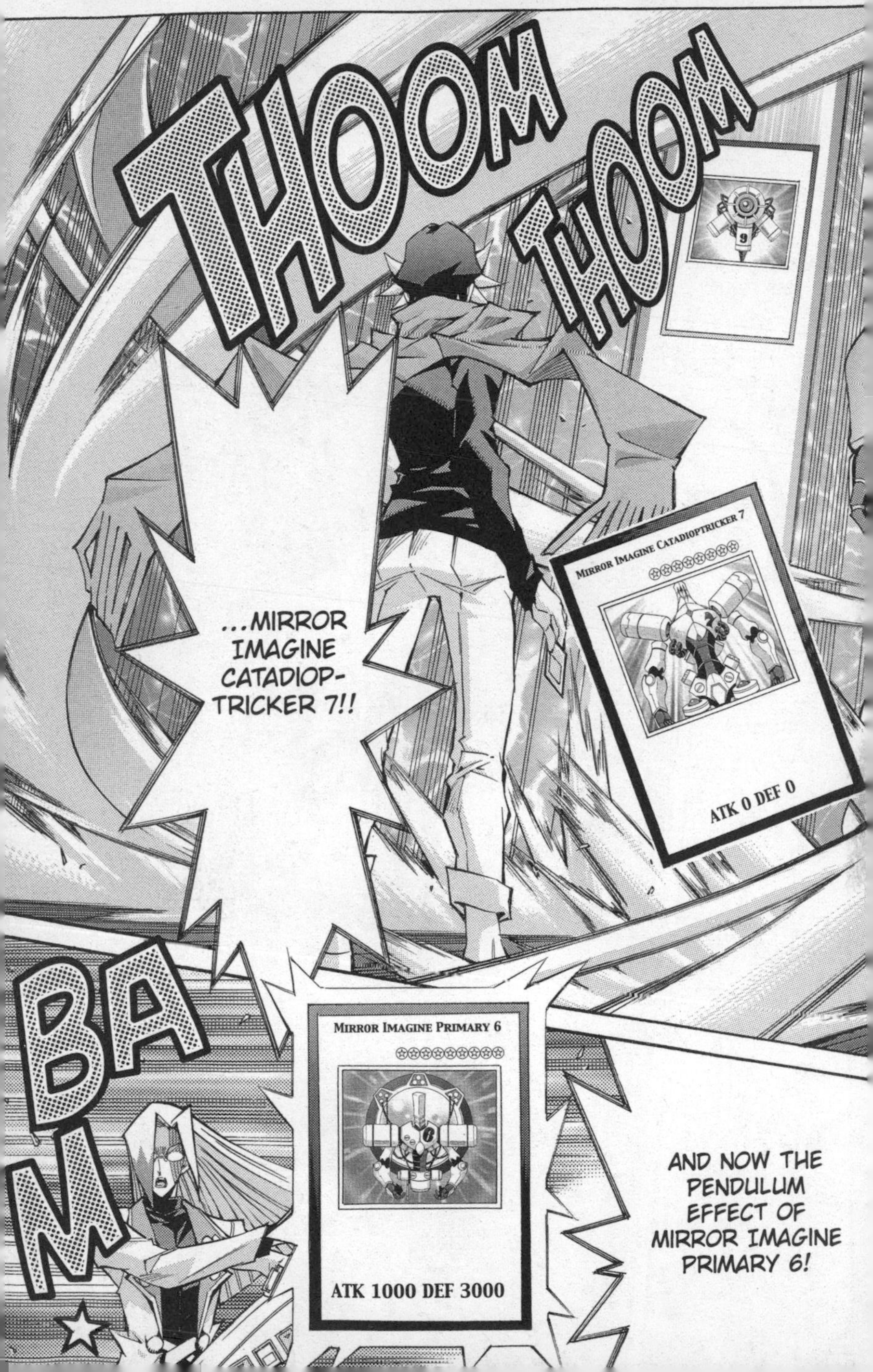
THOOM
THOOM
...MIRROR IMAGINE CATADIOP-TRICKER 7!!
MIRROR IMAGINE CATADIOPTRICKER 7
ATK 0 DEF 0
AND NOW THE PENDULUM EFFECT OF MIRROR IMAGINE PRIMARY 6!
MIRROR IMAGINE PRIMARY 6
ATK 1000 DEF 3000
BAM

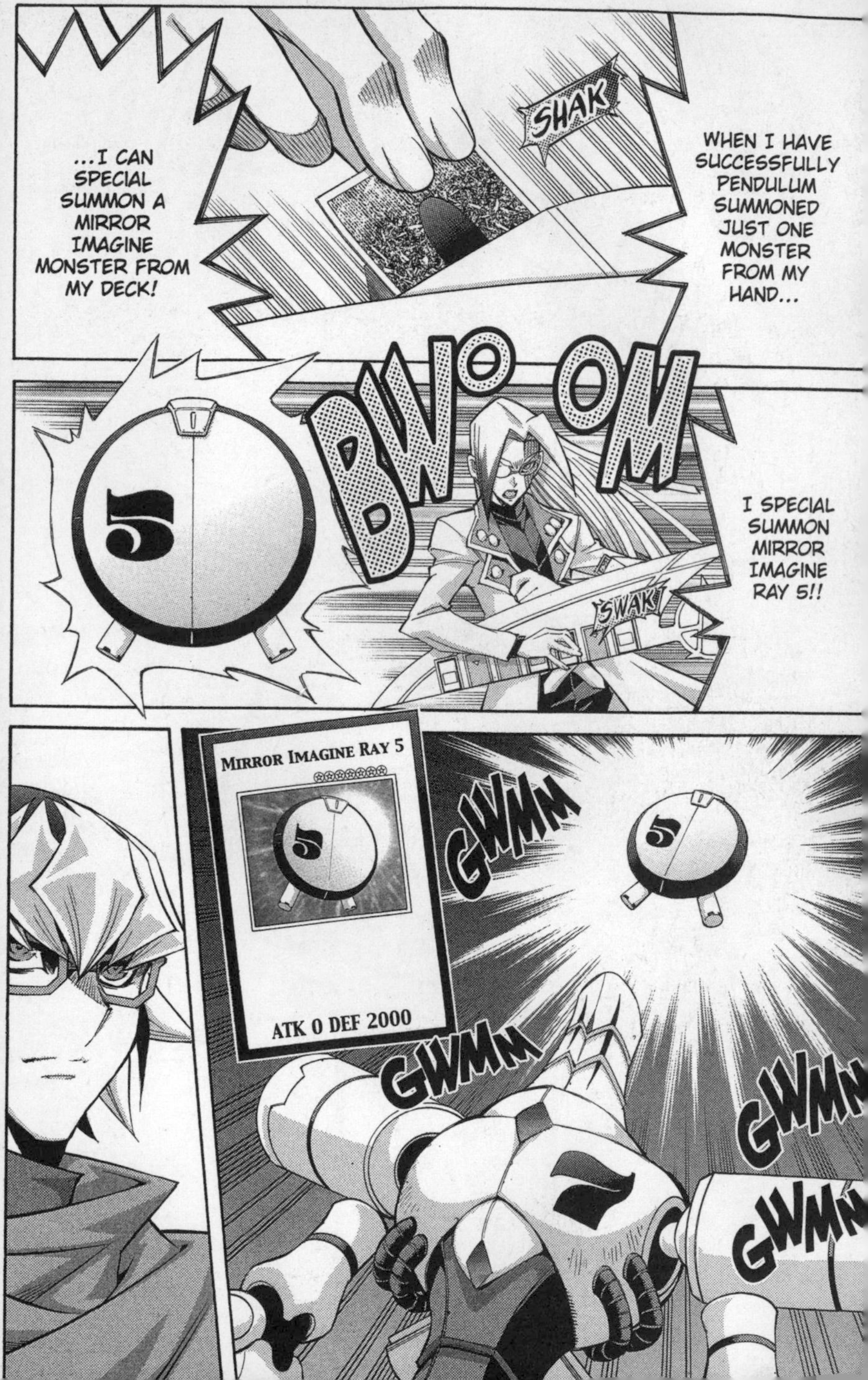
WHEN I HAVE SUCCESSFULLY PENDULUM SUMMONED JUST ONE MONSTER FROM MY HAND...
SHAK
...I CAN SPECIAL SUMMON A MIRROR IMAGINE MONSTER FROM MY DECK!
I SPECIAL SUMMON MIRROR IMAGINE RAY 5!!
BWOOM
SWAK
5
GWMM
GWMM
GWMM
GWMM
GWMM
Mirror Imagine Ray 5
ATK 0 DEF 2000

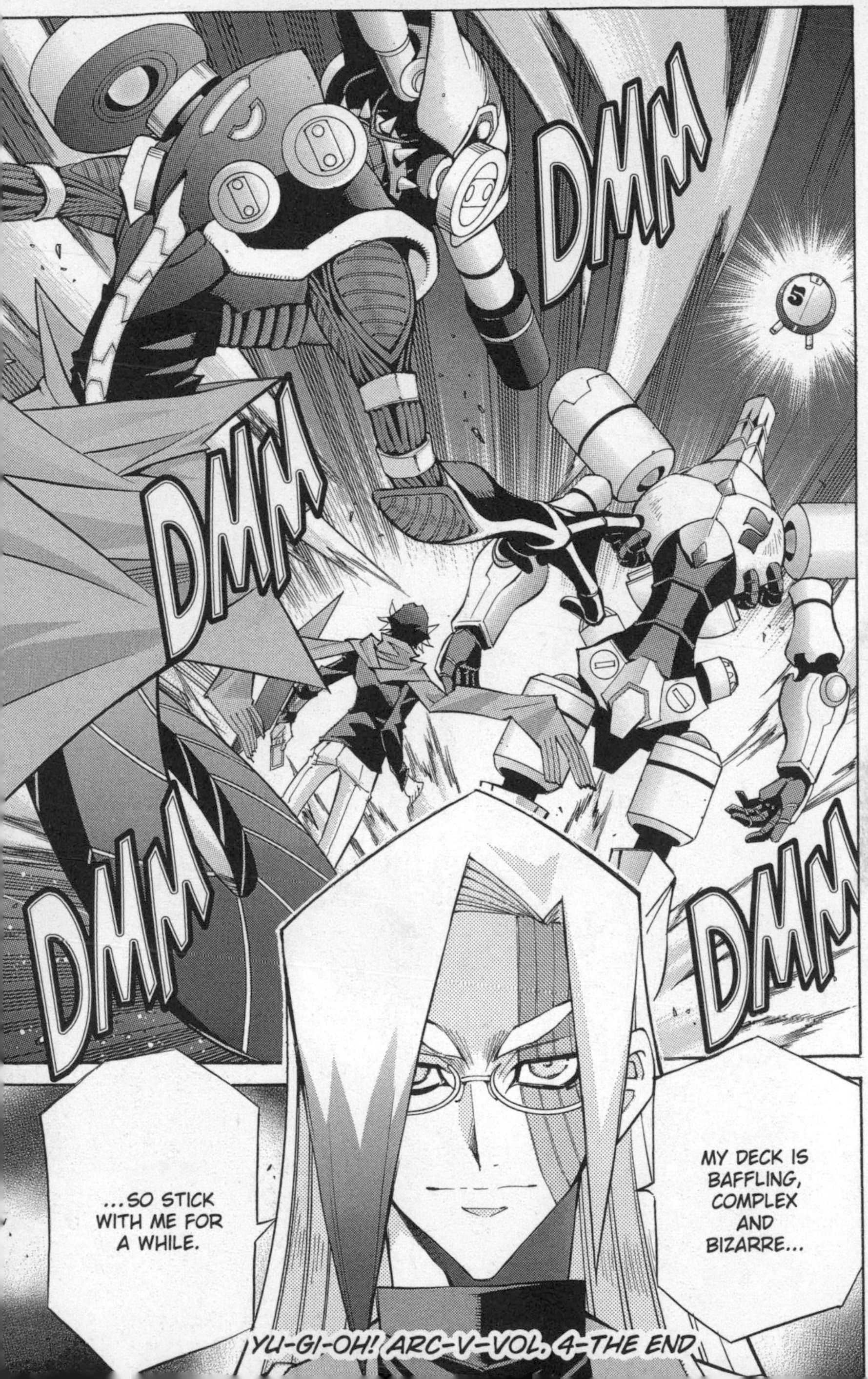
DMM
DMM
DMM
DMM
MY DECK IS BAFFLING, COMPLEX AND BIZARRE...
...SO STICK WITH ME FOR A WHILE.
YU-GI-OH! ARC-V—VOL. 4—THE END

Staff	Junya Uchino Kazuo Ochiai
Coloring	Toru Shimizu
Editing	Takahiko Aikawa

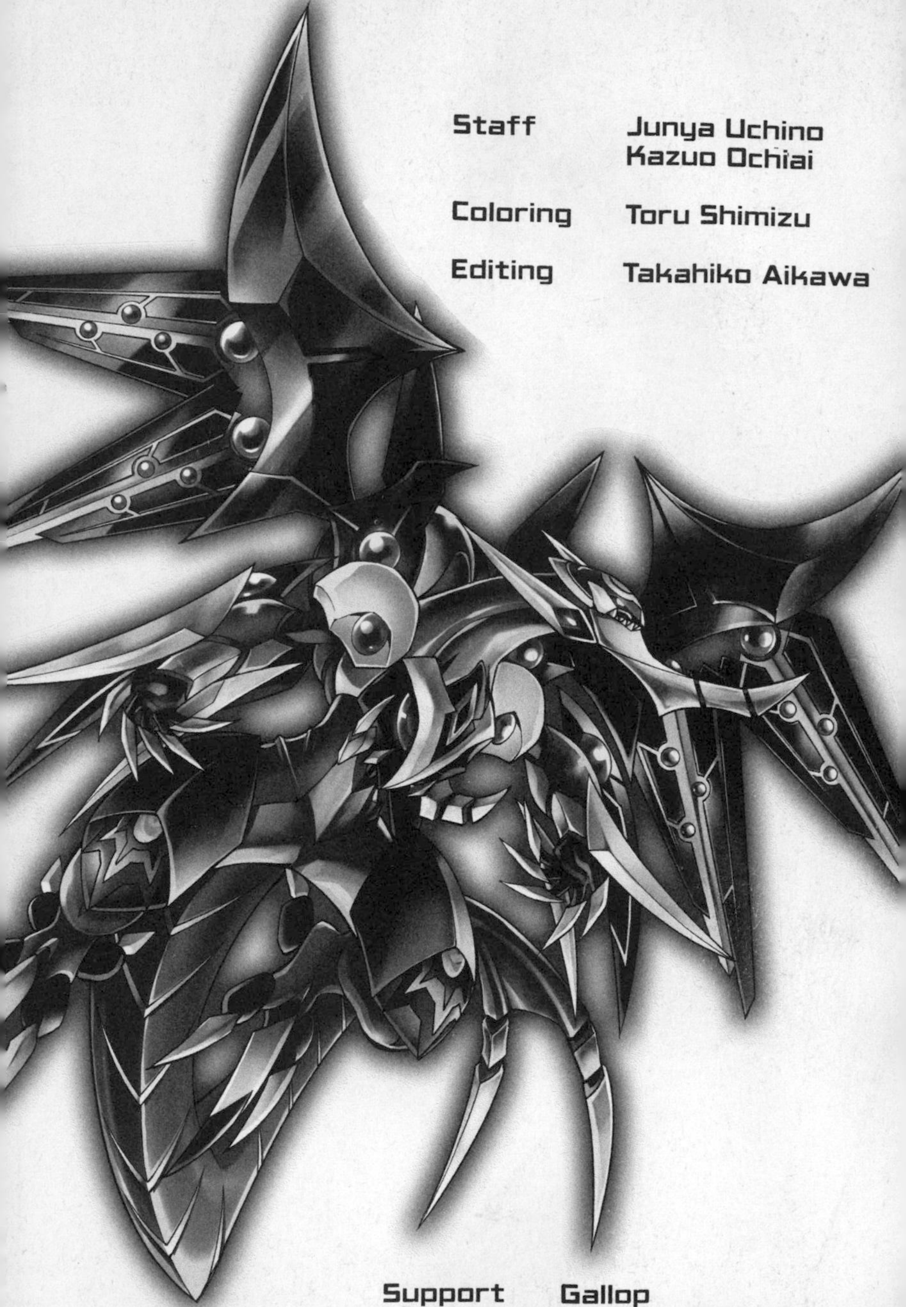

Support	Gallop Wedge Holdings

Hikaru no GO

Story by **YUMI HOTTA**
Art by **TAKESHI OBATA**

The breakthrough series by Takeshi Obata, the artist of *Death Note!*

Hikaru Shindo is like any sixth-grader in Japan: a pretty normal schoolboy with a penchant for antics. One day, he finds an old bloodstained Go board in his grandfather's attic. Trapped inside the Go board is Fujiwara-no-Sai, the ghost of an ancient Go master. In one fateful moment, Sai becomes a part of Hikaru's consciousness and together, through thick and thin, they make an unstoppable Go-playing team.

Will they be able to defeat Go players who have dedicated their lives to the game? And will Sai achieve the "Divine Move" so he'll finally be able to rest in peace? Find out in this *Shonen Jump* classic!

www.shonenjump.com

www.viz.com

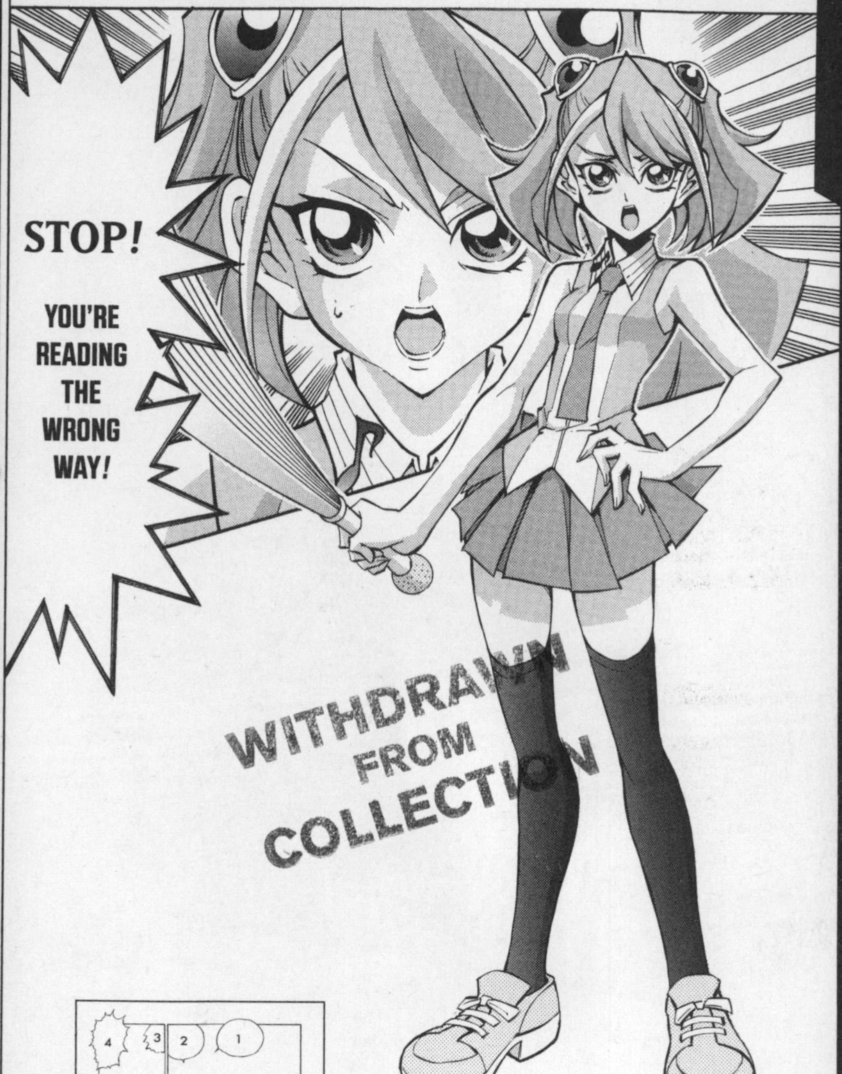

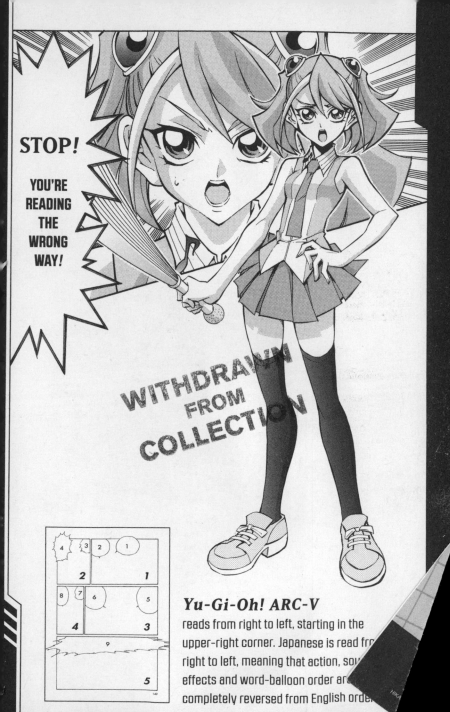

STOP!

YOU'RE READING THE WRONG WAY!

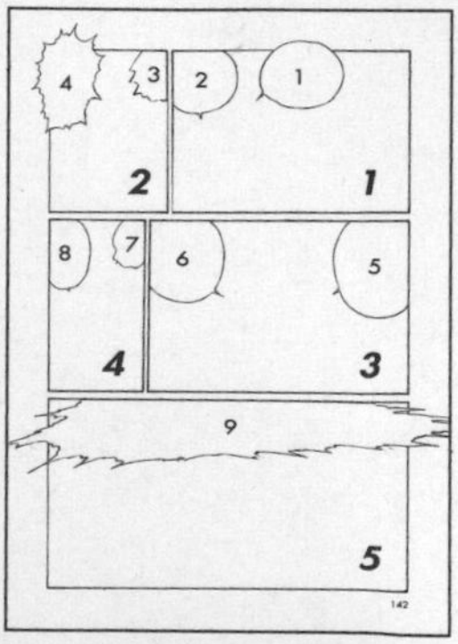

Yu-Gi-Oh! ARC-V

reads from right to left, starting in the upper-right corner. Japanese is read fr right to left, meaning that action, sou effects and word-balloon order ar completely reversed from English orde